ReValuing Care in Theory, Law and Policy

Care is central to life, and yet is all too often undervalued, taken for granted, and hidden from view. This collection of fourteen substantive and highly innovative essays, along with its insightful introduction, seeks to explore the different dimensions of care that shape social, legal and political contexts. It addresses these dimensions in four key ways. First, the contributions expand contemporary theoretical understandings of the value of care, by reflecting upon established conceptual approaches (such as the 'ethics of care') and developing new ways of using and understanding this concept. Second, the chapters draw on a wide range of methods, from doctrinal scholarship through ethnographic, empirical and biographical research methodologies. Third, the book enlarges the usual subjects of care research, by expanding its analysis beyond the more typical focus on familial interconnection to include professional care contexts, care by strangers and care for and about animals. Finally, the collection draws on contributions from academics working in Europe and Australia, across law, anthropology, gender studies, politics, psychology and sociology. By highlighting the points of connection and tension between these diverse international and disciplinary perspectives, this book outlines a new and nuanced approach to care, exploring contemporary understandings of care across law, the social sciences and humanities.

Rosie Harding is a Professor of Law and Society at the University of Birmingham, UK.

Ruth Fletcher is a Senior Lecturer in Medical Law at the School of Law, Queen Mary University of London, UK.

Chris Beasley is Professor of Politics at the School of History and Politics, University of Adelaide, Australia.

Social justice

Series editors: Davina Cooper, *University of Kent, UK*, Sarah Lamble, *Birkbeck College, University of London, UK* and Sarah Keenan, *Birkbeck College, University of London, UK*

Social Justice is a new, theoretically engaged, interdisciplinary series exploring the changing values, politics and institutional forms through which claims for equality, democracy and liberation are expressed, manifested and fought over in the contemporary world. The series addresses a range of contexts from transnational political fora, to nation-state and regional controversies, to small-scale social experiments. At its heart is a concern, and inter-disciplinary engagement with, the present and future politics of power, as constituted through territory, gender, sexuality, ethnicity, economics, ecology and culture.

Foregrounding struggle, imagined alternatives and the embedding of new norms, *Social Justice* critically explores how change is wrought through law and governance, everyday social and bodily practices, dissident knowledges and movements for citizenship, belonging and reinvented community.

Titles in this series:

Law Unlimited
Margaret Davies

Sensing Law
Sheryl Hamilton, Diana Majury, Dawn Moore, Neil Sargent and Christiane Wilke (eds.)

Protest, Property and the Commons
Lucy Finchett-Maddock

Power, Politics and the Emotions: Impossible Governance?
Shona Hunter

The Sexual Constitution of Political Authority
Aleardo Zanghellini

Global Justice and Desire: Queering Economy
Nikita Dhawan, Antke Engel, Christoph H. E. Holzhey and Volker Woltersdorff (eds.)

Law, Environmental Illness and Medical Uncertainty
The contested governance of health
Tarryn Phillips

Forthcoming:

Regulating Sex After Aids: Queer Risks and Contagion Politics
Neil Cobb

ReValuing Care in Theory, Law and Policy

Cycles and Connections

Edited by Rosie Harding, Ruth Fletcher and Chris Beasley

LONDON AND NEW YORK

First published 2017
by Routledge
2 Park Square, Milton Park, Abingdon, Oxon, OX14 4RN

and by Routledge
711 Third Avenue, New York, NY 10017

First issued in paperback 2018

Routledge is an imprint of the Taylor & Francis Group, an informa business

© 2017 selection and editorial matter, Rosie Harding, Ruth Fletcher and Chris Beasley; individual chapters, the contributors

The right of Rosie Harding, Ruth Fletcher and Chris Beasley to be identified as the authors of the editorial material, and of the authors for their individual chapters, has been asserted in accordance with sections 77 and 78 of the Copyright, Designs and Patents Act 1988.

All rights reserved. No part of this book may be reprinted or reproduced or utilised in any form or by any electronic, mechanical, or other means, now known or hereafter invented, including photocopying and recording, or in any information storage or retrieval system, without permission in writing from the publishers.

Trademark notice: Product or corporate names may be trademarks or registered trademarks, and are used only for identification and explanation without intent to infringe.

British Library Cataloguing in Publication Data
A catalogue record for this book is available from the British Library

Library of Congress Cataloging-in-Publication Data
Names: Harding, Rosie, editor. | Fletcher, Ruth, editor. | Beasley, Chris, editor.
Title: Revaluing care in theory, law & policy: cycles and connections / edited by Rosie Harding, Ruth Fletcher and Chris Beasley.
Other titles: Revaluing care in theory, law and policy
Description: Abingdon, Oxon; New York, NY: Routledge, 2017. | Includes bibliographical references and index.
Identifiers: LCCN 2016025149| ISBN 9781138943193 (hbk) | ISBN 9781315672663 (ebk)
Subjects: LCSH: Caring–Social aspects. | Social service. | Kinship care. | Caregivers.
Classification: LCC HV40 .R389 2017 | DDC 361–dc23
LC record available at https://lccn.loc.gov/2016025149

ISBN 13: 978-1-138-60623-4 (pbk)
ISBN 13: 978-1-138-94319-3 (hbk)

Typeset in Baskerville by
Sunrise Setting Ltd, Paignton, UK

We dedicate this book to those who have cared for, with and about us, as well as exemplifying the value of caring for others. Our dedication is especially to Ann, Graham, Laura and Peter, Bev and Vic, and Carol Bacchi.

Contents

Notes on contributors   ix
Acknowledgements   xiii

1 **ReValuing care: cycles and connections**   1
ROSIE HARDING, RUTH FLETCHER AND CHRIS BEASLEY

2 **Negotiating strangeness on the abortion trail**   14
RUTH FLETCHER

3 **Carrying on by *caring with* in the shadow of a South African HIV/AIDS global health intervention**   31
ABIGAIL BAIM-LANCE

4 **Caring for the homeless: Westminster City Council and anti-homeless bye-laws**   48
CAROLINE HUNTER

5 **Paths to social caring: researchers consider their journeys to activism**   65
JENNY BAKER, MARGARET ALLEN AND MAUREEN DYER

6 **Young people who care for a family member with physical or mental health problems: can research better reflect the interests of young carers?**   81
LESTER WATSON

7 **Caring at the borders of the human: companion animals and the homeless**   97
HELEN CARR

8   **Care and relationality: supported decision making under the UN CRPD**   114
ROSIE HARDING

9   **'New fathers' and the right to parental leave: is the European Court of Human Rights satisfied with just breadwinning?**   131
ALICE MARGARIA

10   **Carers as legal subjects**   148
ANN STEWART

11   **Towards a 'reasonable' level of state support for care?: Constitutionalism, care work and the common good**   165
OLIVIA SMITH

12   **Terms of endearment: meanings of family in a diverse sample of Australian parents**   182
CLARE BARTHOLOMAEUS AND DAMIEN W. RIGGS

13   **'It has had quite a lot of reverberations through the family': reconfiguring relationships through parent with dementia care**   198
ELIZABETH PEEL

14   **'Institutions, they're very straight. My god I hope I don't have to go into a care home': spatial inequalities anticipated by older lesbians and gay men**   215
SUE WESTWOOD

15   **Beyond care and vocabularies of altruism: considering sexuality and older people**   233
CHRIS BEASLEY

Index   251

Notes on contributors

Margaret Allen is Professor Emerita at the University of Adelaide. She retired in 2010 after teaching gender studies and history for four decades. She helped establish women's/gender studies in the university sector. She researches whiteness and gendered, transnational histories with a particular emphasis upon India and Australia 1880–1940s. She was Vice President (Affirmative Action) of NTEU in the early 1990s. She is a member of the management committee of the Fay Gale Centre for Research on Gender.

Abigail Baim-Lance is a medical anthropologist affiliated with the City of New York's School of Public Health, and University College London, Department of Applied Health Research. She received her PhD from Johns Hopkins University and has conducted qualitative research in South Africa, England and New York. Central issues animating her work revolve around forms of social participation in healthcare, particularly in long-term care settings, such as in the treatment of HIV/AIDS and other chronic conditions. She also focuses on methods of translating theoretically oriented research into healthcare settings.

Jenny Baker is Associate Professor, University of Adelaide and an indigenous Australian who, before her retirement, held the position of Director of Yaitya Purruna Indigenous Health Unit, in the School of Population Health/Public Health, Faculty of Health Sciences University of Adelaide. She is a member of the Fay Gale Centre and has been active around Indigenous Health for many years. Her recent book is *Theorising Survival. Indigenous Women and Social and Emotional Wellbeing*, Brisbane, Postpressed Publications, 2012.

Clare Bartholomaeus is an adjunct Research Associate in the School of Social and Policy Studies at Flinders University. Her research interests include gender, diversity and childhood/youth.

Chris Beasley is Professor in Politics and founder of the Fay Gale Centre for Research on Gender at the University of Adelaide, and was co-Director of the Centre 2009–13. Her research interests include the knowledge economy and activist teaching, embodied ethics and care, contemporary film, sexuality and intimacy, and innovations in heterosexuality and hetero-masculinity. She is on the editorial boards of *Men and Masculinities* and *NORMA: International Journal for Masculinity Studies*. Her books include, among others, *Heterosexuality in Theory and Practice* (with Heather Brook and Mary Holmes) (Routledge, 2012), *Gender & Sexuality: Critical Theories, Critical Thinkers* (Sage, 2005), and *What is Feminism?* (Sage, 1999).

Helen Carr is a Professor at Kent Law School. Her interests lie in the regulation of housing and homelessness and she has a broader concern with social welfare law. She has recently completed a research project on shared ownership (with Professor David Cowan from Bristol University and Alison Wallace, York University) and is in the process of writing, with Professor Caroline Hunter, a book interrogating the relationship between homeless people and the law.

Maureen Dyer, a sociologist of education, was involved in the establishment of women's/gender studies at the University of South Australia and was deeply involved in advancing gender issues in NTEU. During the 1980s she was involved in the Priority Projects programme to promote equity in education in South Australia. Since leaving the University she has spent over a decade as an International Affairs Gender, Training and Education Consultant, chiefly in Papua New Guinea.

Ruth Fletcher is a Senior Lecturer in the School of Law, Queen Mary University of London. She has published widely on questions of reproductive legality and the connections between socio-legal theory, feminist methods and health practices. Ruth is currently working on a book that considers how formal and informal legalities 'make life difficult' on the abortion trail. She is the Academic Editor of *Feminist Legal Studies* and co-director of the ReValuing Care Network.

Rosie Harding is Professor of Law and Society at the University of Birmingham. Her research focuses on the everyday regulation and legal recognition of intimate and caring relationships and is grounded in questions about care and mental capacity, feminist legal theory and gender, sexuality and law. Her work has been supported by research grants from the AHRC, ESRC and the British Academy. She is editor of *Ageing and Sexualities: Interdisciplinary Perspectives* (2016, Ashgate, with Elizabeth Peel), *Law and Sexuality* (2016, Routledge Critical Concepts) and author of *Duties to Care: Relationality, Dementia and Law* (2017, Cambridge University Press) and *Regulating Sexuality* (2011, Routledge; winner of the 2011 SLSA-Hart Book Prize and 2011 SLSA-Hart Early Career Prize). She co-directed the AHRC-funded ReValuing Care Network with Ruth Fletcher and Chris Beasley.

Caroline Hunter is a Professor at York Law School, University of York, UK. Her research interests lie at the intersection of housing law, policy and practice. She has conducted a number of empirical studies on evictions, regulation of anti-social behaviour and homelessness. She has published extensively on these subjects and is a co-author of Arden and Partington's *Housing Law* (Sweet &

Maxwell). She is currently jointly authoring with Helen Carr a book provisionally entitled *Socio-Legal Encounters with Homelessness: Regulating People at the Margins*.

Alice Margaria is a Post-doctoral Researcher at the Fundamental Rights Laboratory in Turin. She holds a PhD in law from the European University Institute. Her doctoral project investigated the construction of fatherhood emerging from the jurisprudence of the European Court of Human Rights. She has been a visiting scholar at various institutions, such as Emory University and the Max Planck Institute for Social Anthropology. She has also worked with international and non-governmental organisations, including UNICEF Office of Research, OSCE and the Human Rights Law Network. Her current research explores how judges are responding to the challenge of ensuring legal recognition to 'new' family ties that do not conform to the traditional family model, from a comparative perspective.

Elizabeth Peel is a Professor of Communication and Social Interaction at Loughborough University, UK. She is a critical social psychologist and held a British Academy Mid-Career Fellowship for the *Dementia Talking: Care, Conversation and Communication* project. She is a Fellow of the British Psychological Society (BPS) and chairs its Psychology of Sexualities Section. She is on the editorial boards of *Feminism & Psychology*, *Journal of GLBT Family Studies*, *Psychology & Sexuality* and *Qualitative Research in Psychology*. Her co-edited book *Out in Psychology: LGBTQ Perspectives* (Wiley, 2007) won the American Psychological Association Division 44 distinguished book award, and her co-authored textbook *Lesbian, Gay, Bisexual, Trans and Queer Psychology: An Introduction* (Cambridge University Press, 2010) won the BPS award 2013. Her latest books are, with Rosie Harding, *Ageing and Sexualities: Interdisciplinary Perspectives* (Ashgate, 2016) and, with Damien Riggs, *Critical Kinship Studies: An introduction to the Field* (Palgrave Macmillan, 2016).

Damien W. Riggs is an Associate Professor in social work at Flinders University, and an Australian Research Council Future Fellow. He is the author of over 150 publications in the areas of gender and sexuality studies, family studies and mental health, including (with Elizabeth Peel) *Critical Kinship Studies: An Introduction to the Field* (Palgrave Macmillan, 2016).

Olivia Smith lectured on law for many years in Ireland and the UK. She currently works in publishing and as an independent scholar. Her current project is on Irish law and Irish literature.

Ann Stewart is Professor of Law, Warwick Law School, specialising in the area of gender and the law, particularly in the context of international development, and works collaboratively in a number of jurisdictions, particularly in southern and eastern Africa and in South Asia. She was Ford Visiting Professorial Fellow at the Centre for Law and Governance at Jawaharlal Nehru University, New Delhi, in 2010, and is presently co-lead for Warwick University's Global

Research Priority on International Development. Recent work has focused on concepts of care and body work, both within the context of the UK and global value chains.

Lester Watson recently completed his doctoral thesis in the School of Psychology at Charles Sturt University, Australia, from where he previously graduated with an honours degree in psychology. His qualifications also include a political science degree from the Australian National University. He has worked extensively with children and young people in the conduct of qualitative research, most particularly using collaborative/participatory methodologies. His interests include critical psychology and research with a social justice focus. Lester also has wide experience with the Australian Government, having worked in a variety of positions across six departments.

Sue Westwood is a socio-legal scholar with an interest in ageing, gender, sexuality and equality. Sue is a postdoctoral researcher at the Department for Social Policy and Intervention, University of Oxford, researching social policy relating to the care of older people and people with dementia. She also teaches law at Coventry University. Sue's monograph *Ageing, Gender and Sexuality: Equality in Later Life* and co-edited collection (with Dr Elizabeth Price) *Lesbian, Gay, Bisexual and Trans* (LGBT*) Individuals Living with Dementia: Concepts, practice and rights* were published by Routledge in 2016. She has four further edited collections underway: *Intersections of Ageing, Gender and Sexuality* (with Andrew King, Policy Press); *Minding the Knowledge Gaps: LGBT* ageing* (with Dr Andrew King, Dr Kathryn Almack and Dr Yiu-Tung Suen); *Older LGBT* Housing: Inequality issues* (with Dr Andrew King, Tina Wathern and Julia Shelley, Policy Press Shorts); and *Ageing, Diversity and Equality* (sole editor, Routledge).

Acknowledgements

The editors of this volume wish to acknowledge the financial support of the UK Arts and Humanities Research Council which funded the establishment of the ReValuing Care Network, and hence provided the institutional basis for developing an international research network. The AHRC funding generated a workshop at Keele University, UK, in 2012 and a workshop at the University of the Adelaide, South Australia, in 2013. We also acknowledge the participatory and financial support of Queen Mary University of London, which hosted a further workshop in 2014 developing some of the chapters published here. The ReValuing Care workshops were highly productive and, so far, have resulted in the publication of two edited volumes, including this one, many individual publications, key note addresses and presentations in several countries.

We also wish to acknowledge the support we have received from the universities named above, as well as the University of Birmingham, who continue to support the ReValuing Care Network website. The network would not have been possible without the essential involvement of two research centres that originally combined forces to produce the ReValuing Care Network and its subsequent activities and publications, the Centre for Law, Gender and Sexuality (Universities of Keele, Westminster and Kent, UK) and the Fay Gale Centre for Research on Gender (University of Adelaide, South Australia). These two centres provided a highly active and engaged combined research grouping which drew upon their memberships and their broader research communities located in a range of other universities across the globe. While many of the centre members have directly contributed to this volume, the participation and intellectual contribution of other members should also be noted here. In Australia, participants from the Fay Gale Centre included Carol Bacchi, Emily Cock, Pam Papadelos, Victoria Skinner and Anna Szorenyi. In the UK participants from the Centre for Law, Gender and Sexuality included Donatella Alessandrini, Marie Fox, Jane Krishnadas, Ambreena Manji, Harriet Samuels, Michael Thomson and Sorcha Ui Chonnachtaigh. The ReValuing Care Network was supported by an advisory panel of Ann Stewart, Anthony Smith, Louise Rogers and Maria Drakopoulou, whose advice and support was invaluable throughout the ReValuing Care Network activities. Thanks also to Tracey Harrison and Sue Westwood for administrative and research assistance.

There is no doubt that our acknowledgements merely state in the baldest terms the creative and nourishing benefits of a caring research comradeship, a collectivity of companionability, mutual respect and support, and intellectual challenge. The ReValuing Care Network, which produced this volume and more, was indeed itself a practice of revaluing care.

Chapter 1

ReValuing care
Cycles and connections

Rosie Harding, Ruth Fletcher and Chris Beasley

Care is central to life, and yet is all too often undervalued, taken for granted and hidden from view. The ReValuing Care network[1] identified care as a central problematic, a focus of feminist debate for many years, and set about recuperating and developing anew aspects of that debate. This collection of original essays is the product of conversations, debates and discussions that took place at and through a series of ReValuing Care network workshops.[2] In this book, we seek to explore the different dimensions of care that shape social, legal and political relations, looking back through feminist literatures and experiences, and forward to alternative visions of how care can be valued, imagined and accomplished.

Previous feminist research on care has cohered around three key themes: the need to value caring and domestic labour in law and society; the utility of a feminist 'ethics of care'; and latterly, the limitations of care as a normative and conceptual framework. Early feminist work on the concept of care focused on the problems with non-recognition of women's unpaid domestic care work (Barrett and McIntosh 1982; Delphy 1984). This has since expanded to address care as an aspect of everyday life within and without kinship domains through such concepts as social reproduction (Bakker 2007; Bakker and Silvey 2008; Fudge 2014), affective equality (Lynch *et al.* 2009; Grummell *et al.* 2009), and care chains (Stewart 2007; 2011; Hochschild 2000). Similarly, the ethics of care has been routinely drawn upon to explain how relationships motivate choice and action in the social world (Sevenhuijsen 2003; Tronto 1993; Barnes 2012). At the same time as relational subjectivity is becoming a mainstream concept (Nedelsky 2011), some have questioned whether an ethic of care can resolve the crisis of subjectivity for feminism (Drakopoulou 2000).

More recently, critical considerations of care have cohered around questions of how to interrogate the asymmetry of care (Beasley and Bacchi 2007; Cooper 2007). Some efforts to value care-receipt have engaged with ideas about vulnerability (MacKenzie *et al.* 2013; Fineman and Grear 2013) and capability (Sen 1989; 1993; Nussbaum 2011; Fox and Thomson 2013) in normalising and valuing the experience of being cared-for, as well as other kinds of engagement with care. ReValuing Care as a network of scholars, and as an intellectual and political idea, is situated in these efforts to value the diversity, fluidity and publicity of care, while wanting to resist thinking in terms of universal understandings of care (Menon 2002; Mol 2008).

The key research questions that formed the basis of the ReValuing Care network activities, and which now form the intellectual foundations of this edited collection, were concerned with how creative, cross-disciplinary collaborations can advance knowledge of the ways that care is imagined, valued, resourced, supported and regulated. The network also sought to interrogate what the creative methodological approaches and critical theoretical engagements of law, gender and sexuality scholarship contribute to, and draw from, improved understandings of the value of care in society. In the fourteen substantive chapters that follow, this book address these questions in four key ways. First, the contributions expand contemporary theoretical understandings of the value of care by reflecting upon established conceptual approaches (such as the ethics of care) and developing new ways of using and understanding this concept. Second, the chapters draw on a wide range of methods, from doctrinal scholarship through ethnographic, empirical and biographical research methodologies. Third, the book moves beyond the usual subjects of care research, by expanding the analysis beyond the more typical focus on familial interconnection to include professional care contexts, care by strangers and care for and about animals. Finally, the text draws on contributions from academics working in Europe and Australia, across law, anthropology, gender studies, politics, psychology and sociology. By highlighting the points of connection and tension between these diverse international and disciplinary perspectives, this collection outlines a new and nuanced approach to care, exploring contemporary understandings of care across the social sciences and humanities. In *ReValuing Care*, we take a broad approach to care and include the diverse range of theoretical perspectives involved in understanding embodied experiences of responsiveness and affect, both in relation to caring *for* and caring *about* different people, practices and places. Keeping the definition of care open in this way generates the capacity for creative interdisciplinary and cross-sector exchange.

ReValuing care: cycles and connections

Given the great deal of feminist literature that already addresses aspects of care, both empirically and conceptually, we wanted to begin this collection with a justification for why we feel that care remains an important site for feminist research and theorising. There are three key drivers that underpin our commitment to ReValuing Care in theory, law and policy, which are reflected in, through and across the contributions to the collection. We are interested in uncovering and understanding the new moments of regulation and recognition of care across social interconnections that are shaped by legal, social and political responses to care needs and care provision. We also seek to think conceptually about the values that underpin the term care, as a practice and as a description of social (inter)connections. Finally, we propose that considering cycles of care can provide a new conceptual language for understanding, valuing and operationalising care for the future. For us, 'cycles of care' captures how subjects move between and among instances of care-receiving and care-giving over time and space as they generate and value connection with one another through embodied experiences and rights claims.

Legal, social and political responses to care needs and care provision

Recent years have seen the emergence of the carer as a political and legal subject (see Stewart, Chapter 10). In spite of critical and comparative work which has highlighted the diverse locations of care-giving, too often care-giving is treated as almost entirely privatised within the family, undertaken by women and socially constructed as women's responsibility. The twenty-first century explosion in the regulatory domains surrounding both informal care (care provided by friends and family members) and paid care-giving has intensified public scrutiny of care, if unevenly. For example, the introduction of legal recognition and rights for carers in particular national settings has taken place incrementally over the last half century, partly in response to activism through the carers' movement (see Carers UK 2015), and partly as a response to changing patterns of family life, health and social care provision, and population demographics. Lengthening average life expectancies, workplace gains for women resulting from feminist activism, and the long-term effects of equal pay, maternity leave and anti-discrimination legislation, alongside the changing economic contexts of relational lives, mean that the heterosexual, biological, nuclear family as the normative ideal of privatised care-giving has lost whatever explanatory force it had. Rather, care is given and received in and through multiple, diverse situations where overlapping modes of private, informal and professional care-giving interact and interconnect (see for instance, Dimova *et al.* 2015).

Perhaps as a result of these changing social contexts, the provision of care has become a matter that no longer resides within the nuclear family (if it ever did) but instead has become the focus of a great deal of political and legal attention. These regulatory responses to the shifting care contexts in turn require rejoinders from critical, feminist perspectives to uncover the complex and shifting effects of such changes to care law and policy, which are taken up by contributions in this collection. The contemporary regulatory moment takes a multiplicity of forms, including: increasing rights claims, like those that arise from the UN Convention on the Rights of Persons with Disabilities (see Harding, Chapter 8), or those made possible through public dialogue on the appropriate legal recognition of care (see Smith, Chapter 11); or the reprivatisation of responsibility for care into different spaces, like the development of 'voluntary' community care-giving frameworks (see Baim-Lance, Chapter 3); or the use of regulatory tools to move 'public' care provision for the homeless into 'private' spaces (see Hunter, Chapter 4); or the uneven application of equality and anti-discrimination provision, like the limitations of the response of the European Court of Human Rights (see Margaria, Chapter 9) or in formal care spaces (see Westwood, Chapter 14).

As we finalised this collection, a particular example of the shifting legal and political value given to care and carers hit the British news headlines. The UK Government announced in January 2016 that the rules on the controversial benefit cap[3] would be changed to exempt anyone in receipt of Carer's Allowance. This followed a High Court verdict in November 2015 that the inclusion of carers in receipt of Carer's Allowance in the benefit cap was unjustifiably discriminatory on the basis of disability, because it did not recognise the impact on disabled people who rely on family carers to support them.[4] This policy was founded in ideologically conservative attempts to reduce the provision of welfare and to 'encourage' individuals to move into the paid labour force. During debates on the introduction of the benefit cap, the then Minister of State for the Department of Work and Pensions, Chris Grayling, said,

> [t]he reality is that the cap is all about influencing behaviour; it is not about creating hardship. If we succeed in influencing behaviour, the number of cases affected by the cap will be cut to a minimum. However, we will only influence behaviour if we have a simple rule which people can understand, and not one hedged about with numerous exemptions that only welfare rights experts can follow. The simple message to every citizen of this country as they enter adult life is that there is a limit to the amount of financial support that the state will provide to people if they fall on hard times, and therefore they need to adapt their circumstances to reflect that reality.
> House of Commons Hansard, 17 May 2011, Col 944

This challenge to the benefit cap for carers, and the subsequent political response to it, provides an insight into why care and caring remains vitally important to feminist theoretical work, and why the conceptual tools created to respond to the privatised nature of care may not be sufficient to respond to governmental regulation of care in the future. As ideologically conservative governments, not only in the UK, but also in Australia, Canada, the US and elsewhere, seek to contract the welfare state, in service of ideological commitments to 'austerity', small state liberalism and 'the market', it is vital that critical scholars take the opportunity to reflect on why and how these regulatory moments occur. In doing so, feminist strategies and rationales for revaluing care may help us to articulate effective opposition, not only to the re-privatisation of caring responsibilities to within the nuclear family (see Cossman 2002), but also to the governmental 'nudges', however subtle (or not) they may be, to simultaneously push those with caring responsibilities back into paid work. Concerns such as these, the emergent social, legal and political valuing of care and carers, and the implications of the ways care is valued, are taken up throughout this collection.

Theoretical engagements with care and connection

Our concern in this collection is not solely on the practice of care, but also on taking forward conceptual insights into how care can be conceptually and theoretically re-valued. The feminist ethic of care literature has been hugely influential in recent decades both in challenging the privatisation of care in to the domestic sphere and in shaping legal and political responses to care. Attention to conceptual analyses and debates about the value of care within this volume owes much to this feminist legacy. Perspectives regarding the value of care, which draw broadly upon the feminist ethic of care, are nevertheless diverse.

A number of the contributions employ the language of care: to interrogate the legal requirements regarding care provision that includes questions of capacity (see Harding, Chapter 8); to investigate the legal identities of carers (see Stewart, Chapter 10; Margaria, Chapter 9); or to examine the character, the social and the individual impact of caring and connection (see Peel, Chapter 13; Hunter, Chapter 4; Baim-Lance, Chapter 3). In other words, the *content* of care reveals its social significance and is theorised as a means to exploring its value. Other contributors approach this in different ways. Some demonstrate new conceptions of and locations for care, thereby *extending* the meaning of the terminology and providing innovations in theoretical understandings of it. For instance, contributors note that care may also be employed: to encompass intersectional frameworks such as age, gender and sexuality (see Westwood, Chapter 14); to include relationships beyond the human (see Carr, Chapter 7); and to refer to modes of social activism and support (see Fletcher, Chapter 2; Baker *et al.*, Chapter 5). Other contributors however *question* the very basis of theoretical frameworks employed in the literature on care and undertake a critique of well-established terminologies, like family (see Bartholomaeus and Riggs, Chapter 12), or even the language of care itself as a means to conceptualise the value of social connection (see Beasley, Chapter 15).

Alternative conceptual lexicons are offered up in this collection as ways to help navigate the complex normative and regulatory frames that shape the experience of care. Some contributors (Harding, Chapter 8; Smith, Chapter 11) use the language of relationality, following Jennifer Nedelsky (2011), who argues for a re-visioning of autonomy as it is figured in legal and political ideas to take account of the inevitability and necessity of relationships as ways of constructing and supporting autonomy. Others use relationality (Baim-Lance, Chapter 3; Carr, Chapter 7) but also find value for thinking through care in Jane Bennett's (2010) concept of 'vibrant matter', where humans and non-humans are linked together in 'confederations', understood somewhat like Deleuze's 'assemblages', to create and shape possibilities and outcomes. Reflexive practice is drawn upon (Baker *et al.*, Chapter 5; Watson, Chapter 6) to demonstrate the interconnections of research and researcher, the ways that caring about and for others permeate not only the research topic but also the choices we make and the ways that we do research as critical and feminist scholars, and as activists. The place of strangers, figured in both an interpersonal and a legal sense, in supporting and facilitating access to care is also raised in these contributions, whether in relation to abortion care (Fletcher, Chapter 2), supporting and feeding homeless people (Hunter, Chapter 4), or the multiple changes that the experience of caring for a parent with dementia bring to family relationships (Peel, Chapter 13). By bringing these varied conceptual approaches together in this collection we hope to draw attention to the multifaceted ways that care and caring can be valued. By pushing care scholarship beyond the usual spaces, topics and contexts we seek to expand the conceptual (and empirical) possibilities of care in critical, feminist, social justice scholarship.

Cycles of care

Finally, we offer cycles of care as a way of framing our collective contribution to these debates and literatures. Care cycles might be thought of as building on the ways that attentiveness calls unevenly on timespace, energy and knowledge. Attentiveness is a key aspect of the logic of care, requiring sensitivity and flexibility in watching out and relating wisely to surroundings (Mol 2008, p. 32). When considering care, in a sense we are investigating ways that attentiveness makes 'social flesh' as it moves with people and things through time and space to provide a hug, or wipe up the mess (Beasley and Bacchi 2012). Like legal embodiment (Fletcher *et al.* 2008), cycles work through subjects, relationships, matter and symbols when they make social flesh. Nevertheless, the conceptualisation of cycles of care takes us beyond legal embodiment as an analytical framework for generating questions about these fleshy connections, and instead embodies the critical tools for understanding how care works. Through the empirical and conceptual contributions in this collection, we examine the actual processes by which care is done. In this way we throw more light on how care makes timespace 'take on flesh', to paraphrase Valverde (2015, pp. 9–10; see also Kotiswaran 2015).

Cycles build on this understanding of the theoretical significance of actual processes of fleshy connection, by capturing the dynamics of care as it starts, stops, turns back on itself, and thickens or thins out in the process. Both organic and thing-like, we select cycles out from the association with ordinary terms, like lifecycles and bicycles, and give it new life. By being attentive to the ordinary, everyday, micro interactions that shape and are shaped by regulatory forces (Harding 2011), cycles help us to focus on the ways that care shifts and changes through space and time. As a moving combination of organic and non-organic components, cycles allow for movement backwards, to grasp a memorable photograph, while moving forwards as living somewhere new becomes the best care option. Cycles allow for sideways moves if working a solution around the problem, rather than tackling it directly, provides a better way to care. And cycles twist and turn as evaluations of how care is working, for example, happen along the way rather than at the end. Like networks, assemblages and confederations, care cycles move through and around matter in their multi-dimensionality. However, cycles feel and remember unevenly as they move hesitantly through timespace and draw the flesh out of what might otherwise be understood as nodes, actants or vibrant matter.

Care moves people and things in another way, of course, as it energises and wears. Lightening the load that comes with ordinary efforts to make life better can be exhausting or uplifting, depending on circumstances and conditions. The kind of attentiveness that misses its mark in some way may end up being wearing, even though in another time and place that miss might have been energising as a warm responsiveness filled the gap. Gunaratnam (2013, p. 43–56) captures these tensions well in her discussion of Maxine's experience of hypersensitivity as she refuses to allow carers to bathe her. For Gunaratnam (2013), Maxine and her carers alike recognise the way that histories of racism can have such an impact on how a dying body cares for itself through a range of responses from paranoia to twinkles. Cycles then also bring in the complex, nested relationalities that shape our experiences of care-giving and care-receiving.

Third, care cycles as knowledge grows, contracts or stands still as we learn more about how particular techniques of care *do* or *provide* care. Scholars of knowledge networks have taught us how expertise is developed through interaction and adaption (Cloatre 2013). Knowledge crosses professional and jurisdictional boundaries as those in need of drugs or treatment find out how access works. In the process, methods of knowing become more about experimentation along the way, and less about application or implementation of pre-existing knowledge and understanding. Care cycles as knowledge of the interactions between people and things become embedded in the apparatuses and techniques of care. Thinking about information and knowledge as an aspect of care cycles allows for a deeper appreciation of the diverse ways in which stories and objects carry care information. The chapters in this collection tell us about the many different ways in which care *does* care, as it builds relationality, watches for calls for assistance or withdrawal, and gets on with the business of looking after bodies. Methods of doing care critically, like networked methods of knowledge generation, can show a similar commitment to the unevenness of care, to the care labour of those who have gone before and to the care-ful imaginations of those around us.

As editors we offer cycles of care as a deliberately tentative frame, which learns from the contributory chapters as it considers steps for building a care-ful critique of existing approaches. We do not propose cycles as a theoretical framework which is applied and developed by each of the chapters to this volume. Neither do we propose it as an approach which transcends, or is better than, previous approaches to care. Rather, with cycles we want to signal a dialogic and open (Valverde 2015) engagement with that which has gone before, with that which is contained herein, and with that which is yet to come. In doing so we aim to build on a well-established legacy of critical race feminism (e.g. Harris 1990), which asks for tentative categories. Harris cautions we cannot escape theoretical categories, but we ought to use them in a way which presumes partial knowledge. Alongside Mol (2002), we want to find a way to avoid the multi-perspectivism which leaves the object singular and alone. Research into care misses too much if it treats care as something that is already known. For us, cycles of care capture the multi-dimensionality, diversity and movement of care, while acknowledging that care will take particular shapes, speeds and paces. Care practices 'hang together somehow' as cycles move, pick some people and things up, and leave others down.

About the book

The fourteen contributions that follow are not organised into parts or sections, because the ways that concepts, locations and experiences of care run through these chapters defy such easy categorisation. We could have arranged the chapters by focusing on the types of care labour discussed (kinship care, elder care, health care, social care) or the scholarly approach taken (conceptual, doctrinal, empirical), or thematically by focusing on particular concepts or ideas (relationality, spatiality, rights). Instead, these contributions are loosely grouped to provide a narrative journey through the multiple ways that care is valued and revalued, practiced and provided, made public and hidden. In approaching the contributions to the collection in the order we have chosen, we hope that our readers will gain a sense of the various conversations and connections that emerged from discussions across and between the ReValuing Care network activities.

To begin the collection, Ruth Fletcher (Chapter 2) offers an account of the negotiation of strangeness as an aspect of feminist activist care in the context of abortion travel and support networks between Ireland and the UK. Drawing on close readings of two interviews with past coordinators of ESCORT, a Liverpool-based abortion support group catering for Irish women, Fletcher interrogates the different work that 'strangeness' does in the context of abortion travel. She argues that negotiating strangeness is a key dimension of the timespace of abortion travel, though not always a negative element. Conceptually it bridges the displacement and 'out-of-place-ness' of the experience of abortion travel through the provision of home-like resources, with support and facilitation in strange places generating care and connection. In Chapter 3, Abigail Baim-Lance takes us on an ethnographic journey to South Africa to explore the ways that home and community volunteers support people living with (and dying from) HIV/AIDS. Baim-Lance explores the potentialities and limitations of community care projects set up through charitable funding, but which carry on without financial resources. She demonstrates the ways that care-givers and care-receivers work together with the things of care (medications, hospitals, clinics, traditional beliefs and remedies) to *care with* as an alternative to caring for, and to taking care of, to argue not only for better resources, but also for better support for the creative, relational responses that are generated by need.

In Chapter 4, we travel back to the UK to explore the ways that charitable, community provision of care for homeless people is constrained and controlled by spatial regulation. Caroline Hunter tells the story, through a reading of consultation documents and responses, of an attempt to ban the serving of food to homeless people outdoors in Westminster. Her analysis explores the complex interconnections of local authorities, charitable giving and constructions of nuisance that shape the ways outdoor city landscapes become the subject of particular regulatory practices that sit on the margins of formal law. The approach engages with Blomley's (2012) concept of police, which draws on particular rationalities of shaping and preventing negative behaviours. In Hunter's contribution, she demonstrates how the threat of a bye-law was enough to police the provision of care to homeless people through soup kitchens and other outdoor food provision services, moving the provision indoors, to private locations.

In Chapter 5, Jenny Baker, Margaret Allen and Maureen Dyer offer a story of their own journeys, and those of others they interviewed, towards social activism in the Australian context. They consider the pain of the injuries of class, race and gender in terms of bell hooks' view that attending to this pain enables the development of resistance and wanting to produce social change. In this context, social activism is reconceived as a form of care, in that social activism involves caring about how society is structured, about how it impacts upon people and about how to ensure that new generations do not suffer the same injuries. Their reflections on their journeys into and through academia, and the ways that their social caring shaped their experience across different vectors of their professional and personal lives, remind us all that how we engage in and with our research requires attentiveness and care. Lester Watson, in Chapter 6, maintains this reflexive focus, offering us another way in which care shapes methodological concerns. He offers an operationalisation of care, informing a research method to engage with and address the methodological challenges of research with young carers. Instead of constructing young carers as victims, as he argues has often been the case in research into the experiences of caring whilst young, he argues that the use of a collaborative research methodology allows attentiveness to the self-constructions of young carers, and injects positivity and engagement into the research process in a way that is responsive to the complex interrelationships between researcher and researched.

Our journey through cycles of care continues in Chapter 7 with a contribution from Helen Carr, in which she argues that understanding homeless people and their pets as 'actants of care' allows us to revalue care in these often marginalised relationships through shifting our gaze onto the relationality of care. Drawing on a range of published narratives of care by homeless people towards their pets, Carr extends the reach of our collection from interpersonal care and relationships, across species boundaries to provide an account of care between homeless people and their companion animals. Carr focuses on the resources animals provide to enable homeless people to resist instances of cultural misrecognition through their caring assemblages. Keeping with the multiple ways that relationality shapes care and caring, Chapter 8 from Rosie Harding takes up the challenge of exploring the conceptual links between care, relationality and supported decision-making by people with cognitive disabilities. The chapter seeks to use a relational lens to bring into focus a path through the misalignment of the English Mental Capacity Act 2005's focus on best interest decision-making and the emphasis on supporting cognitively disabled people to make their own decisions under the UN Convention on the Rights of Persons with Disabilities. Exploring two recent Court of Protection decisions, Harding seeks to bring into focus the ways that different relationalities of care (formal and informal, personal and professional) work with social and legal norms to shape the everyday experiences of people with cognitive disabilities.

In Chapter 9 from Alice Margaria we consider the ways that international human rights norms influence care and caring. Margaria offers an analysis of European Human Rights jurisprudence on parental leave. She interrogates the persistence of the male-breadwinner/female-homemaker dualism within European Court of Human Rights jurisprudence, to evaluate the possibilities of using the ECHR as a means of challenging gender stereotypes in parental caregiving. Her conclusion, that there is a renewed eagerness from the European Court of Human Rights to challenge gender role stereotypes in relation to child care, offers a hopeful vision for the continuing emancipatory potential of international human rights instruments.

The next two chapters continue with investigations of formal legal responses to caring. Ann Stewart (Chapter 10) explores the emergence of the carer as a legal subject, and the consequent recasting of care away from altruistic constructions of the naturalness of familial, unpaid care, towards a claim for compensation for losses associated with social and economic exclusion in contemporary society, where everyone is expected to find value through economically productive activity. Olivia Smith (Chapter 11) provides a nuanced analysis of the possibilities and challenges facing the redrafting of the Irish constitution to provide 'a reasonable level of support' for carers. Smith demonstrates that rather than focusing on the reconciliation of care with labour market participation, the Convention on the Constitution appeared to re-embed state-supported caring within a privatised domestic sphere, even as it expanded beyond a specifically gendered homemaker/breadwinner dichotomy.

In Chapter 12, we shift from legal regulation of caring towards social experiences of family, kinship and caring. Clare Bartholomaeus and Damien Riggs provide an empirically grounded analysis of the ways 'family' is constructed and understood in the context of different approaches to family formation. Their empirical research includes representatives of families formed through adoption, foster care, commercial surrogacy and giving birth following reproductive heterosex. This dataset provides fertile ground for exploring the ways that meanings given to 'family' shape what it means to care, to be in an intimate relationship, and how these different meanings are shaped by normative demands that proliferate about what family means and does. In Chapter 13, Elizabeth Peel explores kinship care in a different context, where kinship relations are turned around and care-giver becomes care-recipient, and the previous recipient of care becomes the party providing care. Peel analyses discourse from focus groups and interviews that uncovers the complexities and challenges of caring for a parent with dementia that fracture or reconfigure normative familial relationships. She explores accounts of sibling conflict and collaboration, as well as discourses of parentification and infantalisation, while considering how these caring dynamics are mediated by gender, social class and locus of care (quotidian or remote). Caring for a parent living with dementia can generate particular issues for adult children that trouble notions of how we understand familial roles, responsibilities and 'duties'.

We stay with concerns around elder care for the final empirical chapter in the collection. In Chapter 14, Sue Westwood interrogates the concerns that older lesbians and gay men have about the ways that care spaces reproduce heteronormativity and heterosexism and heighten affective inequalities. In the provision of personal care in residential settings for older people, the intersection of age, gender *and* sexuality is crucially important. This chapter investigates the intersectional politics of personal care by focusing upon how older lesbians and gay men experience the heteronormative gaze in residential health care contexts.

We close the collection with a chapter from Chris Beasley (Chapter 15) which reflects back on the literatures and concepts that have been implicated in many of the contributions to the ReValuing Care network and in this book. Beasley interrogates both the potential and limits of care as a feminist response to social developments around individualisation, and the potentially problematic ways that ideas of altruism and charity are embedded in many feminist conceptual approaches to care. In response, she offers 'social flesh' as an alternative conceptual means of constructing social interconnection through embodied intimacy to inform scholarship, policy and institutional care.

Notes

1 Funded by the Arts and Humanities Research Council (AHRC) from 2012–14 [grant number AH/J008516].
2 Keele University, 2012, University of Adelaide, 2013, Queen Mary University of London, 2014.
3 The benefit cap reduces the total amount that a person can receive in welfare payments to below £350 per week for single adults, or below £500 for couples and single parents with resident children (HM Government 2016).
4 *Hurley & Others v Secretary of State for Work and Pensions* [2015] EWHC 3382 (Admin).

References

Bakker, Isabella (2007) 'Social Reproduction and the Constitution of a Gendered Political Economy' *New Political Economy* 12(4): 541–556.
Bakker, Isabella and Silvey, Rachel (eds.) (2008) *Beyond States and Markets: The challenge of social reproduction* London: Routledge.
Barnes, Marian (2012) *Care in Everyday Life: An ethic of care in practice* Bristol: Policy Press.
Barrett, Michelle and McIntosh, Mary (1982) *The Anti-social Family* London: Verso.
Beasley, Chris and Bacchi, Carol (2007) 'Envisaging a New Politics for an Ethical Future: Beyond trust, care and generosity – towards an ethic of "social flesh"' *Feminist Theory* 8(3): 279–298.
Beasley, Chris and Carol Bacchi (2012) 'Making Politics Fleshy: The ethic of social flesh' in A. Bletsas, C. Beasley (eds.) *Engaging with Carol Bacchi: Strategic interventions and exchanges* Adelaide: University of Adelaide Press, pp. 99–120.
Bennett, Jane (2010) *Vibrant Matter: A political ecology of things* Durham: Duke University Press.

Blomley N. (2012) '2011 Urban Geography Plenary Lecture—Colored Rabbits, Dangerous Trees, and Public Sitting: Sidewalks, Police, and the City' *Urban Geography* 33(7): 917–935.

Carers UK (2015) 'Valuing Carers 2015' available at: http://www.carersuk.org/news-and-campaigns/campaigns/we-care-don-t-you/value-my-care/valuing-carers-2015 accessed 5 February 2016.

Cloatre, Emilie (2013) *Pills for the Poorest* Basingstoke: Palgrave Macmillan.

Cooper, Davina (2007) '"Well you go there to get off": Visiting feminist care ethics through a women's bathhouse' *Feminist Theory* 8(3): 243–262.

Cossman, Brenda (2002) 'Family Feuds: Neo-liberal and neo-conservative visions of the reprivatization project' in Brenda Cossman and Judy Fudge (eds.) *Privatization, Law and the Challenge to Feminism* Toronto: University of Toronto Press, pp. 169–217.

Delphy, Christine (1984) *Close to Home: A materialist analysis of women's oppression* London: Hutchinson.

Dimova, Margarita, Hough, Carrie, Kyaa, Kerry and Manji, Ambreena (2015) 'Intimacy and Inequality: Local care chains and paid childcare in Kenya' *Feminist Legal Studies* 23(2): 167–179.

Drakopoulou, Maria (2000) 'The Ethic of Care, Female Subjectivity and Feminist Legal Scholarship' *Feminist Legal Studies* 8: 199–226.

Fineman, Martha and Grear, Anna (eds.) (2013) *Vulnerability: Reflections on a new ethical foundation for law and politics* Farnham: Ashgate.

Fletcher, Ruth, Fox, Marie and McCandless, Julie (2008) 'Legal Embodiment: Analysing the body of healthcare law' *Medical Law Review* 16(3): 321–345.

Fox, Marie and Thomson, Michael (2013) 'Realising Social Justice in Public Health Law' *Medical Law Review* 21(2): 278–309.

Fudge, Judy (2014) 'Feminist Reflections on the Scope of Labour Law: Domestic work, social reproduction and jurisdiction' *Feminist Legal Studies* 22(1): 1–23.

Grummell, B, Devine, D and Lynch, K (2009) 'Gender, Care and New Managerialism in Higher Education' *Gender and Education* 21(2): 191–208.

Gunaratnam, Yasmin (2013) *Death and the Migrant: Bodies, border and care* London: Bloomsbury.

Harding, Rosie (2011) *Regulating Sexuality: Legal consciousness in lesbian and gay lives* Abingdon: Routledge.

Harris, Angela (1990) 'Race and Essentialism in Feminist Legal Theory' *Stanford Law Review* 42: 581–616.

HM Government (2016) 'Benefit Cap' available at: https://www.gov.uk/benefit-cap/overview accessed on 10 August 2016.

Hochschild, Arlie R (2000) 'Global Care Chains and Emotional Surplus Value' in Tony Giddens and Will Hutton (eds.) *On the Edge: Globalization and the New Millennium* London: Sage Publishers, pp. 130–146.

Kotiswaran, Prabha (2015) 'Valverde's Chronotopes of Law: Reflections on an agenda for social legal studies' *Feminist Legal Studies* 23(3): 353–359.

Lynch, Kathleen, Baker, John and Lyons, Maureen (2009) *Affective Equality: Love, care and injustice* Basingstoke: Palgrave Macmillan.

MacKenzie, Catriona, Rogers, Wendy and Dodds, Susan (2013) *Vulnerability: New essays in ethics and feminist philosophy* Oxford: Oxford University Press.

Menon, Nivedita (2002) 'Universalism without Foundations?' *Economy and Society* 31(1): 152–169.

Mol, Annemarie (2002) *The Body Multiple* Durham, NC: Duke University Press.

Mol, Annemarie (2008) *The Logic of Care* London: Routledge.
Nedelsky, Jennifer (2011) *Law's Relations: A relational theory of self, autonomy and law* Oxford University Press.
Nussbaum, Martha (2011) *Creating Capabilities: The human development approach* Cambridge, MA: Harvard University Press.
Sen, Amartya (1989) 'Development as Capability Expansion' *Journal of Development Planning* 19: 41–58.
Sen, Amartya (1993) 'Capability and Well-being' in Nussbaum, Martha and Sen, Amartya (eds.) *The Quality of Life* Oxford: Oxford University Press.
Sevenhuijsen, Selma (2003) 'The Place of Care: The relevance of the feminist ethic of care for social policy' *Feminist Theory* 4(2): 179–197.
Stewart, Ann (2007) 'Who Do We Care About? Reflections on gender justice in a global market' *Northern Ireland Legal Quarterly* 58(3): 358–374.
Stewart, Ann (2011) *Gender, Law and Justice in a Global Market* Cambridge: Cambridge University Press.
Tronto, Joan (1993) *Moral Boundaries: A political argument for an ethic of care* London: Routledge.
Valverde, Mariana (2015) *Chronotopes of Law* London: Routledge.

Chapter 2

Negotiating strangeness on the abortion trail

Ruth Fletcher[1]

In thinking about care as a practice that cycles and connects, this chapter focuses on the negotiation of strangeness as an aspect of care. The abortion care practices of feminist volunteers provide a rich site in which to consider whether and how care may be revalued. As they reach out to those who have been displaced in their search for abortion, activists mobilise an ethic of care in constituting relations with strangers, filling a gap in healthcare, and providing non-judgemental support. Their practice of opening up their homes to travelling abortion-seekers draws on techniques of social reproduction as they deploy material and affective resources in reproducing feminist community. Volunteers also face up to the asymmetry of care as they move between acknowledging the burdensomeness of abortion travel, and discovering how strangeness opens up the potential for connection over critique, dialogue and challenge. For all these reasons, abortion support groups provide a fruitful site of inquiry for thinking through the revaluing of care activities. The specificities of their feminist voluntary practices, as they recognise and rework the significance of being and feeling strange on the abortion trail, make them a rich intellectual resource for theorising cycles and connections of care.

This commitment to 'lightening the load' on the abortion trail provides an opportunity to think through strangeness as it is practised in particular times and spaces. In taking up that challenge I respond to Lentin's call for attention to processes of strangering as she asks researchers to stop taking 'strangers as "surfaces", seeing and knowing them episodically' (2004, p. 303). I draw on Ahmed (2000) and Cooper (2007a) in developing my response. Ahmed has offered a way to think about the stranger that takes us beyond strangeness as a personal attribute. She argues that the identification of the stranger as the person we do not know is a form of stranger fetishism. It conceals the forms of authorisation and labour that bring the stranger into being. The stranger is not the person we do not know, but is a figure bearing the attributes of strangeness already. We recognise particular bodies as strangers because they are 'out of place' in some way. By tracing the relations of knowledge that allow the stranger to enter the community as an 'out of place' figure (Ahmed 2000, p. 21), we can learn more about what makes someone seem out of place.

Cooper has taken this kind of approach to defetishising the stranger another couple of steps. First, she argues that: 'the stranger may be less a location of asymmetrical otherness than a relationship between complexly understood and configured "unknowns"' (2007a, p. 205). In this light, the stranger is an effect of shifting boundaries between the known and the unknown; someone who is unfamiliar and belongs at the same time. Second, she argues that stranger contact can take a positive form and be governed by norms of civil attention. For Cooper, strangers in local spaces of social invention, such as the Toronto Women's Bathhouse, can 'rework the connections between public and private, between recognition and misrecognition, between contact and inequality' (2007a, p. 204). In considering how strangeness features as an aspect of feminist voluntary abortion care in the time and space constituted by Irish women's abortion travel since the 1980s, this chapter contributes to defetishising the stranger as a figure of care. It asks how strangeness comes into being as it moves across the boundaries between familiarity and unfamiliarity, belonging and displacement.

Drawing on Rossiter (2009), I use the term 'abortion trail' to capture the timespace of care that has been landscaped by women's practices of abortion travel and a variety of actors who respond to those practices. Abortion-seekers become part of the trail as they negotiate strangeness in crossing boundaries of familiarity, belonging and jurisdiction in their search for abortion care. The trail as a 'landscape of care' is carved out by 'the institutional, the domestic, the familial, the community, the public, the voluntary and the private as well as transitions within and between them' (Milligan and Wiles 2010, p. 738).[2] Law, regulation and practice come together in different ways to generate conditional pathways to abortion care (Beynon-Jones 2012, p. 59; Sethna and Doull 2013; Fletcher 2013; Brown 2013; Gomperts 2002; Bart 1987). Like Valverde, I'm interested in the ways in which time 'takes on flesh' (2015, p. 10), as the trail becomes tangible through the actions of abortion-seekers and their supporters in moving between familiar and unfamiliar spaces. These trails criss-cross the boundaries of formal legal permissibility as they generate grey zones of provision and access. If we want to understand more about how law is experienced by those who escape domestic legal capture and push governance in new directions, then we need to account for practices that support and sustain escape (Gilmartin and White 2011; White and Gilmartin 2008). As Sims *et al.* note in the context of local authorities and flood support, voluntary caring practices, where people step in to care for each other when official support is deficient, are a key part of such a shifting landscape (2009, p. 310). Irish women's practices of travelling for abortion, the safe and legal provision of extra-territorial abortion in Britain, and the support of pro-choice activists at home and abroad, have all come together to generate the abortion trail, a timespace of uneven and unfamiliar, if accessible, abortion care.

From the establishment of the Irish Pregnancy Counselling Centre and the Women's Information Network in the 1980s to the development of a crisis pregnancy counselling network with a majority of pro-choice providers in the 2000s (Connolly 2002, pp. 155–183; Fletcher 2013, p. 173), there are many ways in which feminist activists engaged in care provision and the politics of protest and reform as they sought to legitimise the search for fertility control. Connolly, among others, has analysed their work as part of the development of the Irish women's movement and noted the tensions between revolution and devolution. But here I want to focus on the particularities of feminist care activism as a practical civic feminism that differentiated itself from political and legal activism by focusing on providing support, even as it stayed in touch with political and legal engagement (Fletcher 2015). The many varieties of feminist activism on the abortion trail (McAvoy 2008; Rossiter 2009)[3] provide rich material for considering how trails come into being as cycles of care move people and things along.

The Irish Women's Abortion Support Group (IWASG) was the first British-based abortion support group to offer care to Irish women travelling for abortion. They operated between 1980 and 2000, often alongside the Spanish Women's Abortion Support Group. They recruited volunteers mainly of Irish descent and provided help with information, accommodation and board. They were particularly busy during the 1980s when abortion information was heavily censored and their phone line was an important lifeline. ESCORT, on the other hand, was a Liverpool-based support group that came together originally as university students wanting to act in solidarity with their fellow Irish students (Fletcher 2015). They organised from the late 1980s to the early 2000s and at points they worked closely with the Irish Family Planning Association. A third group, the Abortion Support Network (ASN), is London-based and a more recent incarnation, having formed in 2009. They provide help with fundraising for the abortion procedure itself, as well as help with information and accommodation if needed. In a computer-mediated age (Jackson and Valentine 2014) they are adept at using social media to gain support and to report on their activities (ASN 2014). They also use a more professionalised mode of organising with an executive of trustees and Mara Clarke as a director.

Like feminist abortion activists the world over, these support groups have addressed issues of financing, empathy, information and strategising around abortion access and all the other hurdles that come with it: finding childcare; escaping violence; and getting away from home or work (see further Silliman *et al.* 2008; Quilty *et al.* 2015). But because they have been particularly focused on helping women who travel from a country where abortion is hardly ever lawful, they also have to deal with: abortion as an unfamiliar healthcare service; with women who are negotiating foreign territory; and with clinics who are serving non-residents who will return home. The experience of being rendered strange is a familiar object of criticism in the stories of Irish women's travel for abortion and of those who support them (Amnesty 2015; Taylor 2015; IFPA 2000; Fletcher 1995), indicating the need to think through strangeness on the abortion trail in more depth.

In taking up Lentin's challenge (2004) and thinking through the different work that strangeness is doing in the context of feminist activist abortion care, this chapter proceeds primarily by providing a critical, contextual reflection on two interviews with past long-serving co-ordinators of ESCORT, whose pseudonyms are Ciara and Liz. I decided to emphasise the role of these two interviews in this chapter for two reasons. The first relates to wanting to foreground the role of these two individuals in providing feminist abortion support and making a difference to women's experiences of abortion access.[4] The second relates more to the effect of the transcripts on me as touchstones in my own thinking about strangeness, care and practices of feeling out the abortion trail.

I first interviewed Ciara and Liz in 2004 as part of a research project that analysed the contours of Irish reliance on British abortion provision.[5] They each had several years' experience, not just of providing abortion support, but also of co-ordinating that provision among a group of volunteers and of liaising with Irish family planning clinics and British abortion clinics. In that role they responded to calls from Irish abortion-seeking women and made hosting or meeting arrangements with escorts. At their busiest they supported about 50 women a year, according to Liz's records. They each oversaw liaison with reproductive healthcare agencies in Ireland, such as the Irish Family Planning Association, and with abortion providers in Britain, such as BPAS and Marie Stopes. Liz was co-ordinator of ESCORT for five years between 1992 and 1997. She now works in the management of a sexual health charity and is based in London. Ciara was co-ordinator for about ten years until ESCORT gradually came to an end in 2005. She worked as an NHS manager for a number of years after graduation, completed a PhD in history and is now self-employed. In short, they had extensive expertise in and experience of how voluntary care worked on the abortion trail, and would be key informants in any effort to document the quieter care-related activism that works alongside the louder reform-related activism.[6] My choice to focus on two ESCORT interviews is also informed by a sense of wanting to flesh out the genealogy of feminist abortion activism with a less heard voice, one from Liverpool rather than from London, and one that has received less media and academic attention.

The other reason why I wanted these two interviews to play a significant role in this account of how strangeness works on the abortion trail is because of their significance for my own thinking about feminist activism, abortion care and strangeness. They have long 'worked on me' as a researcher (Gunaratnam 2013, p. 159). As Gunaratnam says:

> The power of stories in the jargon of the social sciences is said to be 'relational'. The meanings and impacts that a story has on those who participate in it and receive it are a part of continually moving properties, energies and connections.
>
> ibid., p. 159

My reading of the interviews as stories about ESCORT's care work is an account of what they made me think about, of some of their moving properties, energies and connections. That they continue to generate meaning and have an impact on me more than ten years after the actual interviews took place is testament to this movement. In a sense they are 'timepieces' which have something to tell us (Franklin 2015, p. 25) about how a consciousness of strangeness works on the abortion trail, a consciousness that continues to animate stories of harm, help and hope in response to abortion restrictions.

Criticising displacement

Being 'out of place' (Ahmed 2000, p. 21), is the first sense in which strangeness features in the interviews and in the narratives of abortion support groups more generally. Sims *et al.* point out that we can learn much about caring by considering the ways in which 'home' is disrupted as a spatiality of care (2009). When our usual spaces of care are disrupted (see Westwood, Chapter 14), care relations reassemble and new caring practices and places come into being. Being out of place is likely to be just as relational as being in place, to paraphrase Massey (2005), and considering the ways in which this sense of displacement is observed, criticised and acted upon tells us something about how care relations put strangeness to work.

In one sense it was unsurprising that displacement and its critique came up in the interviews, because Irish law and policy has long been critiqued by activists, service providers and scholars for exiling women and generating an abortion trail to Britain (Conroy Jackson, 1987; Smyth 1992; Fox and Murphy 1992; IFPA 2000; Rossiter 2009; McGuinness and Fox 2014). At one point in Irish history, this critique was mobilised against the full coercive power of the state. Injunctions were issued to stop student unions and pregnancy counselling centres from providing abortion information and to stop a young pregnant woman travelling with her parents for an abortion (Fletcher 1998; Smyth 2005). Activists and care providers responded by engaging with that illegality. The Women's Information Network ran an abortion information phone line in Ireland when providing such information was unconstitutional (Connolly 2002), and the IWASG ran an 'underground' operation out of London, including a phone line, guest accommodation and liaison with clinics. Since the adoption of constitutional amendments in 1992, abortion law no longer formally categorises travel and information as constitutional violations meriting preventative injunctions. But the feeling of being treated like a criminal because one needs to exit the country to access abortion care is still a strong feature of women's narratives and of civil society critique (Amnesty International 2015; Taylor 2015; X-ile project[7]). As support groups have organised to intervene in those socio-legal relations and to ameliorate the effects of exile on the abortion trail, it is to be expected that members would articulate a concern for the strangering of abortion-seeking women through their displacement. But the different ways in which they responded to, discussed and adapted this 'strange' feeling of displacement, were particularly illuminating in revealing the diverse ways in which care connects and disconnects.

One key way in which volunteers considered women to be displaced was in the sense that they had to negotiate the unfamiliar while looking for help.[8] As Sims *et al.* note, care at home is often thought to be preferable 'on the grounds that receiving care in familiar surroundings affords a greater sense of autonomy, security, and personal control for the patient or service user' (2009, p. 305). In a Canadian context, those who identified their journey to the abortion clinic as 'difficult' gave logistical reasons, such as having to make travel arrangements, as the key factors (Sethna and Doull 2013, pp. 57–8). Having to negotiate through the unfamiliar is seen as a burden. Liz put it this way: 'It must be absolutely awful for them to be phoning somewhere they've never even thought about before. But I saw a lot of resilience and motivation.' In referring to more contemporary practices, the Abortion Support Network has been explicit in articulating this sense of strangeness as a disadvantage for Irish women. Nick Beard has written: 'How much courage must it take to call a stranger in another country on the phone and beg them for advice and money to terminate your pregnancy?' (2013). Mara Clarke, Director of ASN, has put it this way: 'these women are so desperate they are willing to involve a complete stranger in another country in ending their unwanted pregnancy' (O'Connor 2014; see also Abortion Support Network 2014). For them Ireland's failure to provide abortion care is wrong because pregnant women should be able to rely on the familiar at this intimate moment in their lives.

On the one hand, this recognition that the negotiation of the unfamiliar can operate as a burden is welcome. Those concerned with enhancing access to health services and enabling self-determination in all walks of life have often highlighted the significance of familiarity and accessibility in making use of healthcare effective and beneficial (Sims *et al.* 2009; Migge and Gilmartin 2011). And, as McGuinness and Fox say, travelling for basic care can clearly be harmful for some women (2014). On the other hand, some uses of 'stranger contact' to capture the difficulties of abortion travel could imply that unfamiliarity and strangeness are themselves burdensome. They imagine contacting a complete stranger as something to be avoided. This move can be a kind of stranger fetishism in Ahmed's terms, because it brings the stranger contact into being as a discomforting figure, while travelling as the process producing the discomfort fades into the background. But clearly, coming to know and experience the unfamiliar can be a pleasurable experience, and the expectation of pleasure is a common motivation for other kinds of travel (Mason and Lo 2009). Venturing into unfamiliar places through abortion travel does not have to be burdensome or unpleasant.

Perhaps it is the 'having to' venture into the unfamiliar when one would rather not, that can become burdensome. As Liz, Beard (2013) and Clarke (O'Connor, 2014) express their concern over women having to contact them as strangers, maybe they are saying that the necessity of negotiating unfamiliar people and places can be burdensome. Certainly Liz identified the desire to 'lighten the load' as the main motivation for ESCORT volunteers. Her emphasis suggests it is the burdensomeness of travel rather than its unfamiliarity per se which is the problem to which support groups respond. Making abortion difficult to access does not stop women accessing it, but it does fetishise abortion clinics as strange, difficult places. In the process, the potential for more affirmative and even transformative experiences of unfamiliar people and places is obscured.

As well as criticising the burdensomeness of necessary travel, we can also see a defetishising of the displaced abortion-seeking stranger, as volunteers name themselves as strangers to the woman. To the volunteers, it is not that the women are strangers in the receiving country, it is that the support groups are strange sources of information and help about abortion care. In these practices, strangeness is not an attribute of the unfamiliar 'out of place', abortion-seeking woman, but a feature of the set of relations which displaced her and put her in touch with people unfamiliar to her. We might read this as a form of opening up the category of stranger, so that we are all strangers; a kind of practice which Ahmed (2000, p. 73) has criticised as over-universalising. But I think it is more than this. It is not a negation of strangeness, but a way of imagining oneself as strange to another in order to share and diffuse any burden that might come with 'being strange'. It is not one interpretation of or response to strangeness, but a moment of empathy and burden-sharing[9] to produce an enabling connection to move on and become unstuck.

This moment of naming oneself as stranger and sharing any burden of strangeness is informed by a kind of implicit criticism of the situation. This should not be happening, women should not have to rely on the kindness of strangers; they should be able to access the care they need at home. But when they cannot access that care, then group support comes forward to provide a stopgap form of care. As Clarke and other ASN members often say, they are the sticking plaster or band-aid, pro-choice campaigners are the cure. There is an interesting double move going on here. Support group members are critical of the Irish state for making women rely on strangers, while they take the position of a hospitality-providing stranger. Their criticism of the state's estrangement of abortion-seeking women becomes a point of connection and solidarity. Volunteers generate connections with the women they help by criticising their home country for failing to accommodate the women and by offering them hospitality. But it is a form of support and hospitality they think should not exist. In the process the stranger becomes the source of hospitality rather then the one in need of hospitality. Care of strangers fades into care by strangers.

Providing 'a home'

The second key way in which the experience of strangeness was enacted was by responding to this trigger for hospitality and trying to make travelling abortion-seekers feel more 'at home' (Blunt and Dowling 2006; Cloke *et al.* 2007). In providing hospitality, abortion support groups draw on the home as a key site of care and 'the craved-for remedy of pains and distress of city life' (Lentin 2004, p. 303). As Blunt and Dowling (2006) have argued, home is central to processes of international migration given that movement may result from disruption to one's home and may result in establishing a new home. For Sims *et al.* 'homes are highly emotional landscapes with a strong degree of personal significance for their occupants' (2009, p. 306), whose meaning 'can be transformed from the inside by life events such as birth, marriage, illness, or bereavement'. Here, the meanings of home and being 'away from home' are being invoked, engaged and challenged by the life event of abortion. Volunteers intervene in the felt experience of displacement and draw on home in many different senses to stabilise, re-place and comfort women who find themselves on the abortion trail.[10] Volunteer care mediated the strangeness of abortion travel by literally providing their homes to abortion-seeking women, by matching clients and hosts, and by explaining the unfamiliar.

As Liz explains, opening up their homes and providing accommodation to abortion-seekers was a key part of ESCORT's work: 'it's strange to imagine, but we used to have those women and often their supporters for two nights and two days'. In the days before abortion day-care and cheap flights, abortion travel generated the need for overnight accommodation. Women used to be required to stay over a night at the clinic and sometimes needed to get there the day before.[11] Those accompanying them may need a bed while the women stayed at the clinic. This meant that volunteers also had to think about whether they could accommodate partners or friends:

> some of our volunteers only had room for one person, some of them said that they didn't want to ... They lived on their own and didn't want to look after women who had a male partner with them because then they'd be responsible for the bloke while the woman was in the operation, and that did matter to some of them.

Providing accommodation was a key role and involved volunteers in deciding the terms on which they could provide such accommodation. If the women of Greenham Common 'queered home' (Roseneil 2012), the women of abortion support groups reproduced their homes as feminist spaces by opening them up and deliberating on the terms of that opening.

The provision of accommodation was also taken on because homes were the resources they had to offer. As Ciara said:

> I was fortunate in that I had my own house, I had a spare room. I didn't actually have a spare room because I had two kids, but I could make the kids stay in one room, and I had a car.

Providing a home involved the volunteers in re-arranging their material and physical space (Sims *et al.* 2009, p. 311). It had an impact on their use of material resources, but was preferable to providing material help in the form of cash or direct payment. They didn't have access to funds to help with the direct costs of paying for an abortion and they didn't want to get into handling money, except in emergency circumstances:

> it was never Escort's policy to fund the abortion ... we didn't have the resources, we couldn't afford two hundred quid a time on an abortion ... so

it was always that we would save them the hotel, save them the travel, save them the food costs.

They provided a place to stay because that was practical and do-able, and because this 'in-kind' donation had the material effect of reducing the costs normally associated with abortion travel.

Providing an alternative home could also mean doing the kind of care labour that goes into making the guest comfortable. In particular, co-ordinating provision of accommodation involved thinking about the best matches between volunteer and client. A kind of 'craft of matching' (Jacob 2012) is put to work in arranging relations between strangers for a brief encounter. Liz talked about it this way:

> And then the second thing going through my mind was if I knew anything about the woman that she might make natural links with any of our volunteers, because we have women from all sorts of different backgrounds ourselves. So maybe age, maybe having kids was quite important, I tried to put them with women with kids and perhaps tried to avoid putting younger or women who didn't have children, tried to avoid putting them with families with children not knowing whether they would feel a bit traumatised by it.

Here, matching is a kind of care-work done through attentiveness and guesswork about points of connection to make someone feel less strange and more at home.

At other times, home-like spaces were generated by dialogue and exchange over abortion experiences. Making abortion-seekers feel more at home could involve providing information about how the clinic worked and preparing the women for what to expect in making the journey. This involved thinking about the significance of timing and of stages in preparation for making the appointment to have an abortion. Liz explains:

> We couldn't make the appointment ourselves, obviously ... so we gave them information about making the appointment and about making travel arrangements and that if they could they should try to get this or that time to travel, or bear in mind that it takes that amount of time to get to Dublin airport, whatever, and then say look ring us back when you've got all those details.

De-strangering the experience of abortion travel also involved anticipating the management of the clinical aspects of the abortion, such as fasting beforehand: 'We would say that the clinic would explain everything, but that you can't smoke from such a time, and eat and drink ... and then try to be as sort of calm and practical as possible'.

The unfamiliar space of abortion travel was also de-strangered by providing a listening ear (Rossiter 2015, p. 135). To some extent a listening ear was a response to a perceived need to offload, as Ciara explains:

a lot of the women are really using you to offload on because of the secrecy of the situation in Ireland, a lot of them hadn't even told their boyfriends, or you know their sisters or friends or anybody, so when they arrived in England that was the first person they'd ever had a chance to talk to.

But the interesting thing for my purposes is how stranger contact and the knowledge that you will probably never see this person again, all contribute to the generation of speech and the provision of the listening ear. The promise of the stranger is revealed as unfamiliarity frees up personal expression (Cooper 2007a), and takes communication beyond the usual 'stranger civilities'.[12]

Abortion journeys generated different kinds of home-like spaces as volunteers reached out to women and tried to make the encounter less strange and more familiar. They did this literally and materially by opening up their homes. But providing a home also involved affective calculations, such as matching clients with hosts who might have shared interests or experiences, and being prepared to respond to women's stories 'in the moment', if asked. These interactions show that abortion travel had material costs for abortion-seeking women and their supporters. But we can also see how the fact of unfamiliarity between these people could become an asset which generated dialogue and exchange. Being free of the history and future of their usual relationships meant they could open up and focus on the issue at hand. They did not need to worry about the consequences of that opening up. The transient and temporary nature of this strange care-space could be productive for abortion-seeking women, as it presented an opportunity to make sense of their experience.

Challenging trouble

Care practices can be significant sites of harm, not only when care goes spectacularly wrong, but also through mundane experiences of othering. The asymmetry of care (Beasley and Bacchi 2007; Cooper 2007b) may be expressed by treating people as if they cannot look after themselves, as if they are victims in need of rescue, or trouble waiting to happen (Johnsen et al. 2005). Abortion care, like other forms of care, sometimes operates as a site for the generation of exclusionary and racialised experiences (Fletcher 2005; Roberts 1997), by care-receivers and care-givers. Ordinary mundane practices, such as telling someone off for being late, are part of the everyday practices whereby some people get represented as less deserving of care, or deserving of an ill-fitting, interventionist kind of care. They can have a significant impact on how people use services. In a Canadian context Sethna and Doull noted that the women in their study who contacted a second clinic in their search for an abortion, did so because the staff at the first clinic they contacted 'were rude' (2013, p. 55). Although Sethna and Doull do not locate this finding in relation to racial or other differences, being rude can be one way in which racialised and gendered disapproval is communicated. Understanding how people become the objects of rudeness or other troubling communication can provide clues as to how strangeness works through care practices.

I want to use the opportunity provided by some of Liz and Ciara's stories to think more about practices of challenging trouble as a way of negotiating strangeness. My point is less about the presence of racism and stigmatising forms of care among abortion care providers. It would be surprising if it were otherwise. Rather I'm more interested in what some of the responses to troubling instances have to tell us about how the negotiation of strangeness works, as it moves across boundaries of familiarity and unfamiliarity. These reflections are provoked by the way in which aspects of the interviews 'worked on me' (Gunaratnam 2013, p. 159), as ESCORT's past co-ordinators talked about how their clients could be treated as if they were trouble. Moreover, the tactics they deployed in response made me think about the knowing ways in which negative experiences of strangeness can be disrupted and challenged. I focus on the ways ESCORT responded to accounts of racialised strangering by clinic workers because of what they tell us, not because they were prevalent or more serious than other experiences of racism and racialisation along the trail, including from abortion-seekers themselves.

Although they were careful to emphasise that women's experiences of abortion clinics were positive on the whole, ESCORT's co-ordinators did talk about experiences of racism, a kind of 'victim-blaming', and staff having 'rough days'. Liz talked about ESCORT's consciousness of their role as advocates:

> we always said that we were not only supporting Irish women in a practical way, but we were advocates when needed. And that did happen more times than it should have, where Irish women felt that they had been treated badly.

Ciara talked about the non-verbal way in which the attitude of a clinic worker could invoke the feeling of being racialised and stereotyped: 'you can sometimes tell by the look on the receptionists' faces, that they think "Oh, god, it's just another thick Irish woman who hasn't got a clue"'.

The volunteers developed a range of different tactics to counter these experiences of women being strangered as 'trouble'. As Liz explained, the first and most obvious tactic was to complain:

> we've had a lot of stories told to us by women who for one reason or another didn't stay with us, but had reason to contact us and who told us about some really, really horrible times, and we've made complaints on their behalf, which is difficult.

They thought about how to make the complaint as effective as possible. This might mean involving the IFPA head of counselling at the time, who worked closely with ESCORT volunteers, because, as Ciara said, 'she's got the clout' with BPAS. At the time the IFPA had an informal arrangement whereby they could access one free bed for a client if nine others paid their way. The IFPA head of counselling had clout because she would have been in regular touch with BPAS about clients who went to BPAS clinics for abortion care.

They clearly saw that they had a role in calling out clinic workers for poor treatment of abortion-seeking women. But they also tried to understand things from the clinic worker's point of view and in doing so often highlighted the impact of organisational conditions, longevity in the job and rough days. Ciara said:

> If you put yourself in the staff of the clinic perspective, they've been working and they're seeing a production line of Irish women come through. They've lost the sense of how difficult it is for these women. I think sometimes they are just a little bit insensitive to the women's needs.

Liz put it this way: 'Organisations where people have been around for too long, and they've got total compassion fatigue, they stereotype enormously and I have to say that the stereotyping of women from other countries is phenomenal, it's really disturbing.' Ciara also thought that occasional bad days could contribute sometimes to this racialised strangering, rather than, or as well as, fatigue and insensitivity through routinisation:

> I mean it's just someone having a rough day, you know, and they take it out ... human error ... they didn't mean to, you know. They don't quite understand what was a flippant comment to them could be devastating to somebody who's in an emotionally vulnerable place.

As well as complaining about and trying to understand how such strangering practices come into being, volunteers also acted to turn the troubling speech or attitude back onto its maker. They did this by calling attention to the way in which a clinic worker's response to a woman-caller differed depending on whether the woman was by herself or with an ESCORT volunteer. Liz explained her actions this way:

> And it was interesting that if, on a very simple level, I'd have an Irish woman, take her to the clinic in X Street, ring on the buzzer and you don't speak for anyone unless they want you to. There would be occasions where one or two members of staff at the clinic who would answer the intercom and say 'Hello' and then if I said 'It's Liz from ESCORT' they would say 'OK, love, come up, come up'. They were perfectly nice, really nice to the woman I was with, and it was all great. Then once or twice I would stand behind the woman and she'd introduce herself and say it's so and so for my appointment at ten. 'Oh, you're really late, OK come up', and things like that. I would deliberately go up with the woman and just stand next to her and say 'Hi, so and so' because I would know the person who had been weird, and then they'd be so nice.

Liz mobilised her escorting practice and her own familiarity with the clinic workers in a way which produced a change in the treatment of the woman. At minimum, this kind of practice makes the woman's clinic visit less uncomfortable. In this instance, no one is explicitly 'called out' for strangering the woman, and it's unclear if the interaction produced any change in the clinic worker's attitude or commitments more generally. But the production of a change in tone from 'weird' to 'nice' at least takes some of the trouble out of this particular encounter. It creates the possibility that any impatient or hostile treatment will be recognised as illegitimate, and enables a more empathetic response to a visiting abortion-seeker.

Conclusion

Negotiating strangeness is a key aspect of the timespace that is generated by abortion travel and partially filled by the support activities of feminist activists. Making care 'strange' has been a key technique for making it less accessible, not denying it altogether, but making people work harder to get it. There is an established form of strangering that renders abortion-seekers outsiders, 'out of place' and not entitled to hospitality. But there are other ways in which strangering works in the context of abortion travel. Strangering becomes an object of critique and a point of connection as volunteers identify with abortion-seeking women and criticise the process of sending women away. In a sense, feminist activists are expanding the category of stranger by putting themselves inside it, by identifying as strangers to the women. Sometimes this might work as a mode of seeing strangeness as a problem and flattening it out by universalising it. But this self-inclusion in the category of stranger can work in other ways. It can also be a moment of opening out rather than a universalising process. Sometimes there is a desire to learn from the stranger's experience and critique the conditions that brought that experience into being, rather than a desire to be the stranger. This is interesting because of its double move, the maintenance of critique of the displacing practice while acting to minimise the harsh effects of that expulsion. Care as a connection with travelling abortion-seekers, enables and empowers critique.

A second way in which strangeness gets negotiated, is through the provision of home-like resources: a place to stay; an affective match; a space to chat and exchange over life experiences. The fact that host and guest may never see each other again helps make the space for exchange more comfortable. Its very transience helps the offloading along. At the same time, there is a recognition that this kind of care can be no more than a 'band-aid' solution, which ideally would not be necessary. There is a third kind of negotiation of strangeness which involves tackling the construction of abortion-seekers as trouble, as those who are making life difficult for others. Tactics for challenging trouble involved making complaints, locating the troubling urge in the clinic worker's context and calling attention to troubling acts. Strangeness does not appear in these reflections as simply another burden for activists to reduce. Rather, strangeness has a value and a history that can be mobilised in careful connections through critique, home-like comforts and challenging the trouble.

Notes

1. Earlier versions of this chapter were presented at the ReValuing Care Network workshops (University of Adelaide, September 2013 and Queen Mary, University of London November 2014), and at the European Association for the History of Medicine and Health in Lisbon in September 2013. Thanks to colleagues for their questions and comments, and to Chris Beasley, Rosie Harding, Sue Westwood and all in the ReValuing Care Network for their attentiveness in travelling this particular trail.
2. Thanks to Caroline Hunter for drawing this source to my attention.
3. For a fascinating account of the transformative illegality of the Contraception Action Programme see Enright and Cloatre (2016); see also Connolly (2002, 143-144).
4. As Franklin has argued, personal experience continues to be a rich resource for feminist theorising (2015). Fonow and Cook (2005) discuss developments in feminist mixed methods as a critical response to over-investment in personal experience as a foundational source for feminist research. They note that feminist methodology has experimented with more interactive forms of investigation in order to capture the ways that subjects themselves, including the researcher subject, make sense of their own experiences (124).
5. See further: www.researchcatalogue.esrc.ac.uk/grants/RES-000-22-0407/read and Fletcher (2005; 2013; 2015). For information about Dr Deirdre Duffy's 2016 project researching the Liverpool Ireland Abortion Corridor see: https://liverpoolirelandabortioncorridor.wordpress.com/the-project/ Accessed 1 May 2016.
6. For accounts of the Jane Collective, an underground abortion service known as the Abortion Counselling Service of Women's Liberation, which operated in Chicago, USA, between 1969 and 1973 see Bart (1987) and Kaplan (1997). Other non-medical support activities have taken the form of clinic escorts, abortion funds and talk-lines; see Silliman *et al.* (2008), Kimport *et al.* (2012) and Joffe *et al.* (2004).
7. For information about the X-ile project see www.x-ileproject.com/new-page/. Accessed 15 January 2016. Other key civil society criticisms go to the discriminatory effects of the state's reliance on travel, the hypocrisy of taking a stand against abortion on Irish territory while explicitly relying on abortion provision elsewhere to accommodate women's healthcare needs, and women's need for fertility control as an aspect of equal citizenship.
8. Migge and Gilmartin (2011) identify familiarity as an important factor in patient mobility in their analysis of 60 migrants' experience of healthcare in Ireland. Migrants left Ireland and returned home to avail of healthcare in part because that system was familiar to them when information about Irish healthcare was difficult to access. The other factors in patient mobility were availability, affordability and perception.
9. On the critical potential of 'burden-sharing' see Johnson (2013, p. 124), who provides a rich consideration of the possibility of opening out to the other in just such provision for refugees.
10. McGuinness (2015) has written eloquently about the ways in which anti-choice strategies make the experience of abortion 'uncomfortable'.
11. For a documentary investigating the experience of women who have travelled for abortion care and noting the role of ESCORT volunteers in activities, such as meeting them at the airport, see Thompson (2006).
12. For a classic example of work which sees strangeness as a necessary feature of civility in public spaces, see Simmel (1908).

References

Abortion Support Network (2014) *Annual Report*. Available at www.abortionsupport.org.uk. Accessed 1 November 2015.

Ahmed, S (2000) *Strange Encounters: Embodied Others in Post-coloniality* London: Routledge.

Amnesty International (2015) 'She Is Not a Criminal: The Impact of Ireland's Abortion Law'. Available at www.amnesty.ie/what-we-do/sheisnotacriminal/. Accessed 15 August 2015.

Bart, PB (1987) 'Seizing the Means of Reproduction: An Illegal Feminist Abortion Collective—How and Why It Worked' *Qualitative Sociology* 10(4): 339–357.

Beard, N (2013) 'The Debates on Abortion in the Dáil Won't Change the reality Irish Women Face Every Day' *The Journal* 16 July. Available at www.thejournal.ie/readme/column-the-debates-on-abortion-in-the-dail-wont-change-the-reality-irish-women-face-every-day-993657-Jul2013/. Accessed 10 November 2014.

Beasley, C and Bacchi, C (2007) 'Envisaging a New Politics for an Ethical Future: Beyond Trust, Care and Generosity – towards an Ethic of "Social Flesh"' *Feminist Theory* 8(3): 279–298.

Beynon-Jones, SM (2012) 'Timing is Everything: The Demarcation of "Later" Abortions in Scotland' *Social Studies of Science* 42(1): 53–74.

Blunt, A and Dowling, R (2006) *Home* London: Routledge.

Brown, L (2013) *Contested Spaces: Abortion Clinics, Women's Spaces and Hospitals* New York: Routledge.

Cloke, P, Johnsen, S and May, J (2007) 'Ethical Citizenship? Volunteers and the Ethics of Providing Services for Homeless People' *Geoforum* 38: 1089–1101.

Connolly, L (2002) *The Irish Women's Movement: From Revolution to Devolution* London: Palgrave Macmillan.

Conroy Jackson, P (1987) 'Outside the Jurisdiction: Irish Women Seeking Abortion' in C Curtin, P Jackson and B O'Connor (eds.) *Gender in Contemporary Ireland* Galway: Galway University Press; reprinted in A Smyth (ed.) (1992) *The Abortion Papers* Dublin: Attic Press pp. 119–137.

Cooper, D (2007a) 'Being in Public: The Threat and Promise of Stranger Contact' *Law and Social Inquiry* 32(1): 203–232.

Cooper, D (2007b) '"Well you go there to get off": Visiting Feminist Care Ethics through a Women's Bathhouse' *Feminist Theory* 8(3): 243–262.

Enright, M and Cloatre, E (forthcoming 2016) 'Condompower: Transforming Illegality' in J McCandless and A O'Donoghue (eds.) *Judges' Troubles and the Gendered Politics of Identity* Oxford: Hart Publishing.

Fletcher, R (1995) 'Silences: Irish Women and Abortion' *Feminist Review* 50: 44–66.

Fletcher, R (1998) '"Pro-Life" Absolutes, Feminist Challenges: The Fundamentalist Narrative of Irish Abortion Law' *Osgoode Hall Law Journal* 36(1): 1–62.

Fletcher, R (2005) 'Reproducing Irishness: Race, Gender and Abortion Law' *Canadian Journal of Women and the Law* 17(2): 365–404.

Fletcher, R (2013) 'Peripheral Governance: Administering Transnational Healthcare Flows' *International Journal of Law in Context* 9(2): 160–191.

Fletcher, R (2015) 'Civic Feminism and Voluntary Abortion Care: A Story of ESCORT's Contribution to Reproductive Justice' in A Quilty, S Kennedy and C Conlon (eds.) *The Abortion Papers Ireland: v2* Cork: Cork University Press pp. 137–149.

Fonow, MM and Cook, JA (2005) 'Feminist Methodology: New Applications in the Academy and Public Policy' *Signs* 30(4): 2211–2236.
Fox, M and Murphy, T (1992) 'Irish Abortion: Seeking Refuge in a Jurisprudence of Doubt' *Journal of Law and Society* 19(4): 454–466.
Franklin, S (2015) 'Sexism as a Means of Reproduction: Some Reflections on the Politics of Academic Practice' *New Formations* 86: 14–33.
Gilmartin, M and White, A (2011) 'Interrogating Medical Tourism: Ireland, Abortion and Mobility Rights' *Signs* 36: 275–280.
Gomperts, R (2002) 'Women on Waves: Where Next for the Abortion Boat?' *Reproductive Health Matters* 10(19): 180–183.
Gunaratnam, Y (2013) *Death and the Migrant: Bodies, Borders and Care* London: Bloomsbury.
Irish Family Planning Association (2000) *The Irish Journey: Women's Stories of Abortion* Dublin: IFPA. Available at: https://www.ifpa.ie/Doucments/Media/Publications/Irish-Journey. Accessed 10 November 2014.
Jackson, L and Valentine, G (2014) 'Emotion and Politics in a Mediated Public Sphere: Questioning Democracy, Responsibility and Ethics in a Computer mediated World' *Geoforum* 52: 192–203.
Jacob, MA (2012) *Matching Organs with Donors: Legality and Kinship in Transplants* Philadephia: University of Pennsylvania Press.
Joffe, C, Weitz, TA and Stacey CL (2004) 'Uneasy Allies: Pro-choice Physicians, Feminist Health Activists and the Struggle for Abortion Rights' *Sociology of Health and Illness* 26: 775–796.
Johnsen S, Cloke, P and May, J (2005) 'Transitory Spaces of Care: Serving Homeless People on the Street' *Health & Place* 11: 323–336.
Johnson, T (2013) 'Reading the Stranger of Asylum Law: Legacies of Communication and Ethics' *Feminist Legal Studies* 21(1): 119–139.
Kaplan, L (1997) *The Story of Jane: The Legendary Feminist Abortion Service* 2nd ed. Chicago: University of Chicago Press.
Kimport, K, Perrucci, A and Weitz, TA (2012) 'Addressing the Silence in the Noise: How Abortion Support Talklines Meet Some Women's Needs for Non-political Discussion of Their Experiences' *Women and Health* 52(1): 88–100.
Lentin, R (2004) 'Strangers and Strollers: Feminist Notes on Researching Migrant M/others' *Women's Studies International Forum* 27(4): 301–314.
Mason, G and Lo, G (2009) 'Sexual Tourism and the Excitement of the Strange: Heterosexuality and the Sydney Mardi Gras Parade' *Sexualities* 12(1): 97–121.
Massey, D (2005) *For Space* London: Sage.
McAvoy, S (2008) 'From Anti-Amendment Campaigns to Demanding Reproductive Justice: The Changing Landscape of Abortion Rights Activism in Ireland, 1983–2008' in J Schweppe (ed.) *The Unborn Child, Article 40 3 3 and Abortion in Ireland* Dublin: Liffey Press pp. 15–45.
McGuinness, S (2015) 'A Guerrilla Strategy for a Pro-life England' *Law, Innovation and Technology* 7(2): 283–314.
McGuinness, S and Fox, M (2014) 'The Problems of Travelling to Access Basic Care' *Human Rights in Ireland Blog* 13 October. Available at http://humanrights.ie/constitution-of-ireland/the-problems-of-travelling-to-access-basic-care-repealthe8th/. Accessed 10 November 2014.

Migge, B and Gilmartin, M (2011) 'Migrants and Healthcare: Investigating Patient Mobility among Migrants in Ireland' *Health and Place* 17(5): 1144–1149.

Milligan, C and Wiles, J (2010) 'Landscapes of Care' *Progress in Human Geography* 34(6): 736–54.

O'Connor, A (2014) 'No One among Circle of Friends Willing to Admit They Had an Abortion' *The Examiner* 12 September. Available at http://www.irishexaminer.com/viewpoints/columnists/alison-oconnor/no-one-among-circle-of-friends-willing-to-admit-they-had-abortion-286000.html. Accessed 10 November 2014.

Quilty, A, Kennedy, S and Conlon, C (eds.) (2015) *The Abortion Papers Ireland: Volume 2* Cork: Cork University Press.

Roberts, D (1997) 'The Meaning of Liberty' in *Killing the Black Body* New York: Vintage Books pp. 294–312.

Roseneil, S (2012) 'Queering Home and Family Life in the 1980s' IN *Queer Homes, Queer Families: A History and Policy Debate* 17 December 2012, London. Available at: http://eprints.bbk.ac.uk/7874/1/7874.pdf. Accessed 15 August 2016.

Rossiter, A (2009) *Ireland's Hidden Diaspora, the Abortion Trail and the Making of a London-Irish Underground 1980–2000* London: IASC Publishing.

Rossiter, A (2015) 'On the Run: A Story from the London Irish Underground' in A Quilty, S Kennedy and C Conlon (eds.) *The Abortion Papers Ireland: Volume 2* Cork: Cork University Press.

Sethna, C and Doull, M (2013) 'Spatial Disparities and Travel to Free-standing Clinics in Canada' *Women's Studies International Forum* 38: 52–62.

Silliman, J and Gerber Fried, M, Ross, L and Guttierez, E (eds.) (2008) *Undivided Rights: Women of Color Organise for Reproductive Justice* Cambridge MA: South End Press.

Simmel, G (1950/1908) 'The Stranger' in K Wolff (ed.) *The Sociology of Georg Simmel* New York: Free Press pp. 402–408.

Sims, R, Medd, W, Mort, M and Twigger-Ross, C (2009) 'When a "Home" becomes a "House": Care and Caring in the Flood Recovery Process' *Space and Culture* 12(3): 303–316.

Smyth, A (ed.) (1992) *The Abortion Papers Ireland* Dublin: Attic Press.

Smyth, L (2005) *Abortion and Nation: The Politics of Reproduction in Contemporary Ireland* Aldershot: Ashgate.

Taylor, M (2015) 'Abortion Stigma: A Health Provider's Perspective' in A Quilty, S Kennedy and C Conlon (eds.) *The Abortion Papers Ireland: Volume 2* Cork: Cork University Press pp. 217–227.

Thompson, M (2006) *Like a Ship in the Night (A Documentary)* IPAS. Available at http://abortionfilms.org/en/show/3470/wie-ein-schiff-in-der-nacht/. Accessed 1 May 2016.

Valverde, M (2015) *Chronotopes of Law: Jurisdiction, Scale and Governance* New York: Routledge.

White, A and Gilmartin, M (2008) 'Critical Geographies of Citizenship and Belonging in Ireland' *Women's Studies International Forum* 31(5): 390–399.

Chapter 3

Carrying on by *caring with* in the shadow of a South African HIV/AIDS global health intervention

Abigail Baim-Lance

HIV/AIDS swept the globe in the late 1990s at an alarming pace. By 2000, there were over 36 million people living with HIV/AIDS, 70 percent of whom were in sub-Saharan Africa. South Africa bore the brunt of the disease burden, with a thousand people dying of AIDS every day in 2007 (Coovadia *et al.* 2009). The magnitude of the crisis ushered in a global response, in which both public and private donors pledged billions of dollars towards a multitude of interventions to lessen the epidemic's impact. One prominent type of intervention promoted across Africa was home- and community-based care. It was based on evidence that, as the epidemic surged, hundreds of mostly women were self-organizing and taking care of sick and dying family members and neighbors in localities across Africa. Such celebrated accounts led to donor financing of a 'care agenda' and, in turn, the expansion of home- and community-based care programs (Ogden *et al.* 2006).

This chapter explores global health's interests in home- and community-based care as an appropriate response to HIV/AIDS, and how programs in its name have shaped those designated as caregivers. In particular it questions global health's framing of care, and how, in turn, such notions have informed caregivers' ideas of caregiving, and their practices as caregivers. For this investigation, I draw upon ethnographic research I conducted in KwaZulu-Natal Province, South Africa, between 2007 and 2008 with a large-scale home- and community-based care program called 'The Future Project' (The Project). The Project was initiated in 2004 by ABC,[1] a philanthropic arm of an American multinational pharmaceutical company, and a central global health player. In the years that followed it involved hundreds of caregivers clustered in small, community groups across several rural and impoverished areas in KwaZulu-Natal.

There are two related lines of inquiry in this chapter, which draw upon global health literature, The Future Project's published documents, and field-based research where I recorded observations and conducted semi-structured interviews with caregivers involved in The Project. The first line, discussed in part one of the chapter, examines the construction of care by global health and, in turn, its application in the Future Project. Indeed, global health literature is rife with normative assumptions of caregiving as gendered, familial, and timeless.

I explore The Project as an exemplar of how this logic was deployed programmatically in the Project's "23½ hours of care" model, and later its justification of program funding withdrawal by claiming that caregiving would "carry on" irrespective of The Project's involvement. Feminist scholarship helps us place and problematize these moves as part and parcel of longstanding gendered constructions of care.

Part two of the chapter queries the influence of this arguably problematic, but forceful and normative social reality on caregivers involved in The Future Project. The question is apt because, if we follow our earlier analysis, we might assume that caregivers shared The Project's social reality by carrying on in their roles after the program ended. However, using a socio-material analysis (Mol 2002) of the everyday practices of caregiving and the sense-making processes through which caregivers described their work of "carrying on," we find them expressing an alternative interpretation akin to a developing area in political philosophy called new materialisms. One particular new materialist concept explored by Jane Bennett, "vibrant matter" (2010), offers a way to consider the material, interactional, and processual qualities caregivers ascribed to caregiving, which moves beyond the force of static constructions of the self and the social. After laying out key concepts of vibrant matter, I describe two journeys in which I accompanied caregivers with *iziguli* (ill patients in their care) to local healthcare clinics. The first, with caregiver Lihle and *isiguli* Musa, explores caregiving as vibrant matter. The second visit, with caregiver Sonto and *isiguli* Lindo, examines how caregivers performed "caring with" vibrant matter through their corporeal and cognitive attunements. I show caregivers cultivating caring with a world of vibrant matter as an attempt to create moments of stability within a landscape of vulnerability and limited agency. By way of return, the conclusion offers a reflection on the distance we have traveled in this chapter; from what will come to appear to be global health's ill-conceived assumptions about caregiving, to the creative potential entailed in carrying on when programs end.

Part one: the construction of caregiving through HIV/AIDS global health programs

Lead up, establishment, and running of home- and community-based care programs

The story of home-based care begins in the late 1980s, as people were dying of AIDS in their family homes, and families who had very little and were fearful of stigma and discrimination were "nevertheless providing care" (Iliffe 2006, p. 103). Soon, however, they wore thin, "developed holes" and became "stretched" under the burden of AIDS (Akintola 2008; Iliffe 2006, p. 104; Madhavan 2004; Urdang 2006). Community members, without much resource themselves, stepped in to provide surrogate, "family-like" home-based care, particularly as healthcare systems became equally strained under the volume of sick and dying individuals

(Aantjes *et al.* 2014). In the early 2000s the profile of community-based efforts was raised and celebrated by the international community, with UNAIDS endorsing it as "one of the outstanding features of the epidemic" (Iliffe 2006, p. 106). Calls for a "care agenda" to form a central part of the global response to HIV/AIDS led to the formalization of community- and home-based care (Ogden *et al.* 2006). The World Health Organization became a major proponent of this model with the establishment of a care continuum, and a framework to develop standardized home- and community-based care programs (WHO 2002).

Home-based care may have been of particular appeal in post-apartheid South Africa; one of the first plans on social policy set out by the new government expressed the need for the "restoration of the ethics of care and human development" across social policy (Sevenhuijsen *et al.* 2003, p. 301). Over the coming years, caregiving came to figure prominently in the South African national health and welfare agenda in conjunction with public sector redevelopment schemes (Adams and Claassens 2001; DOH 2004; DoSD 2003; Hunter 2005; SA National AIDS Council 2007; Uys 2002). By the mid-2000s, the government recorded the existence of 892 home-based care programs, with over 50,000 beneficiaries (Iliffe 2006).

The Future Project set up

In lockstep with such priorities, between 2004 and 2007 the philanthropic-pharmaceutical entity ABC spent over a hundred million dollars on The Future Project, a "community-supported treatment" intervention that took place in five African regions, including KwaZulu-Natal, South Africa. The Project's central figure was the home- and community-based caregiver. During the funded years, The Project enlisted approximately 600 caregivers in KwaZulu-Natal, clustered in small, community-based groups and scattered across several areas of KwaZulu-Natal. Each caregiver obtained from The Project a small monthly stipend, but was called a Project volunteer. An NGO in the main town oversaw group activities, and a Johannesburg-based program manager provided additional oversight.

Day-to-day activities consisted of caregivers helping those living near them. Their primary function stemmed from The Project's focus on the distribution of antiretroviral (ARV) medication, which meant that caregivers were charged with finding and linking individuals to HIV testing and treatment at clinical delivery points. Project documents also described caregivers as being responsible for the "23½ hours between a 30 minute medical appointment," which grafted a multitude of activities onto caregiving. This did not mean that they provided around the clock care, but The Project expected caregivers to be available at any time for all sorts of *iziguli* needs, including a variety of domestic tasks such as cooking and cleaning, as well as tending to the bodies of the sick by bathing, feeding, or helping *iziguli* walk, tasks intensified for those with AIDS. Caregivers also minded children whose parents had died, and visited government agencies on behalf of *iziguli* and their families. Though they were volunteers, 23½ hours translated into caregivers spending a significant portion of their daily life helping *iziguli* in a diversity of ways, and doing other Project-oriented activities, like attending meetings and training, and filling out reports and other Project-requested materials.

Global health's construction of caregiving: who cares, why, and how?

Global health ascribed three important features to community- and home-based care, based on the early empirical accounts. The first and most prominent was the observation that "Women and girls [were] the principal caregivers in the vast majority of homes and [bore] the greatest degree of responsibility for the psychosocial and physical care of family and community members" (Ogden *et al.* 2006, p. 333; Iliffe 2006; Sevenhuijsen *et al.* 2003). A second feature was that caregivers were motivated by "selflessness," which was "one of the most heroic features of the epidemic ... evok[ing] remarkable displays of compassion" (Iliffe 2006, p. 98). The third feature was its locus in the domestic; caregiving by non-family members took place in people's homes, with one study citing that 90 percent of caregiving occurred there (Ogden *et al.* 2006). In effect, caregivers became surrogate family members, filling in for depleted families. This characterization was maintained even as caregiving went from helping individuals with a "good death" (Chimwaza and Watkins 2004), to increasingly interacting with the healthcare system to assist in distributing and monitoring medications.

Such observed features became built into donor-funded interventions, but without recognizing their historic antecedents. Instead, planners advanced a care agenda to strengthen the support for these women without regard for the contextual factors that gave rise to such performances. As one study states without qualification, "The issues of care, treatment and support must be seen through the eyes of the women *who are most often responsible* for providing them" (Ogden *et al.* 2006, p. 341, my emphasis). Such a perspective might be considered a pragmatic move to better support those on the frontlines of caregiving. However, as programs began taking for granted who, what, why, and how caregiving occurred, its promotion intensified African women's circumscribed roles and responsibilities. In doing so, programs left little space to question the conditions that gave rise to such observable care norms or whether, indeed, they operated universally. Manifested in The Future Project, we can observe how these assumptions leveraged the seamless folding of disparate tasks—the finding, managing, and monitoring of those needing ARVs and performing domestic chores—to create the 23½ hours of continuous care model.

In thinking through global health's importation and then building up of normative ideas about care through its agenda, we can turn to feminist scholars who have long considered the gendering of the social, and in particular the relationship between womanhood and care. Indeed, there are longstanding analyses showing how moral sentiments—such as empathy, solidarity, interpersonal concerns, and communication—endow the concept of care, and simultaneously construct women as caregivers, given their perceived embodiment of such "moral judgment"

(Gilligan 1982). This has been particularly located in notions like "mother love" cultivated in the domestic sphere (Parsons and Bales 1954). Though some scholars celebrate the unique perspectives afforded to women through such relegated positions (e.g., Ruddick 1987), there are equally, if not arguably more powerful, critiques of the problematic perpetuation of this social understanding on the grounds that it stems from the subordination of women within a gender hierarchy. In turn, such constructions impose limits on expressions and experiences for all individuals, regardless of gender (Friedman 1997, p. 667). Some scholars have called for an alternate ethic of care that retains moral orientations, while cleaving gender from care (Sevenjuisen 1998; Tronto 1993).

The social construction of care in global health discourse, and operationalized in The Future Project, further demonstrates how multiple claims can be built off its logic. In the context of The Project, notions of care not only led to the presentation of particular performances undertaken by particular people, but it also introduced a set of morally motivated practices that were critically independent of global health and its interventions. For example, The Project's North American philanthropic director said in an interview,

> [The Future Project] asked, what are the assets you've got in this community? And we actually enable them, in the financial and technical assistance ... we enable them to create their own solutions ... The community has the means and ways to cope with situations as they come.

Caregiving, as a naturalized construct with specific, always-already features, was an "asset" upon which the program was able to draw. Care in this formulation was timeless. From here, it was a short leap for The Project to claim that the activities performed during the program would carry on once the program was no longer operating. And indeed, by 2007, The Future Project began rolling back its support.

The Future Project slipped out the back door by building upon the purported givenness of caregiving. Returning to the broader global health literature, we can identify resonances in the claim to timelessness with depictions offered by other members of the global health community, such as with Partners in Health (PIH).[2] PIH has used a similar home-based care model to the Future Project in Haiti and Boston, which they claim has been "the answer to the missing health infrastructure" (Biehl 2007, p. 306) with its,

> virtuous social cycle ... set in motion by advancing humane, community-based care ... The continuity and responsiveness of care, the willingness of the [caregiver] to "walk with the patient," ... [the] ability to manage the entire context of the patient's illness experience makes the program successful.
> Behfouz et al. 2004, p. S435

In this depiction, care begetting care in an amplified "virtuous social cycle" animates the goals of global health, rather than positioning the program as making individuals perform in particular ways. As in The Future Project, no attention is paid to the variations or contextual influences from or around a program that might be shaping care. One can also imagine in this formulation that caregivers are conceived of as carrying on, irrespective of program interactions since it is only an amplifying and not a constituting force.

We return to the earlier feminist critique to examine the implications of care dressed up in this particular social garb. While the critique might advance a more nuanced understanding of this elaborated social construction, it leaves questions dangling that gain force in my analysis pertaining to the experiences of caregivers within these constructions of care. One question, in 2007, orbited around finding caregivers continuing to undertake tasks on behalf of their neighbors after The Future Project ended. Did their actions confirm The Project's assumptions? Were caregivers a part of a problematic, but forceful social reality? Or, are there other ways of thinking about care carrying on in the shadow of a global health program? This launches a two-fold query into: the possibility of forms of caregiving that might go beyond the constructions offered by global health; and the effects of global health programs on forms of care if we do not take programmatic independence as a given.

Methodologically, this approach requires a grounded analysis to explore caregiving, not by taking apart discourse, but as day-to-day socio-material practices "brought into being, sustained, or allowed to wither away" (Mol 2002, p. 6). This takes us away from construction and critique (though acknowledging their importance to socio-material realities), and into the material world of caregivers. Ideas within new materialisms, in particular the concept of vibrant matter, are particularly generative in thinking about caregiving differently. In an introduction to a collection of writing on new materialisms, Diana Coole and Samantha Frost describe its emergence out of a moment in which "unprecedented things [are] being done with and to matter, nature, life, production, and reproduction" (2010, p. 4). They argue that matter *matters* in new ways, and pushes beyond a focus on constructionism and deconstructionism in favor of "real embodied selves living in the real world, really load-bearing" (ibid., quoting Archer, p. 25). Caregivers are certainly load-bearers, and so it is on this earthy, active, and fleshy plane that the matter of caregiving comes to help us think with caregivers, while thinking in novel theoretical directions. After introducing relevant concepts, I present some caregiving encounters I observed to work through alternative understandings of caregiving and the work of caring with vibrant matter.

Part two: caregiving and "caring with" vibrant matter

Establishing an alternative conceptual approach: new materialisms and vibrant matter

New materialisms aim to "conceptualize and investigate material reality"—both matter itself, and the process of materialization (Coole and Frost 2010, p. 2). An important focus is on how matter has its own power, a kind of agentic property to "shape society and circumscribe human prospects" (ibid., p. 3). In the words of Jane Bennett, matter is "vital energy ... lively and self-organizing" (Bennett 2010, p. 10), meaning that its energy exists independent of human agency. Humans interact with it, but matter is not "under the direction of ... an active soul or mind" (ibid., p. 10). Bennett provides one example of matter as vital energy through the story of the evolution of human bones. Here, soft tissue—or "fleshy matter-energy"—suddenly and through its own activities "mineralized" into bone. Bennett describes this mineral material as "the mover and shaker, the active power, and the human beings, with their much-lauded capacity for self-directed action, appear as *its* product" (ibid., p. 11). Matter *moves us*, and Bennett encourages a "perceptual style open to the appearance of [this] *thing-power*" (ibid., p. 5; my emphasis).

Once matter is dislodged from the human and given independent force-capacity, it becomes infinitely partible, while at the same time relatable. Vibrant matter is not a concept doting on autonomy but on relationality. The human and non-human—each with its own set of forces—come to be related in "assemblages" (from Deleuze, as noted by Bennett) or "confederations" (from Bennett), which are "ad hoc groupings of diverse elements, of vibrant materials of all sorts ... living, throbbing confederations that are able to function despite the persistence of energies that confound them from within" (Bennett, p. 23). Bodies, for example, are constituted by an infinite array of unique matter-parts, meaningful not in their discrete components but as a "collaboration, cooperation, [an] interactive interference" of matters (ibid., p. 21). These inter-workings are unpredictable and emergent, as forces interact with one another to produce "system effects that are different from their parts ... non-linear consequences that are non-reducible to the very many individual components that comprise such activities" (from John Urry in Coole and Frost, p. 14). Configurations comprised of the churnings of parts may result in harmony or cacophony.

What is matter, let alone vibrant matter, of home- and community-based care? For starters, caregiving can be recognized by its attention to the confederated, unpredictable bodies with which it works, each one a vibrant matter confederation. Caregiving is also comprised of what is done with and around the body for which care is sought and offered. In the context of The Project, this entailed being with the body through practices of washing and tending; providing comfort and advice; housework, like changing bed linen, preparing food, and maintaining a homestead; bringing or collecting documents or materials, like supplies and nutritional supplements offered by food aid schemes; and accompanying *iziguli* and family to government offices to make applications for social welfare grants, and visits to healthcare facilities. These matter-parts brought together documents and pills, soap and towels, ideas, roads, relationships, family members present and absent, and, of course, the global health programs and their resources, real and imagined. Each task brought matter in relation to other matter, relating in unpredictable, grounded, tangible, and force-filled ways.

The following accounts articulate the vibrant matter of caregiving further via journeys I made with caregivers and *isiguli* from home to clinic and back again. The first, with Lihle and Musa, offers an opportunity to describe the forces of caregiving matter coming together in emergent confederations. Any single encounter is also lodged within a broader set of interactions, and so I also include the lead up to the journey.

Journey one: Lihle and Musa

I first met Musa with Lihle in July 2007 in his home on a day in which I accompanied Lihle to call on several *iziguli*.[3] In his late thirties, Musa had grown up in the area and moved to Johannesburg to work in a spice factory. He lived there for some years but, like many young people in the mid-2000s, ill health led him back to his family's homestead.

We arrived at the family compound and entered a single room structure. In a dark small room we found Musa and his mother laying on perpendicular beds. Musa was under blankets, appearing frail. After introductions, Musa's mother quickly launched into an explanation of her son's illness, by pulling out from under her bed a Kentucky Fried Chicken bag filled with medications and listed bactrim, efavirenz, pain tablets, a multivitamin, stavudine, and refinah. When she came to refinah, she said that Musa was taking this medication because he had TB. She felt the medication was not working, though, and asked Lihle if she might take him to the nearby healthcare facility. Lihle agreed, and everyone thought that my car would be helpful for this outing, so we planned a visit later that week.

After we departed, Lihle told me that Musa suffered from HIV along with TB because, again, referring to the medications but now in a new way, "bactrim should be given when the CD4 count is above 200, and stavudine when the CD4 is below."[4]

The pills are a first glimpse of the vibrant matter of caregiving with quasi-independent "thing-power" of forces all their own. In one way, the pills acted by being remiss in affecting Musa's body. The pills offered another kind of force-power, based on what they animated for different individuals in the discussion. For Musa's mother, the pills were powerful in not helping Musa manage his TB. For Lihle, who agreed to his mother's terms publicly, the pills carried a different diagnostic force referring to HIV. This presented implications physically for Musa, but also raised the social significance of pills and what they could reveal about an *isiguli's* condition. Lihle knew that, by Musa's mother avoiding the topic of HIV, she too needed to be discrete and not name the disease. The pills show themselves to be plural in their vibrancy, and also unwieldy. They work in their own ways, shaping the confederation through these different alliances. It is clear that no one person can harness the pills, but each negotiates his or her position in the discussion through them.

The following Friday morning, Lihle and I picked up Musa and drove him to the clinic (Musa's mother did not join us). There, he and I sat on a bench while

Lihle queued for check-in. After some time, we entered a consultation with an HIV counselor who looked over Musa's clinic card and quickly announced that she could do nothing for him, as he would need to go back to the hospital where he had initially been treated to go over his medicines and make changes. Looking to dismiss us, and aware that neither Lihle nor Musa seemed to be speaking up, I asked the counselor how Musa was expected to get to the hospital, which was much farther away and a costly taxi ride. "You can take them," she said. I instead inquired about an ambulance. She responded, "They do not like to take people unless they are in a bad condition." "But how are they supposed to get to the hospital if they cannot afford it?" I continued, to which she responded, while taking a long look at me, "Where are you from?"

This led to my launching into a quick explanation of my research into the Future Project, leading the counselor to say, "The Future Project! They have money; they can drive him." I explained that The Project had ended, but she said of the organization, "But they have money. Just talk to them." When I repeated that there was no longer support, the counselor merely shrugged.

At that point, she left the room saying she would check to see whether there was a government-issued food parcel for Musa. She returned empty-handed and instead turned her attention to him, asking about the side effects from the pills he was taking. Called on to speak for the first time, Musa wound up admitting to no longer taking the medications—now, we were talking about ARVs—he had been prescribed, having heard that they did not work. Instead, his mother was giving him *muthi* (traditional medicine). The counselor quickly replied, "You have to decide yourself which to take because *muthi* can destroy the liver, while ARVs can really help you." She continued by comparing the problems of *muthi* with the virtues of ARVs, and then, abruptly turning to Lihle, she said,

> It is your fault that you last saw him a few days back and you only know now that he does not take ARVs. As you can see it's not even three months on ARVs and he has stopped. You are a neighbor but you do not have information on your patients. As a volunteer you must check the pills daily, and not expect Musa's mother to check the patient.

She continued by relaying her days as a dutiful caregiver. In response, Lihle said quietly, "I can hear. I know I made a mistake but I will change." We left soon after. On our return drive, Musa struggled with his breathing, intermittently whispering, "My chest."

The pills continued to exert force throughout the encounter. What appeared to be a question of their inadequacy when we set out for the visit turned into a case of distrust and pill substitution. Use of *muthi* further suggests how medications are believed to have different powers, but again, not only as effects on the body but also in their moral registers. Use of *muthi* instead of ARVs was treated in itself as a disclosure, suggesting once again that there are powers intrinsic to pill-matter that affect how individuals relate to them, and to each other. The pills also led to a redirection of force between the counselor and Lihle. Here, the revelation regarding the misuse of pills placed the caregiver in a harshly judged light, biomedical authority punishing not the patient but the caregiver who had fallen short of her assigned responsibilities.

Another aspect of vibrant matter is the Future Project and its legacy. In one way it became present through the counselor as mouthpiece for The Project's care-rationality. The Project's norms, wielded by the counselor, show how the social construction can become a disciplining tool to diminish the caregiver. The Project was also presented as an enduring resource, another way in which it exerted force with significant effects. These matters, as they rubbed against one another, changed the course of the visit in dramatic ways. No longer was it a check-up for Musa, but the "matter-energy" moved into unforeseen waters with revelations, unexpected moralizing, and the specter of infrastructure hollowed out but continuing to be perceived as real.

This is a confederation of independently dynamic, but relationally constituting parts, with no part alone causing the highly uncomfortable visit. It could not be known up front, but the exertion of forces produced what Bennett calls a "contingent tableau" (2010, p.5). This was further reworked when we returned to the homestead and Lihle immediately confronted Musa's mother about the *muthi*. Now, it was she who turned to her son and said in a high-pitched voice, "Why did you tell them?" A conversation ensued, the outcome being that Musa's mother said she would stop giving her son *muthi*. I was told that the family would find transport to the hospital; no one asked me to drive them. Though Lihle had apparently reasserted herself, later that day she animatedly shared what had transpired with some of the other caregivers. She acknowledged how embarrassed she was because she appeared to know so little about her patient's condition in front of me. With all the vibrant, unpredictable intensities shaping the encounter, we can glean how a confederation in a care encounter continually coalesces, and then gets drawn anew, as parts come into relation in unpredictable and unfolding ways.

I now turn to a second journey, with caregiver Sonto and Lindo, to look more carefully at the importance of caregiver attunements to cultivate a practice of caring with such vibrant matter, just as a craftsperson might be inclined to do, to productively work with the materials they use. This materialization of care introduces a set of questions I will ultimately tackle regarding the importance of subjectivity in the care confederation, and the importance of striving towards stability in relation to an appreciation for vibrant matter.

"Caring with": journey two, Sonto and Lindo

On another occasion in which I set out with a caregiver named Sonto on her daily activities, she took me to a homestead not far from where she lived to visit three children and their grandmother (*gogo*) who was virtually housebound. When we arrived, we found her in the doorway with a small boy named Lindo sitting next to her. Sonto and *gogo* shared their concerns that Lindo was not well and they decided that we should take him to the clinic. "Would you mind if we drove there?" Sonto asked, and I obliged.

A week later, Sonto and I took Lindo to see a doctor at a nearby clinic. He was bundled in a blanket that she had provided and wrapped him in tightly. We attended on the only day of the week the clinic was visited by the doctor. After a long wait, Sonto, Lindo, and I saw the doctor together. During the examination, Sonto relayed concerns about Lindo and his chest problems. The doctor peppered her with questions, and Sonto continually deferred to Lindo's family who had the letters, documents, and clinic cards that would provide the answers. The doctor asked if she would take Lindo to the hospital's pediatric unit for tests, to which she said, "I will have to talk to his *gogo*." As Lindo put his shirt back on, the doctor asked, "What is the boy's age? He's so small." To which Sonto replied, "He is nine. Well, he's been sick."

After we left the clinic and dropped Lindo off, Sonto began to strategize about the best way to arrange an upcoming hospital visit. Because *gogo* was so limited, the only way she could go to the hospital with Lindo would be in a private car. "But they are really expensive," she noted. She toyed with the idea of taking Lindo herself, but quickly rejected it. Sonto then offered background about the family and her suspicions that Lindo's documents had gone missing because they revealed the child's HIV status, and in turn would identify the parents. She also hypothesized that Lindo's ID document might have been taken because it could be used by a family member to secure a social welfare grant, as grants of this kind followed the document holder. Capping off her deliberation, Sonto turned to me as we drove along and simply said in isiZulu, "I have fear." "What are you afraid of?" I asked, to which she replied, "If something happens badly, they can blame me." And then she quickly concluded, "The family must be involved."

Here, similar types of vibrant matter surfaced as in the encounter with Lihle and Musa. In this case, identity documents and clinic take the place of pills and *muthi* as a volatile force that can run in different directions, at one point revealing and at another concealing what is felt to be vital, but incriminating, information. In comparing encounters, a strong theme is the variability of confederations; Sonto is a pillar of discretion, while Lihle churns in the choppy seas of inadvertent disclosure. Neither resists vibrant matter, but the caregivers seem differently capable of creating horizontal relations and ways to work with that which composes the vibrant matter. In this way, the work of care is predicated upon the capacities for caring with vibrant matter. Caring with does not attempt to take control of the elements, but styles relationships with semi-autonomous, free-spirited elements.

The relationships that caregivers establish in care might be understood by turning to Bennett's depictions of the encounters between those who are "intimate with things" and their "creative materiality with incipient tendencies and propensities" (2010, p. 56). She provides an especially vivid illustration of a metalworker's intimacy with metal that is "full of holes and spaces [with] vacancies … quivering of these free atoms at the edges between the grains of the polycrystalline in the complex dynamics of spreading cracks" (ibid., p. 59). And metalworkers then, are themselves emergent effects of the vital materiality they work: the desire of the craftsperson to see what a metal can do ... *enabled the former to discern a life in metal and thus, eventually, to collaborate more productively with it.*

ibid., p. 60; emphasis added

Caregivers in rural South Africa were caring with their version of metal, equivalents of free atoms and complex dynamics of people, families, diseases, pills, documents, systems, programs, roads, treatments, backpacks, care kits, government supplements, and curious researchers. And like metalworkers, they have honed bodily and cognitive techniques to "collaborate more productively" with the material.

In relation to these configurations, caregivers possessed attunements to develop and monitor, act and react. This manifested in various forms, one of the most powerful being when and how to reveal information and make oneself an active part in shaping the discussion. A kind of continuous "boundary work" (Epstein 2007) was evident for Sonto when she used linguistic turns of phrase to, variously: distance herself from decision-making by bringing an absent family into the room; decline to share what she knew, given her perceptions of the consequences of unwanted disclosures; all while choosing to denote her custodial role during the defense of Lindo's size when the doctor judged his small stature. Another caregiver named Mehlo, who worked with Sonto and Lihle, once focused my attention on the drawing together of bodily and cognitive acuity when, on a home visit with her, she commented on a "hidden" family member who she assumed did not want to show us how sick she was. She demonstrated her attunements by stating that she "listened to how *iziguli* appear" and "learned how to look into their eyes." Such sensing practices particularly articulate the bodily repertoires of both *iziguli* and caregivers, in undulating confederations that—to care well—must "productively engage" them.

Stabilization via "caring with"

Staying with Sonto, I want to place our attention on the fear that Sonto articulated on our drive from the clinic, and the profound pressure she felt leaving herself vulnerable when providing care. In this light, her skills of choosing words and reading landscapes may be related to the risks entailed in an uncertain calculus, and unforeseen contingencies and consequences. Blame and embarrassment were some of the terms caregivers used, but this vocabulary may have encoded fears of deeper consequences.

Such fears raise questions, then, about the dark side of care matter's vibrancy. To "shimmer and spark ... no point of pure stillness, no indivisible atom not in itself aquiver with virtual force" (Bennett, p. 57) might draw emergent, independent, energies into a familiar set of negative experiences. For example, Lihle shows us the consequences of a story with a life running away from you; Sonto shows us the consequences of not letting that happen.

For Bennett, matter, "itself *a* life," is a concept working against predictable structures bereft of active processes and emergences because "much of the time the process of material composition is regular and predictable" and "sometimes the arraignment or various intensities produces unpredictability mobile fault lines or energetic currents" (ibid., p. 60). But what if the starting point in the quotidian is a field of the unknown and harsh consequence? What if caring *with* occurs in relation to a scene more similar to what Jane Guyer calls the "coral reef of formality," in which there is "very little institutional buffering from daily unpredictabilities" (2004, pp. 169, 174)? Then a theory of vibrant matter might not be hollowed out by predictability but an attempt to create it. There, caregivers may seek to rework the coral reef through creative and perceptive dexterities. The point emerged in a discussion with Sonto several weeks after Lindo's medical visit, in which she described her interactions with another *isiguli*:

> There was a woman who was sick. It was her third time going to the *inyanga* [traditional healer who prescribes medications]. She was taken by her family, but it was not helping [which I knew because] I found her looking for the car to take her to me. I told her the car musn't take her to me, but it must take her to the clinic. She was surprised. I saw her tongue, it was full of dandruff. I told her daughter ... that she had to go to the clinic, and her daughter hesitated because she thought her mother had had a stroke. So, I insisted that she take her to the clinic because there were the signs I could pick up, and I told them that it might not be a stroke but it might be the blood pressure. I knew that the nurse would see the signs and test her, because if I told them what I suspected they would say I badmouthed her, *hhayi-ke*! So they ended up taking her to the clinic, and the nurses were so angry and asked why they'd waited so long. They couldn't say why.

In this passage, we again witness Sonto's skilled reading of signs, and her calibrated response given the risk-laden social landscape in which a prime concern was, again, judgment when entangled in the affairs of neighbors. The passage also illuminates caring as acute sensing to move with matter in different directions. Compared to the prior episode in which Sonto moved away from clinical judgment, here she works with the clinic's tendency to judge *isiguli*, "insisting" she visits to guide her towards the right diagnosis and treatment.

Towards the end of the passage, Sonto goes further to talk about another embedded process being worked out in caring *with*:

> At the clinic they gave her something to remove the dandruff, and also said she must come back for a checkup, *so that helped her and also helped me. They came back to thank me and said I'd helped them. The stroke had stopped striking her ... she is better now, she can walk to the clinic. But I do not ask her what they said in the clinic ... but she sometimes tells me I helped her*, and she was tired of going to the witch doctors and at the end she could not get better there. *At the clinic, they helped her a lot and*

sometimes I pray to God to help me not to be afraid. Maybe if she is successful she will come back and tell me what is wrong with her.

[my italics]

The dual site of benefit—*so that helped her and also helped me*—offers a clue that there is a bigger project embedded in caring with vibrant matter. By coupling Sonto and the *isiguli's* welfare, Sonto seems to suggest that there are larger stakes attached to an episode of care. This reminds me of Bennett's suggestion that "all bodies are kin in the sense of inextricably enmeshed in a dense network of relations. And in a knotted world of vibrant matter, to harm one section of the web may very well be to harm oneself" (2010, p. 13). Sonto repeatedly talks of being thanked and given privileged information, as if her fear—her vulnerability—has the potential to be allayed under the right confederation. Caring with draws everyone involved into a precarious but potentially improved situation. The implication of thinking about improvement is a reintroduction of time. In each encounter, hope for a better time can be glimpsed.

Bennett is cautious that a turn to subjectivity might wind up controlling and therefore denying the independence of matter. Yet, caregivers engage in the "delicate work of self-creation" (Das 2006, p. 78) not to wrest control of matter, but to appreciate its power and work with it. Theirs is not a will to power over matter, nor are they taking vibrant matter and its potential lightly. Their quest for stability honors vibrant matter in all its possibilities, but underscores that, in conditions of constraint and unpredictability, vibrancy might need to be recognized as being located in projects seeking its greater restraint. Caregivers could only do this by negotiating vibrant matter with skills that might tether outcomes and therefore make their worlds—everyone's worlds—better.

Carrying on seen anew?

Veena Das suggests that we enlarge a field of vision in which we "place constituent objects of a description in their relation to each other, and in relation to the eye with which they're seen" (2006: 4). Caregivers in South Africa enlarged my field as a medical anthropologist, by introducing new and unexpected relations and a different understanding of the world. They did this by sharing their modes of engaging a confederation of vibrant matter, using a rich repertoire of attunements to navigate insecure and variable contexts, making every body count. In so doing, they calibrated and worked on their interactions in a web of relationality, translating broad-based insecurities into more stable possibilities.

In this light, it is not difficult to imagine that normative assumptions of The Future Project—with all of the fixing potential—might be taken up instrumentally by caregivers striving towards stability. We might consider this the figuration of Mol's observation that practices and accompanying logics can, and sometimes do, rely upon one another to "hang together … and allow different versions of a 'single' object to coexist" (2002, p. 180). These versions do not dissolve into each other, but neither are they totally independent. As a site of imagination, caregivers' aspirational horizons through caring with led them to carry on within programmatic structures as vibrant matter too, not by inhabiting The Project's logics but by drawing upon them as free-flowing potential.

In spite of such creative harnessing of possibilities, however, pitfalls remain when including global health's assumptions within caregiving confederations. Institutional discourse that is mismatched with grounded realities intensifies instability. Perpetuating a static rendition of timeless care also harms those who do the load-bearing of carrying on, particularly under the burden of relinquished resources. It would be better if caregivers had more security—and perhaps then more creative options—for caring with vibrant matter. Said another way, some South African researchers have called for better institutional support for caregivers (Campbell *et al.* 2009), and to this I concur. However, I would add the need to recognize vibrant, creative, and processually rich care. Caregivers invite a revaluation of care and a re-calibration of living and working in relation to others, to let caring with take us into new conceptual and practical futures.

Notes

1 All individual and organizational names have been changed to maintain the anonymity of participants in accordance with the study's ethics requirements.
2 Partners in Health (PIH) is an American-based NGO affiliated with Harvard University and works in 12 countries employing a staff of 13,000 people. Activist-practitioner-scholars prolifically contribute to perspectives on social justice, biomedicine, and public health. PIH has launched the careers of a number of individuals who currently hold positions of prominence in the field of global health.
3 As background, there were 11 members in Lihle and Sonto's community- and home-based caregiving group. All female, their average age was 51 years, and each had an average of six children. Nearly all had been married, and a third were widowed. Most had grown up in the region, and had spent some part of their childhoods working on white-owned farms. The women had limited schooling and many had at some point worked in towns or cities as cooks, in domestic labor, or in factories.
4 The medicines that Musa's mother named are listed as part of the cocktail of a HAART therapy regimen though not a complete 3-drug regime (World Health Organization 2006).

References

Adams, Jolene and Marritt Claassens (2001) 'The Role of Poverty Relief and Home-Based Care within the National Integrated Plan for HIV/AIDS.' *Budget Brief no. 78.* Cape Town: IDASA.

Akintola, Olagoke (2008) 'Unpaid HIV/AIDS Care in Southern Africa: forms, context, and implications.' *Feminist Economics.* 14 (4): 117–147.

Aantjes, Carolien, Tim Quinlan and Joske Bunders (2014) 'Integration of Community Home Based Care Programmes with National Primary Health Care Revitalization Strategies in Ethiopia, Malawi, South Africa, and Zimbawe: a comparative assessment.' *Global Health.* doi: 10.1186/s12992-014-0085-5.

Behfouz, H.L., P.E. Farmer and J.S. Mukherjee (2004) 'From Directly Observed Therapy to *Accompagnateurs*: Enhancing AIDS Treatment Outcomes in Haiti and in Boston.' *Clinical Infectious Diseases*. 38 (Supplement 5): S429–436.

Bennett, Jane (2010) *Vibrant Matter: a political ecology of things*. Durham: Duke University Press.

Biehl, Joao (2007) *Will to Live: AIDS therapies and the politics of survival*. Princeton: Princeton University Press.

Campbell, Catherine, Andy Gibbs, Yugi Nair and Sbongile Maimane (2009) 'Frustrated Potential, False Promise or Complicated Possibilities? Empowerment and participation amongst female health volunteers in South Africa.' *Journal of Health Management*. 11 (2): 315–336.

Chimwaza, A and S. Watkins (2004) 'Giving Care to People with Symptoms of AIDS in Rural Sub-Saharan Africa.' *AIDS Care*. 16 (7): 795–807.

Coole, Diana and Samantha Frost (2010) 'Introducing the New Materialisms' in *New Materialisms: ontology, agency, and politics*, Diana Coole and Samantha Frost, eds. Durham: Duke University Press. pp. 1–46.

Coovadia, Hoosen, Rachel Jewkes, Peter Barron, David Sanders and Diane McIntyre (2009) 'The Health and Health System of South Africa: historical roots of current public health challenges.' *Lancet*. 374 (9692): 817–834.

Das, Veena (2006) *Life and Words: violence and the descent into the ordinary*. Chicago: University of Chicago Press.

DoSD (2003) *Appraisal of Home/Community-Based Care Projects in South Africa, 2002–2003*. Pretoria: Department of Health/Department of Social Development.

DOH (2004) *A Guide to Establish a Home Based Care Programme*. Pretoria: Department of Health.

Epstein, Steven (2007) *Inclusion: the politics of difference in medical research*. Chicago: University of Chicago Press.

Friedman, Marilyn (1997) 'Beyond Care: the de-moralization of gender' in *Feminist Social Thought: a reader*, Diana Meyers, ed. New York: Routledge. pp. 664–679.

Gilligan, Carol (1982) *In a Different Voice: psychological theory and women's development*. Cambridge: Harvard University Press.

Guyer, Jane (2004) *Marginal Gains: monetary transactions in Atlantic Africa*. Chicago: University of Chicago Press.

Hunter, Nina (2005) 'An Assessment of How Government's Care Policy is Working in Practice: findings from KwaZulu-Natal.' *Working Paper 42*. University of KwaZulu-Natal School of Development Studies. pp. 1–47.

Iliffe, John (2006) 'NGOs and the Evolution of Care' in *The African AIDS Epidemic: a history*. Athens: Ohio University Press. pp. 98–111.

Madhavan, Sangeetha (2004) 'Fosterage Patterns in the Age of AIDS: continuity and change.' *Social Science & Medicine*. 58: 1443–1454.

Mol, Annemarie (2002) *The Body Multiple: ontology in medical practice*. Durham: Duke University Press.

Ogden, Jessica, Simel Esim and Caren Grown (2006) 'Expanding the Care Continuum for AIDS: bringing carers into focus.' *Health Policy and Planning*. 21 (5): 333–342.

Parsons, Talcott and Robert Bales (1954) *Family, Socialization and Interaction Process*. Glencoe: The Free Press.

Ruddick, Sara (1987) 'Remarks on the Sexual Politics of Reason' in *Women and Moral Theory*, Eva Feder Kittay and Diana T. Meyers, eds. Lanham, MD: Rowman and Littlefield. pp. 237–260.

SA National AIDS Council (2007) *HIV and AIDS and STI National Strategic Plan, 2007–2011*. Pretoria: SANAC Secretariat (DOH).

Sevenhuijsen, Selma (1998) Liz Savage, trans. *Citizenship and the Ethics of Care: feminist considerations on justice, morality and politics*. New York: Routledge.

Sevenhuijsen, Selma, Vivienne Bozalek, Amanda Gouws and Marie Minnaar-McDonald (2003) 'South African Social Welfare Policy: an analysis using the ethic of care.' *Critical Social Policy*. 23 (3): 299–321.

Tronto, Joan (1993) *Moral Boundaries: a political argument for an ethic of care*. London: Routledge.

Urdang, Stephanie (2006) 'The Care Economy: gender and the silent AIDS crisis in Southern Africa.' *Journal of Southern African Studies*. 32 (1): 165–177.

Uys, Leana (2002) 'The Practice of Community Caregivers in a Home-Based HIV and AIDS Project in South Africa.' *Journal of Clinical Nursing*. 11: 99–108.

WHO (2002) *Community Home-based Care in Resource-limited Settings: a framework for action*. Geneva: World Health Organization.

Chapter 4

Caring for the homeless
Westminster City Council and anti-homeless bye-laws

Caroline Hunter

Introduction

> We offer friendship ... I give people a hug, you're not allowed to do that in many agencies etc. now.
> Soup run volunteer

> Excessive soup run activity helps to maintain a street lifestyle for people unwilling to come indoors, and draws people out of accommodation and back into street culture.
> Westminster Council (both quoted in Lane and Power 2009)

The serving of food to the hungry is an iconic image of human care for those in severe need, particularly those without a home in which to keep and prepare their own food. In this chapter I set out the story of an attempt by one of London's local authorities – Westminster City Council (the council) – to ban, through a bye-law, soup runs serving food to the homeless in part of their area.

In reflecting on what happened in Westminster I want to explore some questions about how, what might be considered, a 'space of care' became subject to potential legal regulation. There is now a growing literature on the geography of care. Milligan and Wiles (2010) suggest that any attempt to understand care needs to consider not just the care-giver or care-receiver, but all those involved in the care relationship. 'Critically the nature, extent and form of these relationships are affected by *where they take place*' (ibid., p. 738, emphasis in original). They point out that these 'landscapes of care' can encompass a wide range 'the institutional, the domestic, the familial, the community, the public, the voluntary and the private as well as transitions within and between them' (ibid., p. 738).

Much of the work on the caring landscapes used by homeless people has focused on indoor spaces. While such spaces are also undoubtedly shaped by law, the soup run specifically provides the care in an outdoor, public space. This inevitably leads to interactions and relationality not just between the care-giver and care-receiver, but with the wider public who may also use those spaces. For Johnsen *et al.* (2005, p. 334), the 'transitory spaces of care' that are soup runs 'engage directly with (and must adapt to) spatial variations in turf ownership and associated behavioural codes ... and often have to negotiate conflict with neighbouring retailers, residents and authorities'.

The concept of a landscape of care is also useful in connecting the literatures on both the spatial specificity of care and the social and political construction of care (Milligan and Wiles 2010, p. 742). Care has received much attention as a gendered concept, which links it to the divide between public and private spaces. The role of care (characterised as mothering) has its place in the domestic setting. This pushes it out of the realm of politics and justice. For Milligan and Wiles an ethics of care provides a framework not just for interrogating who gives care, where and why, but also as a way of challenging our usual public ethics of justice. 'An ethics of justice is a more rationalised approach based on universal rules or laws. Hence an ethics of care is concerned more with responsibility and relationships than rights and rules' (ibid., p. 743).

The idea of a space of care inevitably contrasts with literature which has focused on how the neo-liberal age has seen the rise of the revanchist (Smith 2001) or post-justice (Mitchell 1997 and 2003) city where harsh, often legal, measures are used to oust homeless people from public spaces. Much of the focus of this has been on US cities and on laws that target the homeless. The United Kingdom too has seen a similar growth in legal regulation of public spaces, which has had an impact on the homeless people who use those spaces. What is particular about the soup-run ban was that it was directed at the providers of services – the carers – rather than the users of the soup runs.

In legal terms it has been suggested that the forms of local law used to govern public spaces, often bye-laws, come from a different rationality (police) than other forms of law. Rather than being concerned with the rational autonomous rights bearer, they are concerned with the 'household', since in this rationality the state 'is the institutional manifestation of the household' (Blomley 2012, p. 922). In relation to bans on homeless people, the legal effort in the US has been on how these can be resisted through constitutional challenges. These largely focus on the rights of the individuals (see the discussion of the case law in Feldman 2004). In this chapter I want to take the focus back to the care-givers, the homeless charities themselves. Thinking about the attempt to introduce the soup-run ban in Westminster provides a way in to thinking about how law shapes both the space of care and the care-giver.

The story is told from the documentary evidence – the documents produced by both the council and different homelessness organisations operating in the area in response to the proposals. The quotes which open this chapter are taken from a report commissioned by the council (Lane and Power 2009). The documentation is partial and incomplete. An approach was made to Westminster City Council to access all the responses, but unfortunately they were unable to locate them to make them available. Responses were, however, obtained from organisations' websites, where they had made them publicly available.

I first set out how law has interacted with homelessness. I examine the nature of 'police' in this context and the response of 'big law' to this rationality. The second section looks at the role of homelessness organisations and their relationship with the state, examining the differentiation between those organisations that have been contracted into the state project for homeless people and those which sit outside this governing framework. It is these latter organisations which have primarily provided soup runs. In the final section I explore the particular space of care in Westminster and how the ideas which emerge from the literature played out in the attempt to introduce the bye-law which prevented the soup runs from operating. In particular, I focus on the advice obtained by Liberty (2011b) as to whether the bye-law could be challenged under the Human Rights Act 1998. The story of the bye-law reveals a range of rationalities at play and interplay. The rationality of police is not just adopted by the local authority and demonstrated through its use of the bye-law, but also by the corporate homelessness organisations. This is challenged by Liberty through the use of human-rights law based on the rationality of the autonomous human subject. That challenge recasts care in its image, unconcerned with the desire of the carers simply to provide care should this space be closed down.

The modern punitive turn in law

Much has been made of the growth of anti-homeless legislation, particularly in the US (Mitchell 1997; 2003), with many US states and cities regulating begging and, in some cases, prohibiting sidewalk-sitting and sleeping and camping in public parks.

A similar plethora of laws emerged in the UK at around the same time. While moves to recriminalise rough sleeping nationally failed, many other statutory provisions have provided a range of tools to deal with those who are deemed to be behaving inappropriately in public places. These measures, while primarily targeted at anti-social behaviour, have been used against the street homeless (Johnsen and Fitzpatrick 2010). One of the features of these laws is how much they are focused on localised application. Thus, it is for local authorities and the police working in collaboration to decide that a particular area may be subject to control. So, for example, areas may be designated for dispersal (Anti-social Behaviour Act 2003, s.30) or as a designated alcohol free zone (Criminal Justice and Police Act 2001, s.13).

The use of local bye-laws has also emerged as another form of local law which may be instituted by local authorities. The Local Government Act 1972, s.235 contains a broad power for councils to 'make bye-laws for good rule and government and the suppression of nuisances'.

Blomley (2012, p. 921) characterises these forms of law as police – an ancient form of political rationality that is powerfully evident in urban law. For him city ordinances in the US or bye-laws in the UK are key expressions of such law. Drawing on the work of Dubber (2005) he suggests that police differs from law in the way that the state manifests itself. For law the state is a 'manifestation of a political community of free and equal persons'. By contrast the primary concern of police is protection of the state from within and without. As such, is it concerned with domestic order and has a forward looking intent. The city is 'the quintessential police site' (Blomley 2012, p. 925) where it manifests its concerns with the minutiae of everyday life, particularly life in public spaces.

For Blomley the punitive turn is not necessarily directed at homeless people. In considering the city ordinances of Seattle, which ban homeless people from sitting or lying on the sidewalk, there are other rationalities at play.

> To object that urban regulation, like Seattle's sit/lie ordinance, violates the rights of the urban poor is, therefore, to miss the point. It is to insist on a framing for which police is ill-suited: for to invoke rights is to center the autonomous, liberal subject. We value rights because we value the autonomy of the Kantian self. Yet police is very different. To compare it to civic humanism is not so much as to weigh apples and oranges as it is to contrast apples to, say, colored fowl.
>
> ibid., p. 928

For him the sit/lie ordinance is part of a project of regulation of sidewalks more generally, where circulation is the predominant rationality. One feature of this form of rationality is to equate people with things. Thus the homeless person on the sidewalk is no more or less an obstruction than a vending machine or an improperly parked car. Another feature of police is that it is forward looking; it is concerned with prevention of behaviour rather than punishment for past acts.

This forward looking, preventive conception has proved particularly difficult to tame using constitutional and, in particular, human-rights legislation. Ashworth (2004, p. 267) in looking at the plethora of legal powers introduced under the guise of anti-social behaviour in the UK, notes:

> in European human rights law there is a distinction between penalties and preventive orders. One way of establishing that an order is preventive rather than punitive is to show that it can lawfully be imposed in the absence of a criminal conviction, and that it has public protection as its goal. If an order is held to be preventive, this is taken to allow fairly onerous obligations to be imposed on a person either without a criminal conviction or (if the person is convicted) in addition to the penalty or other sentence.

This is very much reflected in the response of the UK courts to the anti-social behaviour order (see *R. (McCann) v Manchester Crown Court* [2002] UKHL 39; [2003] 1 A.C. 787). It raises questions as to how far human rights, as embodied in UK law, can provide a protection against the advance of police.

Another manifestation of urban law that demonstrates its police rationality is governance through use of land. Valverde (2005) demonstrates this through a residential zoning law in Toronto which required a 250-metre separation between any homeless shelter. A challenge to this ordinance on a constitutional basis of discrimination did not get off the ground. 'The attempt to circumvent the relatively self-contained network of planning law by recourse to "big law" thus failed miserably' (ibid., p. 40).

Thus it is suggested that the types of law which might be used to fight legal ordinances against the homeless may be of limited effect, because they do not address the rationality at play in the type of laws being used. The law is not an attack on the homeless person as an individual legal subject, but on the way the city is being used or obstructed in ways that do not differentiate between humans and objects. As will be discussed below, we also see this play out in terms of the attack on those providing care for the homeless in public spaces, and particularly how relational human-centred care clashes with this law.

The role of homelessness organisations

A corrective to the notion of the revanchist city is found in the work of DeVerteuil *et al.* (2009), who remind us both that this punitive turn cannot be assumed to have taken place in all cities (it is, after all, a phenomenon of local law), and also that there are other spaces into which, having been banished from the public space, homeless people disappear. Many of these spaces are provided by voluntary organisations and it is to the role of these in providing and caring for homeless people that I now turn.

The UK is unusual in having a strong legal safety net for homeless people, first introduced in the Housing (Homeless Persons) Act 1977 (Fitzpatrick and Stephens 2007). The genesis of that legislation came from campaigning by a Joint Charities Group (Thompson 1988). The effect of the legislation was to place much of the responsibility for providing a safety net for the homeless not on charities but on the local state. However, from the outset the Act limited the full assistance of the state to those in 'priority need' and in the case of single 'vulnerable' people. In practice this excluded, and continues to exclude, the vast majority of single people who are 'street homeless', so that for this group there was a continued call on charitable organisations to provide assistance.

As a crisis of rough sleeping unfolded in the late 1980s, the then Conservative government turned to non-statutory organisations through the Rough Sleepers Initiative (May *et al.* 2005). The focus of that policy was to get people off the streets, something which continued under New Labour. Although the labels for the policies changed under the New Labour regime, Cloke *et al.* (2010, p. 19) note 'how little has actually changed with regard to the core characteristics of British single homelessness policy over the past decade or so'.

The Social Exclusion Unit, set up when New Labour first came to power, in its report on rough sleeping noted that some voluntary organisations were suggesting that steps should be taken:

to discourage initiatives such as soup and clothing runs which can undermine efforts to get people into hostels. Outreach workers also vary in the degree of assertiveness they use to persuade rough sleepers into shelter and challenge attachment to life on the streets.

SEU 1998, p. 9

In its way this late-twentieth-century attitude very much mirrored that of the nineteenth century (Humphreys 1999) in its concern that the 'wrong' form of assistance was being provided and that only certain more coercive forms of assistance should be provided. The focus for that assistance should be indoors not outdoors. Here we can see the police rationality at play, preventing nuisances on the street 'both by abating those that exist and prudentially forestalling future threat' (Blomley 2012, p. 927).

The change from New Labour to the Coalition Government in 2010 did not bring a great change in the policy (CLG 2011, p. 16). The government championed a 'No Second Night Out' policy, with local authorities working alongside homelessness charities with a particular focus on reaching new rough sleepers.

While the development of a far more comprehensive welfare state during the twentieth century did not lead to an end of the role for homelessness charities, nonetheless the reframing of the welfare state in the latter part of the twentieth century and into the twenty-first century, as part of the turn to neo-liberalism, has meant significant change in the relationship between such voluntary organisations and the state. As the welfare state has retreated (Peck and Tickell 2002) voluntary organisations have been incorporated as mainstream deliverers of welfare. May et al. (2005 p. 704) characterise a shift under New Labour from:

> welfare pluralism but relatively weak regulatory structures and a certain measure of independence for non-statutory welfare providers (whether non governmental agencies or private citizens), [to] ... the development of ever tighter regulatory controls aimed at securing the self-regulation of non-statutory welfare providers and welfare recipients alike.

These changes led to a homelessness sector 'increasingly populated by large corporatist organisations which represent a voluntary sector which is significantly tied into government approaches and agendas' (Cloke et al. 2007, p. 1091). Thus such groups are also subject to the rationality of police and provide their care in conditional ways (Johnsen et al. 2014).

Running alongside this provision is a group of organisations outside the favoured approach, characteristically running night-shelters, drop-in centres and soup runs (Cloke et al. 2007). Buckingham (2010, p. 117) reaches a similar conclusion, identifying four different types of organisations involved in homelessness provision. Three contract with government agencies, with greater or lesser willingness, to provide services. Her fourth category is of non-contractors entirely independent of government contracts, mainly staffed by volunteers and often faith-based. These groups are characterised by their strong emphasis on offering 'acceptance to users and building relationships with them'.

The role of such organisations in providing soup runs has been documented by Johnsen *et al.* (2005). The picture that emerged from their study of soup runs outside London was 'that of a service strongly dominated by churches and/or other voluntary or charitable organisations' (ibid., p. 326). Furthermore, they were more reliant on volunteers than other emergency services for homeless people. They conclude (ibid., p. 334) that 'soup runs continue to occupy marginal positions within service networks because of the incongruity of their non-interventionist ethos'.

Cloke *et al.* (2007; 2010) have suggested that both the individuals and the organisations provide a post-secular response to the crisis of homelessness. They argue that 'soup runs provide a powerful reminder of a quite different current running through the homeless city; the unconditional outpouring of agape and caritas' (Cloke *et al.* 2010, p. 115). They provide a counterpoint to the uncaring picture of the revanchist city seeking to annihilate homelessness through law (Mitchell 1997) and rather recognise an 'opposing social and political urge to care for and serve homeless people in recognition of their plight' (Cloke *et al.* 2010, p. 50).

While Lacionne (2014) provides a critique of such a positive view of the work of religiously motivated care, suggesting that the care cannot be seen as unconditional, the importance for my argument is not the basis on which it is provided, but the fact that it falls outside the usual homelessness governance structures. It is a form of care which resists the rationality of police which has largely been accepted by the corporate charities. This makes them vulnerable to direct police action themselves. I turn next to how this played out and was resisted in Westminster.

The Westminster bye-law proposal

London is, of course, the major and capital city within the UK, which brings particular housing demands and problems. Local government in London is arranged on a two-tier basis, with the Greater London Authority having some strategic functions and the 32 London Boroughs delivering many of the services and having extensive legal powers.

> Westminster lies at the heart of London, contains its royal residences and royal parks, the Westminster parliament and the Whitehall community ... It contains some of the world's finest art collections and some of its most important historic buildings, its world-renowned theatres, plus the attractions of Soho and Leicester Square, make it the country's capital of entertainment. 550,000 people work in Westminster. It is home to about 222,000 people.
>
> The city's population is growing rapidly and is expected to reach 250,000 by 2021.This leads to considerable demand for new housing of all tenures, yet in

an already densely developed inner city area, development opportunities are becoming increasingly rare.

> Westminster Housing Commission 2006, p. 15

This description is found in the report of the Westminster Housing Commission (2006), indicating the particular geographic situation of Westminster within London. The report goes on to acknowledge the particular housing problems to which this leads. In particular, Westminster has a very high number of rough sleepers. A report in 2006 noted: 'Westminster has always had the highest number of rough sleepers of any local authority area in England: in 2006 they had around a third of the national total' (Randall and Brown 2006, p. 2). In 2007 Westminster Council noted in their *Rough Sleeping Strategy* (WCC 2007, p. 2) that, 'For a number of reasons to do with the "pull" of central London, Westminster attracts very high numbers of homeless people and rough sleepers in a high-pressure housing environment'.

One response to this large number of rough sleepers has been the provision of soup runs by voluntary organisations, particularly Christian groups. This has been a 'contentious issue' for many years (Lane and Power 2009). Various attempts were made by the council both to map the problem and to try and co-ordinate, and ultimately reduce, the number of soup runs operating in the borough. A mapping project in 2004, which was sent to the estimated 65 soup runs operating in the borough, concluded that 65 per cent were run by Christian groups, 33 per cent from Greater London and 25 per cent from outside London (WCC 2005). Following this exercise, a 'soup run summit' was convened, although it is not clear that any concrete changes emerged.

The continuing operation of soup runs was clearly at odds with the Council's strategy to provide services for rough sleepers inside buildings rather than on the streets (Randall and Brown 2006, p. 2). In its 2007 *Rough Sleeping Strategy* one of Westminster's seven priorities was 'reducing the over provision of soup runs in Westminster'. In explaining why this was a priority the document (WCC 2007, p. 34) states:

- It is the council's view that there is overprovision of Soup Runs in the borough. Excessive soup run activity helps to maintain a street lifestyle for people unwilling to come indoors, and draws people out of accommodation and back into street culture.
- A scoping exercise (January 2007) showed that in some areas of Westminster, as many as three Soup Run organisations provide food to exactly the same group of people on the same night and in the same place. This kind of uncoordinated provision does not meet any real need on the streets and causes maximum disruption to the local area.
- Anti-social behaviour is rife before, during and after soup runs, and turns many residential and public areas into virtual no-go areas. The majority of soup run users are not rough sleepers.

At this time the Council sought to gain more legal powers to control soup runs through the inclusion in the London Local Authorities Bill of a provision to control the provision and distribution of free food on public land: 'unfortunately, on this occasion the council was unsuccessful in gaining enough support from other London local authorities and the previous Mayor of London' (WCC 2009, p. 11). This might in part have been due to 'extreme public opposition' (Johnsen and Fitzpatrick 2010).

The particular space of care

A particular location where there were concerns about soup runs was an area in the south of Westminster, around Victoria and the Catholic Westminster Cathedral, known as the Cathedral Piazza. In 2009 the council produced a draft action plan for the area. The plan stated that a 'major challenge' was the impact of soup runs operating in the area: 'other issues that have caused concern to local stakeholders are the presence of street drinkers, rough sleepers and the effects of the soup kitchen's operations' (WCC 2009, p. 9). The plan set out existing measures which had already been used to try and control these issues, particularly around street drinking, including a 'dispersal zone' under the Anti-social Behaviour Act 2003. The entire area was also at the time subject to a designated control zone for street drinking. Thus, a police rationality was clearly at play in the area, but these measures had not been able to prevent the soup runs operating, as the measures were focused on the street users rather than the soup-run providers.

At that time the council, together with Crisis (a national homeless charity), had commissioned an independent research report into the effects of soup runs. The action plan for the Piazza area stated that key homelessness agencies, user groups and other agencies represented on the Soup Run Research Steering Group had agreed to abide by the recommendations from the research. The action plan continued:

> The council plans to use the impartial evidence-based findings from this study to promote more appropriate ways for faith groups to work with more homelessness agencies providing building based services. It may also be used to provide evidence to pursue further an amendment to the next London Local Authorities Bill or for the council to draft its own bylaws (awaiting guidance from the Department of Communities and Local Government) to control the distribution of free food.
>
> WCC 2009, p. 11

The report did not suggest any further legal provisions, but primarily focused on better collaboration and co-ordination through the London Soup Run Forum, together with better joint working between soup run providers and other services. It acknowledged the tensions around over-provision in the Victoria area but simply suggested that a 'working group could be established to discuss and mediate the problems of emergency provision on the streets that resolves or reduces current tensions' (Lane and Power 2009, p. 33).

The Lane and Power report included evidence of the motivations of the soup-run providers. One volunteer is quoted as saying: 'We offer friendship ... I give people a hug, you're not allowed to do that in many agencies etc. now' (ibid., p. 13). One case study organisation, All Souls Local Action Network (ASLAN), underlined their Christian mission: 'ASLAN volunteers reach out to some of the most vulnerable and damaged members of society who are commonly forgotten or ignored. In this way ASLAN hope to demonstrate Christ's unconditional love' (ibid., p. 15).

At the same time as focusing on the soup runs, the Council was also drawing up more general plans for the area. The use of legal measures against the presence of the homeless in public spaces has been analysed by Feldman (2004, p. 43) as an exclusion of poverty from 'prime' consumptive spaces: 'contemporary homeless laws protect a consumptive public (which they constitute) from threats to its security and enjoyment'.

We can see this reflected in the draft action plan for the area (WCC 2009), which refers to giving the public spaces a 'real sense of place and purpose'. In relation to the Piazza in particular it is proposed that events may be run in it:

> Possible ideas are a second-hand book market, an antiques market or a farmers market selling quality produce. To promote the Piazza as a place where people can relax and unwind from the hustle and bustle of Victoria, we will consider small scale arts and cultural programmes ... where people will be able to enjoy some of the unique aspects of the area.
>
> WCC 2009

The recommendations from the soup-run research were clearly considered insufficient to bring an end to the problems. In February 2011 the Council ran a consultation on two proposed bye-laws. The first would have made it unlawful to sleep rough in the designated area. The second proposed outlawing the distribution of any 'free refreshment in or on any public space'. Westminster claimed that 'the bye-law was proposed as a last resort. Despite a decade of efforts to resolve the issue, no solution has been reached which satisfied both local residents and other interested parties.' (WCC 2011, p. 5) The bye-law was framed very much in terms of 'use' (Valverde 2005), it does not target the soup runs specifically but makes unlawful a particular activity in the area.

Responses to the proposal

The responses to the proposals came from a variety of organisations. Over 400 responses were received (WCC 2011, p. 9). Unsurprisingly the majority of local residents' groups were in favour of both bye-laws. The umbrella group for businesses in the Victoria area and the principal landowner for the area were supportive of the soup run bye-law but not the rough sleeping bye-law. Interestingly, the charities providing services to the homeless were not uniformly against the bye-laws. At least one (Thames Reach, 2011) was in favour of both bye-laws, and some others also supported the soup run bye-law.

Those charities advocating the soup-run ban did so partly on the basis of the disturbance to local residents' lives and partly on the fact that the soup runs could not be justified. Soup runs are only justified where they engage homeless people to be helped indoors. That from St Mungo's is typical:

> In our view, the wide availability of outreach services in Westminster means that that justification for soup runs no longer applies.
>
> There is an argument that taking basic services to the streets helps keep people there and that what should instead happen is that essential services should be available inside easily-accessible buildings.
>
> St Mungo's 2011, p. 1

Two responses advocate caution because of the possibility of 'entrenching the opinions of soup run providers who are resistant to change' (Crisis, 2011). Indeed, Housing Justice (the national Christian umbrella group for housing and homelessness) suggests 'the ban will have the opposite effect, encouraging soup run martyrs into civil disobedience' (Housing Justice 2011a, p. 3). Thus we get to the position where it is suggested that not only will this form of caring be outlawed, but also that the carers themselves will become outlaws. None of the mainstream charities advocate for the soup runs on the basis of the type of unconditional care they provide.

Perhaps most interesting response, from the legal point of view, is that of Liberty, a leading civil-rights organisation, which actively promotes civil rights. Unsurprisingly Liberty (2011a) resisted both bye-laws. Liberty's resistance is couched in legal terms of legitimacy and proportionality. These will be explored further below, in the light of the legal advice obtained by Liberty.

The follow-up

Following the consultation, the council concluded that 'there is clearly significant opposition to the Rough Sleeping byelaw' (WCC 2011, p. 11) and withdrew the proposal. However, the soup run proposal was held for progression following an eight-week discussion and resolution period. It was not subsequently implemented, and a process of dialogue continued. When Westminster sought to move ahead on the ban on the 'distribution of free refreshment' Liberty sought advice (the 'Liberty advice', 2011b) from leading public lawyers on the legality of the bye-law. It published that advice (from James Goudie QC and Deok Joo Rhee) on its website.

The conclusion of the Liberty advice is that there is a strong case that the bye-law is unlawful. Whether a court would have agreed with that conclusion we cannot know. The authors of the advice conclude that the bye-law constitutes a disproportionate interference with a number of fundamental rights of the soup-run providers under the Human Rights Act 1998. Thus there was a potential for 'big law', based on the autonomous rational subject – here the soup run volunteers – to be used to challenge the police bye-law.

Article 8 of the European Convention on Human Rights provides for respect for private life. The lawyers conclude that 'the charitable activity of providing food and drink to those in need clearly falls within the ambit of article 8', as article 8 protects personal autonomy and the right to enter into and develop relationships with others. While this does not extend to public activities (see *R (Countryside Alliance) v A-G* [2008] AC 719), the charitable provision of food is fundamentally a private activity, which is undertaken by the volunteers 'for the humanitarian purpose of helping another human being who is in need and giving effect to personal philosophical and ethical convictions' (Liberty 2011b, p. 7). As such, any interference with this form of personal autonomy requires appropriate objective justification. Thus there is some potential, through individual human rights, to accommodate a charitable rationality.

They also consider whether there is a breach of article 9 – the right to freedom of thought, conscience and religion – in so far as volunteers assist the soup runs because of their personal philosophical and/or religious convictions. If they do, it is concluded that the bye-law would plainly constitute an interference with article 9.

Whether the interference with these qualified rights is unlawful depends on whether the bye-law is proportionate and rational. The starting point for considering whether the interference with the rights of the soup-run volunteers is proportionate and rational are the two aims taken from the council's own documents. The first focuses on the soup runs as facilitating and enabling rough sleeping and being bad for the well-being of the homeless themselves; the second on the nuisance and annoyance to the local residents and businesses. In the view of the barristers 'the Court would be likely to accept that these aims, however they might be reformulated, are sufficiently cogent to justify an appropriately rational and proportionate response' (Liberty 2011b, p. 15).

So the starting point of the Liberty advice is that it accepts that the Council could exercise this type of ban, in some circumstances. For the barristers, however, the ban as currently proposed was neither rationally connected to the legitimate aims of the bye-law nor proportionate for a variety of reasons. Much is related to the lack of evidence to justify the ban. Further, it is the broad nature of the ban (beyond the work of the soup kitchens to 'innocent' sharers of food) which makes it disproportionate. Here then the 'use' nature of the bye-law is in fact a weakness and opens it up to challenge (cf Valverde 2005).

The only reference to the actual behaviour and motivations of the soup-run providers come when discussing Westminster's justification for the ban. One part of this was the 'fact that other, different, volunteering opportunities working with the homeless are available in London which volunteers ... could take up' (Liberty 2011b, p. 21). This justification is dismissed by the barristers in the following terms: 'it is difficult to understand the supposed relevance of the availability of other volunteering opportunities working with the homeless. This is entirely incapable of providing any justification for the proposed bye-law' (Liberty 2011b, p. 21).

Ultimately the council decided not to go ahead with even the soup-run bye-law. This was hailed as a victory by Housing Justice in a press release dated 2 November 2011 (Housing Justice 2011b). Interestingly, while it welcomed the decision, Housing Justice also committed itself to working with the Council: 'However Housing Justice and its members are committed to working together with Westminster and all local authorities, homelessness agencies and churches to help develop more indoor venues and to create a better and more effective safety net.'

By the time Westminster came to publish their rough sleeping strategy for 2013–16 they were able to state:

> Following intensive and positive dialogue in the Victoria area of Westminster, the number of soup runs operating in this locality has declined considerably through voluntary agreement. Some of those soup runs now operate out of a local hostel and we want to continue working with those soup runs to ensure the work they are doing maintains its relevance while not impacting on local residents.
>
> WCC 2013, p. 14

This document stresses the options for volunteering that are being offered as an alternative to the soup runs. Thus, for the Council, it was not the charitable act of care they wished to end, but rather its conflict with the police rationality which meant that it was being provided in the wrong space.

Conclusions

The area around Cathedral Piazza provided a transient space of care similar to those of other soup runs described by Johnsen et al. (2005). The motivations of the soup-run providers were similar. Over a long period the providers of that care faced considerable hostility from the local council who made several attempts to remove, or at least reduce, them. On the face of it this may seem like an example of the revanchist city where, in this case, those providing care for the poor are moved off the streets, in order to open them up to commercial activity.

DeVerteuil and others point to the necessity of a nuanced response to what is occurring to homeless people in our cities. In the context of Westminster, it is worth noting that the attempt to introduce what was effectively a law against sleeping rough in part of the borough was relatively easily 'defeated'. In the face of strong opposition, the council retreated. This left the council with their attempt to end soup runs. Here the response was much more ambiguous.

A number of the large charities, which fall into Cloke et al.'s (2010) corporatist description, who were tied into the government agenda, strongly supported the bye-law. The soup runs did not, for them, provide a form of care that was appropriate. Any provision of care had to be far more instrumental to bring people indoors. Simply providing care – the caritas and agape referred to by Cloke *et al.* (2010) – is not sufficient to justify and support the service of food in public spaces. Even the strongest critic, representing the soup-run providers (Housing Justice), has largely bought into this agenda. They have also backed the move indoors to private space. As a space of care for homeless people the public space of the Cathedral Piazza and surround was deemed unsuitable.

Much of what has happened in the control of public space in the UK over the last 20 years falls within Blomley's description of police. He suggests that in relation to bans on sitting on sidewalks the rationale is less to do with upholding commercial interests and more a rationale of dealing with nuisance and obstruction. There is, however, evidence in Westminster that the rationale was in part about commercial interests. The order was not confined to the pavements, but included a much larger public area where the council had plans for other commercial activities. Nonetheless, the references to nuisance indicate a strong element of police rationality. There was a focus on the effects of the soup runs that had nothing to do with the service they were providing, but rather with the domestic order of the city. What was unusual about the bye-law was its focus not on the usual suspects – homeless people, street-drinkers and beggars – but on the providers of care to such people.

Blomley (2012, p. 923, quoting Dubber and Valverde 2006, p. 5) notes the 'fatherly concern [of police] presumes a particular form of prudential wisdom, with the ability to decide, in the particular instance, which specific measure will best promote prosperity, order, and well-being, without being bound by strict law-like definitions'. The Local Government Act 1972 gives a breadth of lawmaking power and, in this instance, the proposed bye-law would have had the effect of criminalising an 'entirely lawful, humane and benign conduct: providing food to another person in need' (Liberty 2011b, p. 5).

Here the patriarchal rationale of police conflicts with the more matriarchal care of the soup-run providers. Again, insofar as the argument about the move indoors was accepted, the care was shifted from the public space to the private space. This was the appropriate site for it. This seems to accord with the police rationality. It also accords with the broader rationality of much municipal law of controlling use of public space.

In so far as the Liberty advice provides an opportunity to see how a legal opposition to police from big law might counter its tendencies not to be bound by law-like definitions, it is interesting to note that the authors consider that the rights of the carers, as set out in articles 8 and 9 of the ECHR, could be trumped by an argument relating to nuisance and the impact of the behaviour that accompanies soup runs. It is the lack of evidence and the making of the argument that is the failure in this case. What is apparently being struck here is a balance between the freedom of the autonomous carer and the need for police in these public spaces. Similar challenges focusing on the religious freedoms of providers have also had to compromise. Langlois (1996, p. 1287) writing about homeless shelters and soup kitchens provided by churches in the US concludes that the 'operation of shelters and soup kitchens must still comply with reasonable municipal restrictions and courts will not excuse a nuisance simply because it results from the free exercise of religion'. In this regard human rights, like constitutional freedoms in the US, provide only a partial bulwark against this rationality.

Yet the council do also recognise, to a limited extent, the fact that if they are going to close down this space for those involved in the soup runs to provide care then other opportunities should be made available. In this they provide some recognition of the urge to care amongst the soup-run providers. The Liberty advice provides an interesting contrast. For the authors, providing alternate opportunities to care is not relevant to the question of whether there has been a breach of the rights of the soup-run providers. It cannot provide a justification. Thus a human-rights defence reveals itself as being uninterested in an ethic of care, in the motivations and desires of the soup-run providers to care.

Ultimately the bye-law was not promulgated, and we shall never know whether, if challenged, it would have been upheld. What has apparently happened is that the soup-run providers were persuaded to change their practices in other ways. It was not necessary to pass the law to get them to move away from Cathedral Piazza itself to other locations, and in particular to indoor locations. The evidence does not show whether this was because of the threat of external regulation or because they genuinely considered that another space provided a better space of care to provide food for homeless people.

References

Ashworth A. (2004) 'Social control and 'anti-social behaviour: the subversion of human rights?', *Law Quarterly Review* 120(Apr): 263–291.

Blomley N. (2012) '2011 Urban geography plenary lecture – colored rabbits, dangerous trees, and public sitting: sidewalks, police, and the city', *Urban Geography* 33(7): 917–935.

Buckingham H. (2010) *Accommodating change? An investigation of the impacts of government contracting processes on third sector providers of homelessness services in South East England*, PhD thesis available at: http://eprints.soton.ac.uk Accessed on 7 August 2013.

Cloke P., Johnsen S. and May J. (2007) 'Ethical citizenship? Volunteers and the ethics of providing services for homeless people', *Geoforum* 38: 1089–1101.

Cloke P., May J. and Johnsen S. (2010) *Swept up lives: re-envisioning the homeless city*, Chichester: Wiley-Blackwell.

Communities and Local Government (2011) *Vision to end rough sleeping: no second night out nationwide*, London: DCLG.

Crisis (2011) Crisis' response to Westminster Council's consultation on the proposed soup run and rough sleeping by-laws available at: www.crisis.org.uk/publications-search.php?fullitem=303 Accessed on 10 August 2016.

DeVerteuil G., May J. and von Mahs J. (2009) 'Complexity not collapse: recasting the geographies of homelessness in a "punitive" age', *Progress in Human Geography* 33: 646–666.

Dubber M. D. (2005) *The police power: patriarchy and the foundations of American government*, New York: Columbia University Press.

Dubber M. D. and Valverde M. (2006) 'Introduction: perspectives on the power and science of police' in M. D. Dubber and M. Valverde, eds., *The new police Science: The police power in domestic and international governance*, Stanford, CA: Stanford University Press, 1–16.

Feldman L.C. (2004) *Citizens without shelter: homelessness, democracy and political exclusion*, Ithica: Cornell University Press.

Fitzpatrick S. and Stephens M. (2007) *An international review of homelessness and social housing policy*, London: CLG.

Housing Justice (2011a) Position statement: Westminster Council proposal to ban rough sleeping and soup runs.

Housing Justice (2011b) Housing Justice: Westminster Council drops byelaw available at: www.housingjustice.org.uk/news.php/31/hj-press-release-westminster-council-drops-byelaw Accessed on 1 August 2016.

Humphreys R. (1999) *No fixed abode: a history of responses to the roofless and the rootless in Britain*, Basingstoke: Macmillan Press Ltd.

Johnsen S., Cloke P. and May J. (2005) 'Transitory spaces of care: serving homeless people on the street', *Health & Place* 11: 323–336.

Johnsen S. and Fitzpatrick S. (2010) 'Revanchist sanitisation or coercive care? The use of enforcement to combat begging, street drinking and rough sleeping in England', *Urban Studies* 47(8): 1703–1723.

Johnsen S., Fitzpatrick S. and Watts B. (2014) Conditionality briefing: homelessness and 'street culture' available at: www.welfareconditionality.ac.uk/wp-content/uploads/2014/09/Briefing_Homelessness_14.09.10_FINAL.pdf Accessed on 22 July 2015.

Lacionne M. (2014) 'Assemblages of care and the analysis of public policies on homelessness in Turin Italy', *City: analysis of urban trends, culture, theory, policy, action* 18(1): 25–40.

Lane L. and Power A. (2009) *Soup runs in central London: the right help in the right place at the right time?* London: LSE Housing.

Langlois M-O (1996) 'The substantial burden of municipal zoning: the Religious Freedom Restoration Act as a means to consistent protection for church-sponsored homeless shelters and soup kitchens', *William & Mary Bill of Rights Journal* 4(3): 1259–1287.

Liberty (2011a) Liberty's response to the consultation available at: www.liberty-human-rights.org.uk/soup-run Accessed on 1 August 2016.

Liberty (2011b) Westminster Soup byelaw – legal opinion available at: www.liberty-human-rights.org.uk/soup-run Accessed on 1 August 2016.

May J., Cloke P. and Johnsen S. (2005) 'Re-phasing neoliberalism: New Labour and Britain's crisis of street homelessness', *Antipode* 37(4): 703–730.

Milligan C. and Wiles J. (2010) 'Landscapes of care', *Progress in Human Geography* 34(6): 736–754.

Mitchell D. (1997) 'The annihilation of space by law: the roots and implications of anti-homeless laws in the United States', *Antipode* 29: 303–355.

Mitchell D. (2003) *The right to the city: social justice and the fight for public space*, London: Guilford Press.

Peck J. and Tickell A. (2002) 'Neoliberalising space', *Antipode* 34: 380–404.

Randall G. and Brown S. (2006) *Evaluation of building based services and other rough sleeping programmes in Westminster*, London: City of Westminster.

St Mungo's (2011) Response to Westminster Council's byelaw consultation available at: www.mungos.org/homelessness/publications/latest_publications_and_research/1216_response-to-westminster-council-s-byelaw-consultation Accessed on 1 August 2016.

Smith N. (2001) 'Global social cleansing: post liberal revanchism and the export of zero tolerance', *Social Justice* 28(3): 68–74.

Social Exclusion Unit (1998) *Rough sleeping: report by Social Exclusion Unit*, London: HMSO.

Thames Reach (2011) Thames Reach's position on proposed Westminster bylaws and soup runs available at: www.thamesreach.org.uk/news-and-views/news-archive/news-archive-2011/thames-reachs-position-on-proposed-westminster-byelaws-and-soup-runs/ Accessed on 1 August 2016.

Thompson L. (1988) *An act of compromise*, London: SHAC/Shelter.

Valverde M. (2005) 'Taking "land use" seriously: toward an ontology of municipal law', *Law Text Culture* 9, 34–59.

Westminster City Council (2005) Soup run scoping and mapping report.

Westminster City Council (2007) Westminster City Council rough sleeping strategy 2007–2010.

Westminster City Council (2009) Westminster Cathedral Piazza draft action plan.

Westminster City Council (2011) Transforming lives: Westminster City Council's approach to rough sleeping.

Westminster City Council (2013) Rough sleeping strategy 2013–2016.

Westminster Housing Commission (2006) Report of the Westminster Housing Commission.

Chapter 5

Paths to social caring
Researchers consider their journeys to activism

Jenny Baker, Margaret Allen and Maureen Dyer[1]

Social activism involves caring about how society is structured, how it impacts upon people, and working to ensure that new generations do not suffer the same social injuries experienced by previous generations. We argue that social activism is a form of caring, and that caring about making society better is basic to social reform. As Tronto says, 'until we care about something, the care process cannot begin' (1995, p. 145) and the context of that caring, or lack of, is as Uma Narayan reminds us, deeply political and often part of an internalised dominant ideology:

> [w]hile contemporary care discourse correctly insists on acknowledging human needs and relationships, it needs to worry about who defines these often contested terms. I conclude that improvements along dimensions of care and justice often provide 'enabling' conditions for each other.
>
> Narayan 1995, p. 133

In exploring these issues, we have interviewed a small number of women activists whose stories are interwoven with our own. We trace our own journeys, and those of our interviewees, to social activism. Understanding our own locations in social hierarchies and in relation to the current nexus of power–knowledge, recognising how we had internalised dominant ideologies led us to see that '[d]ominant and totalising theories were not objectively true … [but rather] our identities had been culturally constructed'. For as 'the scales fell from my eyes', there was a sense of the 'political possibilities' (Newton 1988, p. 93). The pain of the injuries of 'race', class and gender were for us a 'catalyst for change' and impelled us to social action. As bell hooks writes,

> I say remember the pain because I believe true resistance begins with people confronting the pain, whether it is theirs or someone else's, and wanting to do something to change it.
>
> hooks 1990, p. 215

The reflections of these activists are largely set in the state of South Australia, during the 1970s to 1990s, when there was a surge of activism around gender, race and class issues. The 1970s in particular saw a wave of social justice reforms in association with the reformist Dunstan government in South Australia and the national Whitlam governments (Parkin and Patience 1981; Whitlam 1985).

Within this context of social reform, however, different social groups fared rather differently. In particular, Aboriginal people have long been the most disadvantaged social group in Australia, reflected in low life expectancy and high rates of imprisonment. Jenny Baker, and others like Sandra Saunders, women born in the 1940s, were among the first generation of Aboriginal people to gain a tertiary education, taking important roles in the struggle to establish Aboriginal-managed health and legal services. These services were intended to be responsive to the needs of their people and sought to defend their cultural heritage against rapacious economic developments. The activism of these women (often exhausting and personally debilitating), and their passion for change, grew from their experiences as Aboriginal women in a racist society.

Margaret Allen provides a somewhat different story of activism in focusing upon white feminists involved in the development of the women's movement and women's studies. She explores how she and two of our interviewees, Kay Schaffer and Suzanne Franzway, found their ways into feminism and activism, having come to maturity in societies where women's economic and social rights were limited and their public roles constrained. Their involvement in creating feminist curricula and teaching generations of students grew from their determination to create more opportunities for women and girls than had been available to them. Australian feminism was burgeoning in the 1970s and 1980s and they were active in labour unions and involved in creating institutions such as the Working Women's Centre and a feminist library, The Women's Studies Resource Centre. These institutions, like the legal and medical services created by Aboriginal people during the same period, required negotiation and battle with the state for the financial resources necessary for their survival.

Our final story of activism arises out of a narrative of immigration. Maureen Dyer's early years were shaped by the British class system. A working-class child, she managed to get into a grammar school, very much a middle-class institution, which led her into a university education. This education enabled her to analyse the impact of the class system on her own subjectivity. Her anger and indignation about the injustice of a classed and gendered education impelled her, once she had migrated to Australia, to work to open up opportunities for children from underprivileged families.

All these activists were able to create and benefit from the reformist moments in Australian social policy during the 1970s, 1980s and 1990s and to use the state to support their ventures. Sadly, more recent decades have seen the rise of economic 'rationalism', and the de-funding of many of the services and initiatives established during the earlier periods. Thus, it is timely to emphasise the crucial links between care and social activism.

Jenny Baker

In the 1950s, when I was a young school child, my skin was covered in psoriasis, a relatively common skin condition, and I regularly visited a skin clinic in a children's hospital accompanied by my father and younger sister. After these hospital visits we would be rewarded with a currant bun at the Adelaide railway station before we caught the train back to Port Adelaide, a poor working-class suburb of Adelaide surrounded by docks and factories, where my father worked. The reward was for allowing my body to be examined by men in white coats. At that time there were few women doctors and certainly no Aboriginal doctors, either male or female. The doctors spoke to each other about my psoriasis while I remained almost detached from my body.

These experiences had a major impact on my understanding of 'health' and 'care', as well as concepts such as stigmatisation and what Franz Fanon described as the 'epidermalization of existence' (Gilroy 2000, p. 46). Fanon was describing skin colour and the racial hierarchy rather than a skin condition, but this concept also fitted my experience as I am an Australian Indigenous/Aboriginal[2] person through my mother's family, who were of the Mirning nation situated on the Great Australian Bight on the southern coastline of Australia. From 1953 onwards my father, who was non-Aboriginal, was given full legal custody of my sister and me, to the exclusion of our Aboriginal mother. This outcome fitted with the policies of eugenics that legalised the removal of 'part-Aboriginal', or 'half-caste', children from their Aboriginal parent (McGregor 1993). I grew up being very aware of my skin and people peering at me; 'look Mummy that girl has leprosy' was one comment I remember. Other people saw the skin colour. 'Have you got *boongs* [a racist derogatory term for an Aboriginal person] in your class', a non-Aboriginal father asked after looking at the class photo and pointing to my sister and I, his daughter later told me. The realisation came that it was the idea of race, as well as my skin condition, that affected the way people viewed me and other people in my family. In fact 'dirty, diseased and neglected' fitted the racist images that white people had (and many still have) of Aboriginal people (Duguid 1978; McGregor 1993; Human Rights and Equal Opportunity Commission 1997)

Sandra Saunders, an Aboriginal activist interviewed for this project, shared a related childhood experience that shaped her life:

> Well, I can remember the first time that I questioned what was happening in the world was when I was a young girl. I was probably in about grade 4 [between 8 and 9 years old]. My grandparents used to come and visit from Kingston [South Australia] ... and when I went to school on Monday these kids would tease me: 'Who were those black people you were with, Sandra?' ... and then one day I just said, 'Ah, they're my grandparents', and from that day on I was okay – the day I stood up. And that was the day that I recognised what it was about, like it was about racism.
>
> SS

Sandra's activism as a young adult began to develop in the fields of community development, welfare and legal rights for Aboriginal people. My own activism turned towards health. My interest in political power had been a part of my childhood as my father, originally a sheep and wheat farmer on marginal land on the west coast of South Australia, ended up working in factories in Port Adelaide in the 1950s and was a strong trade unionist. I remember distinctly a statement he made at the kitchen table that 'a worker's only got his labour so he's got to fight for wages and conditions'. My mother kept her view of the world to herself. After my own studies on colonial Australia as an adult I began to understand that more clearly, especially considering how, at that time, the Australian Workers Union protected white workers to the exclusion and dispossession of Aboriginal workers (Martinez 1999). This lack of awareness by my father, I think, certainly contributed to their divorce. My younger sister and I were left without the daily presence of my mother and older sisters or brothers.

What is difficult to acknowledge is that caring attitudes can intersect with the repugnant ideas of a racial hierarchy. These ideas 'enabled' the dispossession of Aboriginal people from their lands, then continue to enable the exclusion of those deemed 'racially inferior' from professions and workplaces, such that this becomes 'normal'. The excluded become the strangers, 'uncivilised', 'primitives' a process described by Sara Ahmed as 'the *historical determination of the form of the privileged body or the body-at-home*: the body which comes to matter' (Ahmed 2000, p. 94).

The way power operates in care is ever changing, but Ahmed's analysis provides a deeper understanding of the racist exclusion that Aboriginal people were facing during critical times of my life. When I left the children's hospital to work in the Aboriginal Medical Service in Adelaide, I was exposed to a completely different form of care and health from that of my nursing training and experiences in a children's hospital. The Aboriginal Medical Service was a primary health care service and very different from secondary hospital care.[3] It had an approach to governance that was profoundly different from other health care institutions in Australia; it was an organisation that was Aboriginal-community controlled; that is, controlled by an elected Aboriginal board of management. It owed its origins to the federal Whitlam Labor government reforms of 1972, which sought to address the high Aboriginal infant mortality rate and improve access to health care for Aboriginal people (Foley 1982; Waterford 1982).

Both Sandra Saunders and I were involved in Aboriginal-community controlled organisations during a time of positive change in Aboriginal affairs in Australia; the period of the Hawke and Keating Labor governments 1983 to 1996. Sandra was the director of the Aboriginal Legal Rights Movement (ALRM) in South Australia and I was the clinical manager of the Aboriginal Medical Service (AMS) in Adelaide. As Sandra notes, regarding this time, '[t]here was a real buzz about "Things are happening for Aboriginal people in this country", and it was exciting as well as a terrifying sort of period' (SS).

We were both excited at the prospect of working in an Aboriginal organisation. When I joined the Aboriginal Medical Service I felt the same feelings of being 'at home' as Sandra:

> [i]t was like going home, if you know what I mean. It just felt right being in an Aboriginal community organisation where you've got Aboriginal people around you that understand what you're talking about and you're all arguing or standing up or providing a service for the people who need it.
>
> And so my first task there, that I could see what I needed to do, was ensure that the Aboriginal people within the organisation did have the voice and did have the say, and so I implemented a structure within the organisation where Aboriginal people would meet regularly and talk and ... we'd come up with strategies for the organisation. So that was a big thing.
>
> SS

We were both called upon to represent these organisations at a national level. For Sandra, one of her biggest challenges was in response to the Royal Commission into Aboriginal Deaths in Custody (1991) and the implementation of the recommendations:

> [w]hat a bloody nightmare that was! We set up a unit within Aboriginal Legal Rights, where Aboriginal people were employed to actually look at the whole thing and go and meet with the Education Department, the legal section, welfare, the gaol system – whoever it was who had a responsibility to implement these. So we were forever arguing with these people about, 'Why haven't you implemented certain recommendations which relate to your area?' It was an absolute nightmare. And then you'd have another death in custody and they'd say, 'Oh, yeah, well – yeah, we didn't quite get it right'. And so today we are still dealing with that same thing, where Aboriginal people are still dying in custody because they haven't followed proper procedures.
>
> SS

Following this, the ALRM (under Sandra's leadership), was involved in the Royal Commission into the Separation of Aboriginal and Torres Strait Islander Children from their Families, also called the *Bringing Them Home* report (Human Rights and Equal Opportunity Commission 1997):

> the other thing that we set up or were involved in was the Stolen Generation and that had to be – I mean, it took a while before Australia recognised that they had to do something about it and we had people in our civil section working on that with families, children, people that were stolen, and that was heart-wrenching as well, and out of all that, you know, we had put some good cases together and that went on and people won that. Yeah.
>
> SS

While Sandra was leading this work within ALRM, I was representing the AMS and other South Australian Aboriginal health services at national meetings of Aboriginal health service administrators to draft the National Aboriginal Health Strategy (National Aboriginal Health Strategy Working Party 1989). The strategy was the first one ever by Aboriginal people working in Aboriginal-community controlled health services. The strategy needed to be endorsed by federal ministers from both Aboriginal Affairs and Health before final endorsement from the Council of Australian Governments meeting in Brisbane in 1989.

Even though the National Aboriginal Health Strategy (NAHS) was eventually passed, the state Labor (social democratic) government in South Australia did not support the funding or expansion of the AMS in Adelaide, despite the fact that during this period, 1988 to 1989, it was seeing over 100 new patients a month. One of the state government's senior health bureaucrats had remarked that he saw Aboriginal health services as a form of 'apartheid'. By contrast, Aboriginal people saw it as taking back control over their lives after 200 years of exclusion and denial of rights. A Coalition Committee was formed, aimed at changing the position of the state government. It included representatives from the churches, the trade union council, the South Australian Council of Social Services, the Public Health Association and the Aboriginal board members of the AMS. I was chairperson of this committee. As a result of this political pressure by the Coalition Committee, the UTLC asked the AMS to lead the May Day march in 1989 and the Uniting Church in South Australia presented a petition of 5,000 signatures to the Minister for Health. These were very visible signs of support that the government found difficult to ignore and the AMS finally had increased funding released under the NAHS.

The efforts it took to achieve this were, for me, personally gruelling and had a major impact on my marriage and family life which, looking back, I would have preferred had not happened. Indeed, when a review of the implementation of the NAHS recommendations was done in 1994 the results were very disappointing (Commonwealth Department of Human Services and Health 1994).

However, it was an even more gruelling time for Sandra, who needed to leave ALRM after the outcome of the Royal Commission into Hindmarsh Island Bridge (Rowse 2000; Simons 2003). The Commission became a major political event at the time in Australia, not just South Australia. It involved prominent conservative Adelaide families with family links to the judiciary, academia and politics opposing a small group of local Aboriginal (Ngarrindjeri) women and their supporters who sought to prevent the building of a bridge on the basis that it would destroy a traditional Ngarrindjeri women's site. The application to build the bridge in the southeast of South Australia between the mainland and a very small island was to enable property development for holiday houses and would replace a small ferry. The legal challenge by these women was overturned and the Australian press repeatedly attempted to humiliate them nationally by ridiculing the idea of 'secret women's business' (Rowse 2000; Simons 2003). This political and cultural struggle involved significant costs for activists like Sandra:

when the Royal Commission decision come down, ... it virtually accused the women of fabricating the story. I was absolutely shattered and for months and months I sort of had no feeling, if you know what I mean. I couldn't feel emotion.

I reckon they took my naiveté with the way they tried to destroy myself and other Ngarrindjeri women over that, and it took a long time for me to get back to feeling okay. Yeah. And that was – the only way I could do that was I said it was time to step aside and leave Legal Rights and just have some time for myself and my family, which is what I done. And I went and got a shop (laughs) at Wangary [the only shop there].

SS

The rollercoaster of Aboriginal affairs in the racist Australian political landscape scorched many Aboriginal activists. I left AMS after four years and spent two short periods as a director of an Aboriginal women's and children's shelter and as a bureaucrat in a Commonwealth department of housing while studying for a Masters in Public Health. I entered academia in 1992 to teach Aboriginal health and Aboriginal studies and to develop curricula for nursing and medical students. My insights in that role were shaped by those intense years working in Aboriginal organisations and the short, contrasting period spent in the Commonwealth public service. It grounded my understanding of nursing and, particularly, of primary health care and community development, and the way that these ideas intersected with racism, Aboriginal sovereignty and the state.

Translating concepts into curricula meant remembering and confronting 'the pain' (hooks 1990, 215), and providing critical content that had been absent in my own nursing education. The history of colonial Australia and the ideas underlying the racial hierarchy are intertwined and one cannot understand the legacies of the historical lack of care and caring for Aboriginal people, including their present health status, without that knowledge. Curriculum content that omits that history is not only denying Aboriginal voices but also the basis for conversations that lead to better outcomes in care. Social activism uncovers the shortcomings of social life as it happens and it provides an essential understanding that health and welfare professionals need before they can begin to practise. It is part of what the care profession has been about in Australia, and it is necessarily implicated in their duty of care. Denying cultural rights and health rights was, and is, part of the dispossession and marginalisation of Aboriginal people. In this setting, the role of activist leaders like Sandra Saunders in challenging injustices faced by Aboriginal people when dealing with the judiciary, and knowledge disciplines like anthropology supporting the framework of the law, must be viewed as an act of social care and should not be forgotten. As Narayan points out, justice and care are intimately linked:

[w]hile contemporary care discourse correctly insists on acknowledging human needs and relationships, it needs to worry about who defines these often contested terms. I conclude that improvements along dimensions of care and justice often provide 'enabling' conditions for each other.

Narayan 1995, p. 133

Margaret Allen

My first awareness of difference and injustice came around class and differential social power. My father held a white-collar position but had grown up in a working-class family. My mother had a more middle-class background. A family saying, that we were 'poor but respectable', was said in a joking and self-deprecating way, but really we were middle-class. Experience is, of course, contextual (Scott, 1991).

At our church, St Andrew's Church in Walkerville, we were very aware of the domination of the well-to-do, snobbish families who lived in the neighbouring suburb of Medindie. The minister seemed to pander to these people, ignoring more ordinary members of the congregation, such as my family. I was less aware then of my own class advantage. One incident, however, does stand out. I was about eight years old, playing with a school friend. When she referred to my sister and I as 'youse', my father gave her a little lecture, remarking in a jocular manner that 'ewes' were female sheep. Thus he reminded her she did not speak 'properly' and a line was drawn and I was placed firmly on the superior side. We were always encouraged to speak 'properly', learning that language could be an instrument of differentiation and even of oppression.

As I grew up, I was made aware of my father's views that society was dominated by 'them', a rather unspecified group of the powerful and wealthy. More than a politics of envy, this was an awareness that society was unequal, that some were more than equal before the law. Before the reforming Dunstan Labor government brought in a great slew of consumer protection legislation in the 1970s, I can remember my father rueing the power of various business sharks to defraud and ruin poor and guileless consumers (Davis and McLean 1981, pp. 33–36). His belief that social institutions could and should make for a more equal society was powerful. By comparison, my mother's position was not a political one, but one of a deep Christian compassion for others.

The Vietnam War proved to be a radicalising experience for many of my generation, and it solidified some of the views I had gained from my parents in relation to unequal power relations and injustice. Initially, I could not believe the propaganda critical of the United States. However, as I learned of the web of US bases overseas, I became involved in campaigns against the war. Following these debates and actions had a strong impact upon me and I became involved in the anti-war struggle. This shift towards activism converged with other concerns about inequality.

Learning about Aboriginal experience in my city also contributed to my social activism. In the early 1970s, I was involved with Aboriginal families through the Homework Club, run through Port Adelaide Methodist Mission. This was an offshoot of the Sunday Club, in which young university students organised recreational activities for Aboriginal children in the Port Adelaide district. In the Homework Club, we helped the children with their homework and occasionally went on weekend outings. On one of these outings, as we drew up by a beach kiosk, one of the girls, looking at the man at the counter, said, 'That man said "Look at those black *****"'. She was only about ten years old and I was shocked to realise that she was already attuned to constantly assessing white people's reactions to her. I felt that I learnt a lot from the children and their families about being Aboriginal in Australian society, I began to see the systematic racism of Australian society and history and felt impelled to teach about this in my courses.

While I have been greatly influenced by political struggles around war and Aboriginal exclusion, much of my activism has centred around gender issues. The world I grew up in was largely gender segregated. Men led, men were important, while women looked after others, did the washing-up and unselfishly put themselves last. I wanted to be a teacher, and remember when I was about ten and my teacher was congratulated for having completed a BA degree. I realised that she was better educated than the school headmaster, but that she could never aspire to his position as she was a woman. I wanted to be able to finish high school and go to teachers' college and university. A narrow stream of opportunity was there if you did well in your examinations, and avoided doing typing and shorthand, skills that might lead you into a woman's position in secretarial work. Armed with a teacher's college scholarship, I was the first person in my family to get a university education. At university I learnt almost nothing about women's social position, about women writers or about women's history. Virtually all our teachers were male. Women students were marginal.

After graduation, while sharing a house with a couple of friends, I began to hear of the ideas of the women's movement. I attended some early women's liberation meetings in Adelaide. Women I had known at university, like Anna Yeatman, Anne Summers and Julianne Ellis, spoke. We sat in a circle and listened to each other. At home, my flatmates and I sat up for hours turning over these ideas. I read some of the roneoed pamphlets and suddenly I saw things differently. It was as if the tensions between wanting to be attractive to men and 'fitting in' with a boyfriend, and following one's own interests and being 'true to oneself', were now explained. Feminist analyses gave me a political frame for understanding myself, my personal history, the people around me and society in general.

Judith Newton encapsulated my experience when she wrote,

> [t]he scales fell from my eyes ... it felt like a moment of empowerment, not of impotence. Dominant and totalising theories were not objectively true; they were informed by male bias. Our identities had been culturally constructed, and we were not alone.
>
> Newton, 1988, p. 93

However, for Kay Schaffer, a pioneer of women's studies and a feminist scholar, it was not a moment of empowerment, but more of an evolution. She came from a working-class family and was the first from her family to go to university. Her father's ambition was for her to find and marry a lawyer or a doctor. While she excelled at her studies, she had no career aspirations beyond marriage and motherhood. Later she realised how dominant ideologies affected her younger self:

> I [was] constantly ... stymied by my own sense of low self-esteem and my internalised, you know, patriarchal monitors that were telling me, 'You're a girl. You've got to settle for second-best. That's just the way it is.'
>
> KS

When she insisted upon having a natural birth when her first daughter was born in Pittsburgh in 1968, she recalls,

> [i]t occurred to me how much the most significant events of women's lives are controlled by institutions beyond their control and by rules that are set up to serve – well, I would say now – patriarchal structures and values.
>
> KS

Then, shortly after having her first child, she sat in on an early university course on non-fiction feminist prose and read Betty Friedan's *The Feminine Mystique* and Simone de Beauvoir's *The Second Sex*. These discussions were, in fact, as she puts it,

> [t]he first time I had actually started to think about women being different from men and in the sense of what their capabilities might be because of their embodied identity. And it was quite a shock.
>
> KS

From a Catholic family, she was also active in her church, especially in the left-leaning Pittsburgh Council for the Laity, advocating for women's right to contraception and the ordination of women in the church. However, soon she felt that the church could not accommodate women like her. When she tried to greet the bishop as an equal, he put his hand on her head and forced her to kneel in submission and kiss his ring.

Kay joined a postgraduate group advocating the introduction of a women's studies programme at the University of Pittsburgh, discovering early feminist women's writing and women's knowledge and re-evaluating her life. After migrating to Australia in 1974, Kay worked to promote discussion about women's social position and their rights, hosting women's conferences in Bathurst (NSW) and then applying for an International Women's Year grant that, with a team of Adelaide feminists, established the Women's Studies Resource Centre[4] in Adelaide, in 1975 (Kinder 1980, pp. 31–33). She had come to see that, with her knowledge of women's literature and cultural studies, she could teach and influence young women through her teaching. From 1978 she developed and taught women and gender studies courses for both tertiary and secondary levels.

For Suzanne Franzway, also a pioneer of women's studies and a long-time activist in the Women in Trades Union Network and for the Working Women's Centre, there was no 'light bulb moment'. Her mother had always worked and she did not feel that texts like Friedan's *Feminine Mystique*, with its critique of US suburban domesticity, spoke to her. She said that such works,

> [h]ad no space for the kind of experience that I and many in the small country towns in Australia, and from the bush, from the land, [had] you know, there was no accounting for those stories.
>
> SF

Suzanne recalled a series of events building her views and her activism, a Women's Liberation Consciousness Raising Group in London in the early 1970s, studying in the early community-based women's studies programme at Flinders University, participating in meetings at Adelaide Women's Liberation in Bloor Court and attending the British Trade Union Congress Women's Conference late in the 1970s. These gave rise to her activism around women and trade unions, and the Adelaide Working Women's Centre (founded 1979) (Williams and Cricelli 1980, pp. 55–59; Watson 1998, p. 529; see also www.wwcsa.org.au, accessed 20 January 2016). Her own experience of being employed on temporary contracts for six years and then facing losing her job, strengthened her commitment to unionism. As she said, in these movements 'from the '80s and '90s, that's where some of the best of the battles were fought out about balancing class and gender' (SF).

As for me, I became a socialist-feminist supportive of anti-racist initiatives. Between the ages of 21 to 26 years I had moved from being someone with no strongly held positions, to having the basic framework of the analyses, which have subsequently guided my life. With Kay Schaffer and four other academic women, I was part of the Women's Studies Course Team, which developed a Graduate Diploma in Women's Studies in 1978 at the Salisbury College of Advanced Education, a polytechnic-type institution, later part of the South Australian College of Advanced Education (SACAE). Women teachers, nurses and social workers streamed into it, exploring both their positions in the workforce and the gendered structure of their occupations and teasing out the pervasive influence of male dominance in their own subjectivities and personal lives. Being part of this cohort of like-minded women, of students and teachers, made it easy to explore these new ideas and to move forward together, throwing off 'all that false instruction'. Preparation of new subjects and discussion with students continually pushed me further into new understandings.

Our programme to allow women early school leavers access to tertiary studies, was based upon recognising their life experiences as a form of prior learning. It went against the grain for the academic administration, and we struggled to maintain this programme. With all my teaching, I sought to empower women and to acquaint them with the knowledge I had been denied in my own education. Such teaching is about caring, about empowering students to act for social justice.

With my union activism, I sought to improve women's working conditions. With the amalgamation of a number of small colleges into the new SACAE, many staff on yearly contracts, some for up to 15 years, were informed that their contracts were not to be renewed. Many losing their jobs were women. As the union took a more confrontational stance with management, I was catapulted into the position of President of the SACAE Staff Association in 1982. The arbitrary injustice of people's livelihoods being taken away propelled us into protest action. For a decade or so, I was heavily involved in union activities at federal executive level and on the Women's Committee, helping to steer the union towards gender-equity policies. This led to a study, *Limited Access*, which charted the pervasive discrimination against, and the lack of opportunities for, academic women and women administrative staff in Australian universities (Castleman *et al.* 1995). Caring about gender and racial inequalities and discrimination against women workers led me, Kay Schaffer and Suzanne Franzway into social activism and into social activism in education.

As Beasley notes in this volume, 'care has ... been a means to envisage an alternative direction for social life, indeed an alternative politics' (Beasley, Chapter 15). Indeed, this social activism is itself a form of caring, a caring about the present and the future.

Maureen Dyer

I grew up in a working-class family in England on the largest housing commission estate in the country. This was Dagenham, a huge, sprawling, industrial suburb of Greater London. It had been built to house people relocated from the slums. It had long grey streets, with long grey rows of houses. Chemical, car and asbestos factories provided the livelihoods for most (Dyer 1998, p. 30). No one in my family had ever been to high school and my father, who I did not really meet until 1947 when he left the army, never believed much in education for girls. At primary school I did well, but like every child at that time, I had to take the eleven-plus examination to measure my ability and thus to decide what type of school I would attend: a secondary modern school where, at that time, you were precluded from any public examinations; or a selected school, such as a grammar school, which would allow you to take the examinations that allowed you to go to teachers' college or university or enter other professions.

No one at my primary school was completely successful. I had to be interviewed to gain a grammar school place. Only later in my studies did I find out how culturally specific the eleven-plus was. No one at my school passed straight through, unlike in middle-class areas where whole school forms were successful, due to the middle-class bias in the test and also often as a result of 'intensive year-long coaching' (Marsden and Jackson 1962). I remember the anger I felt that other students at my primary school who, as a result of their failure at the eleven-plus, were consigned to the dead-end secondary modern school and had very limited chances for their futures.

By the skin of my teeth I managed to gain a place at the grammar school. Even so, I thought I was very lucky to have succeeded and not sure that someone like me really deserved to be a grammar school girl. I felt an alien and interloper and never quite became the 'lady' the school wanted to produce – dressed in a proper tunic and a hat. The school had little understanding of my situation and the deputy headmistress upbraided me for what she termed my greed for working on Saturdays, rather than playing hockey for the school. She did not appreciate the financial sacrifice my parents were making, letting me stay on at school and that my family needed the money. I worked really hard and was academically very successful but never really felt that I fitted in or that schooling was anything but something that enabled me to pass exams. It seemed to have no relevance to my life at that stage.

This was really brought home to me very harshly when I went to university. I knew very little about universities and had only applied because of the encouragement of one very sympathetic teacher, also from a working-class background. Most bright girls at the grammar schools were channelled into teachers' colleges. In England at that time one went to university in another part of the country and resided in Halls of Residence. I felt completely out of place; there were very few girls from working-class backgrounds at all, and none studying history and none who spoke with a cockney accent. At the end of the first term the Warden of the Hall asked me if I felt I was in the right place for someone like me. At the time that did very little for my low self-confidence, although it did make me determined to succeed. Little wonder that after my postgraduate studies I became very angry at what had happened to me, and others like me, and wanted to make sure that the same patronising attitudes to working-class children would not be perpetuated.

Certainly, one of the ways of becoming an activist is to have some awareness and experience of discrimination in one's own life and then to see it in a wider context; that is, the moment when one realises that all one has suffered is not only to do with what one perceives as one's own inadequacies but also comes from the exercise of power.

That was certainly the case for me. I did not really become an activist until I was in my twenties and it was postgraduate education that gave me my first 'light bulb' moment. When I was studying Sociology of Education at Master's degree level, I became aware that what Sennett and Cobb called the 'Hidden Injuries of Class' (1972) had led me to accept myself as inadequate. I had so internalised the dominant hegemony of class to see myself as a somewhat inferior girl who did not really fit in – not knowing how to behave properly, speak properly or look right. Through these postgraduate studies, I became conscious of all the class discrimination to which I had been subjected. Later, through the women's movement of the 1970s, I put this together with gender discrimination.

I taught sociology at university level and helped establish women's studies at my university in the 1980s. While I realised that I was in a privileged position at the university, I was also aware that women across all sectors of the university were the underdogs; they were more likely to be casual staff and also unlikely to gain promotion, not to mention being victims of harassment. I worked at gaining affirmative action policies for the university and in my union. When the university was selected as one of the 28 institutions and companies to be part of the pilot programme for Affirmative Action in the 1980s, I represented it on many occasions at the meetings in Canberra. A major outcome of the programme was the passing of the federal Affirmative Action Act in 1986.

In addition, I was fired by the desire to open up educational opportunities for working-class and other disadvantaged children. Thus, I became my university's representative on Priority Project's Task Force of South Australia for several years. Priority Projects was South Australia's name for the Disadvantaged Schools Program (DSP). This programme was established by the Whitlam government's Commonwealth Schools Commission and aimed to provide federal funding to assist schools in improving students' learning outcomes in disadvantaged areas. The South Australian Task Force oversaw the projects that were submitted by schools and allocated funds to them. Task Force members were given a number of schools, which they were required to visit frequently and give reports on the progress of schools' projects. Visiting the schools I was given, I was struck by the poverty and the hard life of the children, and the commitment of the teachers to improving things for the children. The resources given to the schools were small and limited the changes they could make. Life for working-class girls was still very hard and their chances of going to university were miniscule.

My education allowed me to analyse my own experiences of class and gender discrimination. I cared deeply that women and poorer students should not suffer in this manner and this led me into social activism around affirmative action and around the promotion of educational equality.

Conclusion

Our decision to write about our personal reflections on our activism came from bell hooks. We used our own reflections as a basis for our conference presentation in 2013, before we had begun our interviews. We were surprised how much we liked doing that and have enjoyed this opportunity to weave into it some of the interviews that we eventually did complete. Tracing our trajectories along with those of our interviewees and recognising how early experiences shaped our paths was a celebratory experience. We are all now retired from tertiary education and spend a lot of time grandparenting, gardening, travelling and just generally pottering around.

However, as we look back to Jenny and Sandra's activism for Aboriginal-controlled health and legal services and for cultural autonomy, to Margaret, Kay and Suzanne's actions to develop women's studies and to advocate for women workers and to Maureen's work in gender equity in the workforce and to greater educational opportunities for disadvantaged children, we note the strong connections between passions growing from personal experiences and the throwing off of hegemonic ideologies, finding their expression in social activism.

Notes

1   Activist Intellectual Cluster Group of the Fay Gale Centre, University of Adelaide
2   The term Aboriginal was given to First Nation peoples by the colonisers. Many Aboriginal people continue to use this term to describe themselves in preference to the term Indigenous, which is possibly more widely used in academia by Aboriginal/Indigenous scholars. In this chapter I use the term Aboriginal.
3   Primary health care is the first point of care with, for instance, a community health nurse or medical practitioner, while secondary care relates to care in hospital, after referral from a primary service. See Griew (2008) and Navarro (1984).
4   The Women's Studies Resource Centre, established in Adelaide in 1975 was closed around 2011, due to loss of government funding. At its height it held 'over 18,000 items including fiction, non-fiction, videos, DVDs, CDs, cassettes, posters, journals and teaching kits' and 'extensive records concerning many key women's groups and organizations'. The Australian Women's Register at www.womenaustralia.info/biogs/AWE1033b.htm (accessed 13 January 2016).

Interviews

Suzanne Franzway, interviewed by Maureen Dyer, 29 October 2013 (SF)
Sandra Saunders, interviewed by Jenny Baker, 24 October 2013 (SS)
Kay Schaffer, interviewed by Maureen Dyer, 21 October 2013 (KS)

References

Ahmed, S. (2000) 'Embodying strangers' in A. Horner and A. Keane (eds.) *Body Matters: Feminism, Textuality, Corporeality*. Manchester: Manchester University Press, 85–96.
Castleman, T., M. Allen, W. Bastalich and P. Wright (1995) *Limited Access Women's Disadvantage in Higher Education Employment*. Melbourne: NTEU.
Commonwealth Department of Human Services and Health (1994) *The National Aboriginal Health Strategy: An Evaluation*. Canberra: Commonwealth Department of Human Services and Health, 144.
Davis, K. and I. McLean (1981) 'Economic policy' in A. Parkin and A. Patience (eds.), *The Dunstan Decade: Social Democracy at the State Level*. Melbourne: Longman Cheshire, 22–50.
Duguid, C. (1978) *No Dying Race*. Adelaide: Seal Books, Rigby Ltd.
Dyer, M. (1998) 'TakingA/part'. *Women's Studies Quarterly* 1 and 2: 29–40.
Foley, G. (1982) 'Aboriginal community controlled health services – a short history'. *Aboriginal Health Project: Information Bulletin. Australian Institute of Aboriginal Studies* 2: 13–15.
Gilroy, P. (2000) *Between Camps*. London: Allen Lane The Penguin Press.
Griew, R. (2008) *The Link between Primary Health Care and Health Outcomes for Aboriginal and Torres Strait Islander Australians*. Canberra: Department of Health and Ageing.
hooks, b. (1990) '*An Interview with bell hooks by Gloria Watkins: "No not talking back, just talking to myself"*'. *Yearning: race, gender and cultural politics*. Boston MA: South End Press, 215–223.

Human Rights and Equal Opportunity Commission (1997) *'Bringing Them Home'. Report of the National Inquiry into the Separation of Aboriginal and Torres Strait Islander Children from Their Families*. Sydney: Human Rights and Equal Opportunity Commission, 689.

Kinder, S. (1980) 'The Women's Studies Resource Centre' in J. Barber, *Women's Movement, South Australia*. Adelaide: Experimental Art Foundation, 31–33.

Marsden, D. and P. Jackson (1962) *Education and the Working Class*. London: Routledge, Kegan and Paul.

Martinez, J. (1999) 'Questioning "white Australia": unionism and "coloured" labour, 1911–37'. *Labour History* 76(May): 1–19.

McGregor, R. (1993) 'Representations of the "half-caste" in Australian scientific literature of the 1930s'. *Journal of Australian Studies* 36(March): 51–64.

Narayan, U. (1995) 'Colonialism and its other: considerations on rights and care discourses'. *Hypatia* 10(2): 133–140.

Navarro, V. (1984) 'A critique of the ideological and political position of the Brandt Report and the Alma Ata Declaration'. *International Journal of Health Services* 14(2): 159–172.

National Aboriginal Health Strategy Working Party (1989) *A National Aboriginal Health Strategy*. Canberra: Commonwealth of Australia.

Newton, J. (1988) 'History as usual? Feminisms and the New Historicism'. *Cultural Critique* 9(Spring): 87–121.

Parkin, A. and A. Patience (eds.) (1981) *The Dunstan Decade: Social Democracy at the State Level*. Melbourne: Longman Cheshire.

Rowse, T. (2000) 'Hindmarsh Island revisted: review article'. *Oceania* 70(3): 252–260.

Sennet, R. and J. Cobb (1972) *The Hidden Injuries of Class*. New York: Vintage Books.

Scott, Joan W. (1991) 'The evidence of experience' *Critical Inquiry*. Summer 17 (4): 773–797.

Simons, M. (2003) 'Hindmarsh: where lies the truth?'. *The Age* 9 May: 11.

Tronto, J. (1995) 'Care as a basis for radical political judgments'. *Hypatia* 10(2): 141–149.

Waterford, J. (1982) 'The Aboriginal medical services – a uniquely Australian phenomenon'. *Aboriginal Health Project: Information Bulletin. Australian Institute of Aboriginal Studies* 2 (August): 16–21.

Watson, S. (1998) 'Working women's centres' in B. Caine (ed.), *Australian Feminism, a companion*. Melbourne: Oxford University Press, 529.

Whitlam, Gough (1985) *The Whitlam Government 1972–1975*. Ringwood: Viking.

Williams, Betty and Maria Cricelli (1980) 'The Working Women's Centre' in J. Barber, *Women's Movement, South Australia*. Adelaide: Experimental Art Foundation, 55–59.

Chapter 6

Young people who care for a family member with physical or mental health problems
Can research better reflect the interests of young carers?

Lester Watson

Introduction

Over the past two decades many nation-states, including Australia, have seen an increasing number of children and young people providing primary care for a family member with mental or physical health problems. This chapter examines existing research and argues for a new approach to conducting research with young carers that can better serve their interests. It is argued that most young carer research derives from the construction of children in Western society as innocent, partially competent and vulnerable and, as a consequence, has predominantly been adult designed, adult led and conceived from an adult perspective, and hence largely reflects adult-centred interpretations and agendas. This chapter discusses this socially constructed nature of childhood in terms of a Foucauldian-type genealogy and the roles of developmental psychology and the psy-complex, which are brought together with a children's rights perspective to propose an approach to research that can develop a young carer's standpoint. This approach involves collaborating with young carers in the development of the research design, methods, issues to be examined and the analysis, and providing them with the opportunity to stipulate their own terms of participation. The chapter concludes with brief reflections on a research project, based on the above considerations, which sought to work collaboratively with young carers in rural Australia.

The expanding role of young carers[1]

A substantial and increasing number of young people, aged 10 to 18 years, are providing primary care to a family member. This is most often a parent or sibling that is physically or mentally ill, disabled or has a substance abuse problem. In some circumstances young people are also caring for infirm grandparents.

Carers Australia have estimated that there are more than 18,800 young people providing primary care to family members in Australia, and a further 388,800 providing supporting care. Even these significant numbers are considered to be an underestimation. As has been widely discussed (e.g. Banks *et al.*, 2002; Smyth *et al.*, 2011), many young people who provide care do not identify as carers and others are often 'hidden'. This has been attributed to factors such as preserving the privacy of the family, the stigma associated with some disabilities and illnesses, or the fear of children being separated from their parent.

The number of young carers is very likely to increase in coming years and decades. Due in large part to increasing life expectancy, Australia's most notable demographic characteristic is population ageing. The number of Australians over 65 years of age has increased by over 60 per cent in the two decades since 1990 (ABS, 2010). Changing family structures will also have an effect on the part children play in supporting family members. There is a significant trend towards less traditional family structures, with substantial increases in the number of one-parent families (ABS, 2003) and a reduced role for the extended family (ABS, 2004; Lackey & Gates, 2001). Parents in Australia are also having children at an older age (Laws *et al.*, 2010), which increases the likelihood that some will experience chronic illness while their children are still young. There is also evidence that the onset of some illnesses once associated with older people, such as Parkinson's disease, occur at an increasingly earlier age (Shifren & Kachorek, 2003).

An additional major factor in the expanding role of young carers has been deinstitutionalisation. Over recent decades many Western governments, including Australia, have largely withdrawn from providing care facilities for people with physical and mental health problems. In large part, this care must now be provided in the family home. In Australia the major impetus for the process of deinstitutionalisation, and indeed a paradigm changer, was the *Inquiry into Health Services for the Psychiatrically Ill and Developmentally Disabled* (Richmond, 1983). While the Richmond Report appropriately positioned deinstitutionalisation as offering freedom, self-determination, autonomy and dignity to the ill, these emancipatory ideals have been exploited by Australian Governments in the pursuit of cost-cutting measures that have continued to evolve into a 'cheap' family care network. Coinciding with the process of deinstitutionalisation, governments have sought to normalise the view that care is a family responsibility. There is evidence of a political discourse and the social construction of a moral imperative to care; that it is the 'right and proper thing' for family members to be carers. As noted by Dean and Thompson (1996, p. 154) 'informal caring is to be perceived as natural, common sense, and "taken for granted"'. Heaton (1999) has attempted a Foucauldian-type genealogy[2] of the advent of family carers and concluded that 'the contemporary policy discourse ... reinforced an ideology of welfare which places a moral imperative on families, and women in particular, to function as carers' (Heaton, 1999, p. 764). The government is now being positioned as a supporter of the 'family care network', with its role largely limited to providing back-up in times of crisis and respite. This reduced government role has undoubtedly increased the number of young people who are caring and the extent of their caring responsibilities.

The positioning of young carers as victims

Perhaps as a result of the steady growth in their numbers, young carers were 'discovered' by UK researchers in the 1990s and identified and labelled as members of a new 'social welfare group'. The most prominent and prolific of these early UK researchers were Aldridge and Becker, who were explicitly motivated by an agenda to generate assistance for young carers (see Aldridge & Becker, 1996), most particularly for governments to assume some level of responsibility for the situation. Care was, understandably, constructed as a burden and, in particular, there was concern about young people taking on responsibilities and duties considered to be 'adult', contradicting the accepted notion that they required, and were subject to, the protection of adults. This perspective on young carers was established as the dominant research paradigm, driven in particular by Aldridge and Becker, whose work dominated the field and was extensively cited in almost all subsequent research (e.g. Aldridge, 2006, 2008; Aldridge & Becker, 1993, 1994; 1996). As a consequence, research was largely focused on probing the negative effects of caring and predicated on positioning young carers in comparison to an idealised and socially constructed 'normal childhood' that is free from family disability and illness. Not surprisingly, and as noted by Olsen (1996, p. 44), caring was 'portrayed as almost wholly negative' and young carers positioned as 'tragic victim[s] of circumstance' (O'Dell et al., 2010, p. 650).

In pursuing this perspective, other researchers sought confirmation of all possible negative impacts, which included: restricted opportunities for social activities, sport and leisure (e.g. Thomas et al., 2003); poor educational outcomes (e.g. Cree, 2003; Warren, 2007); and mental health problems, such as depression, anger, anxiety and emotional exhaustion (e.g. Thomas et al., 2003). The construction of young carers as tragic, exploited and possibly damaged, with their education and careers compromised, then became the accepted portrayal of 'what a young carer is'. O'Dell et al. (2010, p. 649) describe the 'dominant construct of young carers [as] a profoundly negative view'. Caring was referred to as 'punishing children' (Aldridge & Becker, 1993) and as a 'curse on children' (Sidall as cited by Prilleltensky, 2004). It is argued that this view is ensconced in the foundation and rationale for young carer research, that the premise has familiarity and the status of accepted wisdom which goes largely unchallenged. It is important to emphasise here that this discussion is not included to diminish the very real difficulties faced by young carers, nor to discount the value of all previous research that studies the impacts of these difficulties. Rather, the intent is to question the assumptions underlying this research in order to consider approaches that may better explore and understand the experiences of young carers.

Underlying this research approach are unstated assumptions that: (1) what constitutes a 'normal' childhood and adolescence is an empirically verified and certain truth; and (2) it is problematic for those young people who differ when compared to this taken-for-granted notion of a 'normal' and supposed universal childhood. Stemming from these assumptions is an unquestioned belief that children need and deserve a 'normal' (Western) childhood and hence a further assumption that research is best directed at finding out how the childhood of young carers is disrupted and differs from the 'norm', and how to 'fix it' or at least ameliorate the consequences of this difference.

The extent of these assumptions is well illustrated by frequent references in the literature to nebulous concepts, such as 'mature before their time', 'forced to grow up too fast', 'delay in social development', or the more emotive, 'robbed of childhood' (Charles *et al.*, 2009, 2010). References to 'caring responsibilities greater than their age' and that '*some* degree of caring is valued and encouraged as part of healthy child development [italics added]' (Harstone *et al.*, 2010, p. 41) carry an implicit assumption that there is a known and normal level of age-appropriate domestic chores and caring. Discussion of 'the transition between childhood and adolescence and adolescence and adulthood' (Harstone *et al.*, 2010, p. 41), which draws upon an understanding that there is a need to progress through a particular series of milestones or 'markers' (Blatterer, 2007), implies there is one 'normal' way of growing up.

The outcome from having a field dominated by a particular research paradigm is that the same findings and messages tend to be continually repeated, reinforced and extended. There are an increasing number of overview or summary articles which draw together the 'well-documented' status of young carer research (for example: Charles *et al.*, 2009; Harstone *et al.*, 2010; Moore, 2005; Simon & Slatcher, 2011). It is significant that O'Dell *et al.* (2010) surmised from their study that young carers were constrained from discussing positive outcomes from caring because they could not reconcile this aspect of their experience with the dominant (negative) representation. This situation would be more understandable if young carers were given opportunities to tell of their experiences through meaningful involvement in research.

It is significant that throughout much of the research there is an underlying assumption that children are partially competent and fragile. This view acts as a barrier to young carers being recognised as competent individuals able to engage collaboratively with the research process. The outcome is research that will necessarily be biased towards adult perspectives and agendas. At its most extreme is the considerable body of research on young carers that does not involve young carers at all, but instead seeks the views of adults. This includes: parents' accounts of their children caring (Aldridge & Becker, 1994); adults' recollections of earlier times as a young carer (Charles *et al.*, 2010; Lackey & Gates, 2001; Shifren & Kachorek, 2003); and the views of professionals from the health and social care sectors (Gray *et al.*, 2008; McClure, 2001). While these 'adult' studies offer an important perspective, they also serve to highlight the extent to which the research is often detached from direct engagement with young carers. Significantly, young carers report being 'excluded from discussions and decision making processes, as they were considered too young to be involved' (Underdown, 2002, p. 59).

The only significant challenge made to the dominant research paradigm has been from a disability-rights perspective (Keith & Morris, 1995; Olsen, 1996; Olsen & Parker, 1997). These authors have criticised the research for portraying young carers as exploited victims and, by implication, parents as selfish and inadequate. They also suggest that the focus on young carers serves to obscure fundamental problems of lack of support and poverty, which force children into caring roles. Most significantly, it is also argued, young carer research has helped normalise the role of young people as carers, and that the resultant channelling of resources towards propping up the young carer network paradoxically diverts focus and resources away from supporting disabled and ill people, which would lessen or remove the need for young carers. These factors suggest that children will increasingly be drawn into caring roles and that the responsibilities and caring workloads attached to these roles may also escalate.

More recently there has been an emerging recognition that researchers need to seek deeper insights by engaging more directly with young carers (Aldridge, 2006; Doran *et al.*, 2003; Gray *et al.*, 2008). However, it is telling that almost two decades after Aldridge and Becker first commenced a programme of young carer research, the attempt by Rose and Cohen (2010) to conduct a meta-analysis of qualitative research on young carers using 'first person accounts' (p. 476) was hamstrung by a lack of studies. While the studies identified by Rose and Cohen (2010) provide some access to 'first hand' accounts, it is notable that most sought to explore aspects that had already been identified by the dominant research paradigm, such as educational difficulties, mental health and access to services. Those studies which might be presented as participatory were, in the main, still highly managed by researchers and can be characterised as 'adult-led, adult-designed and conceived from an adult perspective' (Kellett, 2004, p. 329). Young carers have not had the opportunity to influence the structure, substance or outcomes of their participation.

To summarise, young carer research in large part continues to reflect the established research paradigm and the associated taken-for-granted assumptions about childhood, children and adolescents on which it is based. Most particularly, the research has been devised without the involvement of young carers.

Contextualising young carer research

Research and literature such as the body described above does not emerge in a vacuum; it reflects cultural norms as much as it influences them. The concept of childhood, as it is generally understood in Western society, presents an important context to young carer research. There are two aspects to the contemporary and widely accepted manner in which childhood is perceived in the Western world which, it can be argued, underlie how the young carer research paradigm developed and became entrenched. First, childhood is a period characterised by innocence, dependence and vulnerability (see for example the discussion in Lansdown, 1995). Childhood is seen as a time for play and no responsibility (Cannella & Viruru, 2004). Second, children are considered to develop according to a natural, universal, timeless and biologically driven progression through to adolescence and adulthood (e.g. Turner & Helms, 1995). This understanding of childhood is so powerful in the community that it is very difficult to problematise. As Crafter, O'Dell, de Abreu and Cline (2009, p. 178) argue, it 'pervades and mediates our understanding of childhood and, therefore, the treatment of children and the development of policy governing this group'. The construct of childhood is examined below in order to subsequently consider the implications for a different approach to young carer research. This examination focuses on: (1) a historical perspective of childhood; and (2) the role of developmental psychology and the psy-complex[3] in constructing the contemporary understanding of childhood.

1) The concept of childhood – a historical perspective

It is instructive to examine (and question) the 'accepted' concept of childhood from a Foucauldian 'genealogical' perspective. The seminal work of Philippe Aries, *Centuries of Childhood* (Aries, 1962), a historical analysis of the development of the concept of childhood, has been likened to the genealogies of Foucault (Hook, 2010). Aries' historical research into the lives of children from the Middle Ages onwards describes the socially constructed nature of many aspects of childhood that are assumed to be 'natural' and unchangeable.

Significantly, Aries concludes that the notion of childhood 'did not exist' in medieval society (Aries, 1962, p. 125). He argues that in the Middle Ages children were not afforded a special or distinctive social status and, from an early age, participated in society according to their *physical abilities*. There was not, Aries argues, any awareness that children might require a different and specific kind of social experience. A fundamental change in the construction of childhood arose from the introduction of anti child-labour laws in the nineteenth century. With young people not able to work, there were then concerns about their idleness, anti-social behaviour and delinquency. This concern to keep unemployed young people 'off the streets' led to compulsory education, which was to become a cornerstone of what constitutes a 'normal' modern childhood.

While Aries' research has been criticised for flawed methodology, in particular his reliance on iconography for an accurate depiction of children's lives (e.g. Pollock, 1983; Wilson, 1980), his contribution is nonetheless profoundly significant in that it recognises childhood as a modern invention; a social construction rather than a presumed 'natural' given. In a similar vein, Burrows (1999, p. 28) has discussed the more recent 'invention' of adolescence, suggesting that the concept arose 'in response to some very special sets of social conditions linked to the extension of the length of compulsory education' and a desire to control a part of the population. Adolescence is now widely regarded as a natural developmental stage. The advent of developmental theories, such as that conceived by Erikson (Turner & Helms, 1995), lends scientific credibility to the idea that there actually exists a phase in the lifespan between childhood and adulthood. The significance of these understandings is that the current concept of a 'normal childhood' underlying young carer research is neither universal across cultures nor permanent across time.

2) The role of developmental psychology and the psy-complex in constructing the contemporary understanding of childhood

The adoption of a historical perspective also enables an assessment of the role of the psy-complex in constructing knowledge of childhood and, in turn, the impact on the conduct of research with children. The late twentieth century saw an explosion of 'micro-powers' engaged in childhood, with children and their development becoming a 'proper' subject for scientific study. The growth of psychology as a discipline, and developmental psychology in particular, is in part related to the role it played in the increased surveillance and regulation of childhood (Burman, 1994; Clarke, 2004). Developmental psychology, founded on biologically driven stage-related phases and a belief in a natural, knowable and observable process, reflects mainstream psychology's underlying concept of linear progress towards a better and more advanced state. This viewpoint is exemplified in developmental theories, such as those of Piaget, Erikson, Kohlberg (Turner & Helms, 1995). The corollary is the testing, measuring, ranking and categorising of children – deciding what is normal and abnormal, based on age-related or stage-related 'norms' (Foley, 2001; Prout & James, 1990). The principles of developmental psychology have been recycled and massified through medical and welfare agencies, schools and the popular media, such that its origins are not always visible.

The problematic outcome of this construction of childhood and the role of the psy-complex is the pathologising of children and adolescents whose progression through these 'natural' stages does not conform to the 'norm'. As noted earlier, disruption to a 'normal' educational path is deemed to be one of the most detrimental outcomes for young people caring for family members. Young people who lead different lives may be labelled as incompetent, abnormal, inferior and, in the case of young carers, 'viewed as non-normative and deficient' (O'Dell et al., 2010, p. 643). This discursive regime limits the possibilities for considering children differently and, by extension, young carers.

Children's rights perspective

A further consideration that emerges from a historical understanding of the construction of childhood is the denial of children's rights as independent, intelligent beings. It has been mentioned how the positioning of children has legitimised the right to observe, test, judge, create discourse and intervene in their lives and those of their families. Such positioning also renders it unnecessary, and perhaps even inappropriate, to seek children's participation and collaboration in research. As noted by Fox (2007, p. 11): 'Their [young people's] voices are rarely heard in a meaningful way that is not tokenistic, and they have little control or opportunities to make decisions, even over matters that directly affect them.'

Lansdown (1995) has challenged these concepts of children from a human-rights perspective. She argues that the notion of being incapable and innocent is contradicted by the level of responsibility taken by children in many other countries for 'adult' caring and domestic tasks (which also highlights our Western-centric, culturally specific notion of childhood). She further notes that children in difficult medical situations have shown they can 'develop a capacity for understanding and decision making which far exceed commonly held perceptions about children's capabilities' (Lansdown, 1995, p. 23).

Lansdown (1995) also persuasively argues that the manner in which children are perceived as vulnerable is historically contingent and derives from assumptions about the nature of childhood. She, however, turns the commonly held viewpoint about the vulnerability of children 'on its head', arguing that a 'self-confirming cycle is established' wherein children are construed as vulnerable and in need of protection, and hence adults are given power to act on their behalf; because children are denied the opportunity to participate in decision making, they are in turn *more* vulnerable to adults (pp. 22–3). A similar argument is presented by Boyle (2003) in her consideration of the manner in which the term vulnerability is used to pathologise. Boyle asserts that designating particular groups as vulnerable leads to 'a set of behaviours associated with passivity, and possibly gratitude' (p. 28). It is useful to also discuss these arguments on children's vulnerability in the context of recent feminist literature on this issue. Mackenzie, Rogers and Dodds (2014) offer a taxonomy of three sources of vulnerability that can usefully describe how children are positioned. In addition to their *inherent* vulnerability (intrinsic to the human condition) and *situational* vulnerability (context specific), Mackenzie *et al.* (2014, p. 9) also argue that *pathogenic* vulnerability can result from attempts to ameliorate inherent or situational vulnerability, but 'have the contradictory effect of increasing vulnerability' through the undermining of autonomy and exacerbating the sense of powerlessness. This is consistent with the arguments of Lansdown and Boyle. The diminishing of children from the way in which the adult world behaves and acts toward them is well summarised by Cannella and Viruru (2004, p. 2): 'What is controlled, lost, disqualified, and even erased through our expectations [of children]?'

To summarise the key issues to this point, there is an increasing number of young people providing primary care to a family member as a result of changing demographics and family structures and, most importantly, because of a government process of deinstitutionalisation that has included normalising the view that caring is a family responsibility. Research on young carers often derives from the construction of children as fragile and partially competent. This construct, in turn, stems from a temporary and culturally specific developmental model of childhood underpinned by the psy-complex. The result is that children and young people are denied the right to have a meaningful role in research on matters that impact most directly on them. Instead, the research is predominantly adult conceived, adult designed and led, and is argued to reflect adult agendas and perspectives.

Towards a collaborative methodology

It is axiomatic that all research findings are produced in a particular context. Adopting a particular epistemology directs the design and construction of research into quite specific modes. From the largely genealogical reading of the literature and past research, it is evident how the epistemological foundations and assumptions that underlie young carer research are reflected in their findings. These considerations present imperatives for research methodology, and this section argues for a different approach to young carer research – one that embraces collaboration with young carers and seeks to disrupt the influence of decisions made by the researcher. This involves grounding the research in the fundamental belief that it must fully involve those whose lives are being researched. Moreover, it requires positioning young carers as the subjective experts of their experiences and creating spaces for them to express their lives and their selves on what matters to them and the ways in which it matters.

This argument draws in part on standpoint theory. In Harding's work on feminist standpoint theory, she argues that less powerful members of society experience a different 'reality' because of their marginalisation (Swigonski, 1994). Accordingly, different understandings will emerge when research begins from the standpoint of a particular marginalised group who have experienced the phenomenon being researched; that is, standpoint theory allows for insights into a reality that is only available to those within the particular group. This is not, however, to argue an essentialist position on young carers; it is recognised that their situations and experiences are very diverse and research should seek to capture that diversity.

There are a number of components of research that are argued to be essential for developing a young carer's standpoint. The foremost strategy is to seek the input and participation of young people in developing the format of the research and how it should be conducted. This approach has not appeared in young carer research to date, but does have some precedence in participatory studies with (non-caring) children in other disciplines (for example, sociology, social welfare and education: Bagnoli & Clark, 2010; Holland *et al.*, 2010; Kellett, 2004; Oldfather, 1995). Punch (2002) argues that making young people central to the process, and enabling them to stipulate their own terms of participation, is empowering and disrupts the power imbalance that exists in research involving an adult researcher and child participants.

It is also suggested that participation needs to be fluid, flexible and different for different young people. Unlike traditional research, which usually supposes uniformity in how participants are involved, as a starting point it should be assumed that different young carers will want to participate in different ways, at different times, and may wish to join or leave the research project at different stages. This should be integrated into the research rather than being 'ironed out', which is akin to the 'informal mechanisms of participation' advocated by Vromen and Collin (2010).

There is also a need to reflect upon different methods and techniques that can create better spaces for young carers to collaborate, rather than the more formal, traditional methods. It can be suggested that quantitative methods are unsuitable for their fundamental distancing from participants, while conventional methods of qualitative researching, like interviewing, are likely to be too formal and may reproduce problematic relations of power between adults and young people. Importantly, young carer research needs to encourage participants to nominate their preferred method of participation, recognising that they best understand what is most suited to their own particular age, social competencies, skills, interests and life experiences. As Freeman and Mathison (2008, p. 59) have argued, multiple approaches give young people a range of opportunities 'to express their thoughts and share their experiences in ways that build on individual differences and styles of interactions'. Bagnoli and Clark (2010, p. 116) concluded that basing their 'research methods on the expectations and ideas of its potential participants ... produced research that was better suited and more relevant to young people ... [and] produce[s] data that is closer to the everyday realities of young people's lives'.

Finally, it is argued that the most important (and ambitious) component of a research project that seeks to prioritise young carers is to provide them with the opportunity and the environment whereby they can be actively involved in the analysis of the data. This is seen as diminishing the influence of the researcher, being empowering for the young people and as being critical for producing a final account that better reflects a young carer's standpoint.

Reflections on collaborative methodology in practice

Having advanced the argument for a different research agenda, it is instructive to reflect on a project which sought to implement such an approach. A research project was conducted which involved working collaboratively with young carers, aged between 12 and 17 years, in rural Australia. The starting point for any research is rarely young people themselves, and this project was no different. The initial phase of reviewing literature and producing research plans was adult led and theoretical. This aspect was itself reflected upon carefully, and there was a desire for the young people to challenge and disrupt this planning on meeting with them. Planning was therefore undertaken with the expectation that, as far as possible, it would be undone by working with the young carers. This had some surprising consequences for the project, as was hoped, which led to innovative research in quite unexpected ways.

The initial step was a series of 'consultation' discussions with each young carer to obtain their input in developing the format and design of the research. During these sessions the young people discussed which methods they thought would be most appropriate, what research questions they thought might be most important and who should be involved. The young people were able to choose their own level of involvement and to be part of as many or as few stages of the research as they wished. Many young people took dominant roles, while some were more passive and reactive. Some strongly advocated their parent being interviewed ('I definitely think ... talking to the parents would be a great thing as well'), while others were horrified at the prospect ('oh god, imagine if you asked my Mum about me').

A particularly important part of these 'consultation' discussions was young people choosing their preferred method, or methods, of participating in the research. Possible methods 'floated' by the researcher included such things as: video diaries; Internet-based methods; social media; interviewing each other; and group meetings. It was assumed that not only would multiple methods be chosen, but also that the young people would favour non-traditional and, so-called, innovative research techniques. This assumption was surprisingly and comprehensively contradicted. All participants expressed a firm preference to participate through a series of one-on-one conversations in their homes; that is, the traditional method of interviews the researcher was trying to avoid! The prevailing sentiment was well captured by a 12-year-old boy who said he 'liked to talk' and felt 'absolutely comfortable being interviewed'.

Notwithstanding this unexpected direction for the research, it remained of paramount importance to adhere to the original standpoint of listening to the young people; and, indeed, the interviews that eventuated were (in general) profoundly notable for being articulate and thoughtful, and for providing great insight into the complexities of the young person's caring situation and family life. This outcome reinforced the criticism about adult researchers making assumptions about how young people should participate in research and what is 'best for them'.

The fluidity and non-uniformity that so strongly characterised this research is argued to be a very positive outcome for participatory work with young people. It was unarguably a positive for the young people that they could be involved in any manner they wished: those who had much to say were not constrained by a researcher's 'limited' set of questions; and conversely others were not coerced into trying to discuss issues they did not wish to, or could not, address. Some young people spoke about a wide range of issues; others were more limited in their discussions. The parent was interviewed if the young carer thought it important, but not when the young carer was uncomfortable with the idea.

The demonstration of agency and the level of positive engagement and insight was very significant and supported the criticism of past research for implicitly not seeing young people as competent participants. The young carers' agency was expressed in many ways, sometimes subtly and sometimes very overtly. All participants at times were overtly dismissive of viewpoints that were 'floated' ('I don't think like that at all'; 'I don't believe in that ... I think that is a complete joke') and presented and argued alternative viewpoints. In some cases, young carers took control of interviews. They were remarkably open about their personal lives, family relationships and the physical and/or mental health problems of family members. The strongest collaborative outcome of the research was the successful involvement of the participants in the data analysis. A final meeting with each young carer was conducted after some initial and very tentative analysis had been conducted by the researcher. The young people provided sophisticated feedback on this analysis, which included putting forward opposing interpretations of the data (13-year-old boy: 'it [caring] is *not* a negative thing!').

The research dispensed with the need for a uniform set of data, which is usually considered a standard requirement for traditional research where differences are assumed to need smoothing out. Instead, this project assumed that differences are very significant and non-uniformity was embraced as an important part of seeking a genuine participatory approach with young people. This approach did place additional onus on the researcher to interpret carefully the often widely varying accounts and to be very careful not to privilege the accounts of those young people who were the most talkative and articulate. The methodological outcome of this fluid approach was to create some increase in labour for the researcher, and an enhanced approach for the young carers to construct knowledge.

The outcomes from this research project cannot be adequately canvassed in this chapter. However, it may be useful to note that a very complex and sophisticated understanding of the experiences of young carers emerged from this collaborative work. The accounts varied greatly, portraying a less essentialised and more nuanced understanding of childhood and young carers. To comment very briefly on one aspect of the findings, there was a strong focus by many young people on some positive aspects of caring, most particularly around issues of family loyalty and strong family relationships and connectedness. These factors, together with a catalogue of positive personal qualities that the young people attributed to caring, enabled them to describe themselves and their families as 'better off' and 'better than' non-caring children and families. Significantly, these were the terms in which they most often discussed their experiences as a family carer, rather than practical aspects such as chores, missing social activities or difficulties at school, the focus of much previous research. This suggests that different outcomes most certainly emerge when the voices of young carers are heard more clearly.

Conclusion

This chapter has sought to provide an argument for a new approach to conducting research with young carers and, by extension, young people generally. It has been argued that there is a range of compelling reasons to work collaboratively with young carers in conducting research, a major one being to produce an outcome that better reflects a young carer's standpoint.

Involving young people in decision making about the conduct of the research did add complexity to the process, but it was an important part of fostering genuine participation and collaboration. Relinquishing some control of the research and the resultant uncertainty about its direction helped to diminish the power of the researcher and provide an environment where the new and the unexpected could emerge. This was an important part of disrupting taken-for-granted assumptions about conducting research with young people.

An important point to take from the surprise outcome of young carers choosing the traditional research method of interviews is not to presuppose a particular view about how young carers want to be involved and end up with 'directed' collaboration that may inadvertently impose an unwanted research relationship on participants. A matter for reflection is whether it is the kinds of methods that necessarily make research participatory, or whether it is the depth of involvement participants have in the process of choosing the methods (Kindon *et al.* cited in Bagnoli & Clark, 2010).

This is not to suggest that conducting participatory research is without difficulties. The adult–child binary is clearly a barrier to collaborative research with young people. As has been discussed, children are marginalised in an adult-centred world (Lansdown, 1995) and there is a largely unquestioned assumption that adult knowledge is superior to that of children. There is a cultural expectation that children defer to adults. Adults exert influence on children simply by their adultness, and this impacts negatively on collaborating with young people, no matter how well intentioned the researcher. In this research it was felt that, at times, some younger children had not fully understood the extent of the collaboration that was being sought. Given dominant understandings of traditional research methods, there also remained a concern that the young people may have been inhibited in considering other methods when they chose conversations (Smith, 1997).

Given the entrenched assumptions about children (and adults) and traditional 'scientific' research, it cannot be argued that it is possible to fully overcome the constraints on collaborative research with young people. However, the important point to take from this research project with young carers was their compelling demonstration of enthusiasm, positive engagement and capacity for sophisticated insight and analysis – an outcome that strongly supports the position taken in this chapter. For the researcher, this participatory project was exciting, surprising and often unnerving, but ultimately very rewarding to be able to provide the opportunity for young people to be directly involved in researching the issues which dominates their lives.

Notes

1 Young people who perform a family caring role do not necessarily identify with the term young carer. It is a label that has been adopted by (adult) researchers and service providers and is used in this chapter in the context of interrogating the assumptions that have been made about young carers.
2 This refers to a major aspect of Michel Foucault's work. He used the term 'genealogy' to describe his historical analysis of the origins of present systems of knowledge and associated discourses. He sought to show that there have been other ways of thinking and acting and, most importantly, that many modern discourses are not self-evidently 'true', but are the product of the workings of power.
3 A Foucauldian-related term coined by Nikolas Rose to describe the wide-ranging network of theories and practices within and around psychology and which act to create abnormality, pathologise, regulate and control thinking and behaviour.

References

ABS (2003). Changing families. (4102.0). Canberra: Author.
ABS (2004). Scenarios for Australia's aging population. (No. 4102.0). Canberra: Author.

ABS (2010). Population by age and sex, Australian States and Territories. (3201.0). Canberra: Author.
Aldridge, J. (2006). The experiences of children living with and caring for parents with mental illness. *Child Abuse Review*, 15, 79–88.
Aldridge, J. (2008). All work and no play? Understanding the needs of children with caring responsibilities. *Children and Society*, 22, 253–264.
Aldridge, J., and Becker, S. (1993). Punishing children for caring: The hidden cost of young carers. *Children and Society*, 7, 376–387.
Aldridge, J., and Becker, S. (1994). *My child my carer: The parents' perspective*. Loughborough: Young Carers Research Group.
Aldridge, J., and Becker, S. (1996). Disability rights and the denial of young carers: The dangers of zero-sum arguments. *Critical Social Policy*, 16(48), 55–76.
Aries, P. (1962). *Centuries of childhood*. London: Jonathan Cape.
Bagnoli, A., and Clark, A. (2010). Focus groups with young people: A participatory approach to research planning. *Journal of Youth Studies*, 13(1), 101–119.
Banks, P., Cogan, N., Riddell, S., Deeley, S., Hill, M., and Tisdall, K. (2002). Does the covert nature of caring prohibit the development of effective services or young carers? *British Journal of Guidance and Counselling*, 30(3), 229–246.
Blatterer, H. (2007). Contemporary adulthood: Reconceptualizing an uncontested category. *Current Sociology*, 55(6), 771–792.
Boyle, M. (2003). The dangers of vulnerability. *Clinical Psychology*, 24, 27–30.
Burman, E. (1994). *Deconstructing developmental psychology*. New York: Routledge.
Burrows, L. (1999). *Developmental discourses in school physical education*. Doctor of Philosophy, University of Woolongong.
Cannella, G. S., & Viruru, R. (2004). *Childhood and postcolonization: Power, education and contemporary practice*. New York: RoutledgeFalmer.
Charles, G., Stainton, T., and Marshall, S. (2009). Young carers: Mature before their time. *Reclaiming Children & Youth*, 18(2), 38–41.
Charles, G., Stainton, T., and Marshall, S. (2010). Young carers in immigrant families. *Canadian Social Work*, 12(1), 83–92.
Clarke, J. (2004). Histories of childhood. In D. Wyse (Ed.), *Childhood studies: An introduction*. Oxford: Blackwell Publishing, 3–10.
Crafter, S., O'Dell, L., de Abreu, G., and Cline, T. (2009). Young people's representations of 'atypical' work in English society. *Children & Society*, 23(3), 176–188.
Cree, V. E. (2003). Worries and problems of young carers: Issues for mental health. *Child and Family Social Work*, 8, 301–309.
Dean, H., & Thompson, D. (1996). Fetishizing the family: The construction of the informal carer. In H. Jones and J. Millar (Eds.), *The politics of the family*. Aldershot: Avebury, 145–165.
Doran, T., Drever, F., and Whitehead, M. (2003). Health of young and elderly informal carers: Analysis of UK census data. *British Medical Journal*, 327, 1388.
Foley, P. (2001). The development of child health and welfare services in England (1900–1948). In P. Foley, J. Roche, and S. Tucker (Eds.), *Children in society: Contemporary theory, policy and practice*. Basingstoke: Palgrave.
Fox, R. (2007). Research with young people: Methodologies, challenges and implications. *The Community Psychologist*, 40, 11–16. Retrieved from www.scra27.org/documents/tcp/tcp2007/website.

Freeman, M., and Mathison, S. (2008). *Researching children's experiences*. New York: Guilford Press.

Gray, B., Robinson, C., and Seddon, D. (2008). Invisible children: Young carers of parents with mental health problems – The perspectives of professionals. *Child & Adolescent Mental Health*, 13(4), 169–172.

Harstone, A., Bergen, S. J. R., and Sweetgrass, M. (2010). Young carers: Children caring for family members living with an illness or disability. *Relational Child & Youth Care Practice*, 23(1), 39–45.

Heaton, J. (1999). The gaze and visibility of the carer: A Foucauldian analysis of the discourse of informal care. *Sociology of Health & Illness*, 21(6), 759.

Holland, S., Renold, E., Ross, N. J., and Hillman, A. (2010). Power, agency and participatory agendas: A critical exploration of young people's engagement in participative qualitative research. *Childhood*, 17(3), 360–375.

Hook, D. (2010). *Foucault, psychology and the analytics of power*. Basingstoke: Palgrave Macmillan.

Keith, L., and Morris, J. (1995). Easy targets: A disability rights perspective on the 'children as carers' debate. *Critical Social Policy*, 15(44–5), 36–57.

Kellett, M. R. N. S. (2004). 'Just teach us the skills please, we'll do the rest': Empowering ten-year-olds as active researchers. *Children & Society*, 18(5), 329–343.

Lackey, N. R., and Gates, M. F. (2001). Adults' recollections of their experiences as young caregivers of family members with chronic physical illnesses. *Journal of Advanced Nursing*, 34(3), 320–328.

Lansdown, G. (1995). Children's rights to participation and protection: A critique. In C. Cloke and M. Davies (Eds.), *Participation and empowerment in child protection*. London: Pitman Publishing, 19–38.

Laws, P. J., Li, Z., and Sullivan, E. A. (2010). *Australia's mothers and babies 2008*. (Perinatal Statistics Series No. 24.). Canberra: AIHW.

Mackenzie, C., Rogers, W., and Dodds, S. (Eds.). (2014). *Vulnerability: New essays in ethics and feminist philosophy*. New York: Oxford University Press.

McClure, M. (2001). School-age caregivers: Perceptions of school nurses working in Central England. *Journal of School Nursing*, 17, 76–82.

Moore, T. (2005). Young carers and education. *Youth Studies Australia*, 24(4), 50–55.

O'Dell, L., Crafter, S., de Abreu, G., and Cline, T. (2010). Constructing 'normal childhoods': Young people talk about young carers. *Disability & Society*, 25(6), 643–655.

Oldfather, P. (1995). Songs 'Come back most to them': Students' experiences as researchers. *Theory Into Practice*, 34(2), 131–137.

Olsen, R. (1996). Young carers: Challenging the facts and politics of research into children and caring. *Disability & Society*, 11(1), 41–54.

Olsen, R., and Parker, G. (1997). A response to Aldridge and Becker – 'Disability rights and the denial of young carers: The dangers of zero-sum arguments'. *Critical Social Policy*, 17(50), 125–133.

Pollock, L. A. (1983). *Forgotten children: Parent-child relations from 1500 to 1900*. Cambridge: Cambridge University Press.

Prilleltensky, O. (2004). My child is not my carer: Mothers with physical disabilities and the well-being of children. *Disability & Society*, 19(3), 209–223.

Prout, A., and James, A. (1990). A new paradigm for the sociology of childhood? Provenance, promise and problems. In A. James and A. Prout (Eds.), *Constructing and reconstructing childhood: Contemporary issues in the sociological study of childhood*. London: Falmer Press, 7–34.

Punch, S. (2002). Research with children. *Childhood*, 9(3), 321–341.
Richmond, D. T. (1983). *Inquiry into Health Services for the Psychiatrically Ill and Developmentally Disabled (The Richmond Report)*. Sydney: NSW Health Department.
Rose, H., and Cohen, K. (2010). The experiences of young carers: A meta-synthesis of qualitative findings. *Journal of Youth Studies*, 13(4), 473–487.
Shifren, K., and Kachorek, L. V. (2003). Does early caregiving matter? The effects on young caregivers' adult mental health. *International Journal of Behavioural Development*, 27(4), 338–346.
Simon, C., and Slatcher, C. (2011). Young carers. *InnovAiT*, 4(8), 458–463.
Smith, S. E. (1997). Deepening participatory action research. In S. E. Smith, D. G. Williams, and N. A. Johnson (Eds.), *Nurtured by knowledge: Learning to do participatory action research*. New York: Apex Press, 3–43.
Smyth, C., Blaxland, M., and Cass, B. (2011). 'So that's how I found out I was a young carer and that I actually had been a carer most of my life'. Identifying and supporting hidden young carers. *Journal of Youth Studies*, 14(2), 145–160.
Swigonski, M. (1994). The logic of feminist standpoint theory for social work research. *Social Work*, 39(4), 387–393.
Thomas, N., Stainton, T., Jackson, S., Wai Vee, C., Doubtfire, S., and Webb, A. (2003). 'Your friends don't understand': Invisibility and unmet need in the lives of 'young carers'. *Child & Family Social Work*, 8(1), 35–46.
Turner, J. S., and Helms, D. B. (1995). *Lifespan development* (Fifth ed.). Fort Worth: Harcourt Brace & Company.
Underdown, A. (2002). 'I'm growing up too fast': Messages from young carers. *Children and Society*, 16, 57–60.
Vromen, A., and Collin, P. (2010). Everyday youth participation? Contrasting views from Australian policymakers and young people. *Young*, 18(1), 97–112.
Warren, J. (2007). Young carers: Conventional or exaggerated levels of involvement in domestic and caring tasks? *Children and Society*, 21, 136–146.
Wilson, A. (1980). The infancy of the history of childhood: An appraisal of Philippe Aries. *History & Theory*, 19(2), 132–153.

Chapter 7

Caring at the borders of the human

Companion animals and the homeless

Helen Carr[1]

> If you find me dead, please take care of my dog, she is all I have in the world and she has stuck by my side when no one else would.[2]

Introduction

The epigram encapsulates the two starting points of this chapter. The first is the surprising absence of animals in socio-legal thinking about homelessness given their visibility on the street and in the media. The second is that care provides a dominant theme in the stories that homeless people tell of their relationships with their pets/companion animals. The chapter therefore seeks to fill a significant gap in the literature by reflecting on care-receiving and care-giving and the connections between humans and non-humans in the context of homelessness. My argument is that understanding homeless people and their pets as agents/actants of care enables a revaluation of care through a focus on care's relationality and a significant and potentially progressive reframing of homeless people.

The chapter draws on Franklin, who points out that where humans live 'very closely and purposefully with other species, ... it goes without saying that [their] stories cannot properly be told without including the full cast of supporting actors' (Franklin 2006:138). It therefore amplifies more standard socio-legal accounts of homelessness with stories told of, and by, homeless people about their caring relationships with companion animals. The purpose is to reveal the animal's value to a homeless person, and to demonstrate that homeless people can be simultaneously providers and recipients of care. This disrupts the normative asymmetry of care and dependency, which can entrench the power of the care-giver and demean the recipient as passive and helpless, incapable even of self-care. It also makes visible significant connections between homeless pet owners and the domiciled, rather than understanding the homeless person as a distinct and problematic other. More broadly, I want to use the stories and the consequent revaluation of care as a challenge to a particular injustice inflicted on homeless people, what Feldman describes as their cultural 'misrecognition'(Feldman 2004).

For Feldman there are four strands to cultural misrecognition:

> The first is a form of complete nonrecognition – the homeless as *non-persons* whom domiciled citizens 'see right through' and seek to remove from valued urban spaces ... The second is a conservative individualist image of *disruptive subjects* responsible for their plight – unconstrained profane outlaws of public space. ... The third is a 'compassionate' yet ultimately degrading construal of the homeless as *helpless victims* ... to be sheltered and kept alive with a bed, a blanket and some soup. The fourth is a therapeutic vision of *clients with pathologies*, who, through appropriate classification, surveillance and intervention can be reintegrated into society.
>
> ibid., p. 92

Feldman argues that cultural misrecognition is a form of cultural injustice that is both distinct from and as problematic as the economic injustices that face homeless people. As he explains,

> To treat homelessness as a problem solely of maldistribution is to displace attention from the materialized values and norms that polarize society into home-dwelling citizens and homeless bare life.
>
> ibid., p. 91

In addition to the fundamental injustice of failing to recognise people for who they are, cultural misrecognition is stigmatising, distorts policy responses and negatively impacts upon how homeless people see themselves. Whilst caring *for* the homeless, for Feldman, is part of the political problem of homelessness, my argument is that the caring relationships *between* homeless people and their companion animals are quite different. They provide a useful opportunity to revalue care as something other than an exercise of power that embeds the injustices of cultural misrecognition.

The chapter begins by outlining the role of pets/companion animals in contemporary society and the challenges posed by an emergent academic interest in human–animal relations, before turning to the narratives that homeless people provide in connection with their pets.

Companion animals in contemporary society

Whilst pet keeping dates back millennia (Podberscek *et al.* 2005), the commercial pet industry did not become a feature of Western societies until the nineteenth century, and it was not until the mid twentieth century that pet keeping became widespread. More recently it appears to have increased exponentially – Franklin points to a 66 per cent increase in dog ownership and a 75 per cent increase in cat ownership in the UK between 1963 and 1991, at a time when the UK's human population grew by roughly 10 per cent (Franklin 1999, pp. 89–90). The increase has been accompanied by an increase in the sophistication and economic significance of pet products and services. Nor did the recession have much of an impact.

In 2012 the *Independent* reported that the pet industry was worth more than £2.7 billion and pet owners would cut back spending on their own food rather than that of their pets (Youde 2012). Franklin's explanation relates to the misanthropy, the heightened awareness of risk and the ontological insecurity that many theorists argue are characteristic of our times. He suggests,

> Humans began to build social and emotional ties with animals because it had become increasingly difficult for them to establish and maintain such ties among themselves.
>
> Franklin 1999, p. 36

The growth in pet ownership and the amount that people are prepared to invest in their animals is accompanied by a changing attitude towards pets. Franklin points to a greater emphasis on companionability as opposed to the instrumental or decorative functions of pets (ibid., p. 89). This transformation, I suggest, is key to this chapter as it reveals the potential for caring and sustaining connections between the pet 'owner' and pet, as the narratives I explore below demonstrate.

The extensive services that are available to meet every imaginable need, from psychological counselling through to horoscopes, reinforce the suggestion that pets are increasingly considered as quasi-family, with needs that mirror those of humans. However, the contemporary proximity between companion species and their owners has consequences. New demands are being placed upon owners. For instance, intimacy, as well as a concern with animal health, requires that pet breath is managed. Franklin describes how: 'New companies have emerged to provide pet dental products such as toothpastes with appropriate dog and cat flavours, dental brushes that fit over human fingers and other hygiene items.' (ibid., p. 91)

More generally, Power notes an increasingly coercive edge to pet ownership:

> Dogs are being disciplined in new ways that reflect changing social, cultural and economic imperatives around homemaking and pet-keeping that have emerged across post-industrial nations since the 1980s. In this context a disciplined dog is part of the performance of respectable middle-class identities.
>
> Power 2012, p. 371

In Britain, criminal legislation reinforces responsible pet ownership. The Dangerous Dogs Act 1991 requires that dog owners make responsible choices about their choice of breed in order to protect the public, and the Animal Welfare Act 2006 imposes responsibility on the pet owner to prevent animal suffering.[3] This recent legislative activity is further evidence that contemporary pet ownership is not cost free. Pets are a responsibility; they are expensive, time consuming and difficult to manage. They pose risks to human health and safety, they pollute and they use up scarce resources. The continued commitment to pet ownership, despite the dominance of economic rationalities and a heightened awareness of environmental issues, demonstrates that it offers something people particularly value. For Veevers, pets 'earn their keep' because of the major roles they play in our lives: 'They provide a medium of expression for the personality and preferences of the owner; they facilitate sociability; and under some circumstances they provide a supplement to human companionship, or an alternative to it' (1985, p. 27).

There is no reason to believe that homeless people are distinct from the general population in the value they place upon their relationships with companion animals. Indeed, as the epigram to this chapter indicates, their particular physical, emotional and social vulnerability suggests they are likely to place a premium upon those relationships and, perhaps, pay a higher cost for the privileges of the relationship. As Irvine observes: 'In this world, people must protect their dogs from being confiscated and even shot. They must sleep with their dogs tied to their legs at night. They face numerous risks and confront fears with only their animal as company' (2013, p. 6).

Below I consider Irvine's analysis of narratives that homeless people in the United States use to explain the significance of these relationships. First, however, I consider academic interest in human–animal relationships. I argue that there is a particular value for socio-legal scholarship in theoretical approaches that prioritise the plurality, contingency and permeability of legal and social categories and the recognition of the agency of non-humans.

Theoretical concerns

The growth of human–animal studies

Interactions and relationships with non-human animals, and interactions with other humans about animals, saturate our lives and yet, until recently, have received relatively little academic attention. DeMello (2012, p. 7) notes the paradox, 'This invisibility – in scholarly inquiry – was perhaps as great as the presence of animals in our daily lives'. For Michael it is the scientific objectification of animals and their subservience to human need which explains their absence from modern thinking (2000). Human–animal studies have emerged during the last 20 to 30 years as one response to this academic deficit. Both interdisciplinary and multi-disciplinary, human–animal studies is informed by, but distinct from, scientific studies of animal behaviour. It draws on both humanities and social sciences to seek to understand animals in the context of human society, their social construction, their use in medical research or agriculture, the literary and artistic use of animals and to consider animals wherever they exist – be it the zoo, the laboratory, the wild or the home, or indeed in our imaginations, in legend, myth, film or the theatre. Human–animal studies have proved theoretically productive as the limits of humanist-modernist projects have been recognised.

Challenging conventional categories

The dominant theoretical concern of human–animal studies is animal rights, described by Seager as 'one of the most intellectually challenging, paradigm-shifting, innovative, and radical (in the best sense of that word) areas of intellectual activity and social activism' (Seager 2003, p. 168). Feminist philosophers have made a critical contribution to the debate by pointing to and overcoming the limitations of animal-rights advocates, such as Peter Singer and Tom Regan, whose arguments for the extension of rights to animals are based primarily on their sameness to humans. As Seager points out they 'elaborate most clearly the importance of developing a feminist animal rights theory that does not sanctify the "erasure of difference," an erasure that almost always works primarily to the advantage of the dominant class' (ibid., p. 170). Whilst feminist arguments draw on the ethic of care,

> The most compelling feminist animal rights theorists insist that developing a care-based ethic cannot rest on an appeal to a 'natural(ized)' extension of women's affinities and experiences but, rather, must also reflect a honed political analysis ... including analysis of power relations in animal exploitation industries, in the commodification of animals, and in the hegemonic export of Western constructions of human–animal relations.
>
> ibid., p. 171

Closely related to questions of animal rights are issues relating to identity. As Franklin notes, at a time, 'when the categorical boundary between human and animals, so fiercely defended as a tenet of modernity, has been seriously challenged, if not dismantled in places' (Franklin 1999, p. 3), human–animal studies bring fresh perspectives to notions of 'otherness', and enable reflections on speciesism, hybridity and the divide between nature and culture (Haraway 2003).

Academic lawyers, particularly those influenced by the humanities, have contributed to this emergent field of study. Sarat, in the editorial to a 2010 issue of *Law, Culture and Humanities* dominated by legal contributions to human–animal studies, makes clear where theoretical legal concerns may lie,

> In coming to terms with 'otherness' perhaps no distinction is more dramatic than the difference drawn between humans and other non-human animals. Non-human animals seem, at once, to need legal protection but not to be the bearers of legal rights. The law forbids certain forms of inhumane treatment and enjoins humans to avoid treating non-human animals in particular ways. Yet the law allows, tolerates or sanctions humans in doing things to other species that would constitute grave offenses if done by one human to another.
>
> Sarat 2010, p. 7

In addition to thinking through the bases for the allocation of rights to animals, animal rights raises issues about exploitation and categorisation, questions that are ripe for feminist scholarship. So feminist approaches include,

> Elucidating the commonalities in structures of oppressions across gender, race, class, and species; developing feminist-informed theories of the basis for allocating 'rights' to animals; and exposing the gendered assumptions and perceptions that underlie human relationships to non-human animals. At the same time, the serious contemplation of animal rights makes a considerable contribution to destabilizing identity categories and adds new dimensions to theorizing the mutability of identity.
>
> Seager 2003, p. 168

Fox, in particular, urges lawyers to take human–animal relations more seriously, and argues that to do so they need to pay attention to legal technicalities. She argues that what is needed is,

> a commitment to tackling the animal/human boundary which remains deeply embedded in and constantly reified by law, even as the boundary itself becomes increasingly unstable. ... I aim to take that project a stage further, by suggesting that an attempt to take animals seriously also requires us to problematize the category 'animal'.
>
> 2010, p. 38

Fox's work, urging critical engagement with the problems of legal categorisation from the perspective of the 'animal', shares an interest in disrupting the privileged position of the human with other theoretical developments, particularly those concerned with materiality and clustered about Actor Network Theory.

Expanding understandings of agency

The starting point for these perspectives is on theorising the non-human animal and the object, recognising their potential equivalence to humans as actors with agency.

The perspective asks that we remain open to the possibility that non-humans add something that is of sociological relevance to a chain of events: that something happens; that this something is added by a non-human; and that this addition falls under the general rubric of action and agency. It is the action itself that is the important thing to trace (Sayes 2014, p. 145).

What is particularly interesting about these approaches, in the context of this chapter, is their focus on relationality and connectedness between humans and non-humans. So, for instance, Michael, suggesting we focus on the multiplicity of bodies and things which together make something happen, a grouping he imagines as 'co(a)gents', contrives the 'Hudogledog', which comprises dog, dog lead and human dog walker. He uses the Hudogledog, 'first by pre-emptively deconstructing it, then by tracing its comings and goings, that is, its ephemerality ... to expose those normally undetected pathways, those routes along which pass signs and materials that mediate the heterogeneous (dis)orderings of the Hudogledog' (Michael 2000, p. 118). His task is to explain everyday mundane social and cultural interactions in local parks. However, I suggest that this approach may be productive for understanding care in the context of homelessness. It draws our attention away from the standard dyadic understanding of care, so tellingly problematised by Feldman (2004), and instead make us identify more hidden pathways, for instance by considering the relationships between homeless people and their pets. For Bennett too, non-human agency prompts a move away from an individualistic notion of agency and a concrete notion of matter. What she advocates is a congregational or distributive understanding of agency and a blurring of the borders between human and non-human. For her, 'an actant never really acts alone. Its efficacy or agency always depends on the collaboration, cooperation, or interactive interference of many bodies and forces' (Bennett 2010, p. 21).

What Bennett opens up, with her insistence on assemblages of human and non-human and in common with other theoretical challenges to the human/non-human divide, is the possibility of thinking afresh about moral responsibility and political accountability. This is a very useful move in the project of revaluing care as it enables care to be understood as something potentially distinct from an exercise of power that the privileged 'we' extend to the vulnerable 'other'. When care is framed as an assemblage or relationally then not only are its complexity and nuance revealed but also its potential as a productive force.

Policy implications

The concerns are not solely theoretical. Human–animal studies are having an increasing impact upon social policy. For instance, research has demonstrated the link between animals and human violence, particularly domestic violence, and highlighted the need for services to provide care for the animals of women fleeing violence (DeMello 2012, p. 149). More positively, the therapeutic value of relationships between animals and humans has been recognised as leading to tangible benefits for human health and well being, particularly for elderly people, the vulnerable and the socially isolated. Franklin points to the precariousness of contemporary life where 'divorce, separation, single parenthood, economic depression, the migration of young people from country areas, insecure local labour markets, all serve to increase the numbers of people living alone or households stranded away from former kin', and highlights research which shows that 'participants living entirely alone were more lonely than those living with pets' (Franklin 2006, p. 141), to demonstrate the increasing significance of companion animals.

The interface between policy and theory makes a focus on human–animal relationships attractive to scholars working within social welfare law and has the potential to overcome some of its limits. Whilst I am sympathetic to the dominant concerns of contemporary social welfare scholarship – the punitive exclusion and surveillance of the poor (Wacquant 2009, Standing 2011), and the expansion of categories of welfare subjects – I have argued elsewhere that these concerns can be problematic (Carr 2013). Advocating new categories of inclusion can provoke competition for limited resources amongst the vulnerable and result in new and often intensified exclusions, whilst a focus on the punitive consequences of neo-liberalism's hegemony can operate, in part, to reinforce its power and eradicate complexity and nuance. As De Vertueil argues, such limits can lead to a 'failure to recognize differences within the homeless population, to give voice to homeless people themselves, or recognize the (many and diverse) ways in which homeless people continue to 'get by' and survive in the city' (De Verteuil *et al.* 2009, p. 660). Rethinking the social to include the non-human provides, at the very least, a useful opportunity to think differently. Fox puts it thus,

> This 'lived intersubjectivity' of two beings sharing a messy, awkward, loving relationship provides an ideal opportunity for thinking practically about some of the real-life dilemmas presented in recent theoretical challenges to the animal–human divide and helps us go beyond theories of destabilized categories to the complex theorizations and practices of everyday life.
>
> 2006, p. 535

Fox's aim is to enrich understandings of our relationships with the non-human world. My aim is different, arguably, and, ironically, more humanistic, as I turn to the stories that homeless people tell of their relationships with their animals. My interest is in the resources animals provide to enable the homeless person to resist cultural misrecognition and in revealing the significance of care within the stories the homeless people tell. In the first part of this section of the chapter I provide a brief summary of Irvine's rich and detailed ethnography – published as *My Dog Always Eats First: Homeless people and their animals* in 2013 – in which she provides a personal narrative analysis of interviews with seventy-five homeless pet owners in various cities in California and Florida, whom she accessed through veterinary clinics for the pets of the homeless. The material is particularly useful for the insights it provides into how people construct the identities of their animals and simultaneously construct identities for themselves, and how this relates to their particular experience of homelessness.

Homeless people and their pets

Irvine's analytical focus is on the narratives homeless people provided to explain their relationship with an animal or animals. These provide evidence of the person's experience of their relationship and, simultaneously, evidence of how society 'speaks itself' through peoples' lives (2013, p. 28). Irvine responds to the problematic label of homelessness, which eradicates complexity and nuance, by using a typology comprising four distinct categories of homeless people. Her first category is the recently dislocated – people experiencing homelessness for the first time and for a short while, 'many had recently become disabled, become unemployed, been evicted or some combination of the three'. Irvine identifies her second category as straddlers, 'people experiencing homelessness for the second or third time and some of whom had "bounced" between housing and the street numerous times throughout their lives' (ibid., p. 36). The third category is outsiders – homeless people for whom street life has become a taken for granted way of life. Irvine distinguishes two types of outsider. Her first sub-category is settled outsiders, people who are chronically homeless having lived on the streets for five or more years. The second is travellers, young people, generally under 25 years of age who define themselves as houseless rather than homeless, who avoid homelessness services, other than those provided for youth, and who are 'entrenched in street culture and life on the road' (ibid., p. 37). The final category comprises formerly homeless people who are now housed or living stably, which Irvine included because they had had animals whilst living on the streets or they attributed their success in staying off the streets to their companion animals.

Irvine identifies four strong narrative themes from the accounts of relationships with companion animals. These provide a dramatic counterpoint to the forms of cultural misrecognition identified by Feldman. The first narrative theme, in which the pet is described in terms of 'friend and family', was used mostly by the recently dislocated and straddlers.

> The narrative of the animal as friend or family has this story line: 'I once had a home and a different kind of life. I no longer have those things. I don't know what the future holds, but this animal will be with me'.
>
> ibid., pp. 68–9

The particular power of the friend and family narrative identified by Irvine is that it bestows or restores a moral identity and a sense of self-worth (ibid., p. 82). Caring appears to be central:

> Just having the animal to care for brings responsibility, reliability and consistency to lives that have few conventional means of attaining these qualities. At the same time, the feeling of being needed that comes from the animal's dependence brings emotional benefits.
>
> ibid., p. 81

Irvine's second narrative theme is captured within the phrase, 'Pack of Two'. In these accounts of relationships with animals the pet is described as meaning *everything* to its owner. For Irvine this is about *mattering*, about being noticed and having significance. Caring is again fundamental to this narrative theme. The homeless person *matters* because of the care received from and provided to their animal.

Irvine points to an interesting consequence of the collapse of the distinction between the human and the animal that emerges from the narrative of the Pack of Two: 'Defining oneself in coexistence with another species represents a form of borderland thinking. A borderland is a shared space, often a site of negotiation and struggle over who holds power within it.' (ibid., p. 104) For Irvine this represents an important gesture of moral solidarity, an acknowledgement of human coexistence with other species and an exemplification of animals' social power, a subject I shall return to below.

The third narrative, the animal as protector, almost inevitably a dog, applied mostly to the young homeless outsiders who self-categorised as travellers:

> Stories of animals as protectors unfold from a setting that places the main characters of the Traveller and the dog alone, often sleeping or attempting to do so. 'One time, when we were setting up camp', Chris's story began.
>
> ibid., p. 114

The story continues, there is a happening, a threat, 'it depicts the approach of a stranger, or just the vague sense of something wrong, as triggering the dog's response, which requires a subsequent response from the story teller' (ibid., p. 115). Typically, the dog barks and the traveller is safe. The narrator then reflects on the story and describes what they have learnt from the event.

The travellers constructed themselves as recipients of care from their dogs. They also felt a responsibility to provide appropriate care for their dogs, to constrain their behaviour and keep themselves out of trouble. Irvine concludes, 'Although having a dog can bring on trouble, including negative feedback from others, Travellers' personal narratives also construct dogs as supportive significant others, providing positive self-reflections' (ibid., p. 130).

The final narrative theme identified by Irvine is of animals as life changers and life savers. This was deployed almost entirely by those who were no longer living on the street. Irvine provides several examples of how the pet provides the motivation for escaping addiction and notes that, for some formerly homeless people, it is their pet that keeps them alive. So for Trish her dog was a barrier to suicide, even when she couldn't get the help she desperately needed, 'I couldn't give up because I had something else to take care of besides myself. So he kept me alive' (ibid., p. 142). Once more, care is fundamental to the narrative. When Irvine asked another interviewee why he had said his dogs were keeping him alive, he explained that it was about love:

> 'It's unconditional. Its like mine for them'. I could tell he felt embarrassed speaking this way. Just to ease the awkwardness I said, 'so they just care for you no matter what?'. 'Yeah', he said softly, stroking his dog's smooth copper coat and avoiding my eyes.
>
> ibid., p. 145

These are stories of redemption, in which the animal plays a crucial role. Irvine explains, 'The narratives constructed around animals make sense of the tellers' moves from negative to positive from instability to relative security through fulfilling responsibilities to an "other"' (ibid., p. 152).

As Irvine points out, redemption in general casts identity in a positive light, portraying the possessor as deserving forgiveness and salvation. In stories that emphasise the commitment between the homeless person and their animal, the accounts of the activities associated with caring for and about an other particularly help to construct a distinctly moral identity. Stories of commitment thus bestow a sense of self-worth – essential for everyone, but especially difficult to accomplish when resources for establishing personal significance are scarce.

In general, Irvine's account focuses upon the dyadic relationship between the homeless person and the companion animal. The narratives that homeless people construct about these relationships, I argue, provide them with resources to respond to and manage cultural misrecognition. However, I would like to suggest that the relationship between the homeless person and their companion animal provides something more, a resource for the domiciled to re-orient this cultural misrecognition.

In the next section of the chapter I consider three stories which provide a snapshot of the animal's transformative role in social interactions between the homeless person and the domiciled population. I argue that the presence of the animal is a key constituent in the encounter between the homeless person and the domiciled person, a presence that not only has the potential to undermine cultural misrecognition, but can also be politically disruptive. Although I focus on the productive elements of the stories, I also acknowledge their complexity as I note alternative readings of the stories that are told.

Animals as disruptive social power

The social power of animals goes beyond the immediate relationship. The animal is a medium through which the homeless person can connect with the domiciled population. As Sayes explains,

> Nonhumans that enter into the human collective are endowed with a certain set of competencies by the network that they have lined up behind them. At the same time, they demand a certain set of competencies by the actors they line up, in turn. Nonhumans, in this rendition, are both changed by their circulation and change the collective through their circulation.
>
> Sayes 2014, p. 138

The starting point of the first story, that strangers initiate conversations with people accompanied by animals when they would not do so with a person alone, is a quotidian, but nonetheless powerful, example of the transformational power of animals. However, when the domiciled public interacts with the homeless who have pets, the interaction is not necessarily positive, as Irvine et al. (2012) observe:

> On the one hand, interactions with the public can result in gestures of goodwill, such as a contribution of pet food ... On the other hand, interactions can also mean confrontation: an attack on the homeless person's character in which he or she is deemed unable to care for the animal, and therefore undeserving of animal companionship.
>
> 2012, p. 28

In their analysis of interviews with homeless people asking for their responses to negative comments on their ownership of pets, Irvine *et al.* reveal that, whilst open defiance or ignoring negative comments were not uncommon, the majority of homeless pet owners respond by redefining what it means to be a caring pet owner. The redefinition emphasises the qualities that are peculiar to the care provided by the homeless person to their animal,

> They pointed out that they could provide what other dogs lacked and that their way of caring for an animal surpassed the typical standards, which require a house. They asserted their ability to provide food for their animals, even at personal sacrifice, and to offer enhanced quality of life through constant companionship, an outdoor environment, and freedom.
>
> ibid., p. 38

The redefinition is assisted by donations of pet food from sympathetic members of the public, enabling the homeless people to resist, or at least manage, the negative effects of the abuse.

I suggest that thinking about co(a)gents or distributive agency provides us with another way of seeing the transformations prompted by the donations of pet food. The story involves a particular circuit or assemblage of human and non-human, there is: the homeless person; those members of the public who support, or at least do not condemn, his or her pet ownership; and the pet. Drawing on Bennett (2010) I add a further participant, the pet food itself. In this assemblage the non-humans matter: the animal because it prompts the donation of food; and the food because it sustains the animal and provides material support for the care inherent in redefined pet ownership – the animal can eat first because of the donations. As the food becomes a gift, the pet becomes a privileged beneficiary, the homeless person a model of redefined pet ownership – as well as a co-recipient of the gift – and the donees of the food resist the limitations of neoliberal citizenship as they demonstrate an 'urge to care' (De Vertueil *et al.* 2009). As Bennett points out, food matters. So my claim is that donations of pet food to the homeless are politically radical actions. They demonstrate cross-species solidarity and challenge conventional understandings of ownership, as they recognise a collective, rather than individualised, responsibility for the pets and simultaneously, because of the close relationship between the pet and the homeless person, a collective, rather than individualised, responsibility for homelessness itself. The subversive nature of pet-food donations is underscored when juxtaposed with contemporary attempts to control soup kitchens and other public provision of food to the homeless, and the domiciled populations' resistance to this (see Hunter, Chapter 4 in this collection).

The challenge to conventional ownership posed by cross-species solidarity is also key to the second story, the story of the homeless man, John Byrne, who, in July 2011, jumped into the River Liffey in Dublin to save his pet rabbit, which had been thrown in there by a young man.

One blog post describes the events as follows:

> John jumped to the rescue of his beloved rabbit named Barney, and risked his life to brave the freezing river. River Liffey is known to be filthy and have very strong currents, claiming lives every year. Miraculously, he managed to save Barney from drowning. After jumping into the water and successfully finding Barney, he had to pump air back into Barney's lungs, and help the rabbit regain consciousness. However, he then became stranded below the bridge. Freezing cold and unable to reach the bank, John had to wait for his own rescue by Dublin firefighters. Half way through the rescue, John is seen scuffling with the rescue team because the rescuers were taking John away from the bridge where his dog was waiting.

When John was asked why he risked his life for Barney by jumping into the Liffey, he said, 'Because he is my child, I love him and I just wanted to save him. I didn't think, I just jumped.'[4]

The story is a dramatic representation of the intense emotional bond that typifies accounts of relationships with animals that Irvine characterises as a Pack of Two. As she explains, 'By describing an animal as "everything" narrators attest to social bonds and obligations. This can provide a buffer against isolation and insignificance, and a contrast to claims that characterize the homeless as disaffiliated' (Irvine 2013, p. 101).

Cultural misrecognition is shattered by this story. First, saving his rabbit from drowning gets the relationship between Byrne and the rabbit noticed. A crowd gathers on the bridge, videos are uploaded on to YouTube and the rescue is applauded. Second, his relationship with his animals dramatically disrupts the normal asymmetry of care. Not only does he care sufficiently to put himself at risk, he also rejects the assumptions of the firefighters who rescue him. They want to take him somewhere to be cared for. He insists on returning to the bridge as he has caring responsibilities to his dog.

There is, however, more to be said here than simply marking the dramatic disruption of cultural misrecognition. Once more I stretch Irvine's insights beyond demonstrating the resources that the animal provides to the homeless person. The assemblage of river, crowd, homeless man, rabbit and rescuers is potent. Byrne is recognised differently, perhaps as a hero – as suggested by 'We can be heroes', a comic strip version of the incident (O'Toole et al., 2014) – or as a compassionate citizen – as the award he received from Animal Rights Action Network (ARAN) attests. However, I would suggest that there is a more political dimension to Byrne's behaviour. When he put himself at huge risk to rescue a rabbit he is rejecting the contemporary paradigm of responsible ownership, which is predicated upon the avoidance of risk. The responsible pet owner, for instance, insures, transferring the risk, making it financial and protecting the insured from 'a destabilizing sense of losing control' (Baker 2002, p. 33). Insurance is not an option open to Byrne; nor has he any illusions that he can control events. Anyway, insurance would not meet Byrne's needs. Since Barney is not a possession, but a 'child', what is required of Byrne is the dramatic gesture of social solidarity that he provides to the appreciation of the public. It is fair to acknowledge here that there is an alternative and more conventional interpretation of Byrne's conduct. Perhaps he is simply emulating the self-sacrifice required of a mother and reinforcing public/private divides that would characterise homelessness as a private problem which requires minimal governmental intervention. Nonetheless, I argue that as long as there is a possibility of an alternative and radical explanation then new and political opportunities are opened up.

The third story is well known. It is the story of James Bowen, a recovering heroin addict, who had been homeless, but at the time was living in London in supported housing, who found an injured cat that he nursed back to health at some cost to himself. Bob, the name Bowen gave the cat, followed him everywhere, including on buses and tubes, so he bought a lead and took Bob busking. The pair were noticed, Bowen's income increased, and eventually a literary agent encouraged him to write his story. Once more it is an animal that ensures Bowen is no longer invisible. In March 2014 the *Guardian* reported that Bowen's books had achieved sales of more than a million and had been sold in more than 30 countries (see Flood 2014).

Bowen's story neatly fits Irvine's narrative theme of animals as life savers and life changers. In an interview with Jeremy Vine in 2013 (BBC, 2013) Bowen suggests Bob demanded a mutuality of care. 'He basically said to me,' he tells Vine, 'I am sticking around and you are going to look after me and I am going to look after you.' Bob saved Bowen, he explains, Bob turned his life around. 'He was Karma ... he brought something together with us.' The story, in Vine's words, 'entranced' the public. Some of the charm of the story I suggest derives from its playful reconstruction of Michael's (2000) Hudogledog, perhaps because of the disruptive insertion of a cat, an animal renowned for its independence. So Bowen and Bob are human/cat lead/cat, and Bowen is a busker accompanied by Bob whilst they work on the street, or an author who is accompanied by his subject on the sofa of a daytime TV studio, rather than on a recreational walk in the park. The public respond to the companionability between Bowen and Bob, for instance by providing scarves for Bob, which somehow materialise the caring connection between Bob and Bowen, and by writing Bob fan mail – Bowen tells Vine that Bob, via his publishers, has received record amounts. The power of the tricks, such as the high five performed by Bob and Bowen for Vine, provide further evidence of cross-species solidarity.

However, the interview also suggests some of the ephemerality of the distributive agency of human/non-human connections. Bowen works hard in the interview to sustain his co(a)gency with Bob, for instance by presenting himself as passive in his relationship with Bob – so he tells Vine, 'I am working for him, he is the master' – and in his relationship with the public – he says he was 'made an Ambassador' for drug addiction and homelessness, a responsibility that he was happy to accept. Perhaps most significantly he summarises the story as 'from rags to [and then a hesitation] to turning our lives somewhere better'. The avoidance of the word riches is significant. Although he tries hard not to suggest that money is the agent of his redemption, rather than Bob, it is difficult to completely avoid that conclusion. Nonetheless, the human/cat lead/cat has survived, prompting an extraordinary transfer of resources both to Bowen and to the charities he and Bob promote.

Conclusion

Accounts of relationships between homeless people and their pets tend to focus on the need to expand welfare housing to include, for instance, provision for animals, or they describe how the contemporary responsibilisation of dog ownership has particularly punitive consequences for the homeless and vulnerably housed. Whilst both these approaches are important, my argument is distinct. I suggest that the presence of the animal in the life of the homeless person, and in the relationship between the homeless and the domiciled population, has remarkable social power. It is, in Latour's terms, a mediator:

> Mediators transform, translate, distort and modify the meaning or the elements they are supposed to carry … No matter how apparently simple a mediator may look, it may become complex; it may lead in multiple directions which will modify all the contradictory accounts attributed to its role.
> Latour 2005, p. 39

Irvine's account demonstrates that the responsibility and the care provided to the animal is translated into a resource for the human that allows, in a variety of ways, the human to be transformed, to recuperate from the losses that are inherent in homelessness and manage the injustice of cultural misrecognition. At the very least, she argues, 'for homeless people and others on the margins of society, the language of commitment can "salvage the self" from reminders of a stigmatised status' (Irvine 2013, p. 153).

My argument goes further; it is not only socially positive, in addition I suggest that the presence of animals in the lives of homeless people is replete with other, more political, possibilities. When the caring relationship between the homeless person and the pet is made visible, and forms a connection with the domiciled public, new forms of social solidarity can emerge to disorientate cultural misrecognition, challenge the outsider status of homeless people, and disrupt the limits of neoliberal citizenship. From this perspective the invisibility of animals in accounts of the lives of the homeless and vulnerably housed is even more surprising, for animals have the potential to change everything.

Notes

1 I would like to thank Chris Beasley, Ruth Fletcher and Rosie Harding who have been caring and inspiring editors and the organisers and participants at the Revaluing Care Workshop, Adelaide, August 2013 and the Dogs and Responsibility workshop, Birmingham University, June 2014 where earlier versions of this paper were presented. I would also like to thank my daughter, Harriet, for the enthusiasm and information she provided as I worked on the chapter and my friends Mandy and David, who always stop to talk to homeless people about their animals.
2 Unattributed quotation from Hearthounds – the website of a charity helping homeless people and their dogs http://bringthedog.co.uk/feature-articles/hearthounds/ (accessed 23 November 2014).
3 The way the law plays out for dog ownership by homeless people is important, and is considered by Carr and Hunter (forthcoming).
4 www.reshareworthy.com/homeless-man-risks-life-to-save-pet/ (accessed 15 August 2016).

References

Baker Tom (2002) 'Risk, Insurance and the Social Construction of Responsibility' in Baker and Simon (eds.) *Embracing Risk: The changing culture of insurance and responsibility* Chicago: The University of Chicago Press.
BBC (2013) 'How a Street Cat Named Bob Saved Busker' *BBC News Online*. Available at: www.bbc.co.uk/news/entertainment-arts-23117382, accessed on 7 May 2015.
Bennett Jane (2010) *Vibrant Matter: A political ecology of things* Durham and London: Duke University Press.
Carr Helen (2013) 'Housing the Vulnerable Subject: The English context' in Fineman and Grear (eds.) *Vulnerability: Reflections on a new ethical foundation for law and politics* Surrey: Ashgate.
Carr Helen and Hunter Caroline (forthcoming) *Socio-legal encounters with homelessness* Palgrave Macmillan.
DeMello Margo (2012) Animals and Society: *An introduction to human–animal studies* New York: Columbia University Press.
De Vertueil Geoffrey, May Jon and von Mahs Jurgen (2009) 'Complexity Not Collapse: Recasting the geographies of homelessness in a "punitive" age' *Progress in Human Geography* 33: 646.
Feldman Leonard C (2004) *Citizens without Shelter: Homelessness, democracy and political exclusion* Ithaca and London: Cornell University Press.
Flood Alison (2014) 'Bob the Street Cat Books Sell 1m Copies in UK' *Guardian* 18 March. Available at: www.theguardian.com/books/2014/mar/18/bob-street-cat-books-sell-1m-copies-in-uk-james-bowen, accessed on 24 May 2016.
Fox Rebekah (2006) 'Animal Behaviours, Post-human Lives: Everyday negotiations of the animal–human divide in pet-keeping' *Social & Cultural Geography* 7(4): 525–537.

Fox Marie (2010) 'Taking Dogs Seriously?' *Law, Culture and the Humanities* 6: 37–65.
Franklin Adrian (1999) *Animals and Modern Cultures: A sociology of human–animal relations in modernity* London: Sage.
Franklin Adrian (2006) '"Be[a]ware of the Dog": A post-humanist approach to housing' *Housing, Theory and Society* 23(3): 137–156.
Haraway Donna (2003) *The Companion Species Manifesto: Dogs, people, and significant otherness* London: Prickly Paradigm Press.
Irvine Leslie, Kahl Kristina and Smith Jesse (2012) 'Confrontations and Donations: Encounters between homeless pet owners and the public' *Sociological Quarterly* 53: 25–43.
Irvine Leslie (2013) *My Dog Always Eats First: Homeless people and their animals* Boulder Colorado: Lynne Riener Publishers.
Latour Bruno (2005) *Re-assembling the Social: An introduction to Actor Network Theory* Oxford: Oxford University Press.
Michael Mike (2000) *Reconnecting Culture, Technology and Nature: From society to heterogeneity* London: Routledge.
O'Toole Darrin, Keegan Barry and Cunniffe Dee (2014) 'We Can Be Heroes' Scribd. Available at: www.scribd.com/doc/235964659/We-Can-Be-Heroes, accessed on 7 May 2015.
Podberscek Anthony, Paul Elizabeth and Serpell James (eds) (2005) *Companion Animals and Us: Exploring the relationships between people and pets* Cambridge: Cambridge University Press.
Power Emma (2012) 'Domestication and the Dog: Embodying home' *Area* 44(3): 371–378.
Sarat Austin (2010) 'Editorial' *Law, Culture and the Humanities* 6(1).
Sayes Edwin (2014) 'Actor–Network Theory and Methodology: Just what does it mean to say that nonhumans have agency?' *Social Studies of Science* 44(1): 134–158.
Seager Joni (2003) 'Pepperoni or Broccoli? On the cutting wedge of feminist environmentalism' *Gender, Place and Culture* 10(2): 167–174.
Standing Guy (2011) *The Precariat: The new dangerous class* London: Bloomsbury.
Veevers Jean (1985) 'The Social Meaning of Pets' *Marriage & Family Review* 8(3–4): 11–30.
Wacquant Loic (2009) *Punishing the Poor: The neoliberal government of social insecurity* Durham and London: Duke University Press.
Youde Kate (2012) 'Pampered Pets UK! Owners would rather spend less on themselves than let their cats go without' *Independent* 6 May. Available at: http://www.independent.co.uk/property/house-and-home/pets/news/pampered-pets-uk-7717640.html

Chapter 8

Care and relationality
Supported decision making under the UN CRPD

Rosie Harding[1]

This chapter seeks to explore the conceptual links between care, relationality and supported decision making by people with cognitive impairments that affect their decision-making abilities. It draws on two recent cases to show how supported decision making under the UN Convention on the Rights of Persons with Disabilities (CRPD), which took effect in 2008, can work with the legislative scheme of the Mental Capacity Act 2005 (MCA).

The MCA was introduced to reform the law of England and Wales as it relates to people who lack or lose the capacity to make decisions for themselves. It applies across all areas of life, and provides the legislative backdrop to how we understand decision making by (and for) people with reduced mental capacity. Many of those who have cause to rely on the provisions therein will do so because of lifelong disabilities. Others will be covered by the MCA because of significant health problems caused by accident or illness, such as brain injury or dementia.[2] Under the MCA, persons who are unable to make a decision themselves because of an 'impairment of, or a disturbance in the functioning of, the mind or brain' (House of Lords, MCA, s. 2(1)) are considered to lack the capacity to do so, and others are then legally entitled to make decisions on their behalf, in their best interests.

In contrast to this English legal framework, the CRPD casts significant doubt on the use of objective 'best interests' tests to make substitute decisions for people with cognitive disabilities. Under CRPD Article 12, everyone is entitled to equal recognition under the law, and 'persons with disabilities enjoy legal capacity on an equal basis with others in all aspects of life' (Article 12(2)). The CRPD also introduces a requirement on state parties to provide 'access by persons with disabilities to the support they might require in exercising their legal capacity' (Article 12(3)). The Committee on the Rights of Persons with Disabilities (Committee RPD) released a General Comment on Article 12 in April 2014 (Committee RPD 2014), to address their view that state parties had misunderstood the scope of their obligations under Article 12, particularly around the need to provide support to enable those with an impaired decision-making ability to exercise their legal capacity. As part of that general comment, the Committee also set out their view that '[t]he "best interests" principle is not a safeguard which complies with article 12 in relation to adults' (Committee RPD 2014 [21]), and the consequent need to replace best interests decision making with an approach that respects the best interpretation of the will and preferences of the individual. It is clear that on the face of things, these two legal frameworks, the MCA and the CRPD, do not align well. Whereas the MCA seeks to provide legal authorisation for the formal and informal caregivers of those who lack a decision-making capacity to make substitute decisions in the best interests of that person, Article 12 of the CRPD considers this approach to be an infringement of disabled people's rights to equal treatment before the law.

The aim of this chapter is to explore the extent to which the MCA approach to mental capacity and decision making might be reinterpreted to follow the spirit of the CRPD, and how effective decision-making support can be achieved for people who have impaired decision-making abilities due to cognitive disability. I argue that utilising a relational lens to view decision making can go some way to addressing the conflict between approaches of the MCA and the CRPD, whilst simultaneously recognising the importance of care and support in everyday decision making. The chapter is in three parts. In part one, I explore the concept of relationality as a way of understanding the interconnected nature of social lives. In part two, I set out in more detail the legal approaches to decision making by people with disabilities under the MCA and the CRPD, drawing out the points of conflict and similarity. I explore the ways that a relational lens could help to shift the interpretation of the MCA towards compatibility with Article 12 CRPD. In part three, I test my proposed relational view of the MCA through exploring two cases, *Cardiff CC v Ross*[3] and *A Local Authority v TZ (No. 2)*,[4] to evaluate the potential of the implementation of the CRPD requirement for equal treatment under the law and supported decision making through the existing provisions of the MCA. I conclude that whilst a relational interpretation of the MCA is both possible and beneficial, some reform of the MCA is nevertheless desirable to formalise in English law the move away from the problematic language of 'best interests'. This would also ensure that courts avoid the temptation to disregard decisions made by people with learning disabilities, cognitive impairments and degenerative brain diseases, when these are made with appropriate levels of support and reflect the wishes and desires of the individual.

Before moving on to the substantive arguments in the chapter, I want to provide a brief note on terminology. I use the phrase cognitive disability as a generic term to describe the types of disability covered by the MCA. There is little consensus on the most appropriate generic term to use, but cognitive disability is gaining in popularity as a non-derogatory approach. There are limitations to any generic descriptor of disability, primarily that such terms tend to locate the disability within the individual (rather than in the social processes that exclude them), and as a result draw attention to deficit, rather than the practices and processes required to facilitate full engagement by disabled people. In keeping with the social model of disability underpinning the CRPD, I use the term cognitive disability with a functional orientation, that is, I understand cognitive disability to include functional difficulties with tasks like: memory, problem-solving, attention and comprehension (reading, verbal, linguistic, mathematical and/or visual). The term cognitive disability certainly includes people with medical diagnoses of learning disabilities, acquired brain injuries, degenerative brain diseases and conditions like dementia, and other cognitive impairments including autism, but my focus is less on the diagnosis and more on the impact of functional cognitive impairments on the individual's ability to exercise her agency and autonomy.

Care, connection and relationality

The rational legal subject is a powerful construct:[5] the man [sic] of law is independent; he is autonomous; he makes his own decisions, without influence from others. This rational, independent, autonomous (adult) legal subject is one that has the capacity to weigh up the advantages and disadvantages of a particular course of action. He uses higher-order reasoning to arrive at an informed decision. He is reasonable and objective, in the legal senses of these words. This is, of course, an overstatement of the construct of an idealised rational person of law. Legal frameworks can and do accept decisions that do not fully align with this 'ideal type'. I set it out here more as a counterpoint to the nuanced, contextualised approach that I argue is required, than as a genuine definitional account of legal personhood (for which, see e.g. Naffine 2008). The competent legal subject has the right to refuse healthcare or treatment even when it would be in his (clinically understood) 'best interests' to follow his doctor's advice. Equally, a rational legal subject has the capacity to understand the difference between right and wrong, and to choose to do wrong, to make an unwise decision, to commit a crime. Few human subjects can or do reach such lofty ideals of rational thought and reasoned decision making. Instead, we mostly make decisions about our lives within the contexts of our relational networks: our family, our friends and our loved ones. When we make a decision, we often think about the effects it will have on those around us, as well as on ourselves. We evaluate whether it is the 'right' thing to do, in part, because of the potential effects on known (and unknown) others.

This is not a new insight, arguments for a reconceptualisation of autonomy as 'relational' have developed greatly over the last two decades (see e.g. Nedelsky 1989; Mackenzie and Stoljar 2000a, 2000b; Harding 2012). Alongside these conceptual arguments in favour of reimagining autonomy as relational, a significant literature has developed that takes forward questions of relational autonomy, particularly as it relates to healthcare decision making in a wide range of contexts (Donnelly 2010; McLean 2010; Priaulx 2007).[6] This rich literature has provided persuasive insights into how people make decisions, and hints at the need to depart from an individual focus when making decisions about medical treatment. My focus here is not on the concept of autonomy *per se*, but rather on the relational part of the equation; I seek to explore what it might mean to approach mental capacity law from a *relational* perspective. On my reading, there are three overlapping approaches to relationality evident in much of the academic literature: relationality as a dimension of care ethics (e.g. Gilligan 1982; Tronto 1993);

relationality as constraint (e.g. Mackenzie and Stoljar 2000b; Priaulx 2007); and relationality as interpersonal context (Herring 1999; Herring and Foster 2012). A fourth approach has also recently begun to emerge: relationality as a lens, which brings into focus the interwoven dynamics of everyday life (Harding 2014; Nedelsky 2011). I will deal with each in turn.

The care ethics approach to relationality is founded on the idea that relationality and relational approaches to decision making are gendered, and are most often understood as a feminine attribute. This is most evident in work that takes forward the insights from Carol Gilligan's *In a Different Voice*, who argued that this different voice was marked by 'a mode of thinking that is contextual and narrative ... this conception of morality as concerned with the activity of care centers moral development around the understanding of responsibility and relationships' (1982, p. 19). Gilligan's work is widely cited as the starting point for the wealth of scholarship in the 'ethic of care' tradition (e.g. Tronto 1993; Sevenhuijsen 2003; Barnes 2012), much of which seeks to differentiate the ethic of care from an ethic of justice (e.g. Held 2006; Slote 2007). The key contribution that an ethic of care seeks to make is to undermine the idea that 'individuals basically make rational decisions to act in their best interests, and that they do this from a position in which they see themselves as (and are) disconnected from others and able to act not only rationally but autonomously' (Barnes 2012, p. 12). Rather, an ethic of care approach seeks to embed an understanding of relationality into legal and political theory (Drakopoulou 2000). There is not space here to do justice to all the rich and thought-provoking scholarship in this area, but the central insight from the care ethics approach to relationality appears to be that a moral focus on care (and thus the human need for interdependence) offers a different, and arguably better, understanding of how people live and interact than an ethic of justice.

The second approach to relationality, relationality as constraint, has developed as an extension of a care ethics approach, but is more specifically concerned with relational autonomy. In the introduction to their collection of essays on the topic of relational autonomy (Mackenzie and Stoljar 2000a), Mackenzie and Stoljar outline five feminist critiques of autonomy: first, the symbolic critique, exposing the fallacy of the abstract, self-sufficient, independent individual; second, a metaphysical critique, which seeks to demonstrate the impossibility of the atomistic individual; third, care critiques, which attack substantive independence along similar lines; fourth, postmodern critiques, using critical and conceptual approaches to demonstrate that 'autonomy is a kind of conceit or illusion of the Enlightenment conception of the subject' (2000b, p. 11); and fifth, diversity critiques, to highlight the multiplicity of perspectives on any given issue and the problematic of intersectionality. These different critiques, whilst being nuanced in their own ways, all seek to highlight the conceptual asymmetry between *autonomy* and the *individual*, leading to arguments for the reorientation of autonomy as a relational value. Where these relational approaches to autonomy have been used in an attempt at practical application, however, relational theorists often appear more concerned with exposing the structural or interpersonal constraints that curtail free choice rather than refocusing on the inherent relationality of the human experience (Harding 2012). Priaulx's exploration of the concept of wrongful conception and wrongful birth is perhaps most useful in demonstrating this 'choices within constraints' model of relational autonomy:

> A relational perspective challenges such narrow approaches to humanity: renders visible the broad spectrum of concerns that motivate human decision making; makes understandable what law sees as contradiction and can explain those instances where individuals are caught between yes/no, black/white and choice/no choice.
>
> Priaulx 2007, p. 170

Here, relationality is used to focus on the ways that relationships (whether these are interpersonal relationships or broader forces that shape everyday life, like regulatory frameworks) constrain decision-making choices and force people to make decisions that do not always align with their individual preferences. In much of this literature, the focus is on the autonomy side of the equation, and demonstrates the limits of autonomy as an individual and independent virtue (see further, Harding 2012).

A third approach to relationality in the literature seeks to embed it as an inevitable aspect of human life, such that legal actors should always consider the relational context of decisions being made. This third approach focuses specifically on the interpersonal relationships that surround an individual. One such approach has been Jonathan Herring's (1999) argument that some of the limitations of the welfare principle in child law (such as those outlined by Reece 1996) could be addressed by taking a relational approach to decision making in the best interests of children, in order to better balance children's welfare with parental rights. Herring argues that: 'The child's welfare is promoted when he or she lives in a fair and just relationship with each parent, preserving the rights of each, but with the child's welfare at the forefront of the family's concern.' (Herring 1999, p. 233) Similarly, he has more recently argued, with Charles Foster, that 'A judge who seeks to assess the best interests of X by taking her out of her social context and examining her in isolation in a forensic petri dish will come to a wrong conclusion' (Herring and Foster 2012, p. 499). At the heart of these critiques is an understanding that interpersonal, relational contexts are fundamental to people. I would not go so far as Herring and Foster in suggesting that making decisions without attentiveness to social context is impossible because the person would 'cease to exist' or become a 'non-entity' (ibid.). Yet it is clear that our social and interpersonal contexts not only constrain action, but can also be enabling and therefore foundational for decision making. The question then arises as to how legal frameworks, which are generally concerned with the individual legal subject, can accommodate our interconnected lives.

Relational contexts can be understood as beneficial when these are positive and supportive, but not every person is fortunate enough to have only good relationships in their life. A key problem that comes up when thinking through the implications of a relational approach based on context, is how to deal with situations where a person's relational context is, de facto, deleterious of her autonomy. Where an individual lives within relational contexts that are not supportive of her autonomy, that person will find it very difficult to exercise any agency over her life (though clearly not impossible; see Kotiswaran 2014). Mackenzie, Rogers and Dodds have recently used the concept of 'pathogenic vulnerability' to describe negative interpersonal contexts (Mackenzie *et al.* 2014). Their understanding of pathogenic vulnerability exposes the additional potential for vulnerable individuals in toxic relational contexts to suffer negative outcomes because of the ways that these contexts can compound existing experiences of vulnerability. In their words:

> People with cognitive disabilities, who are occurently vulnerable due to their care needs, are thereby susceptible to pathogenic forms of vulnerability, such as to sexual abuse by their carers. Likewise, pathogenic vulnerability may result when social policy interventions aimed to ameliorate inherent or situational vulnerability have the contradictory effect of increasing vulnerability. A key feature of pathogenic vulnerability is the way that it undermines autonomy or exacerbates the sense of powerlessness engendered by vulnerability in general.
>
> Mackenzie *et al.* 2014, p. 8

So, we must bear in mind the potential for pathogenic vulnerability when relational contexts are not supportive of vulnerable people. Using *context* as the focus for understanding relationality therefore comes up against some limitations. This is not to say that the relational context of vulnerable people will always lead to pathogenic outcomes. Rather, I would argue that relational context is vitally important, because the quality of the relationships surrounding and supporting an individual will always shape his or her ability to flourish.

This leads me to the final conceptualisation of the value of relationality: as a lens focused on everyday dynamics of lived experience. This approach to relationality seeks to draw together the insights of care, constraint and context perspectives on relationality. It seeks to expose all the varied relationships (interpersonal, social, legal, regulatory) that shape and constrain social action. For example, where a person lives within structures of oppression, a relational view allows us to be attentive to the effects of these structures on her life. It allows us to understand the ways that broader, macro norms impact on her everyday life. As Nedelsky has argued:

> Intimate relations, such as spousal relationships, are shaped by societal structures of relationship such as those formally shaped by family law as well as powerful norms of gender roles. These structures will be shaped by patterns of economic relationships, such as employers' preference for hiring men in high paying jobs, expectations that authority should be exercised by men over women, and governmental policies that ensure the availability of (overwhelmingly female) child care workers from abroad who will accept low pay. The availability of such workers arises from long-standing relations of

global economic inequality. Each set of relations is nested in the next, and all interact with each other. Relational selves shape and are shaped by all interactions

2011, p. 31

This fourth dimension of relationality provides the theoretical tools required to interrogate all the different influences that interact to create lived experiences. By focusing the lens of relationality more widely, not just on the interpersonal relationships that support and constrain the individual (as are often visible through the ethic of care approach and contextual version of relationality), but also on the structural barriers and supports that generate axes of privilege and marginalisation (as are brought to light in some approaches to relationality as constraint), we can see the multiple influences that shape decisions and decision making. Here, I imagine relationality's conceptual value as working like the lenses in a telescope, which can be focused in on different depths of interpersonal, social and structural relationships. It allows us to focus on the embodied individual, whilst also keeping in mind the interpersonal and structural contexts that shape everyday lives. I argue that this approach to relationality can help us reimagine the MCA to comply with the spirit of the CRPD.[7]

Relationality in the Mental Capacity Act and the UN Convention on the Rights of Persons with Disabilities

The Mental Capacity Act 2005

The MCA was slow to come into law. The need for legislation to address decision making by and for individuals with cognitive disabilities, as distinct from acute mental health problems, was identified after the reduction in the scope of guardianship under the Mental Health Act 1959 by the Mental Health Act 1983 (Bartlett and Sandland 2014). The Law Commission started exploring how to address the gaps in this area of law in 1989, and they proposed a comprehensive legislative regime in 1995 (Law Commission 1995). A full decade passed between these proposals and the eventual enactment of the MCA, which largely implemented the proposals. In the intervening years, a complex series of cases had developed the 'inherent jurisdiction' of the High Court to make best interests decisions on behalf of individuals with reduced mental capacity (Donnelly 2009). This case law began with a clear statement that best interests (in medical decisions at least) was determined by healthcare professionals.[8] It was an ostensibly objective standard, and one which could even justify the imposition of treatment by force (and without the consent of the patient).[9] Gradually, the content of best interests shifted in common law beyond the medical to include wider emotional and welfare issues, though not the views of the (incapacitated) person about whom the decision was being made.[10] The relationship between the MCA and the inherent jurisdiction is still evolving,[11] though in broad terms, the inherent jurisdiction enables the courts to continue to make best interests decisions that are intended to protect vulnerable adults who do not lack capacity under the terms of the MCA.

The MCA represented, in many significant ways, a sea change in the way that people with cognitive disabilities were treated in English law. First, the MCA begins with series of principles that include: an assumption of capacity; a requirement for supported decision making; and a clear statement that 'A person is not to be treated as unable to make a decision merely because he makes an unwise decision' (s. 1(4)). The MCA does, however, also introduce a comprehensive legal framework for making decisions on behalf of those who are deemed to lack capacity, which hinges on an assessment of their 'best interests' (s 1(5)). Under the MCA, only if a person is unable to make a decision through meeting the criteria in s. 2 and s. 3 of the Act, can a decision be made in their best interests. Perhaps more importantly, the content of the best interests test also shifted with the MCA, to much more explicitly recognise the views, preferences and values of the person with impaired mental capacity than had been the case under the previous common law regimes (see MCA s. 4(6)(a)). Even so, the recognition, consideration and weight to be given to the cognitively disabled person's 'past and present wishes and feelings' as part of a best interests decision, and the exact scope of best interests under the MCA has been a source of debate and contention within the case law. In *Re M (Statutory Will)*,[12] for example, Munby J stated that 'the weight to be attached to P's wishes and feelings will always be case-specific and fact-specific'.[13]

Aintree v James[14] was the first case regarding best interests under the MCA to make it to the Supreme Court for determination. Lady Hale gave the single collegiate decision of the court, thus providing an unusual level of clarity as to the Supreme Court's view, where she stated: 'the purpose of the best interests test is to consider matters from the patient's point of view'.[15] Lady Hale, after pointing out that the patient's wishes do not always prevail (whether the patient has cognitive disabilities or not), then went on to say that:

> insofar as it is possible to ascertain the patient's wishes and feelings, his beliefs and values or the things which were important to him, it is those which should be taken into account because they are a component in making the choice which is right for him as an individual human being.
>
> *Aintree v James*, at [45]

This interpretation clearly seeks to place the person with cognitive disabilities at the heart of the decision-making processes that concern them. It also provides a framework to guide supported decision making by health and social care professionals and family members, in collaboration with cognitively disabled people, and guided by the will and preferences of the individual affected by the decision.

Unfortunately, however, the interpretation of best interests decision making set out in *Aintree v James* does not appear yet to have influenced the wider body of Court of Protection case law. Instead, the Court of Protection appears to remain focused on balancing the wishes, views and feelings of the person themselves with other considerations when making best interests judgements.[16] Nor does the Supreme Court's version of best interests appear to align well with health and social care practice in best interests decision making, where best interests seem to be intertwined in practice with capacity assessments, and are constructed by practitioners as 'joint affairs, involving the practitioners, people who are close to the person concerned and the actual person lacking capacity' (Williams *et al.* 2014, p. 85). Whilst this approach may be, in practice, successful, the very existence of the term 'best interests' in the legislation, alongside the relative weighting put on the views of the person with a cognitive disability when determining best interests in the courts, places the MCA at odds with the CRPD.

The UN Convention on the Rights of Persons with Disabilities

The CRPD guarantees equal treatment before the law for all, including those with cognitive disabilities. Article 12 of the CRPD is concerned specifically with the right to equal recognition before the law, and affirms the rights of everyone to recognition of their legal capacity, including those with cognitive disabilities. The question of how to balance the competing aims of protection and support for people with cognitive disabilities is a key problematic in contemporary mental capacity law (Wildeman 2013). The CRPD seeks to transform the approach to disability equality in international human rights law, by shifting the focus away from stereotypes based on deficit and diagnosis (sometimes called the medical model) towards a social model of disability, which takes the organisation of society (rather than individual impairments) as its focus.

During the drafting process, the CRPD openly sought to precipitate a paradigm shift in normative expectations of the way that mental capacity is to be treated in law, requiring a move away from 'substituted' to 'supported' decision making. Perhaps unsurprisingly this was controversial, and the exact scope of Article 12 was the subject of much debate during the drafting of the Convention. Reflecting these disagreements, the final text of the article appeared to leave some room for continued substitute decision making (Dhanda 2006). Yet, the Committee RPD have stated that Article 12 requires 'the abolition of substitute decision-making regimes and mechanisms that deny legal capacity and which discriminate in purpose or effect against persons with disabilities' (Committee RPD, 2014: [50(a)]). Whilst the UK government was initially of the view that the MCA complied fully with the CRPD, a range of limitations with the contemporary legislative framework in England and Wales has been identified and a review of compliance has been initiated by the Ministry of Justice (Series *et al.* 2015). These limitations include problems with implementation and the potentially discriminatory nature of the way the Act is framed; its provisions only apply to those who are unable to make a decision 'because of an impairment of, or a disturbance in the functioning of, the mind or brain' (MCA, s. 2(1)). As Bartlett (2012) has argued, the inclusion of these diagnostic criteria could mean the MCA is construed as directly discriminatory. He further argues that even without this diagnostic basis, the MCA is indirectly discriminatory, because its provisions, even if construed as neutral, would be more likely to disadvantage people with disabilities (ibid.).

The Committee on the CRPD have unequivocally stated that to fully implement the Convention, state parties must abolish all substitute decision making, replacing any legal frameworks that deny legal capacity to people with disabilities, whether based on status, outcome or functional tests of capacity, with systems that enable supported decision making: status approaches to denial of capacity follow from a particular diagnosis; outcome approaches cover situations where individual decisions are overruled because they are perceived to have negative consequences; and functional approaches are where the decision-making skills of a person are considered deficient. As discussed above, the MCA, whilst generally considered a person-centred and supportive approach to mental capacity, retains best interests as a central concept, uses a functional approach, and allows a range of individuals (including carers, family members and health and social care professionals) to make substitute decisions for those who are considered to lack the required mental capacity to make a particular decision.

The General Comment on Article 12 seeks to clarify what the Committee RPD have described as a 'general misunderstanding of the exact scope of the obligations of State parties under article 12 of the Convention' (Committee RPD 2014: [3]). There are two key take-home messages from General Comment no. 1. The first is that disabled people must be provided with all the support they need to make decisions for themselves, and substituted decision making must be abolished. This includes, for example, decision making under the auspices of legal regimes such as guardianship or forced treatment under mental health legislation. The second key message is that a best interests approach to decision making for cognitively disabled people is not compliant with Article 12 CRPD, and therefore must be replaced by the decision making which represents the 'best interpretation of the will and preferences' of the individual. It is this second issue that has significant potential to shake the foundations of contemporary legal approaches to mental capacity, because the MCA relies so heavily on substitute decision making, under a best interests framework, as one of the underlying principles of the Act.

Most importantly for legal frameworks surrounding mental capacity, the Committee have stated that:

> all forms of support on the exercise of legal capacity (including more intensive forms of support) must be based on the will and preference of the person, not on what is perceived as being in his or her objective best interests.
>
> Committee RPD 2014, [29(b)]

In contrast, regulatory regimes that provide for decision making by and for people with cognitive disabilities across Europe all retain some element of substitute decision making, most with an objective best interests component. Even the law in Sweden, arguably the most CRPD-compliant framework, and which prefers the use of a supported decision-making 'mentor', retains the possibility of the appointment by a court of a 'trustee' who can make substitute decisions (Herr 2003). Similarly, in Germany, the 'custodianship' law requires a custodian to 'carry out measures for the person under custodianship which are necessary for the best interests of the person under custodianship; his/her wishes are to be taken into consideration' (Germany 2013, p. 27). The MCA, as discussed above, uses best interests as a central underpinning principle, and enables a wide range of decision makers to make best interests decisions on behalf of people with cognitive disabilities. The MCA (s. 4(6)) does provide that, when making best interests decisions, the (substitute) decision maker must 'consider, so far as is reasonably ascertainable' the past and present wishes, feelings, beliefs and values of the person about or for whom the decision is being made, but the extent to which these are taken into consideration varies greatly (House of Lords 2014).

The ways that these two regulatory regimes connect is in need of further interrogation. It may be that the government will, in time, move away from the best interests focus of the MCA (though the government's response to the report from the House of Lords seems to suggest that this is not likely to be the case; HM Government 2014). For now, some way forward must be found that reconciles the best interests approach of the MCA with the right to equal treatment under Article 12 CRPD. I argue that taking a relational view can help achieve this. A relational lens can draw into focus the differential influence that different actors have in deciding what should be done. Rather than always deferring to a professional view, taking a relational approach allows us to look at the range of interpersonal, social and regulatory relationships that both facilitate and constrain decisions. Being attentive to these relational dimensions ensures that those who actually do support the person about or for whom a decision is being made are consulted and their views given appropriate weight. Attentiveness to relationality also allows support to be tailored to the wishes and desires of the individual so that decision making works with, rather than against, their preferences. In the next section, I explore two cases where the Court of Protection has taken a relational approach to best interests decision making.

Relational decision making and cognitive disability

Looking across the MCA and the CRPD, and their respective approaches to decision making, two common themes can be identified. The first is that cognitively disabled people are entitled to receive support to help them make decisions about their lives. The second is that when (specific) decisions are outside the boundaries of the functional abilities of a cognitively disabled person, it is their past and present will and preferences that should guide the outcome of the decision, wherever possible. In this final part, I argue that these two themes can be operationalised with relative ease, if we take a relational approach to decision making by cognitively disabled people. I make this argument through an analysis of two recent cases, *Cardiff County Council v Ross*[17] and *A Local Authority v TZ (No 2)*.[18]

An interesting place to begin an investigation into where relationality fits into judicial decision making about people with cognitive disabilities is *Cardiff CC v Ross*. In this fascinating case, Mrs Ross, an 82-year-old woman living with dementia but physically in good health, and her long-term partner, Mr Davies, successfully defended an action by Cardiff County Council. The Council had sought a declaration that Mrs Ross did not have the capacity to decide whether to go on a 16-day Mediterranean cruise with Mr Davies, and that it was not in her best interests to do so. At the time of the application, Mrs Ross lived in a residential care home run by the applicant council during the week, but spent weekends residing with, and being cared for by, Mr Davies at his home. She required some assistance with the activities of daily living, which Mr Davies provided when she was with him. Mrs Ross therefore had two distinct relational care contexts: one institutional, the other interpersonal. The applicant council put forward a range of arguments that Mrs Ross lacked capacity to make the decision about whether to go on the cruise holiday, and also that it was not in her best interests to go on the cruise. Masterman J in the Court of Protection disagreed. He held that she did have capacity to make the decision:

> One must not forget that this is not a life-changing decision, or a choice between two evils or a decision over which an elderly person without Mrs Ross's impairment would be likely to agonise. It is a choice of whether to go on holiday or not, in familiar circumstances, with one's companion of the past two decades. In these circumstances I find myself unpersuaded that Mrs Ross, whatever her limitations, can be shown on the balance of probabilities to have lacked capacity to make this particular decision.
>
> *Cardiff CC v Ross*, at [12]

He also made a determination (if he were wrong in his decision that Mrs Ross had capacity to make this decision) that it would nevertheless be in her best interests to go on the cruise, following the checklist under s. 4 MCA 2005. It seems that in this case, those who were charged with Mrs Ross' care provision in her residential placement sought to impose their assessments of risk and the protective imperative that permeates institutional caregiving (rather than the s. 4 MCA best interests test), on the decision about whether or not Mrs Ross should go on the cruise. It was as if they sought to impose the institutional rationalities of the care home context on to Mrs Ross and Mr Davies' holiday plans. Rather than taking a wide relational view of Mrs Ross' overall personal context, her relationship with Mr Davies, and his experience of caring for her, the social workers had made their decision about Mrs Ross only in respect of their narrow view of her within the care home, which appeared to include a greater degree of supervision, control and protection than was required.

TZ's case is even more complex, is explicitly concerned with relationships and, in particular, the potential future relationships of a 24-year-old gay man with 'mild learning disabilities, atypical autism and hyperactivity disorder'.[19] This case follows on from an earlier hearing, where it was determined that TZ did have capacity to consent to sexual activity.[20] The court was asked to adjudicate whether TZ had the capacity to decide whether a person he might want to have a relationship with was 'safe', and whether he had the capacity to make a decision about the support he requires when having contact with 'an individual with whom he may wish to have sexual relations' (*TZ* at [18]). The court found that TZ lacked capacity in both these areas. In coming to this decision, Baker J noted that the local authority, consistent with the CRPD, 'is under a positive obligation to take steps to ensure that TZ is supported in having a sexual relationship should he wish to do so' (TZ at [47]). The court set out a range of areas which should be included in TZ's care plan to support him to develop sexual relationships,[21] including 'education and empowerment' activities, involving both education programmes and practical measures, including 'visiting pubs, cafes, clubs and other venues, checking to see if the milieu is likely to be of interest to TZ, and one in which he is likely to be safe' (TZ at [61]). There are many remarkable elements of the decision in TZ's case, not least the sensitive way that the Court of Protection sought to balance TZ's own views about what he would like to do (including meet men with whom he might develop a sexual relationship), with the steps that might be needed to protect him from harm. In this case, it is clear that TZ's will and preferences were prioritised over the views of others, and that Baker J successfully navigated what he described as the 'vulnerable person's protective imperative – that is to say, the dangers of being drawn towards an outcome that is more protective of the adult and thus fail to carry out an assessment of capacity that is detached and objective'.[22]

The MCA has enabled cases like those of Mrs Ross and TZ to be decided on the basis of nuanced understandings of the relational contexts of everyday decision making. Both these cases demonstrate how this legislative framework can empower the cognitively disabled person at the centre of the case to live his or her life by his or her own life choices and values. Both utilise relational decision making, and emphasise the importance of relationship in making decisions. Yet both cases also included discussions of arguments put forward by local authorities or healthcare professionals, charged with caring for cognitively disabled people, that seek to limit their lives on the grounds that their best interests require they be protected from harm. For Mrs Ross, the potential harms were risks like falling overboard, or 'wandering' aboard the cruise ship. For TZ, the risks were of potential sexual abuse if he failed to appropriately identify whether a prospective partner was 'safe'. For both, however, the key to their autonomy, and their freedom from overly restrictive care contexts, was to be found in relationally informed, supported decision making, not best interests determinations.

Concluding remarks

Since the MCA came into force in 2007, and the CRPD in 2008, there appears to have been a gradual, but perceptible shift away from best interests and towards supported decision making in the Court of Protection. This is not to say that the

Court has moved away from best interests decisions, far from it (the legislative context requires best interests decisions in all cases), but it is clear that the views, wishes and preferences of cognitively disabled people are becoming much more central in best interests decisions than they were prior to the MCA. The question remains, however, whether best interests approaches to decision making can continue to be placed centrally in the MCA, given the clear conflict with the focus in Article 12 CRPD on the removal of best interests decision making as a mechanism for ensuring equal treatment under the law. I remain unconvinced that best interests is an altogether helpful way of empowering people with cognitive disabilities, but I am equally unconvinced that the individualistic 'best interpretation of the will and preferences' approach suggested by the Committee on the CRPD is much of an improvement. I would prefer to see a regulatory system that takes full account of the relational nature of everyday decision making, and the centrality of care, support and relationship in all decisions that are made by all of us, with and without cognitive disabilities.

Notes

1. I would like to thank the participants in the ReValuing Care network for their thought-provoking feedback on earlier versions of some of the ideas presented in this chapter at the workshops at Keele University (2012), the University of Adelaide (2013) and QMUL (2014). Sincere thanks also to Ruth and Chris for their kind and thoughtful editorial input to this chapter.
2. Dementia is a collective term for a range of progressive, organic brain diseases, which have as their defining feature a gradual loss of the skills required to carry out the activities of daily living. The most common forms of dementia are Alzheimer's Disease (AD) and Vascular Dementia (VD).
3. *Cardiff CC v Ross* 2011 WL 6329190 Court of Protection Case No. 12063905, 2 November 2011.
4. *A Local Authority v TZ (No. 2)* [2014] EWCOP 973.
5. I am drawing here on an ideological construct of the competent legal person, rather than a more nuanced view of the decision maker that has become evident through case law. For a detailed account of law's persons, see Naffine (2003; 2008).
6. The reach of relationality has not been entirely limited to healthcare contexts – e.g. Jonathan Herring (1999) has argued for relationality in family law, and more recently as an better approach to understanding welfare and best interests decision making (Herring and Foster, 2012).
7. See Smith (Chapter 11, this volume) for a discussion of how law structures relations and generates rights disputes.
8. *Re F (Mental Patient: Sterilisation)* [1990] 2 AC 1.
9. *Re MB (An Adult: Medical Treatment)* [1997] 2 FCR 541.
10. *Re A (Medical Treatment: Male Sterilisation)* [2000] 1 FCR 193.
11. See, for example: *LBL v RYJ* [2010] EWHC 2665 (COP); *X County Council v AA* [2012] EWHC 2183 (COP); *A Local Authority v DL & Ors* [2012] EWCA Civ 253, [2012] COPLR 504.
12. [2009] EWHC 2525 (Fam); [2011] 1 WLR 344.
13. Ibid, at [35].
14. *Aintree University Hospitals NHS Foundation Trust v James* [2013] UKSC 67

15 Ibid, at [45]. Cf *F (An Adult: Sterilisation)* [1990] 2 AC 1
16 For example, in *M v N* [2015] EWCOP 76, Mr Justice Hayden stated 'where the wishes, views and feelings of P can be ascertained with reasonable confidence, they are always to be afforded great respect. That said, they will rarely, if ever, be determinative of P's "best interests"'. Respecting individual autonomy does not always require P's wishes to be afforded predominant weight. Sometimes it will be right to do so, sometimes it will not' at [28]. For a further exploration of best interests in the Court of Protection, see Harding (2015).
17 *Cardiff CC v Ross* 2011 WL 6329190 Court of Protection Case No. 12063905, 2 November 2011.
18 *A Local Authority v TZ (No 2)* [2014] EWCOP 973.
19 *A Local Authority v TZ (No 2)* [2014] EWCOP 973 at [1].
20 *A Local Authority v TZ* [2013] EWCOP 2322.
21 For further consideration of care and sexuality, see the contributions from Sue Westwood (Chapter 14) and Chris Beasley (Chapter 15).
22 *A Local Authority v TZ (No 2)* [2014] EWCOP 973 at [41].

References

Barnes, Marian (2012) *Care in Everyday Life: An Ethic of Care in Practice*. Bristol: Policy Press.
Bartlett, Peter (2012) 'The United Nations Convention on the Rights of People with Disabilities and Mental Health Law' *Modern Law Review* 75(5): 752–778.
Bartlett, Peter and Sandland, Ralph (2014) *Mental Health Law: Policy and Practice* (4th Edition) Oxford: Oxford University Press.
Committee (RPD) on the Rights of Persons with Disabilities (2014) General Comment No. 1 on Article 12 CRPD/C/GC/. Available at: www.ohchr.org/EN/HRBodies/CRPD/Pages/GC.aspx accessed on 25 January 2016.
Dhanda, Amita (2006) 'Legal Capacity in the Disability Rights Convention: Stranglehold of the Past or Lodestar for the Future?' *Syracuse Journal of International Law and Commerce* 34: 429–462.
Donnelly, Mary (2009) 'Best Interests, Patient Participation and the Mental Capacity Act 2005' *Medical Law Review* 17(1): 1–29.
Donnelly, Mary (2010) *Healthcare Decision-Making and the Law: Autonomy, Capacity and the Limits of Liberalism* Cambridge: Cambridge University Press.
Drakopoulou, Maria (2000) 'The Ethic of Care, Female Subjectivity and Feminist Legal Scholarship' *Feminist Legal Studies* 8: 199–226.
Gilligan, Carol (1982) *In a Different Voice: Psychological Theory and Women's Development* Cambridge: Harvard University Press.
HM Government (2014) 'Valuing Every Voice, Respecting Every Right: Making the Case for the Mental Capacity Act' Cm 8884. Available at: www.gov.uk/government/uploads/system/uploads/attachment_data/file/318730/cm8884-valuing-every-voice.pdf accessed on 26 January 2016.
Harding, Rosie (2012) 'Legal Constructions of Dementia: Discourses of Autonomy at the Margins of Capacity' *Journal of Social Welfare and Family Law* 34(4): 425–442.
Harding, Rosie (2014) 'Dementia and Carers: Relationality and Informal carers' Experiences' in C. Foster, J. Herring and I. Doron (eds.) *Law, Ethics and Dementia*. Oxford: Hart, 379–391.
Harding, Rosie (2015) 'Statutory Wills and the Limits of Best Interests Decision-Making in Inheritance' *Modern Law Review* 78(6): 945–970.

Held, Virginia (2006) *The Ethics of Care: Personal, Political and Global* Oxford: Oxford University Press.
Herr, Stanley S. (2003) 'Self Determination Autonomy and Alternatives for Guardianship' in Stanley S. Herr, Lawrence O. Gostin and Harold H. Koh (eds.) *The Human Rights of Persons with Mental Disabilities: Different But Equal* Oxford: Oxford University Press, 429–450.
Herring, Jonathan (1999) 'The Human Rights Act and the Welfare Principle in Family Law – Conflicting or Complementary?' *Child and Family Law Quarterly* 11(3): 223–235.
Herring, Jonathan and Foster, Charles (2012) 'Welfare Means Relationality, Virtue and Altruism' *Legal Studies* 32(3): 480–498.
House of Lords (2014) Select Committee on the Mental Capacity Act 2005 Report, 2013–14 Mental Capacity Act 2005: post-legislative scrutiny London: The Stationery Office. Available at: http://www.publications.parliament.uk/pa/ld201314/ldselect/ldmentalcap/139/139.pdf accessed on 18 March 2014.
Kotiswaran, Prahba (2014) 'Abject Labours, Informal Markets: Revisiting the Law's (Re) Production Boundary' *feminists@law* 4:1. Available at: http://journals.kent.ac.uk/index.php/feministsatlaw/article/view/104/270 accessed on 20 January 2016.
Law Commission (1995) Mental Incapacity Law Commission no 231.
MacKenzie, Catriona and Stoljar, Natalie (2000a) (eds) *Relational Autonomy: Feminist Perspectives on Autonomy, Agency and the Social Self* Oxford: Oxford University Press.
MacKenzie, Catriona and Stoljar, Natalie (2000b) 'Introduction: Autonomy Refigured' in C MacKenzie and N Stoljar (eds.) *Relational Autonomy: Feminist Perspectives on Autonomy, Agency and the Social Self* Oxford: Oxford University Press, 3–31.
Mackenzie, Catriona, Rogers, Wendy, and Dodds, Susan (2014) 'Introduction' in Mackenzie, Rogers and Dodds (eds.) *Vulnerability: New Essays in Ethics and Feminist Philosophy* Oxford: Oxford University Press, 1–29.
McLean, Sheila A. M. (2010) *Autonomy, Consent and the Law* Abingdon: Routledge.
Naffine, Ngaire (2003) 'Who are Law's Persons? From Cheshire Cats to Responsible Subjects' *Modern Law Review* 66(3): 346–367.
Naffine, Ngaire (2008) *Law's Meaning of Life: Philosophy, Religion, Darwin and the Legal Person* Oxford and Portland, OR: Hart Publishing.
Nedelsky, Jennifer (1989) 'Reconceiving Autonomy: Sources, Thoughts, Possibilities' *Yale Journal of Law & Feminism* 1: 7–36.
Nedelsky, Jennifer (2011) *Law's Relations: A Relational Theory of Self, Autonomy and Law* Oxford: Oxford University Press.
Priaulx, Nicolette (2007) *The Harm Paradox: Tort Law and the Unwanted Child in an Era of Choice*. Abingdon: Routledge.
Reece, Helen (1996) 'The Paramountcy Principle. Consensus or Construct?' *Current Legal Problems* 49: 267–304.
Series, Lucy, Arnstein-Kerslake, Anna, Gooding, Piers, and Flynn, Eilionóir (2015) 'The Mental Capacity Act 2005, the Adults with Incapacity (Scotland) Act 2000 and the Convention on the Rights of Persons with Disabilities: The Basics' *Thirty-Nine Essex Street CRPD Discussion Paper*. Available at: www.39essex.com/docs/newsletters/crpd_discussion_paper_series_et_al.pdf#page%3D1 accessed on 26 January 2016.
Sevenhuijsen, Selma (2003) 'The Place of Care: The Relevance of the Feminist Ethic of Care for Social Policy' *Feminist Theory* 4(2): 179–197.
Slote, Michael (2007) *The Ethics of Care and Empathy* Abingdon: Routledge.

Tronto, Joan C. (1993) *Moral Boundaries: A Political Argument for an Ethic of Care* New York: Routledge.

Wildeman, Sheila (2013) 'Protecting Rights and Building Capacities: Challenges to Global Mental Health Policy in Light of the Convention on the Rights of Persons with Disabilities' *Journal of Law Medicine & Ethics* 41(1): 48–73.

Williams, Val, Boyle, Geraldine, Jepson, Marcus, Swift, Paul, Williamson, Toby, and Heslop, Pauline (2014) 'Best Interest Decisions: Professional Practices in Health and Social Care' *Health and Social Care in the Community* 22(1): 78–86.

Chapter 9

'New fathers' and the right to parental leave
Is the European Court of Human Rights satisfied with just breadwinning?

Alice Margaria

Introduction

While the male breadwinner family model had already started to decline during the last quarter of the twentieth century (Lewis 2001; Harkness 2008), preoccupations around work–family conflicts have only been raised in more recent times (Scott and Clery 2013). Women's increased labour market participation and, more generally, a rise in the number of hours of paid work within families (Coltrane 2000; Harkness 2008) have created the need for policy measures that attempt to alleviate potential tensions between employment and family responsibilities and, ultimately, to reduce gender inequalities. One solution is to offer job-protected leave from employment for those periods where care is especially needed.

Feminists have long since responded to the unequal distribution of undervalued care work and the related impact of labour market segregation on women by arguing that the time invested in childcare or domestic work is equally valuable to the time invested in the market economy. Leave policies – as well as other work–family balance policies – are grounded exactly on this argument: 'if time that has been excluded is to be included in some way, then it must be analogised' (Grabham 2014, p. 77). Therefore, work–family balance is also intended to signify that, rather than being two distinct spheres with opposing interests and goals, work and family represent two complementary realms of life. More explicitly, to achieve a good work–family balance, the goal of equal participation of women in paid employment needs to be tied to equal participation of men in the home (Fredman 2014).

While US anti-discrimination law tends to reject paternalism as a threat to individual autonomy, the European counterpart strives for equality 'by promoting a normative vision of the ideal life cycle' (Suk 2012, p. 97). In other words, in Europe equality is not attained upon the condition that individuals' choices to work remain free from group-based stereotypes (like in the US); rather, it is defined on the basis of a set of collectively imposed norms about the role of work in one's life (Suk 2012). This explains why the EU directive on Pregnant Workers[1] requires all Member States to provide at least fourteen weeks of paid maternity leave, two of which are compulsory. As a result, it imposes a period during which women cannot choose to work, under the normative assumption that new mothers should rest and breastfeed, regardless of their own preferences (ibid.). More generally, this clarifies why, with some exceptions, European legal orders have not yet fully committed to gender neutrality as a precondition for gender equality (ibid.). Rather, in most European Constitutions, provisions requiring equal treatment and prohibiting discrimination on the basis of sex are accompanied by provisions or doctrinal interpretations authorising or even demanding public authorities to take measures that differentiate on grounds of sex with the aim of rectifying systemic inequalities and redistributing different forms of benefits (Rubio-Marin 2012). In so doing, European policies make use of assumptions about gender roles, which are likely to be contested as a form of discrimination within US legal culture.

It has been argued that the European approach to work–family balance – as much as the US model – has produced an incomplete and insufficient revolution (Esping-Andersen 2009; Fraser 2013; Scott and Clery 2013). Statistics, indeed, show that women's time remains more tied up in domestic and childcare activities than men's (Ellison *et al.* 2009); and, therefore, what has been mainly altered by the decline of the breadwinner model is women's working behaviour, as they tend to face a double burden of domestic and market work (Harkness 2008). Despite the potential of balance mechanisms to impact the organisation of care and paid work, feminist labour lawyers assert that these measures have reproduced a gendered division of labour and crystallised the key role of women in carrying out the reconciliation between professional and family lives (Grabham 2014). In Europe, although making some portion of maternity leave compulsory has served to regulate the employee–employer relationship by protecting workers from downward pressure to keep their leave as short as possible, special entitlements for maternity have inevitably improved the competitive advantage of those who are not eligible for maternity leave, *in primis* fathers. Moreover, the absence of a 'sister-directive' on paternity leave, and the significantly longer duration of maternity leave compared to paternity leave in all European States have certainly reinforced the association of caregiving with femininity.

The present chapter investigates how the European Court of Human Rights (ECtHR or Court) has reacted to women's changed employment patterns and positioned itself in the debate around paternal involvement in childcare, having regard to its jurisprudence concerning the right to parental leave and related allowances. In particular, it seeks to understand whether and, if so, to what extent the Court challenges what Joan Williams calls the ideology of 'domesticity', according to which 'men "naturally" belong in the market because they are competitive and aggressive, while women belong in the home because of their "natural" focus on relationships, children, and an ethic of care' (Williams 2000, p. 1). The primary question to address is whether the Court maintains a conventional definition of fatherhood, which views fathers as just breadwinners or, rather, adheres to the ideology of 'new fatherhood', which includes expectations of co-parenting and shared nurturing. As defined by Collier and Sheldon, a 'new father' is a:

man who is not (or, at least, not just) seen as a primary breadwinner but is also, increasingly, a 'hands-on' carer, an individual who is (or who should be) emotionally engaged and involved in the day-to-day care of his children.

2008, p. 209

While testing the degree of deviation from the conventional definition of fatherhood as just breadwinning, this chapter attempts to determine to what extent the Court conceives the European Convention on Human Rights (ECHR or Convention) as a reflective and/or a transformative tool, at two different but interrelated levels. First, as displayed by Williams' definition of domesticity, gender stereotyping exercises a strong influence over the organisation of work and family life. Sex-role stereotypes – such as the generalised view that men should be the primary breadwinners, while women should be mothers and homemakers – describe the 'proper roles of men and women not by reference to individuals' personality traits, but by the type of conduct desirable for each sex' (Gans 1995, p. 1877); and, in so doing, they are liable to limit the ability of individuals to mould their personal identities in accordance with their desires and to make decisions about their life paths (Cook and Cusack 2010). For instance, due to the stereotypical belief that men are generally unwilling or unable to engage in childcare, men face significant difficulties in building their identities as primary caregivers and often find themselves coerced into assuming breadwinning roles, with detrimental consequences for both women and children. That said, it will be interesting to consider whether the Court employs the law and, more specifically, Article 8 (the right to respect for private and family life) and Article 14 (the right to non-discrimination) of the Convention as a means of combating gender stereotypes and, therefore, of asserting a new definition of fatherhood untied from stereotypical assumptions or as a means of reflecting and compensating for existing gendered patterns of work and parenting.

While the first regards the interplay between the Convention and social realities, the second level of assessment concerns the relationship between the Court, as an international court, and the Contracting States. It is argued that the ECHR system is the product of a 'tidy arrangement' (Weiler 1999, p. 104), which is preserved by the principle of subsidiarity. This principle provides that national authorities are free to choose the measure they deem appropriate to meet the Convention's requirements, while the Court is responsible for reviewing the compatibility of national choices with the Convention. Therefore, the Court is entrusted with the delicate task of ensuring equilibrium between democratic discretion and diversity at the national level, on the one hand, and the universal dimension of the Convention's standards, on the other hand (Arnardóttir 2003).

At the same time, the Convention enshrines a set of abstract rights that, if not interpreted in the light of present day conditions, risk becoming theoretical and illusory, thus compromising the effectiveness of the ECHR system (Mahoney 1990; Andenæs and Bjørge 2013; Nikolaidis 2015). Against this background, this chapter investigates how the Court has navigated the, at least apparent, interpretative dilemma of ensuring a greater match with changing social realities, while respecting State-specific variations; in other words, to what extent the Court conceives the Convention as destined to impose new legal conditions on the basis of its own perception that fathers' rights could be protected in a more dynamic way or it feels that it is up to the Contracting States to bring about the change through legislative reforms and, therefore, it understands the role of the Convention as that of reflecting national legal realities.

The position of the ECtHR: fighting gender stereotyping, but one step at a time

While the position of fathers with respect to EU work–family policies has attracted a fair amount of scholarly attention,[2] the ECtHR contribution to the debate around fatherhood and parental leave has not yet been thoroughly explored. This can be attributed to the limited number of relevant cases that have been brought before the Court to date. Moreover, the issue of parental leave and related allowances, which is considered to fall within the scope of Article 8,[3] represents a relatively recent area of intervention by the Strasbourg Court. After the case of *Petrovic v Austria*[4] which was settled in 1998, the Court only returned to the issue of parental leave in 2009 and, since then, only two judgements have contributed to discussing and, to some degree, to advancing the roles of fathers in family care: *Weller v Hungary*[5] and *Konstantin Markin v Russia*.[6] In all three cases, the Court was called on to settle the legal question of whether the refusal to grant parental leave to fathers, while available to mothers, amounts to a violation of Article 14 taken in conjunction with Article 8.

Over the last fifteen years, the construction of fatherhood endorsed by the Court has shifted from the male breadwinner model to the ideology of new fatherhood. The starting point coincides with the judgement in *Petrovic*, where the Court upheld a traditional division of labour along gendered lines as a justification for reserving parental leave allowances to women. The process of redefinition is the result of a two-stage process, through which the dissenting opinion expressed by Judges Bernhardt and Spielmann in the *Petrovic* case reaches the stage of majority. The first step is represented by the judgement in the case of *Weller*, where the Court employed Article 14 as a 'magnifying lens' (Arnardóttir 2014, p. 330), thus extending the prohibition of discrimination enshrined in Article 14 to cover those rights that are voluntarily provided for by the State, such as the right to parental leave and related allowances.[7] As a second step, in the case of *Markin*, the Court explicitly incorporated anti-stereotyping in its reasoning. This led it to conclude that gender stereotypes cannot constitute a justification for differential treatment and, accordingly, to consider the exclusion of fathers from parental leave entitlements (in line with conventional gender roles) as a form of sex discrimination.

The main catalyst for these moves has been the progressive establishment of a European consensus in the field of parental leave: while at the end of the 1980s (in *Petrovic*), no common standard in the laws of Contracting States existed, in the case of *Weller* (2009), the Court began to note an 'emerging consensus', whose formation was deemed completed by 2012, in the case of *Markin*. More specifically, the (non-)existence of consensus played a decisive role in determining the outcome of these cases and, therefore, the progressive departure from a conventional definition of fatherhood in two different, but connected, ways. Firstly, by influencing the width of the margin of appreciation enjoyed by the State and, consequently, the standard of review undertaken by the Court. While the absence of a shared approach (or the existence of little common ground) on the issue under scrutiny leads to a lenient assessment, if the disputed distinction is generally disapproved of the Court will undertake a stricter assessment of justifications (Gerards 2005). Secondly, apart from increasing the likelihood of finding a violation, the existence of a European consensus also has an impact on the type of reasoning used by the Court to substantiate such a conclusion. Seemingly, the existence of a common ground is relied on to express the urgency and the Court's own eagerness/responsibility to protect disadvantaged groups against forms of stereotyping and structural discrimination that have been recognised as particularly harmful by Contracting States.

Petrovic v Austria: *the absence of a European consensus as a justification for preserving the male breadwinner model*

In the earliest case of *Petrovic*, the applicant was denied parental leave allowance by the local authorities on the grounds that, under the Unemployment Benefit Act 1977, only mothers were entitled to it. Prima facie, the Court's intervention ought to be praised for taking the critical step of distinguishing between pregnancy and childbirth, on the one hand, and parenthood, on the other. In its view, while maternity leave is primarily designed 'to enable the mother to recover from the fatigue of childbirth and to breastfeed her baby if she so wishes', parental leave concerns the subsequent period and aims 'to enable the beneficiary to stay home to look after the infant personally'.[8] It follows that, as far as parental leave is concerned, both parents are 'similarly placed'[9] and, as a result, the unequal treatment complained of requires justification. Despite its promising beginnings, the Court eventually accepted a gendered division of labour and, therefore, a conventional understanding that equated fatherhood to just breadwinning. This outcome was the consequence of two interrelated dynamics: the prevalence of the lack of a European consensus on the 'suspect' ground of discrimination as a determinant of the intensity of review; and the absence of an anti-stereotyping approach, or at least a mentality, on the part of the Court.

Despite recognising the importance of sex equality as a major goal within the Council of Europe and noting that very weighty reasons were needed for a distinction on grounds of sex to be held compatible with the Convention,[10] the Court never really considered whether the differential treatment was justifiable. Rather, it placed greater, or even exclusive, emphasis on those factors that triggered the award of a wide margin of appreciation to the State (Arnardóttir 2003). Elements taken into consideration included: the date of the events (end of the 1980s); the gradual process towards a more equal sharing of family responsibilities between men and women; and, more importantly, the existence of a significant disparity between legal regulations in Contracting States in the field of parental leave allowances.[11] In light of these factors, the Court did not apply the 'very weighty reasons' test, which constitutes the most stringent version of the assessment of justifications and is commonly required by distinctions based on a 'suspect' ground, such as sex. Rather, it conducted a lenient scrutiny, which led to the conclusion that the Austrian authorities' refusal to grant parental leave to the applicant fell within the State's margin of appreciation.

Although not acknowledged, it is undisputable that the Austrian legislation was grounded on the implicit sex-role stereotypes of women as mothers and homemakers and men as primary breadwinners and, accordingly, it conferred the right to parental leave on mothers, but not fathers. Indeed, as argued by Cook and Cusack (2010), the extent to which the reality of parenthood is actually gendered and if gender-neutral parenting only reflects an aspirational view of fatherhood are irrelevant considerations in determining whether a generalised view can be classified as a stereotype. As long as one's needs, wishes, abilities and circumstances are not given any weight, any generalisation applied to him/her will eventually reach the threshold of stereotyping, even if it does describe the actual position of the individual concerned (ibid.). Nonetheless, due to scant anti-stereotyping efforts, the Court ended up perpetuating the man-breadwinner/woman-homemaker stereotype implicit in the Act on the grounds that there was no European consensus on the provision of parental leave allowance to fathers. In other words, in the Court's mind, the legal realities of the Contracting States were not yet sufficiently convergent to question the environment of legitimacy and normalcy around legislation excluding fathers from parental leave entitlements.

The extent to which a stereotype is detrimental is contingent on, *inter alia*, the historical context in which the contested legislation was developed (ibid.; Timmer 2011). In the case of *Petrovic*, the Court proved itself aware of this and observed that 'originally, welfare measures of this sort – such as parental leave – were primarily intended to protect mothers and to enable them to look after very young children'.[12] However, it failed to undertake a reality check and, therefore, to ask what the current effects of such measures were on individual men and women. In so doing, the majority chose to remain silent on the harmful consequences of gender stereotyping with the de facto result of reproducing the traditional ideology of fatherhood which, in this domain, resonates with the male breadwinner model in which the father cannot afford to stay at home and receive no remuneration because he is expected to provide financially for his family.

Against the majority, the dissenting judges Bernhardt and Spielmann adopt a critical attitude towards the justifications submitted by the State for the distinction complained of. They argued that, apart from reproducing a gendered division of labour, reserving parental leave allowances to mothers entailed that, if parents chose a 'non-traditional' arrangement – i.e. the mother continues her professional career and the father stays at home – the family loses, *ipso facto*, the allowance to which it would be entitled if the mother took time off from work. Despite sharing the majority's view that Article 8 does not impose any obligation on States to pay parental leave allowances, the dissenting judges stated that, when choosing to grant additional rights, States cannot do so in a discriminatory manner. Therefore, unlike the majority, they did not accept the absence of a European consensus and 'traditional practices and roles in family life alone'[13] as sufficient grounds for justifying a difference in treatment and the perpetuation of harmful gender stereotyping. Their opinion eventually proved prophetic and the judgement in *Weller* acted as a bridge in the final journey to the stage of majority.

Weller v Hungary: *relying on the 'magnifying effect' of Article 14 while waiting for an established consensus*

In the case of *Weller*, the first applicant, a Hungarian national married to a Romanian citizen who gave birth to their twin sons, the second and third applicants. The first applicant applied for maternity benefits in his own name and on behalf of his children. His request was rejected as, according to the Family Support Act, only mothers with Hungarian citizenship, adoptive parents and guardians were entitled to the benefit in question and a natural father could only request such an allowance if the mother died. Despite being called a maternity benefit, the aim of the sought measure was not only to reduce the hardship of pregnancy and delivery borne by mothers, but was also to support all those responsible for raising newborns by enabling them to take time off work. Therefore, just like in *Petrovic*, the Court was called upon to decide whether excluding fathers from benefits connected to childcare (in relation to which, both parents are similarly placed) constituted a violation of Article 14, in conjunction with Article 8. However, given that the benefit in question was also conferred on adoptive parents and guardians, regardless of their sex, the Court stated that the applicant father had been discriminated against on the basis of his parental status, more than on grounds of sex.[14]

Unlike in *Petrovic*, in *Weller* the Court (implicitly) refused to accept a justification that was informed by a stereotypical perception of the group to which the applicant belongs and, therefore, found a violation of Article 14, taken in conjunction with Article 8. This reverse outcome appears to result from the combination of two factors: changing conditions in Contracting States; and the effective application of Article 14 as a 'magnifying lens' (Arnardóttir 2013, p. 330) to cover the right to parental leave, although not protected by other Convention rights. As regards the first, the Court proved sensitive to the progressive development of a European consensus towards the extension of childcare-related allowances to fathers as well as to mothers. The existence of an 'emerging consensus'[15] – compared to the finding of 'no common standard'[16] in *Petrovic* – had a concrete impact on the outcome of the case, as it narrowed down the margin of appreciation enjoyed by the State and, consequently, led to a stricter review of the justifications advanced.

Moving on to the second factor, through *Weller*, part of the dissenting opinion of Judges Bernhardt and Spielmann became majoritarian; although acknowledging that Contracting States continued to enjoy a certain margin of appreciation in shaping their social security systems,[17] the Court held that the absence of a common European approach did not free them from the responsibility to grant these allowances without discrimination.[18] In other words, it established that States are under the positive obligation not to discriminate when going beyond the minimum requirements of the Convention. It follows that, since the Hungarian Government had created an additional right to parental allowance (although not strictly required by Article 8), the latter fell within the wider ambit of Article 8 with the consequence that the benefit scheme must be grounded on eligibility criteria that are compatible with Article 14. In this case, therefore, the magnifying effect of Article 14 enabled the Court to make the claim fall within the ambit of Article 8, which per se does not encompass a right to parental allowance, by relying on the grounds of discrimination.

Since no reasonable and objective justification to excluding natural fathers from a scheme aimed at supporting all those taking care of newborns could be found, the Court concluded that Article 14, in conjunction with Article 8, had been breached.[19] In this instance, therefore, the Court felt prepared to find a violation, despite the presence of a merely 'emerging consensus' (as opposed to an established European common ground). Arguably, the employment of Article 14 as a 'magnifying lens' spared the Court from having to uphold conservative national legislation in the name of the States' margin of appreciation. Although the Court did not explicitly embark on an anti-stereotyping analysis, the ultimate outcome of this ruling remains that of refusing the misconception that fathers are unwilling and unable to take care of their children, thus contesting the man-breadwinner/woman-homemaker stereotype.

Konstantin Markin v Russia: *the combination of European consensus and explicit anti-stereotyping reasoning*

The anti-stereotyping analysis underlying the finding of a violation in *Weller* became an integral part of the reasoning in the judgement of *Konstantin Markin v Russia*, which represents the natural continuation of the jurisprudence thus far analysed and the Court's most sophisticated stance on the issue of parental leave. In this case, the applicant was a military serviceman and father of three children. Following his divorce from the mother of his children, the couple agreed that the three children would live with their father, while the mother would pay child support. His children being very young at that time, Mr Markin applied for three years' parental leave but his request was denied because, according to the law, a leave of such duration could only be granted to military servicewomen. When rejecting Mr Markin's claim that this amounted to discrimination, the Russian Constitutional Court explained that 'by granting, on an exceptional basis, the right to parental leave to servicewomen only, the legislature took into account, firstly, the limited participation of women in military service and, secondly, the special role of women associated with motherhood'.[20]

The Grand Chamber's judgement – which confirms the Chamber's finding of a violation of Article 14, taken in conjunction with Article 8 – constitutes further evidence of the decisive weight attached to European consensus as a factor influencing the width of the margin of appreciation, the intensity of review, the outcome of the case and, ultimately, the definition of fatherhood endorsed by the Court. This is expressly acknowledged by the Court itself, which considers it impossible not to take note of the evolution that society has undergone since its judgement in *Petrovic*.[21] Having recalled that, for the purposes of parental leave, the applicant, a serviceman, was in an analogous position to servicewomen, when carrying out the justification test special emphasis was placed on an increased convergence between national legislation: in the majority of Contracting States, including Russia, parental leave entitlements had been made available to both mothers and fathers (in 28 out of the 33 States considered) and, more importantly, to both servicemen and servicewomen (in 23 out of the 33 States considered).[22] The general logic underlying the reliance on comparative data seems to be that a notion which has generally been held true for several decades might be called into question when it becomes obsolete and reflects an old-fashioned vision of the roles of men and women.

Therefore, while in *Petrovic* the Court watered down the 'very weighty reasons' test by granting a decisively wide margin of appreciation to the State, in *Markin*, the 'suspect' ground of discrimination resulted in national authorities being left with a narrower margin of appreciation. The different relationship between the ground of discrimination and the intensity of scrutiny in the two cases reveals a continuity in the Court's jurisprudence concerning parental leave and, more specifically, bears witness to the decisiveness of the 'common ground' approach in establishing whether a violation occurred or not. Hence, leaving aside methodological concerns related to the establishment of consensus,[23] both judgements signal that the Court understands the role of the Convention as reflecting – more than transforming – the legal realities of Contracting States.

In addition to invoking the existence of a European consensus, the reasoning is characterised by the Court's insistence on the adverse consequences of gender stereotyping. Indeed, through the *Markin* judgement, the second part of the dissenting opinion raised by Judges Bernhardt and Spielmann in the case of *Petrovic* becomes majoritarian. For the first time in its case law on parental leave, the Court is explicit in naming and contesting the man-breadwinner/woman-homemaker stereotype – on which the Constitutional Court's ruling was based – as insufficient justification for differential treatment. In order to identify the operative stereotype, the Court engaged in a critical examination of the reasons provided by the Constitutional Court and the government in justifying the exclusion of servicemen from parental leave entitlements. As a first step, it stated that the provision under scrutiny could not qualify as a measure of positive discrimination – as argued by the government – as it did not aim to compensate for the disadvantages suffered by women in society.[24] Rather, in the Court's view, the current effect of excluding military servicemen from parental leave was that of 'perpetuating gender stereotypes and is disadvantageous both to women's careers and men's family life'.[25]

This statement can be regarded as a key step in the process of combating gender stereotyping for at least two reasons. First, it reveals the extent to which the operative stereotype is embedded in institutional structures; more specifically, how the State, through its law and judicial practices, has contributed to its enforcement and perpetuation and conferred an extra layer of legitimacy on social perceptions of gender roles (Cook and Cusack 2010). Second, by acknowledging the two sides of gender stereotyping, the Court shows itself aware of the reality that the maternal wall — namely, gender bias and forms of discrimination faced by working mothers and mothers seeking employment — affects both men and women when they request parental leave or otherwise undertake traditionally feminine nurturing roles (Williams and Segal 2003). In other words, it 'does not penalize people of a certain sex; it penalizes anyone who plays a certain sex role' (ibid., p. 79). While forcing servicemen with primary caregiving responsibilities to choose between their professional and their family lives, gender stereotyping limits women's access to the military, the quality of their careers and places on them the burden of childcare.

Incidentally, what is still not contemplated is the harm that the man-breadwinner/woman-homemaker stereotype causes to children. Although extensive research evidence has cogently proved correlations between parental leave and children's cognitive and socio-economic outcomes (Rhum 2004; Tanaka 2005; Gioacchino 2012), the right to parental leave is herein conceived only as a tool for parents to balance their family and work responsibilities. By failing to consider that the national authorities' refusal to grant parental leave to Mr Markin had the factual result of depriving the child of the care of one of his parents at a very early age, the Court eventually constructs the right to parental leave as essentially adult-centric.

Nonetheless, this judgement displays what Arnardóttir calls a 'social-contextual approach' (2014, p. 663). In other words, in its analysis under Article 14, the Court adds an express reference to social context, thus connecting the personal situation of Mr Markin (the individual case) to the wider implications the parental allowance regulation under scrutiny has for men and women. The attention to social context is certainly one of the techniques through which the Court has developed a more substantive conception of equality (Nikolaidis 2015). In confirmation of this, the final judgement goes beyond mere inclusion, as it does not simply approach the case from the applicant's perspective and expand the group of beneficiaries of parental leave entitlements to include men. Rather, it holds a transformative potential, as it goes beyond the issue of formal equality (i.e. servicemen should be treated like servicewomen in relation to parental leave) and locates the discrimination suffered by the applicant within systemic inequalities that both men and women face due to gender stereotyping.

Having identified and exposed the effect of the man-breadwinner/woman-homemaker stereotype, the Court goes on to contest it. Among the multiple steps taken, it does not stop at declaring Article 14 applicable and subjecting the national courts' refusal to grant parental leave to Mr Markin to the 'very weighty reasons' test, thus leaving the State with a narrow margin of appreciation. Rather, the most progressive passage and, consequently, the most significant added value to the Court's jurisprudence on parental leave, is the conclusion that Contracting States cannot rely on gender stereotyping to justify differential treatment. In particular, the Grand Chamber held that:

> gender stereotypes, such as the perception of women as primary child-carers and men as primary breadwinners, cannot, by themselves, be considered to amount to sufficient justification for a difference in treatment, any more than similar stereotypes based on race, origin or sexual orientation.[26]

Similar to the judgement in *Weller*, therefore, the Court, this time explicitly, refused to accept a justification that underlies a stereotypical image of the group to which the applicant belongs. Indeed, the new 'social-contextual approach' adopted in *Markin* not only contributes to reinforcing the substantive dimensions of Article 14, but it also makes them more evident than before (Arnardóttir 2014). In this specific case, the Court spelt out the previously implicit *ratio legis* behind the finding of a violation in the case of *Weller*, thus making the bearing of the 'suspect' ground of discrimination on the width of the margin enjoyed by State more explicit.

Given that generalisations and references to traditional divisions of labour are not accepted as legitimate reasons for differentiating on grounds of sex, the Court concluded that the exclusion of servicemen from the entitlement to parental leave – while available to servicewomen – was not compatible with the prohibition of discrimination under Article 14, taken in conjunction with Article 8. Apart from conveying the message that fathers are as able and willing to nurture children as mothers, this judgement repudiates a legal construction that equates fatherhood to just breadwinning. In so doing, the Court's definition gets close to the ideology of 'new fatherhood', which presupposes an overlap of the (traditionally gendered) roles – nurturing and breadwinning – and is achievable through an effective work–family balance.

Concluding remarks: the driving force of consensus behind the update of the definition of fatherhood endorsed by the court

Despite declaring mothers and fathers 'similarly placed' with respect to childcare since *Petrovic*, the explicit overcoming of a gendered division of labour is accomplished only in the landmark case of *Markin*. Although a violation of Article 14, taken in conjunction with Article 8, was already found in the *Weller* decision, the Court begins to 'bring men into the frame' (Fredman 2014, p. 442) through what Fredman calls a 'levelling up option' (ibid.), which consists in making women's parental rights available to fathers as well. However, it is only in the judgement of *Markin* that the Court discards references to a gendered division of labour as insufficient justification for discrimination and, explicitly, refuses the stereotypical images of the man-breadwinner and the woman-homemaker as determining factors in the allocation of parental allowances.

Having overturned the traditional distribution of roles between men and women, it seems interesting to identify the successor(s) of breadwinning/economic provision in the legal definition of fatherhood endorsed by the Court. The conventional feature under scrutiny – although under serious challenge by changed employment patterns – is not completely abandoned within the Court's jurisprudence, but rather it coexists (in tension) with the emerging image of the 'father as carer'. Therefore, the Court ends up supporting the complex image of the 'new father', which encloses both change and continuity. According to the emerging definition, a father does not abandon his traditional role as provider, but rather combines it with nurturing responsibilities through the take-up of parental leave.

Furthermore, in encouraging the combination of parenting and breadwinning tasks within fatherhood as essential in ensuring a similar arrangement for mothers, the Court proves ready to deal with one facet of 'fragmenting fatherhood' (Collier and Sheldon 2008). In this domain, what is susceptible to a practical kind of disaggregation is a gendered distribution of labour and, therefore, the persistence of economic provision and nurture as two separate roles. In the case of *Markin*, by supporting the idea that men should be as involved as women in taking care of their children, the Court seems to suggest that nurture is no longer the sole or primary responsibility of mothers, and breadwinning functions no longer fall within men's exclusive competence. Rather, in the Court's view, policies that make parental leave entitlements available to both men and women are to be fostered, as they facilitate a more equal sharing of childcare and financial responsibilities – traditionally undertaken along gendered lines – between mothers and fathers. The extension of parental leave to fathers is therefore viewed as a means of supporting the establishment of the allegedly desirable dual-earner/dual-carer family model.

The driving force behind this redefinition of fatherhood has been the progressive establishment of a European common ground in the field of parental leave. It is argued that the (non-)existence of consensus worked as an empowering tool in the Court's jurisprudence in two ways, at least. First, the case law analysed here confirms the role of the evolutive and comparative methods of interpretation in the development of the Court's jurisprudence. This becomes particularly visible if we compare the decisions in *Petrovic* and *Markin*. While the finding of non-violation in *Petrovic* was grounded on the lack of a European consensus, in the case of *Markin* the Government no longer enjoyed a wide margin of appreciation because – as indicated by comparative data – the majority of Contracting States provided parental leave entitlements to both mothers and fathers and, more importantly, to both servicemen and servicewomen. Therefore, the overturning of *Petrovic* was justified by the completion of the shift in national legislation that started in the late 1980s.

Second, the reliance on consensus has enabled the Court to take advantage of social and legal changes through which certain forms of stereotyping and structural inequality have been recognised as particularly persistent and morally unacceptable by Contracting States or even internationally (Arnardóttir, 2014). In the present context, the appreciation of these developments has empowered the

Court to embark on an anti-stereotyping analysis and, more generally, to enrich or, at least, clarify the substantive dimensions of equality within its case law. This second type of influence exercised by consensus emerges from the transition from *Weller* to *Markin*. In the latter, as a by-product of the existence of a European consensus in favour of extending parental leave allowance to men, the Court felt prepared to take an openly critical attitude towards the justifications put forward by the State and to make the anti-stereotyping analysis implicitly underlying the finding of a violation in the case of *Weller* explicit. As a result, it held the differential treatment of servicemen liable for perpetuating traditional gender roles and spelt out the wider implications of such legislation on both men's family life and women's professional careers.

The adoption of an anti-stereotyping approach certainly fits within a broader legal trend – inside and beyond Strasbourg – to embrace a more substantive interpretation of equality (O'Connell 2009). Although there are various substantive conceptions of equality, this paradigm tends not only to prohibit an unjustifiable difference in treatment (like formal equality), but also to enable individuals to pursue their life options in an autonomous manner (Nikolaidis 2015). Moreover, the judgement in *Markin* can be understood as part of an emerging tendency – identified by the literature (Arnardóttir 2014) – to increasingly provide more substantial justifications for undertaking strict scrutiny by placing value on the fact that certain distinctions come from stereotypical and traditional views of gender roles. To a further extent, therefore, it can be viewed as one step towards the establishment of 'freedom from prejudice and stereotyping' as a distinct human interest animating the application of Article 14 (Nikolaidis 2015).

To conclude, the Court's perception of the role of the Convention emerging from this case law is a mixed one. On the one hand, the decisive weight attached to consensus constitutes evidence of the Court's hesitancy to go beyond the will of the Contracting States and, therefore, of its understanding of the role of the Convention as being that of reflecting national legal developments. This attitude is likely to stem from the Court's awareness of the repercussions that a less prudent approach would have on the States' willingness to comply with its decisions. On the other hand, the judgement in *Markin* demonstrates the Court's eagerness to address instances of structural disadvantage by using the Convention as a means of combating gender stereotypes and, therefore, of asserting a new definition of fatherhood untied from the man-breadwinner/woman-homemaker stereotype. However, as shown by the development of the case law on parental leave, the employment of the Convention as a transformative tool remains contingent upon the existence of a European common ground. In other words, the Court feels ready to contest national legislation as discriminatory and, therefore, to push for legal change at the domestic level only when its views are supported by the majority of Contracting States.

One of the dangers inherent in this approach – as exhibited by the *Petrovic* judgement – is that the Court blindly accepts the dominant legal culture, marginalises the most problematic human rights issues (Arnardóttir 2014) and reduces the Convention to a minimum level of protection (Gerards 2005). In the context of parental leave, the Court manages to alleviate this risk by employing Article 14 as a 'magnifying lens'. This becomes visible in the case of *Weller*, where the 'magnifying effect' of Article 14 enabled the Court to silently depart from a conventional definition of fathers as mere breadwinners, even in the presence of a merely 'emerging consensus' among the laws of Contracting States. In other words, the reinterpreted ambit of Article 14 has allowed the Court to update the definition of fatherhood in line with changing standards of gender equality and social attitudes to gender roles, without having to wait for a European consensus to be fully established. Hence, the employment of Article 14 as a 'magnifying lens' served as a tool for balancing the two opposing and yet complementary needs of ensuring the effectiveness of human rights, while acting with caution and achieving jurisprudential progress only through gradual steps, not to undermine the States' confidence in the Strasbourg machinery.

Notes

1 Directive 92/85/EEC of 19 October 1992 on the introduction of measures to encourage improvements in the safety and health at work of pregnant workers and workers who have recently given birth or are breastfeeding.
2 For instance, see Weldon-Johns, M., 2013. EU Work-Family Policies – Challenging Parental Roles or Reinforcing Gendered Stereotypes? *European Law Journal*, 19(5): 679–81; Caracciolo di Torella, E., 2014. Brave New Fathers for a Brave New World? Fathers as Caregivers in an Evolving European Union. *European Law Journal* 20(1): 88–106.
3 When assessing the applicability of Article 8 to the cases concerning the right to parental leave, the Court consistently concludes that, as parental leave has an impact on the organisation of family life, the issue does fall within the scope of Article 8. See para 45 in *Petrovic v Austria*, para 29 in *Weller v Hungary* and para 130 in *Markin v Russia* (Grand Chamber).
4 *Petrovic v Austria*, Application no. 20458/92, 27 March 1998 ('*Petrovic*').
5 *Weller v Hungary*, Application no. 44399/05, 31 March 2009 ('*Weller*').
6 *Konstantin Markin v Russia*, Application no. 30078/06, 7 October 2010 (Chamber), 22 March 2012 (Grand Chamber) ('*Markin*'). A few months after the decision in *Markin*, the Court was faced by a similar application: *Hulea v Romania* (Application no. 33411/05, 2 October 2012). This judgement will not be analysed as it is primarily focused on the issue of whether the refusal to award compensation to a serviceman for discrimination with respect to his right to parental leave, more than the refusal to grant him parental leave, breached the Convention.
7 The non-discrimination clause contained in Article 14 ECHR is formulated as a guarantee 'accessory' to the enjoyment of the other rights protected by the Convention. Nonetheless, in practice, the Court has tended to apply and interpret this provision in an effective manner, thus expanding the scope of protection provided by Article 14. Arnardóttir uses the expression 'magnifying lens' to illustrate this dynamic. In some cases (like *Weller v Hungary*), the magnifying effect of Article 14 has gone as far as giving this provision an autonomous field of application outside the scope of other Convention rights.
8 *Petrovic*, para 36.
9 *Ibid*.

10 *Ibid*, para 37.
11 Ibid, paras 37–40.
12 *Ibid*, para 20.
13 *Ibid*, Joint dissenting opinion of Judges Bernhardt and Spielmann.
14 *Weller*, para 33.
15 *Ibid*, para 28.
16 *Petrovic*, para 39.
17 *Weller*, para 34.
18 *Ibid*.
19 *Ibid*, para 35.
20 *Markin*, para 19 (Chamber) and para 34 (Grand Chamber). Although the argument pertaining to the limited participation of women in the armed forces is imbued with gender stereotyping as much as the first, the present analysis engages only with the 'motherhood' argument, as it is more relevant to decipher the Court's understanding of fatherhood.
21 *Markin*, para 140 (GC).
22 *Ibid*, para 49 (Chamber), para 140 (GC).
23 Literature dealing with methodological issues includes Dzehtsiarou, K. (2015) *European Consensus and the Legitimacy of the European Convention on Human Rights*. Cambridge: Cambridge University Press; Johnson, P. (2013) *Homosexuality and the European Court of Human Rights*. London: Routledge; Letsas, G. (2007) *A Theory of Interpretation of the European Convention on Human Rights*. Oxford; New York: Oxford University Press.
24 *Ibid*, para 140 (GC).
25 *Ibid*, para 141 (GC).
26 *Markin*, para 143 (GC).

References

Andenæs, M. and Bjørge, E., (2013) National Implementation of ECHR Rights. In: A. Føllesdal, B. Peters and G. Ulfstein (eds.), *Constituting Europe: The European Court of Human Rights in a National, European and Global Context*. Cambridge: Cambridge University Press, 181–262.

Arnardóttir, O., (2003) *Equality and Non-Discrimination under the European Convention on Human Rights*. The Hague; London: Martinus Nijhoff.

Arnardóttir, O., (2013) Discrimination as a Magnifying Lens – Scope and Ambit under Article 14 and Protocol No. 12. In: E. Brems and J. Gerards (eds.), *Shaping Rights in the ECHR – The Role of the European Court of Human Rights in Determining the Scope of Human Rights*. New York: Cambridge University Press, 330–349.

Arnardóttir, O., (2014) The Differences that Make a Difference: Recent Developments on the Discrimination Ground and the Margin of Appreciation under Article 14 of the European Convention on Human Rights. *Human Rights Law Review*, 14: 647–670.

Collier, R. and Sheldon, S., (2008) *Fragmenting Fatherhood: A Socio-Legal Study*. Oxford; Portland, Or.: Hart.

Coltrane, S., (2000) Research on Household Labor: Modeling and Measuring the Social Embeddedness of Routine Family Work. *Journal of Marriage and Family*, 62(4): 1208–1233.

Cook, R. and Cusack, S., (2010) *Gender Stereotyping – Transnational Legal Perspectives*. Philadelphia: University of Pennsylvania Press.

Ellison, G. and Barker, A. and Kulasuriya, T., (2009) Work and Care: A Study of Modern Parents. [online] Equality and Human Rights Commission. Available at: www.equalityhumanrights.com/uploaded_files/research/15._work_and_care_modern_parents_15_report.pdf [Accessed 5 October 2015].

Esping-Andersen, G., (2009) *Incomplete Revolution: Adapting Welfare States to Women's New Roles*. Cambridge: Polity Press.

Fraser, N., (2013) *Fortunes of Feminism: From State-Managed Capitalism to Neo-Liberal Crisis*. London: Verso Books.

Fredman, S., (2014) Reversing Roles: Bringing Men into the Frame. *International Law in Context*, 10(4): 442–459.

Gans, D., (1995) Stereotyping and Difference: Planned Parenthood in v Casey and the Future of Sex Discrimination Law. *Yale Law Journal*, 104(7): 1875–1906.

Gerards, J., (2005) *Judicial Review in Equal Treatment Cases*. Leiden; Boston: Martinus Nijhoff.

Gioacchino, D., (2012) Parental Care, Children's Cognitive Abilities and Economic Growth: The Role of Fathers. *Theoretical Economics Letters*, 2(3): 258–261.

Grabham, E., (2014) Legal Form and Temporal Rationalities in UK Work-Life Balance Law. *Australian Feminist Studies*, 29(79): 67–84.

Harkness, S., (2008) The Household Division of Labour: Changes in Families' Allocation of Paid and Unpaid Work. In: J. Scott, S. Dex and J. Wadsworth (eds.) *Women and Employment: Changing Lives and New Challenges*. Cheltenham: Edward Elgar, 234–267.

Lewis, J., (2001) The Decline of the Male Breadwinner Model: Implications for Work and Care. *Social Politics*, 8(2): 152–169.

Mahoney, P., (1990) Judicial Activism or Judicial Self-Restraint in the European Court of Human Rights. *Human Rights Law Journal*, 11: 57–88.

Nikolaidis, C., (2015) *The Right to Equality in European Human Rights Law – The Quest for subStance in the Jurisprudence of the European Courts*. Abingdon: Routledge.

O'Connell, R., (2009) Cinderella Comes to the Ball: Article 14 and the Right to Non-Discrimination in the ECHR. *Legal Studies*, 29(2): 211–229.

Rhum, C., (2004) Parental Employment and Child Cognitive Development. *Journal of Human Resources*, 39(10): 155–192.

Rubio-Marin, R., (2012) A New European Parity-Democracy Sex Equality Model and why it won't fly in the United States. *American Journal of Comparative Law*, 60: 99–126.

Scott, J. and Clery, E., (2013) Gender Roles: An Incomplete Revolution? In: A. Park, C. Bryson, E. Clery, J. Curtice and M. Phillips (eds.), *British Social Attitudes: The 30th Report* [online]. Available at: www.bsa.natcen.ac.uk/media/38457/bsa30_gender_roles_final.pdf [Accessed 5 October 2015]: 115–138.

Suk, J., (2012) From Antidiscrimination to Equality: Stereotypes and the Life Cycle in the United States and Europe. *American Journal of Comparative Law*, 75: 78–98.

Tanaka, S., (2005) Parental Leave and Child Health across OECD Countries. *The Economic Journal*, 515(501), F7–F28.

Timmer, A., (2011) Toward an Anti-Stereotyping Approach for the European Court of Human Rights. *Human Rights Law Review*, 11(4): 707–738.

Weiler, J., (1999) *The Constitution of Europe – 'Do the New Clothes Have an Emperor?' and Other Essays on European Integration*. Cambridge: Cambridge University Press.

Williams, J. and Segal, N., (2003) Beyond the Maternal Wall: Relief for Family Caregivers Who Are Discriminated Against on the Job. *Harvard Women's Law Journal*, 26: 77–162.

Williams, J., (2000) *Unbending Gender: Why Family and Work Conflict and What to Do About It*. Oxford; New York: Oxford University Press.

Chapter 10

Carers as legal subjects

Ann Stewart

Introduction

Carers, generally understood as individuals who provide unpaid support to others with particular needs, have only recently become legal subjects in UK law and policy. They still have a rather ethereal existence: occasionally flitting into sight in labour law and then out of it; appearing on the outer reaches of property law; emerging into the light within social welfare law, but overshadowed by disability rights discourse. Their presence within some aspects of public policy is larger. They feature as subjects in effusively entitled government policy documents, such as *Recognised, Valued and Supported: New Steps for the Carers Strategy* (DH 2010), and have gained visibility and status through their advocacy organisation, Carers UK. This organisation adds a dose of realism to a roseate public image of selfless altruism, based upon the everyday experiences of providing care.

Jonathan Herring entitles his 2013 book *Caring and the Law* because he is wary of the connotations of a title involving carers. He argues that the focus should be on caring, for a number of persuasive reasons. One of which is to highlight a point, long-established by feminists, that we all give and receive care to a greater or lesser extent throughout our lives, as friends, lovers, family or community members. Privileging 'a carer' is to isolate a particular form of autonomous actor when we need to recognise that all are involved in relationships that are fundamental to the functioning of any society.

Nevertheless, carers now feature in their own right in legal texts (Clements 2012; Sloan 2013). These texts tend to focus on social welfare and family law issues, although many people who care also have jobs (including as social-care workers). As Brian Sloan reveals, certain individuals also appear within the domain of private law when they assert a carer identity to found a property claim against asset-rich care recipients. In his exploration of available remedies, Sloan raises the question of what might be the appropriate basis for any such remedy. Is the individual being 'compensated', 'rewarded' or 'remunerated' (2013: 24)? Each remedy points to a different way of valuing the activities associated with caring. Compensation focuses 'on the loss or detriment suffered by the carer as a result of taking on caring responsibilities' (ibid.). In this context, the carer might be limited to compensation for loss which occurred in reliance on a promise, or their future need for maintenance might also be recognised. It is arguable however that 'the true value of the services performed by the carer as a benefit conferred on the care recipient is recognised only if we are prepared to speak of "remuneration" or "reward"' (ibid.).

This chapter focuses on the way in which carers in the UK are understood in the domain of paid work within recent social welfare legislation, notably the Care Act 2014 and in private law. What do we learn from the way in which carers appear in these different areas of law? What form of value is associated with these different locations? Is there any coherence in the way in which carers are valued for their activities? If so, is carer status associated with a reward for altruism, compensation for the social and economic costs associated with caring, or recompense for labour expended? Are carers valued as workers, as citizens, or as community or family members? Are they valued for doing something 'out of the ordinary'? Through the development of this legal identity are we seeing a value being given to caring as a form of socially reproductive labour more generally?

The chapter draws on debates which place caring within the wider framework offered by insightful, if contested, materialist feminist traditions and recent contributions from feminist political economy, to draw out issues relating to the way in which care is valued. It locates the discussion within the contemporary social enterprise approach to social welfare and, in particular, in relation to the management of ageing. It argues that the distinction between care workers and carers, based upon whether the labour is paid for, is becoming less clear as a diversified and segmented market in care services develops; and that through these developments caring, as a form of socially reproductive labour, is becoming 'claimable' as carers gain legal status.

Valuing social reproduction

Although definitions vary, most of those adopting the terminology of social reproduction (SR) agree that the term covers:

> biological reproduction; unpaid production in the home (both goods and services); social provisioning (by this we mean voluntary work directed at meeting needs in the community); the reproduction of culture and ideology; and the provision of sexual, emotional and affective services (such as are required to maintain family and intimate relationships).
> Hoskyns and Rai 2007, p. 300

It is the 'fleshy, messy, indeterminate stuff of everyday life' (Katz 2001, p. 711).

Feminists highlight the lack of recognition of the subsidy provided by those undertaking SR, which leads to an unequal distribution of any benefits resulting from labour exchanged for wages (Rai *et al.* 2014, p. 88). Recent analysis, provoked in part by economic crises and an ideology of austerity, has focused on the way in which the restructuring of the relationship between the state and the market, and the reduction of social protection, affects the distribution of socially reproductive costs (Fraser 2011). 'This is leading to a situation where the subsidy provided by SR is being increasingly relied upon to fill the gaps in the state provision of welfare' (Rai *et al.* 2014, p.88). 'If too much pressure is put upon the domestic sector to provide unpaid care work to make up for deficiencies elsewhere, the result may be a depletion of human capabilities' (Elson 2000, p.28). Rai, Hoskyns and Thomas use the term depletion, which is associated with environmental accounting, rather than depreciation, which is associated with loss of value in capital goods, because it better captures the 'reduction of quantity in a non-renewable resource or something that cannot be replaced' (2014, p. 88). They define depletion as 'the gap between the outflows – domestic, affective and reproductive – and the inflows that sustain health and well-being' (ibid., p. 86). They therefore argue that it is essential to develop appropriate ways of measuring the net cost of SR. Depleted social reproduction (DSR) is the level at which 'the resource outflows exceed resource inflows in carrying out social reproductive work over a threshold of sustainability, making it harmful for those engaged in this unvalued work' (ibid., p. 88–9). 'Because unpaid work is largely unmeasured, the depletion in and through care work is not aggregated and is only "noticed" in ad hoc and small-scale ways' (Hoskyns and Rai 2007, p. 297). Rai, Hoskyns and Thomas argue that there are 'three strategies to reverse DSR – mitigation, replenishment and transformation' (2014, p. 98). DSR is mitigated 'when individuals attempt to lessen the consequences by, for example, paying for help' (ibid.). It is replenished when 'states or private bodies contribute to inflows' – for instance, through a social wage (Young, 1990, p.55). Restructuring of gender relations and the recognition and valuation of SR are necessary for its transformation (Rai *et al.* 2014, p. 99).

In a care economy and a social enterprise culture

Those undertaking SR become carers when their activities move out of the private sphere and attract public recognition in policy and legal domains. This status forms the basis for a claim aimed at recognising and potentially replenishing depletion. However, this carer identity has emerged during a period in which welfare provision has been restructured as neo-liberal policies have evolved, albeit at different rates and in different forms, throughout welfarist states (Bode 2008). These policies have led to the development of welfare markets transforming the non-market sphere through the introduction of the values and practices associated with competition.

> [A]dvanced liberal governance … [seeks to] … degovernmentalise the State … It relocate[s] experts within a market governed by the rationalities of competition, accountability and consumer demand. It does not seek to govern through 'society' but through the regulated choices of individual citizens, now construed as subjects of choices and aspirations to self-actualisation and self-fulfilment.
>
> Rose 1996, p. 41

In such a society individuals must take responsibility for their own personal decisions, undertake their own life planning and manage their own resources (Fox O'Mahony 2012, p. 48). Citizens are individualised, weaned off 'structured dependency' to become prudent, rational, autonomous consumers. The idealised subjectivity of citizenship is that of an enterprising entrepreneur (ibid., p. 28).

The management of older age has been affected significantly by these developments. The promise to UK citizens after the Second World War, based upon understandings of inter-generational solidarity, was that the welfare state would provide support from the 'cradle to the grave'. Changing demographics, particularly the ageing of the population, coupled with the transition from an industrial to a post-Fordist economy, put this model of state provision under pressure from the 1970s. Old age has become a key social problem for welfarist societies (Bode 2008). With the growing number of the population over the age of 65 and expected to live for 20 years or more, many in good health and able to live active lives, there is no longer any suggestion that they will simply 'fade away', supported by the state. The aim now is to move older people away from their perceived structured dependency on the welfare state. The ability to provide for one's self in older age is presented as 'an opportunity to achieve autonomy, control and self-governance' (Fox O'Mahony 2012, p. 65).

> [T]he changing traditions of 'old age' mean that people lead active lives with ongoing financial needs which must be balanced across early and later 'old age' creating new tensions between life style now and potential health and welfare needs into the future.
>
> ibid., p. 45

As critical scholars have pointed out, this idealised model of liberal subjectivity takes little consideration of wider social contexts or human interdependence (ibid.). Life courses still matter; those with social and economic resources continue to be far better positioned in older age and the poor remain poor. Ageing is risky and associated with much unpredictability. Although the still prevalent 'deficit' model of ageing views older people as a drain on society's resources and as a problem, it does recognise these risks. The 'drain' recast as active ageing individualises them.

A social enterprise society leads to an asset-based welfare culture in which caring is undertaken within a marketised context. Family homes become financial assets that can be used to provide caring services. Caring 'needs' become more diverse and stratified as they are recast as demands for services to satisfy individual choice. Carer identities are being reshaped within this context. It is therefore important to explore the basis for claims within the different domains associated with the development of this stratified social enterprise-based market. How is care valued and claimed from the state, an employer, or a private citizen/asset holder? What impact does the form of claiming have on constructions of cared for and carer identity?

Caring for the unproductive: valuing carers in labour market discourse

The next two sections explore the extent to which a carer identity has emerged within labour law. Feminist labour lawyers have made the case that caring is not valued in the labour market (Conaghan 2014). There have been a number of different aspects to this critique but two are of relevance here. The first is that work undertaken in the labour market is predicated upon socially reproductive labour, which is not recognised in the sphere of production. As a result, those responsible for it, mainly women, are disadvantaged in the labour market. The second is that those undertaking caring labour in the home are often not regarded as workers because of the location and the form that this activity takes. The first section below therefore asks: has a carer identity emerged in the workplace to tackle the depletion that the burden of unrecognised care can create? Can carer workers make claims and if so against whom? The second section addresses the uncertain identity of those who undertake socially reproductive work in 'non-traditional' workspaces.

Carer/worker claiming social reproduction through remuneration

Global-north welfare states have reconfigured responsibilities for social provision between the individual and the state. The deal whereby organised labour bargained for a family wage to be paid to male workers to provide sufficient income, supplemented by social provision, to support a household, while women took responsibility for (unpaid) socially reproductive labour supported primarily through the private institution of marriage, no longer pertains.

Employment has become far more precarious with a rise in informality and commercialisation (characterised by a move to self-employment) (Fudge and Owens 2006); and the power of organised labour has been eroded, first by the decline in industrial production and second by the privatisation of many public services. Now, individual workers take responsibility for their social reproduction within a two worker – or, more often in the UK, a one and a half worker – household model. Given that the family wage model was based upon a subsidy to capital provided by women, has there been an increase in depletion? Is the cost of caring claimed and replenished through the productive domain? How have state interventions shaped our understandings of the value of different forms of caring?

Anti-discrimination and equal pay legislation can been seen as strategies to tackle the under-valuation or exploitation of the labour of women who are, or are assumed will be, mothers. It addresses the impact of nurturing the next generation (of workers). Thus in a post family-wage era, ensuring individual equality between workers protects, to some extent, against the depletion of social production – women (and men) may be able to mitigate and replenish through their remuneration. In addition, employment related (social) protections recognise the claims of those caring for children, particularly in their early years. The Labour government that came to power in 1997 did much to foster the development of a social enterprise culture, but recognised the need for a public childcare policy to support such enterprise (Conaghan 2002). The state also expected employers to support this deal because a 'modern' diverse workforce contributes towards productivity.

These measures construct a parental identity to value care in relation to children, primarily in the very early stages of life, with far more limited measures aimed at recognising continuing parental responsibilities. They aim, in conjunction with social benefits and other child related public provision, to provide a small additional public contribution to the privately borne costs on younger workers to raise the next generation of citizens and workers.

Those who care for others, in particular those caring for the older generation of citizens and retired workers, are not 'parent workers'. An identity as a 'carer worker' has only recently emerged, not only due to activist campaigning but also coinciding with the obligation on all to be enterprising. Despite some discussion in the lead up to the Equality Act 2010, carers are not individual subjects for the purpose of anti-discrimination measures. As a result of the Coleman and Attridge law case in the European Court, carers are included to the extent that they can claim discrimination by association with another protected characteristic, such as disability or possibly age (Stewart ibid., 2011). In relation to employment related social protections, a limited number of the measures designed for 'parent workers' have been extended to 'carer workers', such as the right to request flexible working (Work and Families Act 2006). However, from 2014 this right has been extended to every employee who has worked for 26 weeks, which, it could be argued, recognises that all workers undertake socially reproductive activity, but it also moves carer workers back into the shadows.

There is no carers leave equivalent to that available to new parents, despite the effects on the ability to work of those who are expected to care for someone experiencing a sudden life-changing event. There is no employment related public policy relating to carers. State social provision based upon an explicit carer identity takes the form of a pitifully small carer's allowance. It is available to those who provide at least 35 hours a week to someone in need of substantial care, although there is no need to be related to or live with the cared-for person. Only those earning less than £102 a week (after taxes and other deductions in relation to care costs and pension contributions) are eligible.

Carer identity is thus precarious within work discourse. It is associated with older workers who care for partners and parents or older relatives and, in particular, with older women workers whose presence in the labour market is relatively new. Arguably, neither these workers nor the recipients of the care are seen as valuable in the domain of work in a society organised around production. As a result carers experience considerable depletion, whether they seek to continue with non-commodified caring labour or to substitute their labour through the provision of care services.

Care workers providing social reproduction in exchange for remuneration

The subjectivity of carers distinguishes them not only from parents but also from care workers. We are primarily concerned here with carers. However, a brief look at the way in which care workers are positioned within the labour market shows how boundary setting contributes to our understanding of the processes of valuing SR and the degree to which caring is marketised.

The creation of market care has required the development of a private sector workforce to accommodate the way in which social care is now provided. This has been achieved first by the transfer of the original public workforce into the private sector and then by its transformation into a diverse, often informal, service sector. As feminist labour-process scholars have demonstrated, body work (work which involves intimate contact between the worker and the worked-on body) is difficult to commodify fully (Twigg *et al.* 2011; Wolkowitz 2006). Bodies, particularly older frail ones, are not as easy 'to service' as cars; there is limited potential to capitalise. The cost of providing decent quality care, once transferred to the market, ensures that profitability remains relatively low. Risk is transferred to workers through precarious employment relations (Stewart 2011, 2013; Hayes 2015).

The characteristics of body work, including its messiness and the domestic location in which it often occurs, does not make it attractive to workers. It tends therefore to be undertaken by more vulnerable workers, either drawn from minority communities or migrants, who find it hard to resist considerable exploitation of their labour in a largely un-unionised sector. Consequently, this socially reproductive work struggles to gain recognition and is often remunerated at below the statutory National Minimum Wage (NMW), or the recently introduced National Living Wage (NLW). This contributes to the depletion of the worker's own social reproduction and subsidises employers and the state.

Domestic work undertaken within households can cross the boundary of productive labour law regulation, in which work is remunerated, into a context in which far murkier forms of recompense prevail. The recent campaign to maintain the, already limited, protections relating to foreign domestic workers in the UK provides one illustration (Mullally 2014). As activists point out and research confirms (Mantouvalou 2014), visas that tie workers to individual employers and deny them access to the wider labour market ensures that they move into the area now covered by the discourse of modern slavery and away from that associated with (exploited) work (Fudge and Strauss 2014; O'Connell Davidson 2015). More generally, informal domestic/carer workers can be classified as too familial to attract recognition as productive workers covered by the publicly recognised NMW. Because the employer contributes towards the worker's SR (with accommodation and meals) and the work they do could have been substituted by unpaid familial forms of work, their labour is not recognised as work. If such work is not recognised as attracting the NMW, how is it to be understood? *In extremis* it might be recognised within human-rights protections, as a result of developments within the European Convention on Human Rights Article 4 (now incorporated within the Modern Slavery Act 2015) in relation to servitude and forced labour (Mantouvalou 2015). The case law here recognises that in these circumstances the 'victim' has a claim for the harm suffered. This can sometimes involve compensation based upon loss of earnings for work undertaken, and thus is a claim for remuneration, but often irregular migration status denies worker status and the claim is for 'suffering', compensating for human rights violations or 'victimhood' (Barnard 2014; *Hounga v Allen and Anor* [2014] UKSC 47).

Such workers seem, therefore, to move close to a carer identity while not attracting any of the social-welfare related identity that we see in the next section.

Caring for citizens: claiming value in state welfare discourse

How is the assumed solidaristic altruism associated with familial care transformed into a right to claim an identity as a carer within social welfare law and policy? Here, carer identity has been constructed through the unpaid nature of the relationship between those providing and receiving care. The development of market welfare is reconfiguring this identity to incorporate it within the diversified provision of care services.

As the definition of SR makes clear, caring is part of everyday practice in society. However Carers UK define carers in the following terms:

> 6.5 million people are carers, supporting a loved one who is older, disabled or seriously ill. That's 1 in 8 adults who care, unpaid, for family and friends. ... Whether round-the-clock or for a few hours a week, in our own home or for someone at the other end of a motorway – caring can have a huge effect on us, our lives and our plans.
> www.carersuk.org/about-us/why-we-re-here (accessed 11 August 2016)

It identifies the subsidy provided by this form of SR: '[c]arers are holding families together, enabling loved ones to get the most out of life, making an enormous contribution to society and saving the economy billions of pounds'; and the consequences of its depletion:

> Yet many of us are stretched to the limit – juggling care with work and family life, or even struggling with poor health ourselves. We often find it difficult to make ends meet if we're unable to work or if we've reduced our working hours to care.
> ibid.

Carers first attracted a form of legal subjectivity in the 1986 Disabled Persons (Services Consultation and Representation Act). Local authorities were obliged to take into account the abilities of a carer when deciding on the eligibility for public services of a disabled person. Within this Act (section 8), the disabled person must be 'living at home and receiving a substantial amount of care on a regular basis from another person (who is not a person employed to provide such care …)'. The ability of the carer to sustain the level of care is assessed. Subsequent legislation gradually strengthened the public obligation to consider the needs of carers 'who provide substantial care on a regular basis to an adult or a disabled child' and extended the forms of provision they might receive with the Carers (Recognition and Services) Act 1995, the Carers and Disabled Children Act 2000 and the Carers (Equal Opportunities) Act 2004. Although a more rights-related approach starts to emerge, the carer is still assessed in relation to the person in need of care. This relational approach is also evident in the carer's allowance discussed earlier, in that the cared for must be in receipt of a qualifying disability benefit.

The Care Act 2014 replaces the mass of previous piecemeal legislation associated with the provision of social care. It provides, for the first time, a coherent framework based upon 'core values' which again reflects the shift towards a social enterprise culture and market welfare. It puts 'people in control of their care and support' and 'promotes people's well-being by enabling them to prevent and postpone the need for care and support and to pursue education, employment and other opportunities to realise their potential' (DH 2013, p. 5, 7). Section 1 places the well-being of the individual in need of care at its centre. Public authorities are required to respect their independence and choices. Services must be designed to support well-being, rather than fit the individual into services that are available. This is achieved through a process of 'personal budgeting', whereby the care needs of individuals are assessed and then monetised into a notional budget. This process of 'personalisation' enables those who are eligible for state support to be provided with either a direct payment to buy services to meet their needs or a budget to be managed by the authority or other designated agency on their behalf. This monetisation was to be underpinned by a new financial regime for social care, scheduled for introduction in 2015/16 but now postponed. Each citizen was expected to meet the first £72,000 of their care costs (unless eligible through a means test for state support). Thereafter the state will take over responsibility. Thus, each citizen assessed as in need of care will have a 'notional budget' – a public tab in effect. As Series and Clements (2013) point out these developments contribute significantly to the marketisation of care and its further commodification.

In line with the general philosophy, the Act seeks to put 'carers on an equal legal footing to those they care for and [to] put … their needs at the centre of the legislation' (DH 2013, p. 10). Section 10 defines a carer as 'an adult who provides or intends to provide care for another adult', although such 'an adult is not to be regarded as a carer if the adult provides or intends to provide care' via 'a contract or as voluntary work'. Such a carer now has an autonomous right to an assessment, irrespective of whether the cared for is assessed. This assessment may result in an entitlement to services, such as purchasing substitute forms of care and/or access to funds to support education or training or leisure time. Carers can also obtain a direct payment to assist with their own needs or they can be paid from the direct payment provided to the cared-for person. As originally conceived, direct payments were not available to close family members who lived in the same household as the person receiving care, thereby maintaining a boundary between familial and care-service provision. Close relatives living elsewhere are eligible and a local authority now has authority to waive any restrictions. Statutory guidance makes it clear that a person in receipt of a direct payment who employs a person directly is bound by all the laws that cover employment.

What we learn from these developments is that the legal subjectivity of the social welfare carer involves the transformation of private caring undertaken as part of everyday SR into a public claim for recognition and resources. Individual, family or community members must recast themselves to make claims on the state. As legally constructed this identity is associated with caring for the particularly vulnerable. A carer is not a parent providing 'normal' levels of care to a child, nor someone providing care through 'voluntary and paid forms'. However, the 2014 definition lowers the bar for other adult carers in that there is no longer a need to provide substantial levels of care.

These developments seem to suggest that while the status of carer requires more caring than is socially expected, that expectation is being redefined. The 2014 Act also shifts carer identity further away from a relational towards a rights-based, autonomous subjectivity; although carer identity is still triggered by caring for someone else, it depends on the identity of the cared for. It is the form through which caring is undertaken that is being reconstructed.

There has been a long-standing tension between the relational subjectivity of carers and the disability rights movement, which strongly disassociates itself from the discourse of dependency. Their focus has been on meeting the demands of those with a disability through the enforcement of their individual rights. This movement, associated with younger adults, uses the language of personal assistants rather than social carers for paid care (provided through direct payments or otherwise). The discourse relating to carers in the 2014 Act moves the identity of unpaid carers somewhat closer to that favoured by the disability movement.

What then is the nature of this claim? It can be seen as public recognition, as a 'reward' for altruism. It can be seen as public acknowledgment of the effect that this labour has on those who undertake the care; and can be seen as a claim for compensation for citizens for their socially reproductive labour and, as such, as a contribution towards replenishment, in effect a move away from 'private' mitigation. Where the carer is still potentially 'productive' the claim can address the depletion to carer workers produced by such caring. The compensation might aim to enable younger adults to access the labour market, or older women (and men) to remain within it, as discussed in the previous section. However, overall, with the increasing focus on the care recipient as a citizen/consumer responsible for anticipating and providing for their care needs, carers become part of the bigger jigsaw of mixed forms of care provision. Care funded through state transfers (direct payments) blurs the boundaries between informal/familial care and care work. At what point does 'normal' support for a friend or parent become 'caring', in this context? If someone provides cash or gifts in recognition of help from a friend, does this friend become a care worker rather than a carer? Is this a form of labour relationship, just not one attracting the discourse of remuneration? As we saw in the last section, informal (and cheap) support provided in domestic settings, whether funded by state transfers or other income sources, has a tendency to slip between categories and become invisible.

Caring for the asset rich: valuing care through property discourse

Sloan's work (upon which this section draws) on what he describes as the private law of 'informal carers', shines a light on another shadowy group of people whose identity as carers is primarily moulded through private litigation rather than through an employment relationship or through engagement with the state social welfare system. Such claims only have salience if there are property-based resources available to be claimed and an individual in a position to make such a claim. However, the development of private law would be associated with a shift away from citizen claims for social infrastructural support to replenish, towards mitigatory claims against individuals. The emergence of a private law care subject is interesting in the context of asset-based care provision within a social enterprise culture. Should private assets, often those embodied in the 'family' home, be available to 'reward' carers or, more generally, to reduce the public costs of caring?

Should informal carers expect financial reward and be able to make a claim on these assets? Debates over how to understand 'the gift' (Mauss 1990), particularly its relationship to a commodity in market economies, still interest anthropologists (Sykes 2005). Indeed, their analysis of the intersection between gift-giving and market exchange could shed an interesting light on the nature of reciprocity and claiming in this context but is beyond the scope of the present chapter. Sloan assesses the way in which such claims can be pursued presently under English law. He considers two main situations. 'The first is where a carer receives some indication from the person for whom he cares that his care will be rewarded in some way, and the reward is not forthcoming.' (Sloan 2013, p. 2) In property law terms this relates to unconscionability of dealing. 'The second considers whether a remedy should be available in the absence of such an indication' (ibid.) and relates to unconscionability of outcome. Unconscionability is used here to mean significant normative undesirability (ibid.). The relationships under consideration are not contractual and the main mechanism used to make these claims is proprietary estoppel. Sloan identifies the particular issues faced by carers in establishing their case and compares these to other claimants. He concludes that this form of estoppel can provide a remedy in particular circumstances, but 'it is much less clear *why* the doctrine does so' (ibid., p. 80) and it is not clear whether the individual is being 'compensated', 'rewarded' or 'remunerated' (ibid., p. 24). He suggests that a broad estoppel jurisdiction could lead to an increase in costly and bitter litigation between carer and non-carer family members and between 'pure' carers and family members. Sloan defines a pure carer as someone providing a 'significant amount of support in the absence of a close familial or sexual relationship between the parties' (ibid., p. 137). Although this form of litigation is a 'private' mitigatory strategy to claim for depleted social reproduction, the carer seems to have many of the characteristics associated with the informal carer in social welfare law and the domestic worker in labour law as providing a social service.

Caring in an asset-based welfare society?

Carers emerged into the public light as altruistic family members providing care on the basis of affection. Policy makers and advocacy organisations assert that carers are not in it for the money. However, what place does this altruistic, interdependent care-giving identity have within the wider discourse on social enterprise cultures and care economies? Increasingly, policy makers monetise care. They speak of the 'opportunity costs of caring', the loss for UK carers is considered to be, on average, £11,000 per year. The effect on carers' health is costed. There are attempts being made to reflect caring within official national accounting systems (Rai *et al.* 2014). Do these calculations reflect an assumption that there will have to be more monetised incentives to sustain a supply of informal care? Will monetisation integrate informal carers into a diversified labour market, at the bottom as extremely cheap/precarious workers? Or will a new identity emerge that reflects a proprietorial relationship because it is derived in relation to an asset-based welfare economy? If so, what is the nature of the value upon which legal subjectivity is based? Within a labour market this body work would command a price, but within a proprietorial context would it relate to recompense for disadvantages suffered through caring as elaborated within family law discourse? If so, would it be based on need or desert and how would these concepts be monetised?

Oldham (2001) argues for a restitutionary claim for care work backed by the state, given that the economic value of the contribution made by carers is estimated to be £132 billion in 2014–15 (roughly the same as for the NHS) (Buckner and Yeandle 2015). This would involve the creation of a system of 'successional priority' which would give a person who takes care of a relative a prioritised right of provision from that relative's estate. This 'priority concept could be combined with equity release and a state sponsored loan system to provide a more instantaneous incentive for an informal carer' (Sloan 2013, p. 14). Oldham considers that the proposals are based upon relationships of interdependence rather than dependence, and reinforces the concept of desert, although in an individual rather than societal form. It is also based on the assumption that the possibility of private payment may well be necessary to encourage people to care for others within a social enterprise culture. It also reduces the cost to the state (Wise 2002). Oldham has relatives in mind but such a scheme could include 'pure' carers. Is this the way to promote social solidarity within a social enterprise economy? Or does it undermine claims against the state to recognise and replenish through the provision of adequate levels of social provision or, as Pearson (2014) argues, for social infrastructure?

Conclusion

This chapter has considered the way in which carers have gained a legal identity and how this subjectivity is understood in three domains: within the world of production as regulated through labour law; in the field of social welfare law; and in the private sphere relating to claims against property. Through this discussion of the way carer identity is understood in each of these areas it has sought to shed light on an analysis of the relationship between production and social reproduction within the contemporary social and economic context in the UK. Drawing inspiration from Sloan's discussion in which he suggests that there are three bases for claims by carers – compensation, reward and remuneration – the chapter has considered whether these map on to the three areas under consideration. It has adopted the terminology developed by feminist political economists in their analysis of the relationship between production and social reproduction. In particular, it has used the concept of depleted social reproduction, which occurs when the individual is obliged to bear an excessive proportion of the labour associated with social reproduction without a replenishing contribution from the market or the state.

What do we learn from the discourse associated with labour law? Here carers are valued in relation to their productive capacity as workers. Those who nurture future productive workers are valued more than those looking after those less likely to contribute, or who have already contributed, and are still considered an economic drain on society, despite changes in the way in which ageing is understood in a social enterprise economy. While the deleterious effects of the socially reproductive labour associated with the caring undertaken by those defined in social welfare law as carers can found a claim for public resources, it is barely recognised within labour law. This lack of recognition affects the ability of carer workers to secure and maintain their position in the labour market and leads to their inability to counter depletion in their socially reproductive capacity. Their ability to replenish their socially reproductive labour, either directly through 'work/care balance' (see further, Margaria, Chapter 9) or through purchasing substitute services, is undermined.

When commodified, social care commands little value within the care market and results in the precarious position of the 'mainstream' social care workforce, who currently provide domiciliary and residential care services in highly commodified forms to meet the imperatives of a highly risky care market. Workers find it difficult to maintain their claim to at least the National Minimum Wage, let alone the new National Living Wage. Labour law is unable to encompass social reproductive work that is deemed to be insufficiently commodified – that is, work that is too associated with the familial. Domestic/care workers therefore struggle to claim an identity as workers, despite recent developments within international labour law relating to the recognition of domestic labour as work under the ILO Domestic Workers Convention 2011, and to be entitled to the National Minimum Wage under domestic legislation. Labour law is therefore contributing to the development of a highly diversified and exploitative care economy in which body/

caring work is increasingly being marketised without attracting adequate labour law protections.

The contribution of those who provide care has gained most recognition within the state discourse relating to the provision of social welfare. The carer identity that has emerged here results from the changed relationship between state, market and individual following the development of a social enterprise culture. Carer identity is associated with disabled or vulnerable adults, particularly in the context of a rapidly ageing society. We have seen that caring identities are being reconfigured to reflect the shift in responsibility on to citizens to plan for and resource their care in older age. Autonomous subjects in a risk society demand services to satisfy their choices of life style. Carer identity is being recast from a claim based upon altruism – associated with providing very substantial amounts of unpaid care, usually within a familial context – to one more based upon a claim for compensation for losses – associated with social and economic exclusion in a society which expects everyone to value themselves through productive activity. Caring relationships start to attract forms of value associated with service provision.

A tension between competing concepts of entitlement is much in evidence in private property claims between those claiming through a status of carer due to their actions and those claiming through an assumed familial relationship, often as adult children. Within an asset-based welfare culture these tensions are likely to increase as the family home and other assets are used to fund individual caring services (Fox O'Mahony 2012). The financialisation of property and pensions obliges citizens to monetise actual and potential care needs and to consider actively the extent to which they will use assets to buy services in their lifetime, or attempt to 'shield' whatever assets they may have to benefit those who will inherit.

As care recipients are being reconstructed as socially entrepreneurial citizens with high degrees of autonomy and independence, the care-givers in the areas under investigation here are being recast as precarious providers of services, holders of weak rights and marginal property claims makers. All are being drawn into a highly diversified, very informal, still highly familiarised, care economy. The identity of carers must be seen within this move to limit public responsibility to provide for individuals in need of care and to shift responsibility and choice to the individual citizen. Will carers be obliged to adopt the language of the market for recognition as specialist and customised service providers? What would a progressive transformatory strategy of recognising, valuing and supporting caring entail?

References

Barnard, Catherine (2014) 'Enforcement of Employment Rights by Migrant Workers in the UK: The Case of EU-8 Nationals' in C Costello and M Freedland (eds.) *Migrants at Work: Immigration and Vulnerability in Labour Law* Oxford: Oxford University Press 193–215.

Bode, Ingo (2008) *The Culture of Welfare Markets: The International Recasting of Pension and Care Systems* New York: Taylor and Francis.

Buckner, Lisa and Yeandle, Sue (2015) *Valuing Carers 2015: The Rising Value of Carers Support* London: Carers UK.

Clements, Luke (2012) *Carers and Their Rights: Law Relating to Carers* London: Carers UK.

Conaghan, Joanne (2002) 'Women, Work, and Family: A British Revolution?' in J Conaghan, RM Fischl and K Klare (eds.) *Labour Law in an Era of Globalization* Oxford: Oxford University Press 53–74.

Conaghan, Joanne (2014) 'Gender and the Idea of Labour Law' *Feminists@law* 4:1 http://journals.kent.ac.uk/index.php/feministsatlaw/article/view/102 accessed 11 August 2016.

Department of Health (DH) (2010) *Recognised, Valued and Supported: Next Steps for the Carers Strategy* London: HM Government www.gov.uk/government/uploads/system/uploads/attachment_data/file/213804/dh_122393.pdf accessed 7 January 2016.

Department of Health (DH) (2013) *The Care Bill Explained; Including a Response to Consultation and Pre-legislative Scrutiny on the Draft Care and Support Bill* London: HM Government cm 8627.

Elson, Diane (2000) 'The Progress of Women: Empowerment and Economics' in *The Progress of the World's Women* New York: UNIFEM.

Fox O'Mahony, Lorna (2012) *Home Equity and Ageing Owners: Between Risk and Regulation* Oxford and Portland, OR: Hart Publishing.

Fraser, Nancy (2011) 'The Wages of Care: Reproductive Labor as Fictitious Commodity' Lecture, University of Cambridge, 19 March.

Fudge, Judy and Owens, Rosemary (eds.) (2006) *Precarious Work, Women, and the New Economy: The Challenge to Legal Norms Oñati International Series in Law and Society* Oxford and Portland, OR: Hart Publishing.

Fudge, Judy and Strauss, Kendra (2014) 'Migrants, Unfree Labour and the Legal Construction of Domestic Servitude' in C Costello and M Freedland (eds.) *Migrants at Work: Immigration and Vulnerability in Labour Law* Oxford: Oxford University Press 160–179.

Hayes, Lydia (2015) 'Care and Control: Are the National Minimum Wage Entitlements of Homecare Workers at Risk under the Care Act 2014?' *Industrial Law Journal* 44(4): 492–521.

Herring, Jonathan (2013) *Caring and the Law* Oxford and Portland, OR: Hart Publishing

Hoskyns, Catherine and Rai, Shirin M (2007) 'Recasting the Global Political Economy: Counting Women's Unpaid Work' *New Political Economy* 12(3): 297–317.

Katz, Cindi (2001) 'Vagabond Capitalism and the Necessity of Social Reproduction' *Antipode* 33(4): 709–714.

Mantouvalou, Virginia (2014) 'Organising against Abuse and Exclusion: The Associational Rights of Undocumented Workers' in C Costello and M Freedland (eds.) *Migrants at Work: Immigration and Vulnerability in Labour Law* Oxford: Oxford University Press 381–398.

Mantouvalou, Virginia (2015) '"Am I Free Now?" Overseas Domestic Workers in Slavery' *Journal of Law and Society* 42(3): 329–357.

Mauss, Marcel (1990/1922) *The Gift: Forms and Functions of Exchange in Archaic Societies* London: Routledge.

Mullally, Siobhan (2014) 'Migration, Gender, and the Limits of Rights' in R Rubio-Marín (ed.) *Human Rights and Immigration* Oxford: Oxford University Press 145–176.

O'Connell Davidson, Julia (2015) *Modern Slavery: The Margins of Slavery* Basingstoke: Palgrave MacMillan.

Oldham, MPC (2001) 'Financial Obligations within the Family – Aspects of Intergenerational Maintenance and Succession in England and France' *Cambridge Law Journal* 60(1): 128–177.

Pearson, Ruth (2014) 'Gender, Globalization and the Reproduction of Labour: Bringing the State Back In' in SM Rai and G Waylen (eds.) *New Frontiers in Feminist Political Economy* London and New York: Routledge.

Rai, Shirin M, Hoskyns Catherine and Thomas Dania (2014) 'Depletion' *International Feminist Journal of Politics* 16(1): 86–105.

Rose, N (1996) 'Governing "Advanced" Liberal Democracies' in A Barry, T Osborne and N Rose (eds.) *Foucault and Political Reason* London: UCL Press 37–64.

Series, Lucy and Clements, Luke (2013) 'Putting the Cart before the Horse: Resource Allocation Systems and Community Care' *Journal of Social Welfare and Family Law* 35(2): 207–226.

Sloan, Brian (2013) *Informal Carers and Private Law* Oxford and Portland, OR: Hart Publishing

Stewart, Ann, Niccolai, Sylvia and Hoskyns, Catherine (2011) 'Disability Discrimination by Association: A Case of the Double Yes? *Social and Legal Studies* 20(2): 173–190.

Stewart, Ann (2011) *Gender, Law and Justice in a Global Market* Cambridge: Cambridge University Press

Stewart, Ann (2013) 'Legal Constructions of Body Work' in C Wolkowitz, R Cohen, T Sanders and K Hardy (eds.) *Body/Sex/Work – Intimate, Embodied and Sexualised Labour* Aldershot: Palgrave 61–66.

Sykes, Karen (2005) *Arguing with Anthropology: An Introduction to Critical Theories of the Gift* London and New York: Routledge.

Twigg, Julia, Wolkowitz, Carol, Cohen, Rachel Lara and Nettleton, Sarah (eds.) (2011) *Body Work in Health and Social Care: Critical Themes, New Agendas* Chichester: Wiley Blackwell.

Wise, Katie (2002) 'Caring for Our Parents in an Aging World: Sharing Public and Private Responsibility for the Elderly' *New York University Journal of Legislation and Public Policy* 6(2): 563–598.

Wolkowitz, Carol (2006) *Bodies at Work* London: Sage.

Young, Iris Marion (1990) *Justice and the Politics of Difference* Princeton, NJ: Princeton University Press.

Legislation

Care Act 2014
Carers (Recognition and Services) Act 1995
Carers and Disabled Children Act 2000
Carers (Equal Opportunities) Act 2004
Disabled Persons (Services Consultation and Representation Act) 1986
Domestic Workers Convention 2011 no 189 International Labour Office
Equality Act 2010
European Convention on Human Rights

Modern Slavery Act 2015
Work and Families Act 2006

Case Law

Hounga v Allen and Anor [2014] UKSC 47

Chapter 11

Towards a 'reasonable' level of state support for care?
Constitutionalism, care work and the common good

Olivia Smith

Introduction

The ethics of care scholars have contributed a rich body of literature around the public and collective good of care (Gilligan 1982; Noddings 1984; Tronto 1993), simultaneously highlighting the vulnerability of carers within current institutional arrangements that construe care as a private, familial concern (Kittay 1999; McClain 2001). These vulnerabilities are disproportionately experienced across gender, ethnicity and class categories, in respect of both unpaid and underpaid care work. While theorists have argued that a comprehensive concern with injustice and disadvantage requires collective support for the value and work of care, there was traditionally little enthusiasm for the role of rights in this context (Gilligan 1982; White and Tronto 2004). Many theorists expressed scepticism on the role of rights in transforming the conditions that institutionalise vulnerabilities for care workers and, by extension, the recipients of their care. Rights as conceptualised in the liberal tradition have been portrayed as the antithesis to the value of care (West 2003, p. 88), with the former associated with atomisation, individualisation, autonomy and self-interest, in opposition to the carer subject's concern with connectedness, mutual reliance and relationality. At the same time, the call to abandon rights in the battle for support for caregivers is not unanimous, as others argue in favour of rethinking and conceiving of rights to make them more responsive to social relationships (Minow and Shanley 1996; Nedelsky 2012). West (2003) has argued, for example, in favour of reconceiving liberal rights to include a right to care, despite the fact that the US constitutional tradition, like many constitutional documents, makes no reference to such a concept.

Not all constitutional documents are silent as regards the position of unpaid care and the role of caregivers, however. Provisions of the Irish constitution of 1937, albeit problematic in their current guise, conceptualise, potentially at least, care work as something more than a personal and familial responsibility. The constitution (theoretically) views care work as a collaborative endeavour, with the state expressly recognising 'work in the home', albeit problematically described as women's work, as a necessary element to the achievement of 'the common good'. Article 41.2 acknowledges how unpaid care labour is a 'central social organizing device' (Nedelsky 2012) as part of the constitution's provisions on fundamental rights. As discussed below, the nature and form of this recognition to date has been largely problematic. Article 41.2 has tended, therefore, to be dismissed as an anachronism, a relic of a previous time with little relevance to a modern state, given the rise of the 'adult worker family model' (Lewis 2001) and the changing role of women within the state.

Recently, there has been renewed focus on care in Irish constitutional discourse as part of the Convention on the Constitution's consideration of the role of women in the constitution, and its subsequent recommendations regarding the reconfiguration of the constitutional text that deals with unpaid care work. This interesting engagement with the value of care that arose as part of the Convention's deliberative discussions around constitutional change, contrasts with the very limited engagement on the part of the judiciary with the potential or promise of Article 41.2. However, the Convention's reforming recommendation is currently at a prolonged halt within a governmental working group, which is in keeping with the limited and disappointing fate of the Convention's recommendations more generally (see Carolan 2015). But there remains a possibility (although an admittedly remote one) of a 'constitutional moment' (Ackerman 1991), regarding the recognition of a right to care, should an amendment to its terms be put before the people by way of referendum. In addition, the momentum around the reform of Article 41.2 may also benefit from the renewed attention directed towards the status of social and economic rights that also emerged from the Convention's deliberations.

In this chapter I trace the trajectory of the constitutional concern with unpaid care work that took place with the insertion of Article 41.2 into the Irish Constitution, its interpretation, and the prospects for a 'right to care' consequent upon the recommendation overwhelmingly endorsed by the Convention on the Constitution. The purpose of the chapter is to consider how this burgeoning recognition around the public value of care can be more positively translated into constitutional form, thereby attracting recognition of care as a basic, foundational good. The chapter proceeds by briefly considering how the current arrangements around unpaid care present issues of rights and rights violations. It goes on to consider the judicial approaches taken to the value of care implicit in Article 41.2, which range from typical gendered tropes around self-sacrifice, to the denial of the economic value of social reproduction over established forms of property rights against Nedelsky's approach to rights as relational, which sees rights as the means of implementing core values, such as autonomy and equality. Thereafter, I go on to consider the contribution of the Convention on the Constitution, part of a clear trend emerging in constitution-making processes (Carolan 2015) on the reform of Article 41.2, which is followed by some tentative observations regarding a possible constitutional right to care and its implications.

Unpaid care work: an issue of rights

While care and affect have traditionally been sidelined in major works on justice and rights, care and feminist theorists have added considerably to the debate on the inclusion of care as a matter of justice and rights. At the same time, echoing certain feminist legal scholars' doubts regarding the emancipatory potential of rights (Naffine 1990), care theorists have supported the retreat from rights, asserting that the exclusion of care perspectives from the concept of rights is definitional (Noddings 1984; White and Tronto 2004). However, the tension or dichotomy between care and justice and equality in these debates has been challenged in the literature (Kittay 1999; Nussbaum 2000), particularly as care raises important questions around injustice and inequality and the need for responsive mechanisms. For example, Kittay's work suggests that Rawls list of 'primary goods' is capable of being read as inclusive of love and care as basic human needs. And despite a certain feminist ambivalence towards rights claims, constitutional documents worldwide have embraced the language of human rights as a means of asserting support for individual well-being and challenging injustice and inequality, cementing the view that the turn to rights, if not the content and meaning of those rights, has been won (Nedelsky 2008, p. 14). For the most part, vindicating feminist concerns, these rights pronouncements cover those rights typical of the liberal frame, where rights are viewed primarily as negative liberties protecting individuals from the tyranny of majoritarian governments – although some newer constitutional traditions have taken a more expansive turn as regards the scope of constitutional rights (Smyth 2016). Even within those narrower constitutional traditions, certain rights within the liberal framework arguably straddle the, so-called, civil and political – social and economic rights or negative liberty – positive duty divide, divisions that have been questioned with greater frequency (Gearty and Mantavolou 2011). Notwithstanding the fluidity of these boundaries, it remains largely the case that most constitutional rights assertions do not generally make express reference to the rights of those who carry out care work, a reality that can be explained by the constructed 'private' sphere to which liberal thought assigned this type of work and status. Care workers are simply assumed to be entitled to the same liberal rights that all individuals possess, even though the nature of their work and the context in which this is carried out may, in reality, result in a reduced ability to enjoy such rights on an equal basis with the paradigmatic liberal rights holder. Notwithstanding the range of feminist work that has demolished the fiction of the public–private divide (Boyd 1997), the 'rights as boundary' (Nedelsky 1990) metaphor, protecting the self-sufficient individual from unjustifiable state encroachment, has remained stubbornly intact. One consequence is that it allows the state to construe the inequalities and disadvantage endured as a consequence of care work as private and familial, a matter of choice (West 2003) and beyond the concern or responsibility of the state, other than within the largely discretionary measures gifted through the welfare state.

The work of feminist theorists has provided robust challenges to this incomplete understanding, both of the human condition and justice. It has also been exposed as mythical, given the central and indispensable societal role played by care, which makes it a public good (Fineman 2004). Care theory has exposed the poverty of a conception of justice that fails to attend to the necessary social connectedness and dependency relationships that are essential aspects of the human condition and are critical to human well-being and flourishing (Tronto 1993). By refusing to see the contributions that care relationships make to community endeavours, state concerns and economic institutions, it becomes easy to assign such practices to the 'private' sphere, and to place any public concern with the disadvantages endured by those engaged in care within the sphere of needs, welfare and charity, as opposed to fundamental rights.

However, the array of rights violations endured by unpaid caregivers as a consequence of unsupported caregiving is extensive, while simultaneously denied or diminished as being rights violations (Nedelsky 2012). It is largely uncontested that the assignment of unpaid care work to the private sphere has been highly gendered. Pateman's work (1988) on the 'sexual contract' deftly exposed how the contract between the state and the individual that involved the protection of the individual rights holder against state power was built upon a hidden 'sexual contract'. The autonomous rights bearer in the traditional liberal vision was, in reality, propped up and enabled by the assignment of the necessity and inevitability of the tasks of dependency and social reproduction to the socially constructed private sphere, and mainly to women within that sphere. The consequence of organising structures of care work at the level of the private household, or as poorly paid work, has been various rights violations of those persons who perform such care work, including women, members of ethnic minorities and poor people. The inadequacy of public recognition and support for care work can render it incompatible with paid work. This implicates the right of such persons to earn a livelihood[1] and leaves many carers at risk of poverty. In addition, the empirical evidence suggests that the burdens of care work can impact upon carers' rights to health and well-being (Central Statistics Office 2009). Unsupported care work impacts not just the health status of carers, but also their ability to access leisure and play, one of Nussbaum's essential capabilities (2000). It also has knock-on consequences on the quality of care provided for the care recipient. Further, the shift towards welfare state activation measures, coupled with the impact of austerity driven cuts, creates clear inequalities between carers as regards family status. These failures of the political system and the market to generate substantive protections for carers have generated increasing support for the turn towards rights protection (West 2003).

Care work in the constitutional order: a gendered anachronism masking relational possibilities?

While there is evidence of an emerging right to care in other legal domains, such as that which flickers in the context of labour law protection (Busby 2011; Smith 2012), most constitutional documents contain no reference to the central but hidden role that care plays in the liberal state tradition. Care does not form part of the narrative of constitutionalism, which prefers to assert the (theoretical) availability of access to and enjoyment of liberal rights on an equal basis through the inclusion of a limited formal guarantee of equality before the law.

As noted above, the Irish Constitution stands apart from this pattern through its explicit acknowledgement of Pateman's 'hidden' sexual contract. Powerful, long-standing gendered norms that normatively construct unpaid care work as the natural concern (Mullally 2007) and the responsibility of women, were embedded in the constitutional text in 1937 as part of its highly contested provisions on the family. The full text to Article 41.2.1–2, which provoked considerable disquiet from women's groups at the time of the constitution's formation (Hogan 2012, p. 520), states:

> the State recognises that by her life within the home, woman gives to the State a support without which the common good cannot be achieved. The State shall, therefore, endeavour to ensure that mothers shall not be obliged by economic necessity to engage in labour to the neglect of their duties in the home.

This text immediately invites some conflicting remarks. Most obviously it attracts criticism for its confining construction of women's citizenship, which is laid out in indirect terms. It assigns relationships of responsibility for dependents and household work to women as a group, and later, more specifically, mothers, on the basis of an assumed biological suitability.[2] Through the power of constitutional assertion it normatively entrenches a gendered division of labour and a hard public–private divide that sees women as non-contributors beyond the home and assumes their proper dependence on either a male breadwinner husband or, in default, the state. As noted above, an array of rights deprivations follow from this gendered division of household labour. It also permits the perpetuation of unhelpful gender stereotypes[3] that harm both women and men, including distancing men from the benefits of caregiving (Smith 2014). The provision has drawn frequent condemnation, with calls for its amendment or removal coming from international human rights bodies and state commissions (Second Commission on the Status of Women 1992; Constitution Review Group 1996).

On the other hand, Article 41.2 asserts an understanding of constitutional rights as relational, giving express form to Nedelsky's (2012, p. 17) argument that 'what rights actually do is structure relations, which in turn, promote or undermine core values, such as autonomy, security or equality'. Her assertion is that a relational approach to law and rights allows us to analyse rights claims and contestations in terms of 'how they structure relations' and the consequences of this ordering. She treats rights not as 'trumps' but as 'rhetorical and institutional means for implementing core values such as liberty, security, autonomy and equality' (Nedelsky 2011, p. 74). By values Nedelsky is referring to any of 'the big abstractions used to articulate what a given society sees as essential to humanity or to the good life for its members' (ibid., p. 41). A relational analysis of rights can help reveal how existing law is contributing to the problem and suggest how it could be shifted to promote rather than undermine relations conducive to the value at stake, such as dignity or autonomy, equality or affect. Nedelsky poses a series of questions that usefully allow a relational approach to rights to be examined:

1   Examine the rights dispute to determine what is structuring the relations that have generated the problem. How is law structuring the relevant relations, and how is that structuring leading to conflict?
2   Having established this context, the next question is what are the values at stake?
3   The third is to ask what kinds of relationships would foster those values.
4   The fourth is to determine how competing versions of a right would structure relations differently.

ibid., p.36

What role, then, have existing laws and rights interpretations played in constructing the disadvantage and devaluation that attaches to dependency work, and the relationships that sustain this disadvantage? We know that law has played a powerful, often coercive, role in structuring relationships of dependency to the disadvantage of carers through the taxation and welfare codes, through employment and labour market policy and through its construct of the family. (Smith 2015). Yet Article 41.2 constructs a relationship between the state and the carer that envisages support for the relationship between carers and the recipients of care. As such, the guarantee foregrounds the centrality of the value of care to the collective endeavour, the 'common good', which, if expansively read, arguably binds the state to support care labour to respond to the vulnerability, the 'derivative dependency' (Fineman 2004) that care obligations place on care providers. In this sense there is some recognition of the ethic of care concern for relationality and responsibility, which is expressly referenced as a dimension of the (gendered) rights-bearing legal subject. However, the structuring of the relationship between caregivers and state under Article 41.1–2 has generally not been interpreted in ways supportive of carers' rights to autonomy and equality.

Article 41.2 has not fulfilled its (possible) role of articulating and grounding care as a core value, both in terms of acting as a driver for legislative action or as a strong interpretive norm in constitutional review. The superior courts have preferred not to respond to or query how existing law and policy has played a coercive role in structuring relationships of dependency to the disadvantage of carers, to deny the value of affect while simultaneously reproducing gender inequality, notwithstanding the express role set out for a 'supportive state' within the constitutional text. The rights disputes that have engaged Article 41.2 have fallen under three general categories: 1) the absence of state support for dependency work; 2) the recognition of property rights deriving from unpaid work in the home; and 3) justifying gender discrimination in the social welfare code.

Reliance on Article 41.2 as the basis for state support of the dependency work carried out by its subjects has proven unsuccessful before the courts. In *Sinnott*,[4] the failure of the state to meet the most basic educational needs of the plaintiff mother's disabled son over a number of years, thereby imposing inordinate care burdens on the plaintiff mother, was argued to have violated her constitutional rights under Article 41.2 and Article 40.1. While Ms Sinnott's onerous care burdens arose from the state's failure to meet her son's constitutionally protected right to education, and was a breach of his constitutional rights, her work evoked merely 'respect, admiration and compassion' according to then Chief Justice Keane. This care work did not implicate any constitutional right. The majority of the Supreme Court saw the mother's care work as part and parcel of a woman's ordinary duty of dispensation of love and affection and failed to see any connection between the state's failure to the child and its impact on his caregiver. The trope of the selfless, dutiful mother invited judicial praise, but nothing by way of substantive state support. In this context, therefore, we see how the state's failure to vindicate the constitutionally protected right to free primary education, structures relations of extreme reliance between carer and care recipient, impacting the autonomy and equality rights of both the former and the latter.

Denham J. in her dissenting judgment, was open to how an alternative reading of Article 41.2, in conjunction with the equality guarantee, could structure those relations differently in response to the core values of autonomy, equality and care. In a judgment attentive both to the gender context and the necessary contributions made by women's care work, she accepted that Ms Sinnott's rights under Article 41.2 could ground positive action on the part of the state, noting that:

> Article 41.2 recognises the significant role played by wives and mothers in the home. This recognition and acknowledgement does not exclude women and mothers from other roles and activities. It is a recognition of the work performed by women in the home. The work is recognised because it has immense benefit for society. This recognition must be construed harmoniously with other Articles of the Constitution when a combination of articles fall to be analysed.[5]

This requirement of harmonious construal between Article 41.2 and other constitutional provisions, which Denham J. applied in respect of the relationship between Article 41.2, the equality guarantee in Article 40.1 and the right to education, is a rare isolated attempt to animate a rights-based understanding of care relationships, in this context, by means of the constitutional guarantee of education for disabled children, by reference to the principle of equality, that includes concerns for the autonomy and equality rights of care workers. The values at stake in this rights claim importantly foregrounded include: the public good of education; the availability of that good to all individuals on an equal basis; and the corresponding autonomy deprivation endured by carers when the recipients of their care are denied access to their constitutional rights to education.

Similarly, in *L v L*,[6] the Supreme Court's construal of property rights as capable of being generated only through monetary contributions to the family home, thereby dismissing the contribution made by those performing unpaid work within the family home, overturned the High Court's view that Article 41.2 supported the concept of a constitutional trust in favour of the unpaid care worker. The structuring of property rights in matrimonial relationships on the basis of monetary work alone simply ignores the productive value of unpaid work (Roberts 1997). This additionally diminished the autonomy of unpaid carers and exacerbated the inequality of women care workers, particularly upon marriage breakdown, in the era prior to the introduction of legislative provisions on judicial separation and divorce and continues to impact many women in old age (Smith 2015).

Similarly, the relational consequences of the diminished value of equality between men and women and between all children in the state was in evidence in the interpretation accorded to Article 41.2 in *Lowth v Minister for Social Welfare*.[7] Here the courts choose to judicially affirm women as default caregivers, so as to legitimate the legislature's exclusion of fathers who act as lone parents from social security benefits designed to support lone parenting. The legislative decision to confine such benefits to deserted wives (since reversed through statute law), thereby entrenching relations of poverty and exclusion for lone fathers and their children, was justified, according to the Court, by the Constitution's express reference to the role of mothers, which the legislature was entitled to have recourse to in designing its welfare schemes. It was irrelevant that the consequence of this legislative decision was to increase the vulnerabilities of lone fathers and the children they care, despite it appearing in direct contravention to the view of the importance of (gendered) care work to the common good. Arguably, this inequality could have been offset had the court been willing to consider how an alternative version, along the lines of Fineman's 'Mother/Child dyad' (Fineman 1995), could structure relations more responsively to the common good value of care.

The next section switches the focus to the contributions of citizen-led fora, which have become increasingly popular in discourse on constitutional processes and change. The Convention on the Constitution's engagement with care and affect, which arose from its charge to consider the role of women in the constitution, instituted the possibility of breathing new life into Article 41.2. It also prompts wider conversations about the nature and meaning of 'the common good' or, in Nedelsky's terms, our 'shared values', and the role of constitutional rights in shaping a response.

The constitutional convention: reconfiguring care as a core value

Ireland's Constitution of 1937 has been the subject of a number of commissions and reports suggesting reform and amendment. The most recent, the Constitution on the Convention,[8] a 'hybrid mini public' (Goodin and Dryzek 2006), was an exercise in deliberate democracy designed to increase citizens' forms of participation in and contribution to policy, legislative and constitutional decision making (Harris et al forthcoming). Established in 2012, the Convention was charged with considering seven areas of the Constitution with a view to making recommendations for reform to be submitted for consideration to Government. It was also permitted to consider 'other relevant constitutional amendments' once its reports on its assigned matters were completed. The parliamentary resolution establishing the Convention committed the Government to 'provide in the Oireachtas a response to each recommendation of the Convention within four months'.

The membership of the Constitutional Convention comprised 66 citizens selected randomly from the electoral register, generally balanced in terms of gender, age, region, social class and occupational status (with some notable exceptions[9]), plus 33 parliamentarians and an independent chair. Its budget did not extend to the provision of on-site care facilities, which seems somewhat incongruous in light of the Convention's remit. It was assisted in its work by an academic and legal team whose role included assembling an advisory panel of experts and representatives of advocacy and civil society groups to present at the Convention's plenary meetings. The Convention established a forum for receiving submissions from members of the public and interested groups, which were considered during its interactive panel discussion with interest groups and academics. An important aspect of the Convention's working arrangements was that members were facilitated in small round-table discussions, designed to allow for detail of the issues under consideration to be explored. The Convention's working procedures then provided that the outcome of these discussions were fed back to the full Convention so that all members benefited from the group deliberations at individual tables. The plenary sessions, consisting of contributions from the academic experts and relevant advocacy groups, were recorded and also live streamed on the web. While academic research on the Convention's processes and operation is now beginning to emerge (Carolan 2015), pressures of space only allows for consideration of its discussions around Article 41.2 of the Constitution.

The Convention's second plenary meeting was held on 16 and 17 February 2013 and its purpose was to consider: i) amending the clause on the role of women in the home and encouraging greater participation of women in public life; and ii) increasing the participation of women in politics. Interestingly, the Convention was not directly charged with considering the constitutional position of caregivers per se, rather it was through engaging with the gender dimensions of unpaid work in the home that the wider issue of constitutional support for unpaid carers more generally emerged in its deliberations.

Following the weekend's presentations, discussions and deliberations, the Convention voted on a range of questions pertaining to Article 41.2 of the Constitution: 88 per cent voted to amend the clause; only 11 per cent voted in favour of its retention in its current guise; similarly, only 12 per cent voted in favour of deleting the provision in its entirety; as compared to 88 per cent in favour of its modification; 98 per cent recommended a change to make the clause gender-neutral to include other carers in the home; with 62 per cent voting to include carers beyond the home within the scope of the constitutional guarantee. Interestingly, the Convention then went on to consider the extent of the obligation to be placed on the state using a scale of 1–5, as set out below:

Noting that Article 41.2.2 says:

'The State shall ... endeavour to ensure that [mothers] shall not be obliged by economic necessity to engage in labour to the neglect of their duties in the home', what level of obligation should be placed on the State (on a scale of 1–5)?

1. Endeavour to Support	20%
2.	4%
3. Provide a reasonable level of support	35%
4.	12%
5. Shall support	30%

The average position held on this five-point scale was 3.22, which indicated that the Convention as a whole favoured a 'reasonable level' of state support for unpaid care. This dimension is of interest given the overwhelming vote in favour of providing support for carers in the home. It affirms in a deliberative democratic setting both the extent of the popular support for care as a public value and the need to untether care from strict gender roles.

The Government's response to the Convention's recommendation on Article 41.1–2 was to establish a task force in the Department of Justice, Equality and Law Reform to consider the matter. This shift from the reference to 'women's work in the home' to the possible reference to carers requires, according to the Minister, 'extensive consultations in relation to these new elements and to the appropriate choice of language for incorporation into the Constitution'. This task force was due to report in October 2014, but the report has yet to emerge. Indeed, only two of the Convention's 18 recommendations for constitutional amendment have resulted in governmental commitment for referenda.

Care as a constitutional right: some reflections

In the absence of the working group report on the Convention's recommendations, and in the face of governmental silence on the issue, I offer some very tentative reflections on the question of a revised commitment to care in the constitutional order.

From the debate and the text ultimately adopted by the Convention on the Constitution it is clear that it envisaged something more than a right in the form of a negative liberty that permits a choice to become a caregiver; a choice that depends upon the derivative dependency needs of the caregiver to be met through the private family or at the discretion of the welfare state. The Convention's deliberations show how it was cognisant of the realities of the human need for interdependence

(Harding, Chapter 8), which requires the strengthening of the public commitment to care work. To this end, it proposed to respond to the inequalities associated with care work by increasing the obligation on the state to provide such caregivers with a 'reasonable level of support'. The proposed amendment of the constitutional text is to strengthen the provision, shifting it away from a guarantee of 'imperfect obligation' (Whyte 2013) and towards a more definitive, albeit simultaneously contestable, standard of 'reasonable level of support'. This shift, were it ever to be realised, would reflect a collective choice by means of a referendum to place care and affect at the core of our democratically held values, as essential to our human endeavours. It expresses a key dimension to care ethics that a focus on care provides a better understanding of how people live and interact (see Harding, Chapter 8). This conceptualisation of the care right is positive in nature and demands efforts on the part of the state to ensure its realisation, vindication and protection. It would bind all organs of government, requiring the legislature to give effect to that collective choice and subjecting it to the oversight and protection of the courts through judicial review.

However, the contours of the right that might make it successfully into the constitutional text by way of a referendum are still very unclear and remote. The notion of constitutionalising a reasonable level of support for carers in the home suggests both a possibility of a shift in the nature and status of current supports for caregivers and in the nature of rights claims currently viewed as cognisable by the courts. In respect to the latter point, the Irish courts have been traditionally hostile to the kinds of rights claims that could possibly be made under the terms of Article 41.2 and other constitutional guarantees. This point invokes the distinction made by Costello J. between commutative and distributive justice in *O'Reilly v Limerick Corporation*,[10] where he stated that claims for material conditions to a minimum standard of living should be advanced before the legislature and not the courts. This line of reasoning was subsequently endorsed and repeatedly reiterated by the Supreme Court.[11] The current supports for carers, such as income support and other support services structured through the welfare state, are not, according to the Supreme Court, constitutional obligations. However, the direct language of the Convention's recommendation would suggest that these supports would, were such an amendment to succeed, no longer be beyond the direct scope of constitutional review. Indeed, the express inclusion by way of public plebiscite would expressly counter one of the reasons relied upon in the judiciary's continuing insistence as to the non-justiciability of social and economic rights, namely, the failure to include them in the various referenda to date on amending the Constitution.[12]

Further, the language suggested by the Convention makes possible reference to the requirement for state support as a universal entitlement. This requirement to provide support is not expressed as being predicated on the needs of carers, but rather as being supportive of the work that carers do. This would suggest a need for a rethink around the design of current supports, including income support, that are structured around the contributory principle, or around family means testing.[13] It also could suggest that any legislative attacks on the range, nature and quantum of care supports become subject to an independent rights standard, and would no longer be capable of being judicially explained away simply as desirable policy (Fennelly 2010).

Of course, the right to reasonable support could be furthered in other ways beyond state provision of income support, such as, for example, by state action around the reconfiguration of property rights within marriage or dependency relationships and the equalisation of social security rights for partners who carry out care work. However, the Supreme Court, in response to the legislature's attempt to provide for the equalisation of ownership of the family home among spouses, viewed this legislative wish to offset the economic vulnerability of the unpaid carer partner, as an impermissible intrusion into the autonomy rights of the family in *Re Article 26 and the Matrimonial Homes Bill*.[14] It is unclear whether a more substantive underpinning to Article 41.2 would be capable of tempering the dominance of proprietary rights and its structuring of relations of power and relations of inequality. Indeed, on this point, Nedelsky has argued against the constitutionalisation of property on the basis that property is a 'second order value' and a means to the values we seek to attain by way of constitutional rights, such as equality, life, liberty, autonomy and security (Nedelsky 2011, p. 255). Indeed, Ireland has direct experience of the problems created by property rights for legislative endeavours designed to tackle inequality, as the initial duty placed on employers to make reasonable accommodation for people with disabilities was found unconstitutional by the Supreme Court as a breach of employers' property rights (Smith 2001; 2010).[15] Thus, the proposed amendment to the text of Article 41.2 does not, of itself, unseat the privileged position accorded to property within the Irish constitutional hierarchy.

Given the reliance on the classic form of 'rights as boundary' judicial reasoning in this context, it is important to issue a note of caution about any possible advances thought implicit in the strengthening of the obligations of support for care workers under the terms of a redesigned Article 41.2. This shift in language as currently suggested can hardly prompt a move towards the wider institutional change required to underpin support for care work. Nedelsky suggests that what we need is a 'dialogue of democratic accountability' to offset the limitations of constitutionalism as a means of protecting rights from violation by democratic decision making via judicial review (Nedelsky 2008). The application of the traditional judicial review model assumes that the consequences of such a constitutional amendment is to hold the legislature's actions to account by reference to the meaning attributed to that right, to be worked out by the judiciary. And in the context of claims for care supports as rights, this has been approached largely within the traditional boundary model of rights protection, for example, as bolstered by the Supreme Court's concern for property rights and the autonomy of the family as a whole, as opposed to the attempt by the legislature to structure relationships of autonomy and offset the vulnerability of members within the family. This boundary model of rights protection leaves insufficient room for a relational analysis of rights, which, in the context of Article 41.2 jurisprudence as discussed above, remains largely unacknowledged.

Nedelsky's relational understanding of constitutional rights asserts that when constitutional rights hold ordinary laws to account they structure relations and this 'must be consistent with basic mutual respect, dignity and autonomy'. Thus, when actions of the legislature are held accountable to constitutional rights, the enquiry is whether the relations it structures – for example, those that currently persist with respect to carers – that create disadvantage, denial of autonomy, or deprivation, are consistent with core constitutional values, which includes the value of care to the common good. Nedelsky's argument is that, to further this dialogue between the legislature and courts about our core values, we need to rethink a system of rights protection that implicates not just the courts but broadens the means of deliberating over the meaning and extent of rights. Her specific example is an alternative social charter model put forward by a coalition of antipoverty groups in Ontario, which made disadvantage central to its commitment to social rights and which created institutional structures for broadening the means of reflecting on and implementing rights beyond the courts (Nedelsky 2011, p. 265–76). An opportunity for such broader reflection and engagement could yet emerge from another of the Convention's recommendations, referenced below, which has direct relevance to the question of care as a core constitutional value.

While it could be argued that the recommendation in favour of a redesigned Article 41.2 would entrench a clear social right within the constitution, the Convention on the Constitution did not expressly go on to consider the institutional dimensions to its enforcement. However, when the Convention completed its assigned tasks, it was permitted to consider two additional topics from a number of categories set out under 'any other amendments', following an extensive public consultation process. The Convention devoted its final plenary meeting to the question of economic, social and cultural rights (Convention on the Constitution 2014). While 85 per cent of the Convention favoured changes to the Constitution in order to strengthen the protection of economic, social and cultural rights, a considerable minority (43 per cent) voted in favour of referring the issue elsewhere for further consideration of the implications of possible reforms. Such a development, should it be progressed, would seem a suitable forum for considering ways of deepening the means of developing institutional reforms to rights advancement, understanding and interpretation.

Conclusion

The Convention on the Constitution's recommendation that the state would be required to provide a reasonable level of support for carers provides an enforceable (if unclear) standard by which the state's actions towards carers can be assessed. The Convention on the Constitution has provided an interesting impetus for the state to deliberate and reflect on the valuable role played by care in our collective endeavours. While the process, including the Convention's composition, procedures and outcomes, has attracted some media and academic criticism, it remains a useful start towards public deliberation over the content of our core values, and is in keeping with Nedelsky's vision for rights as a means of holding governments to account over core values through a dialogue of democratic accountability. Its recommendation was ultimately in favour of adding another clear social right into the constitutional text. To this extent, it supports those who assert that social rights are of equal weight to the civil and political rights traditionally provided for in constitutions (Gearty and Mantouvalou 2011, p. 108). The constitutionalisation of a right to care would require that legislative and administrative action is compatible with this right, which places it above the discretionary politics of the welfare state.

Some notes of caution around this development should be flagged, however. Given the judicial hostility that continues to persist around the status of social and economic rights within the Irish Constitution, it is important to reinforce that a shift in the constitutional text of Article 41.2 towards gender neutrality may be insufficient to ground support for care as a public value and an issue of rights. This is because this development takes place against the backdrop of pre-existing institutional provisions for rights protection and interpretation, and it does not move on to consider broader forms of accountability beyond the traditional judicial review model. There may yet be scope for future developments in this regard, following the recommendations made by the Convention on the question of economic, social and cultural rights, and it would be useful to consider the development of systems for deliberating the meaning of such rights to help ground a relational analysis of rights more generally, an approach that is, arguably, already implicit within Article 41.2.

Finally, the shift to gender-neutral language within the constitutional text does not, of itself, suggest an advancement as regards gender equality in the distribution of care work (Department of Justice, Equality and Law Reform, 2007). While 'a just structure of household relationships is crucial for the enjoyment of rights', the adoption of the language of gender neutrality against a backdrop of considerably gendered institutional structures around care and labour market work limits the nature of advancing our responses to care inequality. Given that the legislature, as the primary organ of advancing rights protection, continues to subscribe to gendered policy measures as regards care supports (Smith 2014), it might have been useful to consider the utility of binding the state towards guaranteeing the rights of both women and men to engage in care work, so as to include the performance of care work alongside labour market work. The proposed reformed constitutional text, as envisaged by the Convention on the Constitution, seems to confine state support for caregivers within the home, which leaves uncertain the constitutional position occupied by those who undertake other roles in conjunction with dependency work, or who would wish to do so given the availability of supports. In this sense the Convention's recommendation risks an adherence, particularly in the context of orthodox family forms, to a hard division between a caregiver and a breadwinner.

As Nancy Fraser has pointed out, the competing models of universal breadwinner and caregiver parity model will not achieve the kind of transformative change required given the pervasiveness of institutional structures that operate to disadvantage caregivers irrespective of sex. She suggests a universal caregiver model that assumes all persons should be permitted to choose to combine paid work with caregiving, which is ultimately dependent on a norm of good quality, well paid, part-time work, requires support in public policy (Fraser 1994). To this end, it would have been useful for the Convention to interrogate more deeply the links between Article 41.2 and the second aspect of its remit, namely, measures to encourage greater participation of women in public life. While the Convention recommended that the Constitution be amended to include an explicit provision on gender equality,[16] issues of the, broadly conceived, more equitable distribution of care work between the state, the market and the family requires attention to its gender (and race and class) contexts. To this end a consideration of the intersection of the terms of Article 41.2 with a reconfigured equality guarantee attentive to disadvantage, could usefully have been contemplated alongside a right to reconciliation, such as that included in Article 33 of the EU Charter of Rights and Fundamental Freedoms. In the meantime, it will be interesting to observe whether voters will get a chance to contribute to the collective concern around care as a core value and a possible constitutional right.

Notes

1 The right to earn a livelihood has been recognised as an unenumerated right under Article 40.3 of the Irish Constitution.
2 In an isolated decision, *DT v CT* (2002), Judge Murray sought to extend Article 41.2 to cover the care contributions of fathers, noting 'the Constitution … is to be interpreted as a contemporary document'.
3 A shift to gender neutral language was also recommended by the All-Party Committee on the Constitution, *Tenth Progress Report – The Family* (Constitution Review Group, 2006) p.120.
4 *Sinnott v Minister for Education* [2001] 2 IR 545.
5 [2001] 2 IR 545, 665.
6 [1989] ILRM 528; [1992] IR 77.
7 [1998] 4 IR 321.
8 See www.constitution.ie
9 Certain minority groups (for example, new Irish citizens and members of the Traveller community) were not represented, nor were members of the homeless community. The use of random sampling for such a small number of participants may explain this, though see Carolan (2015) for criticism.
10 [1989] IR 181.
11 These comments were endorsed by three Supreme Court justices in *Sinnott*. See also the comments of Murphy J. in *T.D. v Ireland* [2001] 4 IR 239, 316.
12 See Murray J at 316–17.
13 The current structure of qualifying conditions for carers means that less than 30 per cent of carers qualify for income support: The Carers Association (2009).
14 [1993] IR.
15 *Re Article 26 and the Employment Equality Bill* [1997].

16 Although the results here were not as emphatic as might have been expected: with 62 per cent voting in favour of an express clause on gender equality and 37 per cent voting against.

References

Ackerman, B. (1991) *We the People* Cambridge, MA: Belknap Press of Harvard University Press.
Boyd, S. (ed.) (1997) *Challenging the Public Private Divide: Feminism, Law and Public Policy* University of Toronto Press.
Busby, N. (2011) *A Right to Care? Unpaid Care Work in European Employment Law* Oxford: Oxford University Press.
Carolan, E. (2015) 'Ireland's Constitutional Convention: Behind the hype about citizen-led constitutional change' *International Journal of Constitutional Law* 13: 733–748.
Central Statistics Office (2009) *Quarterly National Household Survey – Carers*.
Constitution Review Group (2006) *Report of the Constitution Review Group* Dublin: Stationery Office.
Convention on the Constitution (2014) *Eighth Report of the Convention on the Constitution, Economic, Social and Cultural Rights*.
Department of Justice, Equality and Law Reform (2007) *National Women's Strategy* Dublin: Stationery Office.
Fennelly, N. (2010) 'Judicial Decisions and Allocation of Resources' *Advocate* 23: 48.
Fineman, M. (1995) *The Neutered Mother, The Sexual Family and Other Twentieth Century Tragedies* New York: Routledge.
Fineman, M. (2004) *The Autonomy Myth: A Theory of Dependency* New York: New Press.
Fraser, N. (1994) 'After the Family Wage: Gender equity and the welfare state' *Political Theory* 22: 591.
Gearty C. and Mantouvalou V. (2011) *Debating Social Rights* Oxford: Hart.
Gilligan, C. (1982) *In a Different Voice: Psychological Theory and Women's Development* Cambridge, MA: Harvard University Press.
Goodin, R. and Dryzek J. (2006) 'Deliberative Impacts: The macro political uptake of mini publics' *Politics and Society* 34: 219–244.
Harris, C. Farrell D., Suiter J. and O'Malley E. (forthcoming) 'Deliberation in Practice: Reflections on Ireland's Convention on the Constitution' *Journal of Policy Deliberation*.
Hogan, G. (2012) *The Origins of the Irish Constitution 1928–1941* Dublin: Royal Irish Academy.
Kittay, E.F. (1999) *Love's Labor: Essays on Women, Equality and Dependency* New York: Routledge.
Lewis, J. (2001) 'The Decline of the Male Breadwinner Model: Implications for work and care' *Social Politics* 8: 152–169.
McClain, L (2001) 'Care as a Public Value: Linking responsibility, resources, and republicanism' *Chicago-Kent Law Review* 76: 1673.
Minow M. and Shanley, M. L. (1996) 'Relational Rights and Responsibilities: Revisioning the family in liberal political theory and law' *Hyptia* 11(1): 4–29.
Mullally, S. (2007) 'Substantive Equality and Positive Duties in Ireland' *South African Journal of Human Rights* 23: 291–316.
Naffine, N. (1990) *Law and the Sexes: Explorations in Feminist Jurisprudence* North Sydney: Allen and Unwin.
Nedelsky, J. (1990) 'Law, Boundaries, and the Bounded Self' *Representations* 30: 162–189.

Nedelsky, J. (2008) 'Reconceiving Rights and Constitutions' *Journal of Human Rights* 7: 139–173.
Nedelsky, J. (2011) *Law's Relations: A Relational Theory of Self, Autonomy, and Law* Oxford University Press.
Nedelsky, J. (2012) 'The Gendered Division of Household Labor: An issue of constitutional rights' in B Baine, D Parak Erez and T Kahan eds. *Feminist Constitutionalism: Global Perspectives* New York: Cambridge University Press 14–47.
Noddings, N. (1984) *Caring* Berkeley, CA: University of California Press.
Nussbaum, M. (2000) *Women and Human Development: The Capabilities Approach* Cambridge: Cambridge University Press.
Pateman, C. (1988) *The Sexual Contract* Stanford: Stanford University Press.
Report of the Second Commission on the Status of Women (1992) Dublin: Stationery Office.
Roberts, D. E. (1997) 'Spiritual and Menial Housework' *Yale Journal of Law and Feminism* 9: 51–80.
Smith, O. (2001) 'Disability, Discrimination and Employment: A never ending legal story' *Dublin University Law Journal* 23: 148–174.
Smith, O. (2010) *Disability Discrimination Law* Dublin: Thomson Roundhall.
Smith, O. (2012) 'How Far From a Right to Care? Reconciling paid work and unpaid care work in Ireland' *Irish Jurist* 47: 143–167.
Smith, O. (2014) 'Litigating Family Status Discrimination' *Feminist Legal Studies* 22: 175–201.
Smith, O. (2015) '"Respect and Admiration": The invisibility of older women's care work in Ireland and the limits of formal equality'. Conference paper on file with author.
Smyth, C. M. (2016) 'Socio-Economic Rights in the Irish Courts and the Potential for Constitutionalism' in L Cahillane, J Gallen and T Hickey eds. Judges, *Politics and the Irish Constitution* Manchester University Press.
Tronto, J. (1993) *Moral Boundaries* New York: Routledge.
West, R. (2003) 'The Right to Care' in E Feder Kittay and E Feder eds. *The Subject of Care: Feminist Perspectives on Dependency* Lanham: Rowman and Littlefield 88–114.
White, J.A. and Tronto, J. (2004) 'Political Practices of Care: Needs and rights' *Ratio Juris* 17: 425–453.
Whyte, G. (2013) 'Amending the Clause on the Role of Women in the Home'. Presentation made to the Convention on the Constitution.

Chapter 12

Terms of endearment
Meanings of family in a diverse sample of Australian parents

Clare Bartholomaeus and Damien W. Riggs

Introduction

Terms such as 'family', 'child' and 'parent' are both over-determined and ambiguous in their lexical meaning. They are over-determined in the sense that each of these terms brings with them a number of normative assumptions (of, for example, genetic-relatedness between family members), whilst at the same time being so expansive as to encompass any number of family configurations and practices of care. The words people use to describe family, then, can constitute terms of endearment (i.e. they can express affective connections), yet at the same time endearment can be defined on very specific terms that may serve to exclude as much as they include. 'Terms of endearment' is thus used in this chapter as a broad category for how people describe those they consider kin, focusing on social experiences of family, kinship and caring. The contents of this category are explored here through a thematic analysis of the ways in which a sample of 60 Australian parents from across a diverse range of families spoke about what the word family meant to them, and how extended family members engaged with them when they had children.

Of course, terms such as family, child and parent differ significantly across geography and history. As a number of writers have noted, in many parts of the world families have changed from being about obligation to centring on care, intimacy, love, trust and mutuality (Gabb & Silva 2011; Jamieson 1998; Padilla *et al.* 2007). Furthermore, the forms families take also differ according to place and time. In many Western societies, for example, families are increasingly diverse (de Vaus 2004), therefore providing possibilities for broadening, and at times challenging, normative models of the family. De Vaus writes that whilst families have always come in 'many shapes and sizes', in contemporary society 'the range of choice and the do-it-yourself character of family making mean that there will be an enormous diversity of family forms' (ibid., p. xv). Authors such as Mason (2011), however, argue that with such diversification comes greater challenges in terms of how kin relationships are described. She argues that 'people are sometimes uncertain about and often work quite hard to negotiate and decide upon their kin relationships in these "new" (some are not so new) circumstances. What is more, there is not always a consensus in a family about it' (ibid., p. 64). Such uncertainty, Mason suggests, potentially serves to perpetuate normative assumptions about families due to the fact that, when faced with an ever-broadening range of ways to talk about families, individuals may often resort to commonly used and familiar ways of making sense of their experiences. This helps to explain Stiles' query as to how 'the nuclear family lives on in the discourse of family in the West, despite the majority of so-called "blended" families, single mums, single dads, the extended families of many different cultures, adoption, fostering and gay and lesbian relationships' (2002, p. 16).

Mamo's (2005) research with lesbians who had used commercial sperm banks to have children provides a clear example of how relatively 'new' family forms are often reliant upon normative narratives of kinship. Mamo argues that her participants' constructions of family were influenced by broader discourses about families and what is considered 'normal'. Thus, she argues, whilst assisted reproductive technologies and sperm banks can be used to have children in ways other than reproductive heterosex, the social meanings of family and who is counted as family are less often challenged (ibid., p. 248). Normative assumptions and models of families have also been identified in as diverse contexts as heterosexual parents conceiving via donor sperm (Grace & Daniels 2007) and transnational adoptive families (Howell 2003).

One particular normative assumption that appears in accounts of a diverse range of families is that of genetic relatedness. As several writers have noted (e.g. Grace & Daniels 2007; Logan 2013), despite increased diversification in terms of modes of family formation, genetic ties continue to be privileged. As a counter to this, there has been an increased focus on alternate ways of conceptualising families beyond genetic relatedness. Critical studies of families have, for example: 1) emphasised the importance of viewing families as constituted through practices (Morgan 1996; 2011) rather than genetics; 2) suggested the utility of thinking about 'family as a verb' (Stiles 2002); 3) noted that families are as much about relationships as they are about the way such relationships are 'displayed' to others (Finch 2007); and 4) explored the ways in which families are created beyond the norm of adult-child relationships, in the form of 'families of choice' (Weston 1991).

Taking up the points raised thus far in terms of family diversification, kinship norms, ways of describing family relationships and care, this chapter explores issues relating to the meaning of family and recognition, inclusion and exclusion, through the analysis of interview data collected from a diverse sample of Australian parents. The sample differed in regard to mode of family formation, and included people who became parents via adoption, foster care, commercial surrogacy or giving birth following heterosexual intercourse. This unique dataset of diverse families allows for an in-depth comparison of ideas about family and care, extending previous studies focused only on one family form. We explore similarities and differences across the cohorts in regard to ways in which they described what the word 'family' meant to them, and the terms on which recognition and inclusion was offered to participants by their extended family members. In doing so, we consider the ways in which meanings of family have implications for how we understand what it means to care, what it means to be in a relationship with another person, and how much of this is regulated by social norms in regard to what is most commonly seen as constituting a family.

Methods

The research reported in this chapter draws on interviews conducted as part of a project undertaken by the second author between 2011 and 2013. The research sought to identify similarities and differences between four cohorts of parents according to mode of family formation. Included in the total sample of 60 interviews were four cohorts of 15 interviews, with cohorts representative of families formed through adoption (A), foster care (FC), commercial surrogacy (CS) and giving birth following reproductive heterosex (RH). The research was approved by the Social and Behavioural Research Ethics Committee at Flinders University. Participants were recruited via support networks (e.g. Surrogacy Australia), through postings on social media and through snowballing from participants recruited through those sources.

Interviews typically lasted for 60 minutes and covered topics such as: journeys to becoming parents; decision-making in regard to mode of family formation; support experiences (in regard to general community, family and the government); and understandings of what constitutes family. The majority (n=45) of the participants were female, and the overall sample included both heterosexual (n=36) and lesbian or gay (n=24) participants. Most participants were members of a couple (n=54), with the remainder being single at the time of the interview.

For the purpose of the present chapter, interview responses to two questions were examined: 1) what does the word family mean to you?; and 2) how did your extended family and friends respond to you having children? Interview responses to these two questions were analysed thematically, in the approach advocated by Braun and Clarke (2006). All the extracts were read repeatedly by the first author to identify the most common responses given. Common responses were then grouped into themes, and the extracts within each theme were then read by the second author to ensure that the themes generated were indicative of broad trends across the data set in regard to the two interview questions under examination. Having grouped the extracts into themes, a representative sample of extracts (i.e. those from each mode of family formation that best illustrated each theme) was then selected for closer examination in this chapter. The analysis presented below thus reports on the most common themes identified amongst responses to each of the two interview questions, and within each theme examines differences and similarities between the interview cohorts.

Meanings of family to participants

Participants from all family forms, for the most part, described families expansively and inclusively. Key themes identified from the interview question that focused on the meaning of family to participants were: 1) family as togetherness, including living together; 2) family as love and support; 3) family as broader than genetics; and 4) family as a bounded entity. Each of these themes is now explored in turn.

Families as togetherness: sharing lives and living together

Ribbens McCarthy (2012) argues that 'togetherness' is a theme commonly drawn on when people discuss families in places such as the UK, Australia and the US, where it is used in terms of claiming identity through shared memories and a sense of collectiveness. Togetherness was the most common theme drawn on by participants to describe family in the sample analysed here. Amongst the sample 'family as togetherness' related to sharing lives and spending time with others, and was sometimes specifically discussed in terms of living together. Thus, emotional and physical aspects of togetherness were viewed as key to family, emphasising family as a practice of care.

Participants discussed family as the people they share their life with, thus suggesting an everyday intimacy and closeness:

> Sarah (FC): family – it's people with whom you are intimately bound, who you share your life with, who you support, who are the most important people – your core people in the world.

Another participant, Anne, brought up a number of ideas as to what family means, particularly that of togetherness and living together or closely, as well as caring for one another. In her response to the question about the meaning of family she also mentioned 'longitudinal commitment' and multiple generations, themes that were most likely to be mentioned by participants forming families via reproductive heterosex:

> Anne (RH): basically it means people, together, in some shape or form, who have some kind of shared journey, you know? Some kind of idea about growing together, a longitudinal commitment in some form or another. And intergenerational, and responsibilities for each other and care and commitment and, beyond biological. And often it's about living together, or living closely, or having shared arrangements or care for one another.

The theme of living together, as may be expected, was key to the families formed through adoption and foster care. Whilst some writers have argued that family does not mean household (see, for example, Finch 2007, pp. 68–9), people who 'do' families with few or no legal or genetic ties may draw on living together as a way to define their families. Indeed, living together and undertaking caring practices can develop emotional connections in foster care families (Nutt 2013). In these responses, family was often discussed only in relation to the family unit that lived together. Jane drew on this theme and also highlighted that family are the people 'you do life with', thus emphasising family as practice:

> Jane (A): a family is the members of a household in which you do life with really.

Other participants included both those in their household and their extended family:

> Emily (FC): it's a combination of things, including that the family all live in our household together, so my partner's family, my children's family, but also my family that I was raised with, my extended family and now my partner's extended family.

As these extracts suggest, for many of the participants physically being together, doing things together and sharing aspects of lives, were important to creating and maintaining a sense of family. This theme of families as living together was particularly important for the foster and adoptive households. For other family forms not targeted in this study, such as step and blended families, living together may be less relevant due to family members residing in or moving between more than one household (see, for example, McCarthy et al. 2003). Thus, whilst the participants in the study represented diverse family forms, parent/child families tended to be viewed as units of people who shared their lives and lived together.

Families as closeness: love and support

The interrelated themes of love and support were drawn on by participants from all four family groups, highlighting how these practices appeared to be valued regardless of household or legal or genetic ties. There is an increasing interest in the concept of intimacy in terms of families and personal relationships (see, for example, Gabb & Silva 2011; Jamieson 1998; Roseneil & Budgeon 2004). Jamieson argues that whilst intimacy is often understood in terms of 'knowing' and 'understanding' (disclosing intimacy), often more important in many relationships are 'unconditional love, support, help, and care' (1998, p. 160).

The theme of love was one commonly drawn on by interviewees who had engaged in commercial surrogacy. For example, Mark said:

> Mark (CS): [Family] means a whole lot of things in a way, but really what it comes down to is a group that support and love one another.

A number of participants in the cohort of foster parents also discussed the themes of love and support along with togetherness, emphasising things such as the emotional values of belonging and feeling at home:

> Amy (FC): Family means to me a place of security where you always know that you belong, you are accepted and that you are loved.

> Tom (FC): For me it means togetherness and support and unconditional love, and a place where you can be yourself and feel at home and not have to worry about what people think.

In these extracts families were framed as loving places where people were supported. It is perhaps unsurprising that the theme of love was emphasised by families formed through surrogacy. Given the fact that social opinion about commercial surrogacy is often negative and focuses on the commodification of both women's bodies and children, the narrative of love serves to rhetorically shift the focus away from these concerns and towards a normative understanding of loving families (Riggs & Due 2014). Similarly, the emphasis upon love amongst participants who were foster carers potentially reflects the fact that, in Australia, media representations of foster carers often depict them as mercenary and 'in it for the money' (Riggs & Delfabbro 2008). The binary of love and money has long been emphasised in research on foster care, and it is logical that participants who had undertaken foster care as a mode of family formation would emphasise the former over the latter. Family support was also important in terms of relations with and inclusion by the extended family, which is discussed later in the chapter.

Families of the heart: the (un)importance of genetic ties

The relative unimportance of genetic ties was another key theme identified across the interviews. Despite the increasing acceptance of diverse family forms, as discussed in the Introduction, there remains an emphasis upon genetic connectedness in Western societies (Finkler 2001; Grace & Daniels 2007; Nash 2004). This has been influenced by technological advances (such as in the ability to trace genetic origins), and can be seen in the popularity of television programmes such as *Who do you think you are?* (Logan 2013; Mason 2008). Participants in this research often mentioned genetic ties (referred to in terms of blood and biology), but also tended to suggest that family was not limited to them. As might be expected, addressing the (un)importance of genetic ties was salient for adoptive and foster parent participants, where they were not the genetic parents of their children. However, it was also evident in several responses from the families formed through reproductive heterosex.

A number of adoptive and foster parent participants explicitly stated that families were not necessarily genetically related. This included using family terms such as 'son' to describe the relations between family members:

> David (FC): I am not biologically related to my son but I consider him very much to be my son.

Another participant, Frieda, spoke about family broadly, and included friends made through adoption support groups:

> Frieda (A): I think that you can still have a family even though they are not biological. So yeah, family, I think is more about that relationship and how you consider those people. ... in terms of our connectedness we have made our own family and it's not all people that are related biologically or through adoption but also through friends as well.

Beyond the cohorts of adoptive and foster parents, other participants noted the ways in which the norm of genetic relatedness impacted upon their experiences of family. For example, Martha, who had undertaken commercial surrogacy, discussed her goddaughter's distress at not being able to include her on a family tree for school, which resulted in her claiming there was a family of the heart and a family of the blood. Martha explained this by saying:

> Martha (CS): I think you have the traditional family which is, you know, the family that you're related to by blood, and you have the family of the heart, which is people that are part of your family that you choose to be part of your family because they are.

Most of the participants who had formed families via reproductive heterosex also stated that family was broader than genetic ties (sometimes after being asked about this specifically), with no participants restricting family solely to genetics. For example, Megan emphasised diversity in terms of who is counted as family, relating this to support, rather than genetic ties:

> Megan (RH): I guess I think it's a very broad term, so it's not just like mum, dad, kids, its wider ranging than that – and not just extended family but just maybe, it could be anyone that you feel particularly close to. Doesn't have to be biologically related or anything like that. I think, I just think, for different people family is different things, so for a lot of people whose biological family hasn't been there or been supported or whatever, they might see family as people who aren't biologically related, more as people who have been there and been supported.

Overall, most participants explicitly discussed family as not restricted to genetic ties and were fairly broad with their definitions of who could be included as family. Some participants related this to choice and making their own family. However, it was clear that despite the diversity of families and the general acceptance that non-genetically related people can be family, genetics were a reference point for how people were able to discuss who was included as family (i.e. statements that genetics did not matter necessarily mentioned genetics). Whilst such statements were made, as shown in the following section, friends were not often included in ideas of family, even though non-genetically related children usually were.

Family as a bounded entity

Whilst genetics were not emphasised as central to parent/child relationships amongst the sample, understandings of genetic relatedness did play a role in the inclusion or exclusion of extended family and friends in definitions of family. Mason (2011) emphasises that who is seen as kin may be related to closeness, such as being close to one sister and not another. However, alongside family as relating to choice and whether people are liked or not, she also argues that '[m]ore conventionally defined relatives' were included as family regardless of closeness (ibid., p. 69). In the sample, some participants viewed particular friends as family, in some cases due to a lack of support from their families of origin.

Some participants included friends amongst those they counted as family in their lives. This was the case for some of the adoptive parent participants, who viewed friendships with other adoptive families in terms of being family. This was demonstrated by Emma who used family terms to describe friends' children:

> Emma (A): We have other adoptive families around us and I consider their children our nieces and nephews. And one family in particular, their son, he will tell everybody, 'cos our children come from the same children's home and they were in at the same time and he just automatically tells everyone that my son is his brother. And they get away with it (laughs). And I think ... I've found this with a lot of families.

Another participant included her extended family and friends in her definition of family, and excluded immediate family:

> Amanda (RH): including friends, maybe including immediate family – maybe not including immediate family, maybe including extended family. For me it is extended family and friends, mainly, and not so much immediate family.

Other participants were explicit in the limits of who was included in family, where friends were most often excluded. This was explained by Tess, who viewed family as meaning specific things which excluded friends, regardless of how close they were:

> Tess (RH): some of my family are not biologically connected to me but I don't see, I don't see friends as family – I see close friends as sometimes more intimate relationships than family but I don't see them as family. Family doesn't mean that you are intimate or that you are close, it's a different relationship.

These extracts highlight diversity amongst the sample in terms of who is included or excluded from the category of family. For some of the participants it was clear that there were parameters defining who was included in the family, whilst for others notions of family were much more expansive and nebulous. As Morgan writes, when discussing family practices, people are usually referring to certain practices which are viewed as 'different' somehow from other practices (1996, p. 11). Participants in the sample analysed here viewed parent/child relationships as family, yet did not always view broader relationships with extended family and friends in the same way. As will be explored in the next section, for extended family members, certain parent/child relationships were not automatically treated as constituting family, and not all children were recognised and included as family members.

Extended family members: meanings of family and varying levels of support and inclusion

In terms of the second interview question focused on in this chapter – and in comparison to the broadly inclusive responses participants gave in terms of defining family – participants typically reported that their extended families tended to have narrower views of family, resulting in varying levels of support and inclusion. Participants were asked about their extended family members' support of and responses to them having children. Across the four cohorts (adoption, fostering, surrogacy and giving birth following reproductive heterosex) there tended to be more similarities than differences in extended family support and inclusion. Importantly, there were a number of contextual reasons for levels of support, many of which did not directly relate to mode of family formation. Key themes relating to this question were: 1) full recognition and inclusion of children regardless of how families were formed; 2) uncertainty and misunderstanding due to unfamiliarity with a family form; and 3) the influence of an existing limited relationship with extended family.

Recognition and inclusion

A number of participants from all four cohorts emphasised that their child(ren) were fully recognised and included by their extended families. This was described in numerous ways, from child(ren) being 'embraced' by the family to legally changing a will to include grandchildren who were not genetically related.

One of the foster parent participants emphasised the inclusion of her son and the practical and emotional support provided by extended family. As with other participants, she described her son's relationship to other family members using family terms:

> Tamara (FC): [My extended family have] embraced him right from the start, as if he was my biological child. My mother's very supportive, she's a grandmother to him and my nieces and nephews are cousins to him ... mum's given me a huge amount of practical support – babysitting, transporting. My brother and sister give very strong emotional support.

What is interesting about Tamara's response is the use of the phrase 'as if he was my biological child', suggesting that being treated as genetically related is the privileged form of family. As mentioned earlier, families formed via genetic relatedness are often used as the norm against which diverse family forms are measured. Some participants felt it necessary to emphasise that their family relationships were like, and thus equal to, those formed through genetic relatedness.

Evelyn, who adopted her child, spoke of her mother's initial dislike of her plan to be a single mother, but then how she embraced her child, even changing her will to be legally inclusive:

> Evelyn (A): [My mother] changed her will to say that things get divided between her grandchildren and she wrote specifically it doesn't matter if they are blood grandchildren or adoptive grandchildren. So she just wanted to make a gesture you know, to say that they were included and she considers them her grandchildren.

In some cases, the strong support and inclusion of children by extended family can be interpreted to reflect the dominant view that wanting and having children is 'natural', however it occurs. For example, a family created through surrogacy was well-supported by their family and friends, which was linked to a long-standing desire of one of the partners to have children:

> Adam (CS): All of our family and friends were just happy for us and excited, and you know especially my partner's family, with him wanting a child all his life and everyone knowing it, they were extremely happy.

Together these extracts demonstrate that for some participants there was full inclusion offered by extended families, emotionally, practically and legally. Nonetheless, in some ways this acceptance reflects dominant ideas about families, where being 'like' a genetically related family is privileged, and the view that it is natural to have children.

Mixed responses: uncertainty and misunderstandings of unfamiliar family forms

Recognition and inclusion was less straightforward for some extended family members, where they were unsure about how children fitted into families, demonstrating unfamiliarity with different ways of 'doing' family. The ways in which some participants became parents challenged extended family members' preexisting concepts of families and how to have children. Thus, sometimes family members were both supportive and unsupportive or initially unsupportive but then more so.

A lack of familiarity with a particular family form was most evident amongst the extended family of participants who were foster parents. The unfamiliarity with this family form, including uncertainty about the children and the process of fostering, led to a reported lack of support and inclusion. This included participants saying that they were questioned as to why they would foster 'other people's children'. The view that foster parents are only carers of other people's children is evident in legislation and broader discourses about fostering (Riggs *et al.* 2007), thus likely influencing extended family members' responses. For example, Tom detailed the contradictory and uncertain acceptance of his children by extended family members, particularly his mother. It appears that a lack of understanding can lead to the devaluing of foster children, in that they are viewed as tenuous and able to be 'given back' if, for example, their behaviour is difficult to manage:

> Tom (FC): [Extended family is] one of those funny things, I mean they are there, they babysit, but it's this funny battle and a funny love hate thing that I have with my family around my children. Because on the one hand they would be the first ones to punch you in the face if you said 'oh they are not your children', but on the other hand they do these subtle things that I think 'oh would this be different if they had been born to me?'. Things like mum saying frequently in regard to out of control behaviours 'I don't suppose you could give him back' and I just think what are you on? You wouldn't say 'just give them to the orphanage' if you'd given birth to them.

Another foster parent, Angela, discussed the lack of support from extended family, relating again to a misunderstanding of fostering itself. Angela also noted that her extended family were somewhat supportive of her children to whom she is genetically related, suggesting both the privileging of children entering families in certain ways, as well as difficulties with existing relationships (discussed further below):

> Angela (FC): My extended family and especially my husband's extended family, they have not been supportive – 'what are you looking after other people's kids for? You're taking on other people's problems. They'll be nothing but trouble.'

A lack of understanding of a particular family form was also experienced by the extended families of adoptive parents. In one family, whilst the mother (i.e. the children's grandmother) changed her will to include her adoptive grandchildren, as discussed above, one sister did not understand what adoption meant, viewing the child as temporary:

> Evelyn (A): She definitely doesn't understand, she doesn't understand that he's mine, she seems to think that he's some temporary child that I am just minding. Definitely has the opinion that he is a foster child and he's not my child, she thinks of him as being – belonging to his birth mother. But I'm not

sure that she even gets adoption, like, I'm not sure if she understands that once you've adopted someone that they are totally yours.

Compared to this sister, Evelyn said that her younger sister was 'very supportive and as far as she's concerned they are her niece and nephew'. However, she received mixed responses from extended family members, including comments like 'I hope the child doesn't think that I'm going to pass on family heirlooms to her 'cos they are not real kids in the family'.

Some of the participants found that although there was initial apprehension or uncertainty with regard to their mode of family formation, this changed once extended family met the child(ren). For example, Mike expressed this clearly by emphasising a difference in what people imagine a child coming into the family will be like and what happens when they arrive:

> Mike (A): My family became – well my sister particularly – it's really only my sister, you know, loves them to death really. She, after being initially – they were both very cynical her and her husband – really embraced it so I think a different story between what people are imagining and then when they arrive.

However, the initial lack of support followed by acceptance may have related not to extended family members necessarily changing their mind about the family form, but accepting an individual into the family. In other words, individual children may be accepted but this does not mean that the idea of the normative family is challenged.

The extracts included in this theme highlight the dominance of a narrow, traditional version of family. So-called new family forms are measured against traditional family forms, not only in relation to genetic ties, but also in terms of children being permanent additions to the family (rather than temporary or for an unknown amount of time) and belonging to their parent(s) (where they cannot be given back to others). Thus, caring practices between adults and children are not always read in straightforward ways as constituting family.

Existing limited relationship with family

Importantly, the lack of support and inclusiveness experienced by some of the participants was sometimes the product of existing limited relationships with extended family members. Some participants did not necessarily have close, caring relationships with their extended family. This was sometimes, but not always, related to physical distance.

Limited relationships with extended family members were mentioned particularly by families formed via reproductive heterosex. For example, Ingrid noted that whilst she was emotionally close to her own family, she did not have a close relationship with her partner's family, even though they lived nearer to them:

Ingrid (RH): I speak to my family every day. But they don't live close. So I don't see them all the time. I normally end up seeing them every fortnight kind of thing. My partner's family we don't see as often, even though they actually live closer but we see them less and we don't speak to them as often either.

Other participants offered similar views of extended families and their involvement in their children's lives. For example, one participant stated that 'my mother overseas is not really someone I want them to have contact with' (RH).

A lack of closeness to extended family members was also mentioned by other cohorts. In one interview, an adoptive parent suggested that whilst her son was largely accepted by many family members, she was estranged from both sides of the family due to other reasons. These participant responses are a reminder that broader contexts of family relationships are important to understanding the inclusion and recognition of children entering families, in whatever form.

Discussion: policy and practice implications

Having outlined the findings of our thematic analysis, we now turn to consider the policy and practice implications of the findings in terms of care. Specifically, we return to the point we made in the introduction to this chapter, namely that the meanings people attach to family and practices of care have implications for how we understand what constitutes care and relationships, and how this is regulated by social norms. Perhaps the clearest implication of our findings is that for many people family recognition is contingent. Whilst it was certainly the case that many of the participants experienced inclusion from their extended family members, many of the participants did not. As we noted, in some cases this was unrelated to having children; some families simply are not that close.

Further, in terms of the contingent nature of recognition, there are three key implications of the findings that we believe have relevance to both policy and practice. The first of these relates to the ongoing hegemony of genetic relatedness, which has been documented elsewhere, including in the work we discussed earlier. In terms of policy and practice, our findings are interesting in terms of how even those who were critical of the norm of genetic relatedness were reliant upon it as a normative category against which to contrast other forms of relatedness. We are, of course, not naively suggesting that the privilege accorded to genetic relatedness can be easily done away with. Instead, our suggestion is that those working in the areas of policy and practice need to be finely attuned to the often subtle and nuanced ways in which genetic relatedness is continually treated as the norm. Our point, then, is less about the need for diverse families to be addressed in every policy or mode of practice (this should already be the case), but rather that policies and modes of practice should attend to the ways in which they may often be premised upon a norm of genetic relatedness.

The second implication is derived from the accounts provided by participants who had children through foster care (and, to a lesser extent, adoption). For many of our participants in these cohorts, there was a keen sense that their family was not adequately recognised, because both foster care and adoption are often viewed as not permanent. For us, this raises two concerns that have implications for policy and practice. The first of these is perhaps the most obvious: the need for public awareness campaigns that address misconceptions about foster care and adoption. Such awareness raising is important given the impact assumptions about permanency potentially have upon a willingness to provide care. Increasing awareness, it has been suggested, might help to address the current dearth of people willing to provide care (Riggs 2015). The second concern is perhaps counterintuitive to our first concern. It is important for spaces to be created in which care (and family) can be spoken about without permanency. The example of residential care, where paid staff provide care for children who cannot be housed elsewhere, illustrates the fact that a caring, family environment can be established without this necessarily being reliant upon the permanency of the adults involved (Riggs & Ogilvy 2015).

The final implication relates to the emphasis upon living together as a central definition of family. Research on couples who live apart continues to emphasise the relational strains that result not simply from being away from one's loved ones, but the strain that comes from non-recognition of relationships where partners do not live together (such as in the case of couples who 'live apart together', see Reimondos *et al.* 2011; Roseneil 2006). In addition to research on the non-recognition of couples who do not live together, research on families who live apart (such as in the case of Fly In Fly Out employees) suggests both the practical strains that can result from living apart (such as reduced support, sadness resulting from distance, challenges that arise when a family member returns home), and the symbolic strains that come from the relative invisibility of these family forms. Whilst increased attention has been paid to the practical strains in regard to industry policies and practices (e.g. see Gallegos 2005), less attention has been paid to the symbolic effects upon families of living apart. The symbolic dimensions thus warrant further attention in terms of how families who live apart are recognised.

Whilst there are potentially other implications to be derived from our findings in terms of care-related policies and practices, our focus above upon the effects of social norms in terms of how people understand care and relationships is the central point to be derived. As our findings suggest, no matter the family form or mode of family formation, social norms can impact negatively upon people's experiences of family. Whilst this may be most true for the most marginalised families, it is important to recognise the effects of social norms upon everyone.

Conclusions

The analysis that we have presented in this chapter highlights similarities across parents from the four cohorts (adoption, foster care, surrogacy and reproductive heterosex), in addition to issues that appear to pertain specifically to certain cohorts. The inclusion of four cohorts extends previous research by allowing a comparison of understandings and experiences of family amongst those who parent in diverse family forms. What is consistent across the four cohorts are the ways in which a norm of genetic relatedness and a focus on cohabitation remain a dominant way of thinking about families. This is perhaps unsurprising, given the fact that all the participants are, by fact of their status as parents, constantly negotiating their relationship to normative expectations about what it means to be a family. In other words, whilst some of the participants challenged normative expectations, they nonetheless recognised that such expectations exist. Rather than suggesting any of our participants (or their extended families) were dupes of normative discourses in relation to family, this appears to demonstrate the power inherent in social norms, and how even in sites of resistance such norms still shape what is made intelligible.

In conclusion, our findings from a unique dataset of four family forms have supported the claims of previous research carried out internationally by demonstrating that in the Australian context too there are normative demands that circulate in regard to families, despite the proliferation of new family forms. Indeed, we have demonstrated that even when inclusion is offered, in many cases it comes with conditions, or at the very least a comparison to normative understandings of family. As we noted in our introduction, then, terms of endearment – the ways we think about and describe those we consider kin – are inherently dilemmatic. They can engender feelings of belonging, love and care, whilst at the same time those very feelings can serve to exclude, especially when they are normatively framed in relation to particular privileged forms of family.

References

Braun, V., and Clarke, V. (2006) Using thematic analysis in psychology. *Qualitative Research in Psychology*, 3(2): 77–101.

de Vaus, D. (2004) *Diversity and Change in Australian Families: Statistical profiles*. Melbourne: Australian Institute of Family Studies.

Finch, J. (2007) Displaying families. *Sociology*, 41(1): 65–81.

Finkler, K. (2001) The kin in the gene: The medicalization of family and kinship in American society. *Current Anthropology*, 42(2): 235–263.

Gabb, J., and Silva, E. B. (2011) Introduction to critical concepts: Families, intimacies and personal relationships. *Sociological Research Online*, 16(4).

Gallegos, D. (2005) *Fly-in Fly-out Employment: Managing the parenting transitions*. Perth: Centre for Social and Community Research, Murdoch University.

Grace, V. M., and Daniels, K. R. (2007) The (ir)relevance of genetics: Engendering parallel worlds of procreation and reproduction. *Sociology of Health & Illness*, 29(5): 692–710.

Howell, S. (2003) Kinning: The creation of life trajectories in transnational adoptive families. *Journal of the Royal Anthropological Institute*, 9(3): 465–484.

Jamieson, L. (1998) *Intimacy: Personal relationships in modern societies*. Cambridge: Polity.

Logan, J. (2013) Contemporary adoptive kinship: A contribution to new kinship studies. *Child and Family Social Work*, 18(1): 35–45.

McCarthy, J. R., Edwards, R., and Gillies, V. (2003) *Making Families: moral tales of parenting and step-parenting*. Durham: Sociology Press.

Mamo, L. (2005) Biomedicalizing kinship: Sperm banks and the creation of affinity-ties. *Science as Culture*, 14(3): 237–264.

Mason, J. (2008) Tangible affinities and the real life fascination of kinship. *Sociology*, 42(1): 29–45.

Mason, J. (2011) What it means to be related. In V. May (Ed.), *Sociology of Personal Life* (pp. 59–71). Basingstoke: Palgrave MacMillan.

Morgan, D. H. J. (1996) *Family Connections: An introduction to family studies*. Cambridge: Polity Press.

Morgan, D. H. J. (2011) *Rethinking Family Practices*. Basingstoke, Hampshire: Palgrave Macmillan.

Nash, C. (2004) Genetic kinship. *Cultural Studies*, 18(1): 1–33.

Nutt, L. (2013) Foster care in ambiguous contexts: Competing understandings of care. In C. Rogers, and S. Weller (Eds.), *Critical Approaches to Care: Understanding caring relations, identities and cultures* (pp. 122–131). Abingdon: Routledge.

Padilla, M. B., Hirsch, J. S., Muñoz-Laboy, M., Sember, R. E., and Parker, R. G. (2007) Introduction. In M. B. Padilla, J. S. Hirsch, M. Muñoz-Laboy, R. E. Sember, and R. G. Parker (Eds.), *Love and Globalization: Transformations of intimacy in the contemporary world* (pp. ix–xxxi). Nashville: Vanderbilt University Press.

Reimondos, A., Evans, A., and Gray, E. (2011) Living-Apart-Together (LAT) relationships in Australia. *Family Matters*, 87, 43–55.

Ribbens McCarthy, J. (2012) The powerful relational language of 'family': togetherness, belonging and personhood. *The Sociological Review*, 60(1): 68–90.

Riggs, D.W. (2015) '25 degrees of separation' versus the 'ease of doing it closer to home': Motivations to offshore surrogacy arrangements amongst Australian citizens. *Somatechnics*, 5: 52–68.

Riggs, D. W., Augoustinos, M., and Delfabbro, P. H. (2007) 'Basically it's a recognition issue': Validating foster parent identities. *Family Matters*, 76, 64–69.

Riggs, D.W. and Delfabbro, P.H. (2008) Economies of care: Recognition and remuneration of foster carers. *Journal of the Association for Research on Mothering*, 10(1): 94–104.

Riggs, D.W. and Due, C. (2014) 'The contented faces of a unique Australian family': Privilege and vulnerability in news media reporting of offshore surrogacy arrangements. *Feminist Media Studies*, 14(5): 869–872.

Riggs, D.W., and Ogilvy, R. (2015) Professional carer experiences of working with young people in specialist care placements in South Australia. *Children Australia*, 40, 361–366.

Roseneil, S. (2006) On not living with a partner: Unpicking coupledom and cohabitation. *Sociological Research Online*, 11(3).

Roseneil, S., and Budgeon, S. (2004) Cultures of intimacy and care beyond 'the family': Personal life and social change in the early 21st century. *Current Sociology*, 52(2): 135–159.

Stiles, S. (2002) Family as a verb. In D. Denborough (Ed.), *Queer: Counselling and narrative practice* (pp. 15–19). Adelaide: Dulwich Centre Publications.

Weston, K. (1991) *Families We Choose: Lesbians, gays, kinship*. New York: Columbia University Press.

Chapter 13

'It has had quite a lot of reverberations through the family'

Reconfiguring relationships through parent with dementia care

Elizabeth Peel[1]

Introduction

In this chapter I explore the accounts of adult children caring for a parent with dementia. Dementia is typically understood to be an umbrella term for a large number of conditions, the most common of which are Alzheimer's disease, vascular dementia and fronto-temporal dementia. These are progressive – ultimately terminal – conditions that affect memory, communication, mood and behaviour. I examine the accounts of interactions with parents with dementia that fracture and reconfigure normative familial relationships. In so doing I suggest that, in the absence of a primary spousal carer, caring for a person living with dementia can necessitate particular issues for adult children that trouble notions of how we understand familial roles, responsibilities and 'duties'. This issue impacts a significant minority of British adults. There are estimated to be 670,000 informal family carers of people living with a dementia in the UK (Alzheimer's Society 2014). The total cost of dementia to UK society is estimated to be £26.3 billion, with £11.6 billion being contributed by the work of unpaid carers (Prince *et al.* 2014). Unpaid care to older or disabled people provided by a family member is typically understood to encompass personal care and/or practical household tasks and/or paperwork and administrative duties.

A classic memorial lecture given by Elaine Brody (1985), reflecting on the state of gerontological research in the USA thirty years ago, has many current resonances. Brody argued that 'parent care has become a normative but stressful experience for individuals and families'. And, moreover, she suggested that the experience of caring for a parent was not a brief or short-term concern for adult children, but rather that 'it is *long-term parent care* that has become a normative experience – expectable, though usually unexpected' (p.19/21 original emphasis). What is interesting and resonates today, I would suggest, is the tension between the notion of a lengthy period of parent care as being normative *and* unexpected. In many contexts, and in many families, there is a cultural expectation that care work will be undertaken by adult children at some point during the life course, but at an individual level this (often) gradual move into a carer role may not be anticipated or prepared for. Caring for a parent with dementia provides a particularly illuminating focus for considering issues of familial care provision for older adults, because care is needed long-term (on average ten years following diagnosis), and the degree and reach of dependency increases incrementally and covers cognitive, communicative, social and practical domains. Returning to Elaine Brody (1985), she used the term 'family homeostatis' to signal the destabilising effect that a parent's increased dependency has on families – 'whether it is precarious or well-balanced – [it] must shift accordingly' (p. 22).

It is also important to acknowledge that parent care does not necessarily map on to a particular age or stage in an individual's life course. There is extensive literature on young carers (for example, Aldridge and Becker 2003), and in the context of caring for a parent with dementia – which is the focus here – while the majority of those informal carers engaged in parent care will be in their 50s onwards, a significant minority of people (estimated to be over 40,000 in the UK alone, Prince *et al.* 2014) are diagnosed with dementia under the age of 65. Hence, children in their teens and adult children in their 20s and 30s are also positioned as engaging in parent care (Allen *et al.* 2009; Svanberg *et al.* 2010; 2011). In this context, Allen, Oyebode and Allen's (2009) grounded theory study, based on data from twelve young people (aged 13–23) caring for a father with younger onset dementia, identified five main elements impacting on their well-being, which they labeled 'damage of dementia', 'reconfiguration of relationships', 'strain', 'caring' and 'coping', and described as constituting an overarching theme of 'one day at a time'. In terms of the reconfiguration of relationships – a theme I explore later in this chapter – they found that most participants 'said that they had lost their "real father"' (p. 466), and that all their participants had a role in the care of their father. These authors suggest that their study 'highlighted the ways in which stress related to having a father with dementia proliferates and affects almost every area of life, leading to very high levels of distress' (Allen *et al.* 2009, p. 477). Therefore, it is important to recognise that parent care in the context of dementia is not solely the preserve of middle-aged adults onwards, although numerically this is the largest group of familial carers in this context.

Caring for a dependent parent is a stressful thing to do (Starrels *et al.* 1997), and there is extensive psychological and social scientific literature that documents the association between negative mental and physical health and well-being and providing this type of informal care (see Amirkhanyan and Wolf 2006; Etters *et al.* 2008; Lilly *et al.* 2012; Shulz and Sherwood 2008). In terms of the early literature focusing on negative mental health experiences in adult children caring for a parent with dementia, Dura *et al.* (1991) found 34 per cent met the Diagnostic and Statistical Manual (DSM) depression or anxiety criteria, compared to eight per cent of the matched controls in their study during the same time period. More recent survey research with 120 US and Australian carers (O'Dwyer *et al.* 2013) found that 26 per cent had contemplated suicide in the previous year and almost 30 per cent reported they were likely to attempt suicide in the future. Depression predicted the presence of suicidality in this sample, and the authors concluded that their findings suggest 'an alarming number of people contemplate suicide while caring for a family member with dementia' (p. 1188). The overarching message from this literature has been summarised as 'caregiving often results in chronic stress, which compromises caregiver's physical and psychological health. Depression is one of the common negative effects of caregiving. ... Caring for a person with dementia is particularly challenging, causing more severe negative health effects than other types of caregiving.' (Shulz and Sherwood 2008, p. 26) As I go on to discuss, this well-established finding of high levels of carer stress and strain was echoed in my own research with Rosie Harding. Most questionnaire respondents in our 'Duties to Care' project (78.5 per cent, 142) were 'under strain' as defined by their responses to the, well-used, Caregiver Strain Index (Robinson 1983) that formed part of a more wide-ranging questionnaire (Harding and Peel 2013). In the following section I describe the empirical data on which the rest of this chapter is based. However, before doing so, it is worth emphasising that this chapter contributes to a number of arguments associated with a critical health and discursive psychological perspective (Murray 2014; Edwards and Potter 1992; Peel et al. 2005).

First, and most obviously, the literature on informal carers generally, and in the dementia context specifically, has largely focused on the experiences of heterosexual spousal carers (Braun et al. 2009; Calasanti 2006; Hellstrom et al. 2007; Hong and Coogle 2016). While this particular group of informal carers is, of course, significant and many insights from this group are transferrable into other relational contexts, this focus has arguably led to a marginalisation of the perspectives of adults who provide parent care. In my dementia projects, of the total sample of 185 original questionnaire participants[2] 33 per cent (62) were caring for a parent (see also Harding and Peel 2013; Peel and Harding 2014; Peel 2014). The study was explicitly framed as adopting an inclusive definition of carer. The participant information sheet stated:

> The study aims to be inclusive of all people who care for someone with a diagnosis of dementia. The person that you care for could be a relative or friend that either lives with you or lives in a residential setting. You may provide day-to-day care or you may not (or no longer) be responsible for daily care. Caring for a person with dementia includes emotional care, or emotional and practical care.

This construction of carer may have contributed to a third of participants caring for a parent. I contend that foregrounding the experiences of this sub-set of carers may offer a critical lens on family dynamics and the processes and practices of caring more broadly. Thus the framing of the study as explicitly inclusive, and the desire to draw attention to the understandings from an under-researched subgroup of family carers, fits with a critical psychological perspective (see also Riggs and Peel 2016).

Second (some), forms of critical psychology and discursive psychology enjoin us to take language seriously, and view discourses – as marshalled by people – as actively constructing particular representations of the social world and, in this instance, caring relationships. Thus, bearing these concerns and foci in mind, in the analysis that follows I take a broadly discursive psychological approach to these carers' talk (Edwards and Potter 1992), being mindful of the types of actions (that is, justifying, complaining) participants are accomplishing, as well as the topical focus of their accounts of caring. However, I apply a critical realist rather than a thoroughgoing social constructionist perspective to carers' accounts for feminist/political reasons. Social constructionism may risk *potentially* presenting participants' accounts in a somewhat detached, even slightly ironic fashion. This sits uncomfortably alongside my own position as an ex-carer of a parent with dementia who is personally and politically supportive of carer's experiences and perspectives (Peel and Harding 2015), therefore a critical realist epistemological stance recognises the grounding of participants' accounts in their lived reality. Having said this, I am mindful of the *actions* accounts are achieving in their local context, for instance, presenting oneself positively by attributing responsibility to external factors, or through comparison. To offer one concrete example from later in the chapter, while Laura's account of her brother's contribution to their father's care – 'unfortunately my brother just said "I don't care, let-you do it, you do it"' – is a reflection of her reality, it simultaneously functions to construct her via contrast as a responsible, caring daughter. So the positioning, by participants, of siblings as behaving in problematic, infantalising or disruptive ways also serves as a form of positive self-representation.

Third, my aim in this chapter is to tease out some of the different ways that concepts of duty, worry, care and vigilance are talked about in these interview and focus group data with informal carers currently, or previously, providing parent care. The dialectic tensions of dependence versus interdependence (Brody 1985) can be felt particularly acutely in the dementia care context wherein the person with dementia may exhibit behaviours that challenge those around them, and become increasingly 'child-like' (see also Riggs and Peel 2016). The risks of infantilising[3] people with dementia, communication difficulties and cognitive impairments are real and problematic, and the notion of role-reversal has been argued to be 'a superficial concept at best' (Österholm and Samuelsson 2015, p. 23). Role-reversal may well, on one level, be a superficial concept, but as I go on to highlight in this chapter, the role demands associated with caring for a parent with dementia are such that normative familial relationships are fractured and reconfigured, in ways which can leave families negotiating conflictual situations.

Duties to care and dementia talking: method

As mentioned earlier, this chapter is based on qualitative data collected through the interlinked 'Duties to Care: A socio-legal exploration of caring for people with dementia' and 'Dementia Talking: Care, conversation and communication' projects. As Table 13.1 indicates, semi-structured interviews and focus groups were conducted with eleven adults caring for either a mother (n=9) or a father (n=2)

Table 13.1 Interview and focus group participant demographic information

Pseudonym	Age	Class	Person care for/age	Dementia type	Residence of PWD	Caring status
Victoria (I)	63	Middle class	Mother, 88	Alzheimer's	Own home	Current
Carlos and Anne (I)	58	Working class	Father, 87	Alzheimer's	Own home	Ex-carer
Jan (I)	58	Working class	Mother, 87	Vascular dementia	Residential home	Current
Sue (I)	59	Working class	Mother, 87	Vascular dementia	Residential home (self-funding)	Current
Derek (I)	65	Working class	Mother, 86	Vascular dementia	Own home	Ex-carer
Maureen (I)	60	Middle class	Mother, 95	Alzheimer's	Nursing home (self-funding)	Ex-carer
Chloe (FG1)	58	Middle class	Mother, 84	Vascular dementia	Nursing home	Ex-carer
Laura (FG1)	55	Working class	Father, 88	Vascular dementia	Nursing home	Current
Peter (FG1)	58	Working class	Mother, 92	Mixed: Alzheimer's and Vascular	Own home	Current
James (FG2)	47	Middle class	Mother, 77	Vascular dementia	Own home	Ex-carer
Alan (FG4)	59	Working class	Mother, 89	Alzheimer's	Own home	Current

with dementia. The mean age of participants was 58 (range 47–65). All participants were white and heterosexual, aside from one bisexual interviewee (Sue). Interviews (averaging 1 hour 37 minutes) were conducted in participants' homes between November 2011 and January 2012. Most interviews were conducted in the Midlands, three were conducted in the north of England and two in the south. Fifteen participants attended four focus groups held in two large cities and two towns in central and southern England between September and December 2011. In total 8 hours 40 minutes of focus data were collected, with each group lasting around two hours.

The focus group questions placed more emphasis on the legal and practical aspects of caring, while the interviews were more focused on communication. There was, however, overlap in the questions asked in the interviews and the focus groups. Participants were asked in both studies about their experience of caring for someone with dementia, and what, if any, support they received from others. Focus group participants were asked about both negative and positive views about dementia care services, while interviewees were asked about 'low' and 'high' points in their experience of caring.

Fracturing and reconfiguring normative familial relationships

In the analysis that follows I explore core concepts connected to duty, worry, guilt and vigilance, and the ways in which caring for a parent with dementia can fracture and reconfigure normative familial relationships with reference to two main themes. The first is *sibling conflict and collaboration*, the second is *parentification and infantalisation*. Parentification is a term used to describe how carers' 'felt that they were cast in a more parental role' (Allen *et al.* 2009, p. 467) and, as we see below, this concept can be usefully applied to these data. With regard to overt reference to duty, it was the men in this sample who made reference to filial relationships creating the conditions for them taking on caring responsibility for their parent (McDonnell and Ryan 2013). As identified in the literature on male caregivers in dementia (ibid.), the men who were carers in this research talked about their experiences in a way that was less 'emotional' than the women caring for parents. A 'factual' account of a sense of duty and familial role was presented by Derek, for example:

> I think when I actually became my mum's fulltime carer, it would have been very, very difficult to move her. ... I don't expect a medal or anything but the reason I did it was because she's my mum, and it was my duty. I'm her son. And it was my duty to care for her. You know, she cared for me when I was a child, so I-you know, I felt, I've got to do this, because she's my mum ... in a nutshell, I-I took it on because it was my mum.

Here, Derek explicitly accounts for the caring work he undertook with his Mum in terms of duty and in terms of reciprocity of roles – 'she cared for me when I was a child'. This emphasis on familial caregiving expectations is reminiscent of the 'custodial' task-focused and deficit-based style of caring identified in Ward-Griffin *et al.*'s (2007) Canadian study of mother–daughter dementia caregiving relationships; an approach in which they identified duty as the defining characteristic. In contrast to findings from a study of, predominantly female, Australian Italian dementia caregivers (Benedetti *et al.* 2013), Carlos – an Italian male carer in this study – drew on the familist values associated with southern European societies: 'I didn't want to look after my dad but I promised, on me mum's deathbed I promised that I'd look after him, er and I won't go back on my promise. So I took on that responsibility, but not knowing what I-what was-what was ahead of me.' (Carlos) So, for Carlos, a promise and commitment to his mother underpinned the caring role he undertook for his father. Other participants who were acting as full-time carer for their parent, such as Alan, positioned themselves as being 'on a knife-edge myself', but the demands of caring were also discussed by those participants whose parent was now residing in a care home.

The ongoing demands of caring in a non-resident capacity were most often framed in terms of worry, vigilance and guilt. Jan – whose mother had moved into residential care – explicitly recounted how: 'the worry never goes away, you wake up with it, you wake up with this sinking feeling (laughs) in the pit of your stomach, oh, you know, what's going to happen today, is she going to be all right'. The extreme case formulation (Pomerantz 1986) 'never' and the ever-present constancy of the worry, conveyed as both unconscious and conscious, worked to highlight the embeddedness and the degree to which this sense of worry permeates Jan's relationship with her mother now she is not providing day-to-day care. Chloe, reflecting on her relationship with the nursing home care provision during the last months of her mother's life, also emphasised some of the challenges and concerns connected to care being provided in this context.

> One of the most important things for me was knowing, especially when Mum was in bed, that she wasn't left for hours. ... the thought of her, not having anybody go in that room for three hours was horrendous, and that always used to worry me and-and I often used to think at different times during the day, I wonder if Mum's seen anybody today. ... And, of course, once she was in bed, they did have to go every two hours to turn her. But it was that-it was that horrible feeling of thinking that-have they forgotten she's in her room, that was really really important to me.

We can see in Chloe's account a similar emphasis on the anxiety created through not 'knowing' whether and when her Mum was having contact with care staff when she was bed bound. Chloe had worked with staff in the nursing home to operationalise a chart in which staff documented when they went into her mother's room (Edwards 2014). Previous research has emphasised the difficulties experienced by long-distance caregivers, for example, over half of the participants in Koerin and Harrigan's (2002) study reported at least one negative impact on employment and having given up leisure activities, hobbies and holidays. Relationships with partners can be strained and friendships can be lost due to the commitments of providing care and the associated lack of time (Edwards 2014; Suitor and Pillemer 1993). Chloe, here, conveys the 'horrendous' 'worry' and 'horrible feeling' created through caring at a distance and being reliant on care workers to ensure regular contact with her mother. Sue also conveyed this sense of anxiety regarding her mother: 'she's gone into a nursing home now but my sister and I both still have to be quite vigilant, I'd say'. Thus, keeping a careful watch for potential danger or difficulty, when parents were in a residential care setting, was in part about monitoring the provision and quality of care in these settings, as well as the deterioration of the parent with dementia. Edwards (2014, p. 176) used the phrase 'orchestrator in the background' to reflect the demanding commitment that monitoring and arranging care and services is for distance caregivers.

Further examples of the fracturing of normative familial relationships were conveyed through the challenges of remote caregiving and the lack of control or certainty regarding the parent with dementia's health: 'It's a horrible thing to have to put your mother in a home; you have to get over that one. And then the slow decline and then the phone might ring any minute, your mother's had another blah, blah.' (Sue) Or as Maureen emphasised:

> the constant worry of who was going to be on the phone next; was it going to be the police again to say she'd been found wandering, ah, was it the neighbours to say that she'd been aggressive and unpleasant and erm, didn't know where she was; erm, was it going to be the carers to say she'd had a fall, or what was the next crisis going to be?

The concept of compassion fatigue has been well documented with respect to professional healthcare providers, but has only been explored in a limited sense with familial caregivers (Day *et al.* 2014). Day, Anderson and Davis's (2014) interview research with adult daughters caring for a parent with dementia concluded that this group are at risk of the combination of helplessness, hopelessness, inability to be empathic and sense of isolation that results from prolonged exposure to perceived suffering. Chloe, for example, emphasised another difficulty with distance care-giving, 'if you don't go, you then feel terrible for not going', and Victoria articulated the chore-like character of caring for her mother who was living in her own home:

> It feels like sort of like a chore, you know you've got to keep communicating with this person because if you don't it's going to get even worse so that-because the faster she deteriorates the bigger the problem for my sister and I looking after her. You know, even if we're paying other people to do it, it's still actually, in one way or another, is more of a problem because it's us who's having to take decisions, it's us who's having to be the intermediary, even if we do less and other people do more. So-so keeping her healthier for longer, there's like a-there's something in it for me, but it is a chore. There-no, I would say there's no pleasure in it whatsoever, no, no.

Therefore the lack of 'pleasure' in caring for a parent with dementia, the worry, guilt and vigilance were all evident in the fracturing of normative familial relationships between adult child and parent, for the adult daughters. Duty and responsibility were also foregrounded, most explicitly in the adult sons' accounts. The reconfiguring of relationships – particularly regarding being mis-perceived – was present in adult sons' but not daughters' accounts. Derek, for example, provided a lengthy account of his 'mum wanting me to- to go to bed with her', which precipitated her being admitted to hospital:

> It's terrible to think that your-your own mother doesn't know you. ... she came up to my bedroom, and erm, it-it was quite obvious from the things that she was saying to me that she thought I was her husband, because she was saying things like 'you don't want to get in-you don't want to be in bed with me, do you? Why? What have I done? Why won't you get in? Why won't you come to bed with me?' So I said 'look, Mum, I'm not Dad. I'm Derek. I'm your son'. 'How can you be my son? I'm not-I haven't got a son.' Well, she-she became very, very aggressive. We came back downstairs, and uh, then she started banging and slamming all the doors, and knocking on the walls ... I didn't know how to cope with it, Liz, so I thought 'what am I going to do?' So in the end, I phoned ... and a very, very nice doctor came out ... [he said] 'it's not fair on you. You can't possibly cope with your mother in this condition.' So he got my mum admitted.

Behaviour that is challenging to others – known as behavioural and psychological symptoms of dementia (BPSD) – is a common experience in caring for a person with dementia, and often precipitates a move into a hospital or residential setting and the initiation of anti-psychotic medication (Harding and Peel 2013). In Derek's case their relationship being (temporarily) reconfigured as wife and husband, rather than mother and son, was vividly recounted, and Derek's challenge to his mother's perception of reality precipitated not only 'very aggressive' behaviour but her removal from her home. The gulf between who, and how, the person was and their current behaviour was especially marked in the accounts of sons caring for their mothers. Derek also, for example, reported the disconnect between his mum swearing at him and his understanding of her previous self: 'my mother wouldn't say boo to a goose she was a very gentle lady'. James discussed the reconfiguring of his relationship with his mother in different terms:

> Strange to say, even though she wouldn't recognise me as her son, deep down there was something there, because I was the one person she would be at most ease with, is probably the best way I can put it. But it got to the stage whereby, for example, my Mum would see my car in the front drive and say 'oh my boyfriend is here, my boyfriend is here'. ... The first time this happened I thought 'now what do I do now?' [Laughs]. So I decided to change my clothes, my top and trousers, and suddenly I was her boyfriend. And this went on for quite a few months and it was not only just once a day, every time she saw my car – it might be four, five, six times a day. ... That was the most, you could say, the strangest story I could, I could quote. Erm, but I took it as, erm, a compliment, because I was assuming she was going back to times when she-when my father-late father was, ah, courting my-my Mum.

James, here, recounts engaging in role-play with his mother in order to maintain her reality that he was 'my boyfriend' rather than her son. While use of deception, on both sides, has been described with respect to mothers and daughters (Ward-Griffin *et al.* 2006) it is interesting in James' case that by actively engaging in his mothers' reality — and rationalising the situation as 'a compliment' — this circumvents any BPSD-related aggression. James' positioning of these relationship reconfiguring events as the 'strangest story' in his experience of caring for his late mother sits very differently to Derek's experience of not 'know[ing] how to cope'.

There were other ways in which caring for a parent with dementia fracture and reconfigure normative family relationships: sibling conflict and collaboration; and parentification and infantilisation. I now go on to to discuss these before drawing some conclusions about the nature of parent care in this context, and what might be understood about care more broadly from these data.

Sibling conflict and collaboration

Previous research has emphasised that 'stresses experienced during the development of parental dementia seemed to increase conflicts in the family' (Barca *et al.* 2014). An Australian survey, for instance, identified family conflict in the context of younger onset dementia by a large minority of carers (41 per cent) (Luscombe *et al.* 1998), and in these data it was only Maureen — who had been estranged from her brother for many years prior to her mother developing dementia — who reported that having 'everything … on my shoulders' would have been alleviated by 'having a sibling to share it with'. For most participants relationships with siblings were recounted as a significant source of additional stress: in the case of brothers, 'unfortunately my brother just said "I don't care, let-you do it, you do it"' (Laura) and 'I did feel angry about it, because I didn't get any help from him' (Derek); or because of role conflict; or other differences created by the demands of caring for a parent who does not have capacity. Conflict about money — and discomfort about having uncertainty or distrust in their siblings' approach to spending money under power of attorney regulations — was discussed in a number of the female carers' accounts. Chloe, while emphasising that her sister 'didn't do anything remiss' did not 'know if she ever paid Mum back for those few bits she bought that day', and Sue discussed a range of issues that she and her sister had 'come to blows about', including money:

> What I'd like is a calm interchange because Bev's got her own views about how to deal with my mum. … And we have come to blows about I don't think we should do that. … I think maybe we were just so stressed [in the hospital] and we just had a big bust up. … And the money was a big thing, keeping an eye on the money. Bev would just go into her account and I'd say 'what's the money going on?' 'Why are you saying I'm pinching mum's money?' 'Well no, I'm not, we need to keep a check on it', we've got power- … And I thought

we're going to need this money. ... it's going to run out and we need as much as we can to pay this bill because once it's run out we're in shit street. So we've fallen out about-not about the money but, you know, we needed to sort all that out and the actual day to day caring. ... she's got the cash card but I keep my eye on the bank account. ... I think it has affected our relationship, definitely, my sister and I. We're okay but it's not what it was, there are still a lot of things unsaid.

We can see in this account that differences in approach to engaging with their mother, stressful situations (such as hospital admission), and the ongoing provision of practical and emotional support now that their mother is in a residential home all impact on the relationship Sue discusses having with her sister. However, the worry about ending up in 'shit street' if their mother's finances did not enable them to continue to pay for her care is a particularly stressful aspect of dementia care in England and Wales, which relies on joint powers of attorney adopting a similar approach to financial management that can be difficult to negotiate and achieve. While Sue claimed that her relationship with her sister was 'okay', Jan's relationship with her sister had 'totally broken down' during the course of caring for their mother and her being moved by Social Services into a residential home:

The worst thing was trying to communicate to my siblings how bad mum was. I-I was very close with my sister and our relationship's totally broken down over it because she was just in denial. ... I really thought she would understand. And when mum was diagnosed and we came to register the Power of Attorney she totally backed out of it all, she just said 'No, I don't remember signing anything' and-and wouldn't do anything, wouldn't-just wouldn't get involved. And the only phone calls I ever got from her were sort of, sort of criticisms of what we were doing, you know 'Oh mum's like that cos you do too much for her' and 'Mum's always been content to sit back, if you cook her meals course she won't bother' and things like that, you know, really unhelpful stuff. ... she would even come and have rows in front of mum, you know, it was, that was awful. I would say if anything that was the worst, that was the worst aspect of it, you know? [After mum went into a care home] I had her [sister] crying on the phone and saying how awful I was-and I was grieving myself, I didn't want to do that either, you know, and we ended up having a real humdinger and me saying 'Look, this isn't about you, this is about mum, we're keeping mum safe and don't you think it's hurting me as well?' you know 'I've been in there every single day for nearly eighteen months, you know, don't you think it's hurting me?' ... it's gutted me cos we were always so close ... I was just gutted that she weren't there when I needed her, you know.

The interpersonal conflict and the perceived lack of support for Jan, who was their mother's main carer, are very present in her account of this sibling conflict as 'the worst thing' she had experienced with regarding to caring for her mother.

Although conflict and difficulty between siblings was most evident in participants' accounts there was, in line with some previous research (for example, Allen *et al.* 2009), some evidence from Victoria of siblings supporting each other. Victoria compared the experience of sharing caring responsibilities with her older sister in a comparatively favourable light to caring for a partner with dementia as 'we're equals':

> We keep each other sane, yes. (laughter) I-I actually sort of like feel-erm I go to Alzheimer's Society er carer's coffee mornings and I actually, I don't know how people who are like married to somebody cope because there isn't like somebody else that you can say-cos like my sister and I are in the same sort of place, you know, like we're equals so you can be honest with each other … when we're both in town we sort of like share it out week-by-week because we're now at the stage where my mother has a daily check. … And it depends like on who's there, who happens to be there on the day, who finds out what needs doing and then we sort of like liaise between us.

Victoria's account contrasted quite sharply with those of other participants in that equality, honesty and ongoing liaison are emphasised, whereas in much of the other data regarding interaction with siblings an implicit lack of honesty and an absence of a collaborative approach to parent care was evident. The final theme that connects to fracturing and reconfiguring normative family relationships is parentification and infantalisation, which I now go on to discuss. With regard to the latter it is also important to note that infantalising talk to the parent with dementia was also articulated as a source of sibling discontent. For example, as Alan suggested: 'my sister speaks to her like she was a child and I don't think that's a good thing'.

Parentification and infantalisation

There were numerous examples in these data of participants' being cast in a parental role and utilising many of the strategies and approaches which their parents may have used with them as children (for instance, using time out as a strategy to manage their frustration with their parent's behaviour – 'furious enough that I've just walked away', Victoria). All the participants talked in ways which suggested that they were mindful of simplistic role-reversal notions regarding the progression of dementia; yet, as Victoria suggested, as symptoms of dementia worsen and parental dependency increases over time 'the adult relationship has gone and all you're left with is the fact that you're mother and child and therefore you are irrevocably tied together'. Victoria and Sue, especially, reflected on the changed relationship with their mother. Victoria's account highlights how deception and concealment reconfigure the relationship in ways outside normative patterns 'at this stage of life', which positions a woman in her 50s as a 'teenager'.

> VI: I've learnt to lie, I lie to her. ... I've learnt to deceive her. You know, like my sister erm, when she was at the stage of-sometimes she'd like appear on my sister's doorstep for the fifth time, erm and sometimes it would be to ask the same question again, and my sister was like oh, going completely crazy, it's like she would not answer the door even though she was in the house.
>
> EP: Right.
>
> VI: Cos she said 'If I'm not there she'll just go off and wander back home, and it won't be the end of the world and she'll cope and she'll get on. No, no, it doesn't matter, if it really is urgent she'll come back again another hour later.' You know, so-you know, that's a lie isn't it?
>
> EP: Yeah, yeah, yeah. And I mean how does it feel being-like doing-like you and your sister doing that with your mum?
>
> VI: A bit of a surprise (laughs) no, a bit of a surprise. And-and odd because it's the sort of thing you do when you're a teenager (laughs) you know, yeah, and I'd say it's the same sort of feeling, you feel you're being a bit of a naughty teenager. You're hiding things from them that at this stage of life you weren't expecting to, you know, you would be open with them. ... it's just that like the truth is going to be more hassle than I can cope with, I'm not going there today, you know.

That Victoria was 'surprise[d]' by her own behaviour and the way she interacts with her mother is reminiscent of James' 'strange' role-playing and Derek's verbalised distress at his mother wanting him 'to go to bed with her'. These aspects of care within this particular context are more complex and challenging than the provision of emotional, practical and personal care might suggest. The negotiation of care for caregiver and care recipient is shaped by the cognitive and BPSD aspects of dementia, as well as historical and contemporaneous familial relationships and roles. Elderspeak, or infantilising communication, has been highlighted within dementia research (see Österholm and Samuelsson 2015) and in these data problematic communication from siblings was also highlighted, as in the case of Alan (above) and as Sue commented, 'my brother's not very good with her, he takes the mickey out of her a bit, makes jokes. ... and she looks at him and she doesn't understand'. But what was also interesting was the ways in which the provision of hands on caring could be produced as infantilising by the parent with dementia:

> The hands on caring ... She was awful, I didn't do anything right. 'Don't treat me like a baby' and, you know, it's very difficult to get it right, isn't it? She was doing things which- 'I can walk, I'm not an invalid'. ... the path from

independence to dependence ... For us as a family, perhaps not for the professionals because she'll take it from them, but for the family it's been really difficult.

Sue, here, formulates her mother's journey from independence to dependence as one that has been, and continues to be, 'really difficult' for the family particularly.

Concluding remarks

As I noted at the start of this chapter, the academic literature about informal carers in general, and dementia carers in particular, has predominantly explored the experiences of heterosexual spousal carers. This emphasis has meant that the perspectives of adult children who provide care – broadly conceived – to a parent with dementia have received less attention and are eclipsed by the partner–carer experience. I have focused here on interview and focus group talk about caring from daughters and sons, and highlighted some of the ways in which normative familial roles, responsibilities and 'duties' are fractured and reconfigured in the context of dementia care. There are many difficulties that form part of informal dementia carers' experiences – including behavioural and psychological symptoms (Harding and Peel 2013), incontinence (Drennan *et al.* 2011), financial management (Langan and Means 1996) and difficult decisions towards the end of life (Wilkinson 2015). While there is much to be done to explore the perspectives of people with dementia themselves, especially women who are disproportionately affected both directly and as formal and informal carers (Erol *et al.* 2015, 2016), this analysis has offered a perspective on family dynamics and the processes and practices of caring more broadly.

Notes

1 I gratefully acknowledge the support of the British Academy (Small Grant no. SG1000017 and Mid-Career Fellowship no. MC110142) for funding the projects giving rise to this research, and Chris Beasley and Rosie Harding for helpful editorial input.
2 Ethical approval was granted from university ethics committees. The recruitment strategy for this study involved third sector organisations (for example, Dementia UK) advertising the study, and is described in detail elsewhere (see Harding and Peel 2013; Peel and Harding 2014). All but five of the focus group and interview participants were recruited from the original 'Caring for People with Dementia' questionnaire – there was no overlap between interviewees and focus group participants.
3 This is sometimes referred to as elderspeak.

References

Aldridge, J. and Becker, S. (2003) *Children Caring for Parents with Mental Illness: Perspectives of young carers, parents and professionals* Bristol: Policy Press.

Allen, J., Oyebode, J.R. and Allen, J. (2009) Having a father with young onset dementia: The impact on well-being of young people. *Dementia: The International Journal of Social Research and Practice*, 8(4), 455–480.

Alzheimer's Society (2014) Statistics. Carer support position statement. Available at: www.alzheimers.org.uk/site/scripts/documents_info.php?documentID=546 Accessed 10 August 2016.

Amirkhanyan, A.A. and Wolf, D.A. (2006) Parent care and the stress process: Findings from panel data. *Journal of Gerontology Series B: Psychological Sciences and Social Sciences*, 61(5), S248–S255.

Barca, M.L., Thorsen, K., Engedal, K., Haugen, P.K. and Johannessen, A. (2014) Nobody asked me how I felt: Experiences of adult children of persons with young-onset dementia. *International Psychogeriatrics*, 26, 1935–1944. doi:10.1017/S1041610213002639.

Benedetti, R., Cohen, L. and Taylor, M. (2013) 'There's really no other option': Italian Australians' experiences of caring for a family member with dementia. *Journal of Women & Aging*, 25(2), 138–164.

Braun, M., Scholz, U. and Bailey, B. (2009) Dementia caregiving in spousal relationships: A dyadic perspective. *Aging & Mental Health*, 13, 426–436.

Brody, E.M. (1985) Parent care as a normative family stress. *The Gerontologist*, 25(1), 19–29.

Calasanti, T. (2006) Gender and old age: Lessons from spousal care work. In T. Calasanti and K. Slevin (Eds.), *Age Matters: Re-aligning feminist thinking* (pp. 269–294) New York: Routledge.

Day, J.R., Anderson, R.A. and Davis, L.L. (2014) Compassion fatigue in adult daughter caregivers of a parent with dementia. *Issues in Mental Health Nursing*, 35(10), 796–804.

Drennan, V.M., Cole, L. and Iliffe, S. (2011) A taboo within a stigma? A qualitative study of managing incontinence with people with dementia living at home. *BMC Geriatrics*, 11, 75. www.biomedcentral.com/1471-2318/11/75 Accessed 24 August 2016.

Dura, J.R., Stukenberg, K.W. and Kiecolt-Glaser, J. K. (1991) Anxiety and depressive disorders in adult children caring for demented parents. *Psychology and Aging*, 6(3), 467–473.

Edwards, D. and Potter, J. (1992) *Discursive Psychology*. London: Sage.

Edwards, M. (2014) Distance caregivers of people with Alzheimer's disease and related dementia: a phenomenological study. *British Journal of Occupational Therapy*, 77(4), 174–180.

Erol, R., Brooker, D. and Peel, E. (2015) *Women and Dementia: A global research review*. London: Alzheimer's Disease International. Available at: www.alz.co.uk/women-and-dementia Accessed 24 August 2016.

Erol, R., Brooker, D. and Peel, E. (2016) The impact of dementia on women internationally: An integrative review. *Health Care for Women International* doi: 10.1080/07399332.2016.1219357 Advance access.

Etters, L., Goodall, D. and Harrison, B.E. (2008) Caregiver burden among dementia patient caregivers: A review of the literature. *Journal of the American Academy of Nurse Practitioners*, 20, 423–428.

Harding, R. and Peel, E. (2013) 'He was like a zombie': Off-label prescription of antipsychotic drugs in dementia. *Medical Law Review*, 21(2), 243–277.

Hellstrom, I., Nolan, M. and Lundh, U. (2007) Sustaining 'couplehood': Spouse's strategies for living with dementia. *Dementia: The International Journal of Social Research and Practice*, 6, 383–409.

Hong, S. and Coogle, C.L. (2016) Spousal caregiving for partners with dementia: A deductive literature review testing Calasanti's gendered view of care work. *Journal of Applied Gerontology*, 35(7), 759–787.

Koerin, B. B. and Harrigan, M.P. (2002) P.S. I love you: Long-distance caregiving. *Journal of Gerontological Social Work*, 1/2, 63–81.

Langan, J. and Means, R. (1996) Financial management and elderly people with dementia in the UK: As much a question of confusion as abuse? *Ageing and Society*, 16, 287–314.

Lilly, M.B., Robinson, C.A., Holtzman, S. and Bottorff, J.L. (2012) Can we move beyond burden and burnout to support the health and wellness of family caregivers to persons with dementia? Evidence from British Columbia, Canada. *Health and Social Care in the Community*, 20(1), 103–112.

Luscombe, G., Brodaty, H. and Freeth, S. (1998) Younger people with dementia: Diagnostic issues, effects on carers and use of services. *International Journal of Geriatric Psychiatry*, 13, 323–330.

McDonnell, E. and Ryan, A. (2013) Male caregiving in dementia: A review and commentary. *Dementia: The International Journal of Social Research and Practice*, 12, 238–250.

Murray, M. (2014) (Ed.) *Critical Health Psychology* (2nd Edition) London: Palgrave Macmillan.

O'Dwyer, S.T., Moyle, W., Zimmer-Gembeck, M. and De Leo, D. (2013) Suicidal ideation in family carers of people with dementia: A pilot study. *International Journal of Geriatric Psychiatry*, 28(11), 1182–1188.

Österholm, J.H. and Samuelsson, C. (2015) Orally positioning persons with dementia in assessment meetings. *Ageing and Society*, 35(2), 367–388.

Peel, E. (2014) 'The living death of Alzheimer's' versus 'Take a walk to keep dementia at bay': Representations of dementia in print media and carer discourse. *Sociology of Health and Illness*, 36(6), 885–901.

Peel, E. and Harding, R. (2014) 'It's a huge maze, the system, it's a terrible maze': Dementia carers' constructions of navigating health and social care services. *Dementia: The International Journal of Social Research and Practice*, 13(5) 642–666.

Peel, E. and Harding, R. (2015) A right to 'dying well' with dementia?: Capacity, 'choice' and relationality. *Feminism & Psychology*, 25(1), 137–142.

Peel, E., Parry, O., Douglas, M. and Lawton, J. (2005) Taking the biscuit? A discursive approach to managing diet in type 2 diabetes. *Journal of Health Psychology*, 10(6), 779–791.

Pomerantz, A. (1986) Extreme case formulations: A way of legitimizing claims. *Human Studies*, 9, 119–229.

Prince, M., Knapp, M., Guerchet, M., McCrone, P., Prina, M., Comas-Herrera, A., Wittenberg, R., Adelaja, B., Hu, B., King, D., Rehill, A. and Salimkumar, D. (2014) *Dementia UK* (2nd edition). London: Alzheimer's Society.

Riggs, D.W. and Peel, E. (2016) *Critical Kinship Studies: An introduction to the field*. London: Palgrave Macmillan.

Robinson, B.C. (1983) Validation of a caregiver strain index. *Journal of Gerontology*, 38(3), 344–348.

Shulz R, Sherwood P.R. (2008) Physical and mental effects of family caregiving. *American Journal of Nursing*, 108 (9 Suppl): 23–27.

Starrels, M.E. Ingersoll-Dayton, B., Dowler, D.W. and Neal, M.B. (1997) The stress of caring for a parent: Effects of the elder's impairment on an employed, adult child. *Journal of Marriage and the Family*, 59(4), 860–872.

Suitor, J.J and Pillemer, K. (1993) Support and interpersonal stress in the social networks of married daughters caring for parents with dementia. *Journal of Gerontology*, 48(1), S1–S8.

Svanberg, E., Stott, J. and Spector, A. (2010) 'Just helping': Children living with a parent with young onset dementia. *Ageing & Mental Health*, 14(6), 740–751.

Svanberg, E., Spector, A. and Stott, J. (2011) The impact of young onset dementia on the family: a literature review. *International Psychogeriatrics*, 23, 356–371. doi:10.1017/S1041610210001353.

Ward-Griffin, C., Bol, N. and Oudshoorn, A. (2006) Perspectives of women with dementia receiving care from their adult daughters. *Canadian Journal of Nursing Research*, 38(1), 121–146.

Ward-Griffin, C., Oudshoorn, A., Clark, K. and Bol, N. (2007) Mother-adult daughter relationships within dementia care: A critical analysis. *Journal of Family Nursing*, 13(1), 13–32.

Wilkinson, S. (2015) Refusing to live with advanced dementia: contemporaneous and prospective decision making. *Feminism & Psychology*, 25(1), 148–154.

Chapter 14

'Institutions, they're very straight. My god I hope I don't have to go into a care home'

Spatial inequalities anticipated by older lesbians and gay men

Sue Westwood[1]

Introduction

This chapter explores the spatial inequality implications of older lesbians' and gay men's concerns about their future care needs. Drawing upon the work of social geographers and feminist care ethicists, it analyses a subset of data derived from interviews with older lesbians and gay men, taken from a wider research project on ageing, gender and sexuality, and later-life equality (Westwood 2015a, 2016). There is a growing body of literature documenting older lesbians' and gay men's concerns about the provision of housing, health and social care for older people (Westwood 2015b; King and Cronin 2016), perceived to be 'heteronormative at best and homophobic at worst' (Westwood 2015c, p1). So far the literature, while recognising there are major inequality issues involved, has not yet explored how they are constituted. In my analysis of these data, I propose that older lesbians' and gay men's concerns about future care needs are spatial concerns, based on the anticipated occupation of older-age care spaces (domiciliary care, residential and nursing home care) perceived to be sites of inequality framed by the social reproduction of heteronormativity and heterosexism.

Davina Cooper defines equality as no one having 'an inherent right to impact more on their social and physical environment than anyone else' (Cooper 2004: 77). Previous analyses of spatial (in)equalities distinguished between lesbian and gay spaces (bathhouses; cruising spaces; public sexual spaces; urban commercial sexual spaces) and other spaces normalised as heterosexual. However, there is now a growing appreciation that space is co-occupied and co-produced (Browne and Bakshi 2011), performative, as 'in the process of becoming and produced between actors and actants' (Browne 2007, p. 996), and involving intersecting identities of varying spatial power and dominance (Podmore 2013). As Gill Valentine has observed, 'the ability to enact some identities or realities rather than others is highly contingent on the power-laden spaces in and through which our experiences are lived' (Valentine 2007, p.19). In her study with a deaf lesbian, Valentine demonstrated how that woman felt marginalised by disablism when among hearing lesbians and gay men, and by heteronormativity and homophobia when among heterosexual deaf people. Valentine observed,

When individual identities are 'done' differently in particular temporal moments they rub up against, and so expose, these dominant spatial orderings that define who is in place/out of place, who belongs and who does not.

ibid.

A key dimension of such spatial ordering relates to sexuality. Heterosexism (the systematic privileging of heterosexual identities) is a 'pervasive cultural phenomenon' (Peel 2001, p.544) operating individually, culturally and institutionally. Individually, it is maintained through everyday interactions: the operation of norms (Butler 1999); the discursive reproduction of 'everyday sexualities' (Coates 2013, p.536) and of homophobia (Gough 2002, p.219) in 'everyday talk-in-interaction' (Kitzinger 2005, p.221). Institutional heterosexism is 'expressed through society's structure, institutions, and power relations' (Herek 2004, p.11) and involves the systematic discursive and performative reproduction of heterosexuality, heteronormativity (the assumption that heterosexual identities and relationship formations are the norm) and homophobia (prejudice and discrimination against lesbians and gay men).

Resistance to unequal power relations, including those of heteronormativity and heterosexism, can take many forms. It can involve action (oppositional acts, both overt and covert) and inaction (silences and absences) (Ewick and Silbey 1998). For older lesbians and gay men the dual strategies of concealment and visibility have been fundamental to their resistance. Concealment ('the closet') is:

A strategy of accommodation and resistance which both reproduces and contests aspects of a society organized around normative heterosexuality.

Seidman *et al.* 1999, p. 10

Visibility (coming out of the closet) was a central feature of the gay liberation movement, which opposed the subjugation of lesbian and gay sexualities, their invisibilisation and iterated marginalisation through concealment. Despite binary notions of 'being out' or 'not being out', in reality 'coming out' is an ongoing process rather than a one-off event (Orne 2012). Lesbian and gay men often strategically deploy both concealment and visibility in their public identity management, as in being selectively 'in' or 'out' according to context, to enable them to navigate spaces perceived to be more or less safe for non-heterosexuals.

Despite legal and structural gains in relation to equality for lesbians and gay men, 'these forms of sexual legitimation have been socially and spatially uneven' (Podmore 2013, p. 263). Many public places continue to be 'coded' as unsafe for the overt performance of same-sex sexuality identities and intimacies (Hubbard 2013). Feminists have long-critiqued notions of the privacy of home as a 'safe' space for women (Mallett 2004) and lesbian authors have highlighted how the lesbian home is not totally free from the heteronormative gaze, as it still comes under the surveillance of heterosexual others (biological family, friends, neighbours, service providers) (Johnston and Valentine 1995). Historically, however, many lesbians united together in discrete home-based networks of solidarity and support 'below the radar' (Robson 1992, p. 184) of public life. Many older lesbians and gay men, in particular, rely upon home as a comparatively safe space for open identity performance (Simpson 2015) and as a means of resisting both ageism and 'the erasure and/or discipline of the heteronormative gaze' (Gorman-Murray 2013, p. 103).

Spatiality is interwoven with temporality (Casey 2013). Not only do geographical spaces change across time, a single space can be differently experienced according to time of day or night, and according to how old the person is who is occupying that space (Simpson 2015). Importantly, people, including LGB individuals, occupy different spaces as they age. One of the key triggers to occupying the same homespace differently, or new homespaces altogether (permanently or transiently), is the need for care (Phillips 2007). For further consideration of the spatialities of care, see Hunter, Chapter 4 in this collection and for a useful discussion of the disruption of home in the provision of care, and the importance of strangeness in the spatiality of care see Fletcher, Chapter 2. Care spaces are not only sites for the material practice of physical care but also one where the 'social body' is or is not secure (Dyck *et al.* 2005, p. 173). My argument in this chapter is that older LGB people experience older-age care spaces differently *both* because of their age and age-related care needs *and* because of the particular norms and normativities that are reproduced in those spaces.

Despite the relevance of spatiality for the performance of sexualities/sexual identities, the relationship between sexuality/sexual identity and spaces of care has received very little attention. Indeed, apart from lesbian and gay parenting, there is a conceptual disconnect between sexuality and care (Cooper 2007). This is compounded in older-age care contexts where older people are considered not to have a sexuality at all or, if they do, it is a risky sexuality which is subject to monitoring and control (Ward *et al.* 2005). The central feature which distinguishes older lesbians and gay men from older heterosexual women and men is thus obscured and/or subject to heightened surveillance.

Many older lesbians and gay men have supported friends and family in older-age care spaces and have witnessed many of their shortcomings, which in turn has raised concerns about their own future care (Price 2012). In my analysis of the data I show how participants perceive such spaces of care as being sites of inequality through: the discursive and performative reproduction of heteronormativity and heterosexism; heightened exposure to prejudice and discrimination; and constraints upon all three types of resistance (visibility, concealment and solidarity). I then consider the ethical implications of this and suggest a range of ways in which they might be addressed.

Methodology

The data subset analysed here is drawn from a wider dataset comprising the empirical component of my PhD thesis, which interrogated how the intersection

Table 14.1 Profile of participants

	Women	Men	Total
Total no of participants	36	24	60
Age range	58 to 92	58–76	n/a
Single	14	11	25
Couple	22	12	34
Polyamorous	—	1	1
Children	17	7	18
No children	19	17	36
Grandchildren	13	3	14
No grandchildren	23	21	44

of ageing, gender and sexuality impact later-life equality (Westwood 2015a, 2016). Semi-structured interviews were conducted with 60 older LGB individuals. Participants were recruited via online advertising, networking, opportunistic and snowball sampling. Data were analysed using a staged process of thematic analysis (Braun and Clarke 2006). The data subset analysed here is drawn from one identified thematic stream relating to anticipating future care needs and formal care provision.

Obtaining a representative sample with LGB individuals is extremely difficult, because it involves accessing hidden, marginalised populations of uncertain constituencies. All but one of the participants this study identified were white British, and the majority were well-educated and relatively affluent, reflecting the standard profile of LGB samples (Grossman 2008). For a more detailed profile of the participants, please see Table 14.1.

Of the 60 participants only ten, five women and five men, were living in sheltered accommodation, the other 50 were living independently. Only one participant was in receipt of domiciliary care in her sheltered accommodation. Although the majority of participants were considering anticipated, rather than actually experienced, care provision, their views were not constructed in a vacuum. Some of the participants had worked and/or were still working in social care contexts and many had supported and/or were still supporting friends and family members residing in sheltered accommodation and care homes. As a result, their thoughts and fears about older-age care provision were informed by their direct experiences, and/or witnessing, of such provision.

Social reproduction of heteronormativity and heterosexism

Participants were concerned about the social reproduction of heteronormativity and heterosexism in older-age care spaces:

> I live in an incredible amount of fear about my future. Not just as an older person. But as a gay older person. Institutions, they're very straight. My god I hope I don't have to go into a care home, I really do … When I think about it, I find it quite scary. It frightens me that I am just going to be invisible, a nobody, that I am just going to be lost. And what I would want to do is just die.
>
> May, aged 64

May is describing here the perception that older-age care spaces have a (hetero-)sexuality. She is worried that this will lead to a lack of recognition and cultural devaluation. This creates such feelings of despair that she imagines wanting to die.

How care institutions are understood to be discursively and performatively rendered 'straight' is demonstrated in Lewis' interview. Lewis is on a committee supporting his local day centre for older people. But he would not go there himself:

> I can't see me fitting into somewhere like that … Because of entrenched attitudes and because it's all geared to heterosexual people … Everything that happens, what they talk about, and their past, things that don't relate to me as a gay man … everything's heterosexist, really. They can't relate to your needs. … You don't have 'Gay Times' on the table, but you'll have something for heterosexuals on the table.
>
> Lewis, aged 65

Lewis is highlighting the power of heteronormativity and heterosexism, reproduced in social norms ('attitudes'), visual representations ('You don't have "Gay Times" on the table'), performance ('everything that happens') and discourse ('what they talk about, and their past, things that don't relate to me as a gay man'). Alastair also spoke about 'family talk':

> They talk about their families the whole time. Their sons, their daughters, their cousins, their nephews, their nieces, and if you say anything about your boyfriend, they say 'oh you have to go on about being gay don't you?' You feel like punching them.
>
> Alastair, aged 76

Alastair – estranged from his own biological family who have not accepted his sexuality – perceives everyday talk about biological family relationships as reinforcing heterosexist reproductive norms and excluding other (non-heterosexual) relationship forms.

The perceived power of heteronormativity in care spaces is summed up by Cat (aged 60): 'We see it as being heterosexualised, being put into a care home.' Mixed care was seen as a key component of that heterosexualisation. Many women participants did not want to co-occupy care spaces with men: 'I really, really hope I don't have to share accommodation with men' (Judith, aged 71); 'going in mixed accommodation, I don't think I could cope with that, I'd find that really, really difficult. Just would. Find men's habits not very pleasant' (Claire, aged 65); 'I couldn't bear to be in close proximity with men' (Ellen, aged 64). Many older lesbians and gay men lead parallel lives, having very little to do with one another – 'One of the things about a gay man is that he probably prefers the company of other men' (Ken, aged 69). The idea of sharing care spaces together is an unappealing prospect, for both some men and women:

> I am terrified of a nursing home where all the staff are female, and they treat me as if I fancy the women. Just awful … Not a woman in sight would be fine by me. I know that sounds awful … I just relate to men so much better … the vast majority of women that I know, pass me by, they're just part of the scenery that I can't avoid.
>
> Phil, aged 62

Phil is articulating here the position of those gay men who prefer not to be in the company of women. The prospect of being in a care space where women are in the majority fills Phil with fear. Participants were also concerned about not being able to maintain contact with their personal communities.

> If I'm in a sheltered unit or an old people's home, I want to be able to read and get information and I want to be able to connect with my community. I want to go to [older lesbian group] still. Now how am I going to get to [older lesbian group] if my mobility is compromised? Is somebody going to get me a special bus? If I'm lucky I'll have friends who'll take me there once a month. But what if I have Alzheimer's? Will it be assumed I'm heterosexual and I don't need my friends to come and talk to me about my past?
>
> Diana, aged 69

This extract highlights the importance of retaining connections with one's community (in this case an older lesbian community) and fears that such connections will not be maintained in formal care spaces.

All the participants were agreed that there should be choices of care provision ('One size doesn't fit all', Martin, aged 62; 'I think people should have choice and there should be homes for gays and lesbians definitely', Jack, aged 66; 'I would like to see a choice of care homes', Rene, aged 63). There is, at present, no such choice of provision in the United Kingdom (UK).

Heightened exposure to prejudice and discrimination

Participants were also concerned about spatially reproduced and reinforced prejudice and discrimination: 'It will make you feel more isolated if you're treated as straight or if you're treated as peculiar if you're not straight' (Iris, aged 61).

Iris is expressing two sets of concerns: the fear of isolation caused by the assumption of heterosexuality; and the fear of exposure to prejudice and discrimination if recognised as non-heterosexual. Frances expressed fears about abuse:

> Because of our sexuality there's more to be abusive about potentially and because we're still considered less than, then the idea of stealing from us, or you know being abusive in some other way, is even more attractive. Well who cares about the fag, who cares about the dyke, they don't need the money, so in that sense we're more vulnerable.
>
> Frances, aged 66

Frances is concerned about exposure to targeted abuse because, according to her understanding, lesbians and gay men are culturally devalued. A more common concern among participants related to 'everyday' prejudice. Diana spoke about a friend living in sheltered accommodation, who is not open about her sexuality:

> She lives her life privately. But she has to get involved in this sheltered unit, because there are coffee mornings and things like that and, you know, she doesn't want to be unfriendly. She wants to feel part of that community. She also happens to be Black. And she's had to listen to things, when people have been reading the newspaper, listen, when there's some gay issue or something, to things like 'Oh, if my daughter was like that I'd kill her'. Now what does she do with that? If she challenges that she outs herself and then puts herself in a very vulnerable place.
>
> Diana, aged 69

Highlighted here is the tension between wanting to be part of a shared community, and yet feeling marginalised because of heterosexism and homophobia. Diana's friend has chosen to remain hidden in order to feel safe and (partially) accepted. Being Black (which she is unable to conceal), and therefore (implied) in a minority among White service users and staff, compounds her marginalisation.

The need to conceal was evident in the narratives of the ten participants already living in sheltered accommodation, only one of whom had chosen to be open about their sexuality. That person, Graham, took a 'resistance by visibility' stance:

> I am certainly an out gay man and will remain so. I don't intend to go back into the closet, you know. And there are a number of friends of mine who are concerned about the future and feel they may well have to go back into the closet. Now that's not going to happen to me.
>
> Graham, aged 70

While Graham is very deliberately open about his sexuality, the nine other participants living in sheltered accommodation (all different places) were not open. This was informed by fear: 'What if they took a dislike to me? I don't think many people here would understand it or accept it somehow' (Agnes, aged 92); 'I do not need what might be a headache or provoke an adverse reaction' (Frank, aged 70); 'It's a general feeling that they would treat me differently if I was out to them' (Rene, aged 63). Les was outed by a noisy friend 'and the people in the flat above me heard, and she told the people behind me, and the same day there were shouts of "Poof, poof" … over three years of abuse' (Les, aged 62). Les was eventually relocated by his local authority to another sheltered housing complex.

Constraints upon resistance

As noted in the introduction, resistance to heteronormativity can involve both concealment and/or visibility. As Donald (aged 76) observed:

> We didn't change attitudes to gays in the lesbian and gay movement by being completely in a ghetto. Partially we needed some places to hide, but mostly we did it because we came out … Visibility is always the crucial thing.

Residential care spaces pose challenges to both visibility *and* concealment. Each will now be considered.

Resistance by visibility

Some participants (approximately 50 per cent of the gay men and a third of lesbians, Westwood 2015c) wanted integrated housing, sharing care alongside heterosexual women and men:

> I think we need something that is integrative. I think there will be, if there aren't already, LGBT nursing homes or care homes. It wouldn't be something I want. I wouldn't want to live in that bubble. I don't live in a bubble.
>
> Bob, aged 60

Understandings of equality among those who wanted integration cohered around ideas of equality of outcome, of being treated as equal to, but not the same as, older heterosexual people:

> We should all be able to live together in harmony, but in order to do that, the staff must not assume everyone to be heterosexual and must treat everyone equally. Not necessarily the same, but equally.
>
> Bernice, aged 60

A number of participants thought they would actively resist discrimination in mainstream care spaces:

> I don't want to be in an enclave. I'd rather challenge inequalities when they happen.
>
> Marcia, aged 66

> I think when you're confronted with something as outrageous as being driven up to Shady Pines, we'll open the door and jump out or do whatever we can do … [laughs] … And the principle has always been, unless you act and do it yourself, it don't happen.
>
> Martin, aged 62

The problem with this strategy of anticipated resistance is that it may be compromised by age-related disabilities and associated care needs. As Alex, who still works in social care, observed:

> In ten years' time the people entering care homes are going to be so enfeebled, so dependent, many of them with dementia, that the element of choice, and the ability to exercise that choice is almost going to be non-existent.
>
> Alex, aged 60

Moreover, with older age, a reliance upon others for care and institutionalisation (Wiersma and Dupuis 2010), older people are often reluctant to complain:

> A lot of older people … will do anything not to upset their carers because they're scared of the repercussions … Daphne's mum wouldn't let Daphne speak up on her behalf, because she was scared about how she would be treated … is it, as you get older, that you're scared of upsetting the people that you are relying on for something?
>
> Sandra, aged 61

The reluctance to complain – and fear – associated with age-related frailty was understood by Audrey as having particular implications for older lesbians and gay men in care spaces:

> As you get older you begin to lose confidence and when you're very old you can become very unconfident. And I think it's to do with losing physical strength and ability … and I think, therefore, people put up with things and don't feel that they can fight back. And I think when you hear these things about old gay men and lesbians going into residential care homes and going back in the closet, because they just don't feel they can cope with the prejudice, that's terrible. But you can understand it, because I do think as you get older, many people do get more afraid.
>
> Audrey, aged 67

Audrey is making a connection between embodied age-related changes and increased fear informing those older lesbians and gay men who choose to conceal themselves in care spaces. However, such concealment can also be compromised in care spaces.

Resistance by concealment

Care spaces can also place constraints on concealment, as this extract from the interview with Les (living in new sheltered accommodation after homophobic harassment in his previous sheltered housing) demonstrates:

> When I first came I met a woman in the laundry and she invited me to join them all for a coffee morning. And so I did. First question: 'Have you any children?' 'No'; and then, 'Have you been married?' 'No'. And you can hear their brains working away [laughs] you know. And some of the people at the coffee morning don't live here, they live on the estate, and it only takes one person to know ... Then, that's it, everybody knows.
>
> Les, aged 62

Les is describing the difficulty in concealing life histories in communal living, and the (implied) implications for personal safety. This is nuanced by class. Les is bankrupt and living on benefits. He has limited choices about where he can live. Whereas more affluent participants felt that they did have more choice:

> I have a regular income. So I'm not on benefits ... I will probably have access to more housing options than people who have less money than I do. And will probably be able to take a stand because I'm independent. Whereas someone who is dependent on say the council or some other government body and would live in fear of losing their housing if they came out.
>
> Frances, aged 66

As this extract highlights, access to economic resources creates greater choice, and thereby greater power for some older people.

Care spaces also place constraints on the strategic mobilisation of identity, for instance being 'in' or 'out' according to context. Rene, living in sheltered housing, removes signifiers of her lesbian identity when strangers enter her home:

> I've got some explicitly lesbian fridge magnets stuck on the side of my fridge and if I have tradesman in I tend to hide them in a drawer cos I don't want to be treated less favourably.
>
> Rene, aged 63

In residential care provision Rene would be unable to selectively reveal or conceal her identity. She would need to be 'all in' or 'all out', depriving her of choices about when and how she resists heteronormativity.

Resistance by solidarity

The majority of lesbian participants (almost two-thirds), and just under half the gay men, wanted sexuality/gender-and-sexuality specific accommodation (Westwood 2015c). The lesbians favoured women-only/lesbian-only accommodation and the gay men favoured gay-men only accommodation. The men who wanted gay-men exclusive accommodation included those who preferred not to be in the company of women as well as those who did not want to be in a minority in care homes ('90 per cent of it's females in nursing homes', Ian, aged 69). Nine of the ten participants living in sheltered housing said they would have preferred to live in specialist accommodation: 'Can I just say that if there was a gay [retirement complex], I would have lived there' (Des, aged 69).

The desire for specialist care spaces was linked to love, care and solidarity:

> Physically I [don't] think my needs would be any different ... if I can't walk up the stairs then I need a lift, just like anybody else does, and if I need a wheelchair, my wheelchair, it may have a rainbow flag on it, but you know, it's not really any different. But it's something cultural and it's about shared experience and maybe even shared values, but I'm not sure about that. And I think it has a lot to do with friendship and support and knowing that there's a good possibility that, you know, I won't be mobile and that I want the people around me to have some sense of who I am, from their core to my core.
>
> Frances, aged 66

In this extract we can see the key distinction between physical care needs and sociocultural needs, and in particular the importance of being among like-minded others, especially for individuals belonging to minority groups. Several of the women spoke about wanting co-operative living spaces:

> My ideal, what I'd really like to do, is to sell my house, and put it together with other women selling whatever they've got, and having a big place, and living with other women, just for the camaraderie, the possibility that between us we might be able to make sure that we have the support that we need because we're older.
>
> Rachel, aged 64

Here Rachel is talking about shared solidarity and support and the collective commissioning of care by a collective of women. There are no such projects at present in the UK, and only one, the Older Women's Co-Housing project in North London,[2] is under development.

Discussion

This chapter adds to our understanding of the concerns older lesbians and gay men have about their future care needs in several ways. The analysis of the participants' narratives highlights how their concerns are spatialised, relating to the health and social care spaces they may be required to occupy due to age-related care needs. Those spatialised concerns relate, in turn, to perceived and/or anticipated inequalities in those spaces. The discursive and performative privileging of heterosexuality in sheltered housing and care institutions is read by the participants as operating in four main ways: in everyday talk among staff and service users, which assumes heterosexuality to be the norm; in heteronormative relationship discourse, which again assumes heterosexuality to be the norm; in implied or explicit cultural devaluation of lesbian and gay sexualities; in the presence of heterosexual-privileging media and the absence of media which reflect lesbian and gay lives. All serve, separately and together, to reproduce and reinforce heterosexuality, heteronormativity and heterosexism. Additionally, participants perceive those spaces of care to be particular sites of heightened exposure to prejudice and discrimination from which there is no escape.

A key insight from this analysis is the significance of anticipated occupation of older-age care spaces for resistance. The participants' concerns were underpinned by themes relating to the three key resistance strategies deployed by older lesbians and gay men (visibility, concealment and solidarity). Visibility was understood to be undermined by both a lack of recognition and/or unsafe recognition. Concealment, and its selective mobilisation, was understood to be threatened by the public performance of home in front of and alongside others. Solidarity was perceived to be denied by the separation from other lesbians and/or gay men and the compulsory co-occupation of care spaces dominated by heterosexual-identifying individuals.

As the participants' narratives highlight, formal older-age care spaces problematise the 'doing' of home (Milligan and Wiles 2010), because the 'privacy' of home itself is being performed in a 'public' place, in that the home for older people in receipt of care is also: a place of work (care staff, ancillary staff, tradespersons, etc.); a place of unelected co-occupation through 'enforced engagement ... with other older people that under different circumstances they would have chosen not to' (Milligan 2012, p. 1562); and a place of *both* surveillance (Kontos and Martin 2013) *and* heightened exposure to a heteronormative gaze (both formal, by staff, and informal, by peers and their visitors). This results in a loss of home as 'a place of retreat into a private world, away from public scrutiny, where the individual can control decisions about who to admit or exclude' (Milligan 2012, p. 1562). While this is problematic for all older people, this loss is heightened for older lesbians and gay men who rely more on home as a site of sanctuary from, and resistance to, the heteronormative gaze.

In this way, older age and older-age care needs serve to dislocate older lesbians and gay men from the relative safety of the homespaces and networks of solidarity they have constructed for themselves, relocating them into new spaces in later life which are particular sites of the reproduction of heteronormative power and of exclusion from lesbian and gay collective resistance. The lack of appropriate mainstream provision and the lack of alternative specialist provision (e.g. services exclusively for older lesbians and/or gay men) compounds the situation. Both combine to produce profound spatial and affective inequalities for older lesbians and gay men in later life. They are spatial in that, returning to Davina Cooper's definition of equality (no-one having 'an inherent right to impact more on their social and physical environment than anyone else', Cooper 2004, p. 77), heterosexuals and heteronorms are perceived as/do have greater impact than non-heterosexuals on the social and physical care environments of older people. They are affective, in the denial of access to love, care and solidarity (Lynch *et al.* 2009) and of safe housing environments (Barnes 2012) for lesbians and gay men in later life.

This study also highlights the significance of temporality for the spatiality of care, in two main ways. First, personal chronologies inform spatial location. School-age children who identify as LGB and/or are exploring their sexuality have no choice but to occupy normative educational spaces through and against which they navigate these issues and concerns. Despite growing acceptance of sexuality and gender identity diversity, such young people continue to experience bullying and intimidation in those spatial contexts (Monk 2011). Similarly, older LGB individuals and/or those who are sexuality/gender non-conforming, are compelled by care needs to occupy older-age care spaces which are also highly normative. It is, therefore, the intersection of age (and age-related needs) *and* specific kinds of normative spaces which produce the spatial inequalities about which older LGB people are so concerned. Second, as Judith Butler (2008) has highlighted, different spaces can operate different norms at the same time. Older-age care spaces may reproduce different (and less liberal) norms relating to sexuality than other contemporaneous spaces in the wider community. Through their (ageing) chronologies and associated care needs, older LGB people are relocated into different normative spaces where they experience different levels and types of in/exclusion than those which they might experience in mainstream society.

This study adds to our understanding of spatial inequalities in three main ways. First, it highlights how care spaces are sexualised, normative spaces. Care in older-age care spaces, these findings suggest, has a sexuality attached to it. It is heterosexual care, produced in heterosexist ways, predicated upon heteronorms, and directed at (assumed) heterosexual subjects by (assumed) heterosexual care providers. That care has a (hetero-)sexuality is a striking feature of these findings, posing a considerable challenge to the traditional conceptual disconnect between sexuality and care (Cooper 2007). Second, building upon Gill Valentine's (2007) work, the findings show how older age relocates lesbians and gay men into care spaces where they 'rub up' (p. 19) against the dominant spatial orderings exposing the privileging of heteronormativity and heterosexism. These dominant spatial orderings serve to position older heterosexual people as 'in place' and older lesbians and gay men as 'out of place'. The third insight from the findings is in relation to how the privileging of heteronormativity and heterosexism can be understood to operate in those care spaces, through the discursive and performative reproduction of heterosexuality.

If we understand formal care spaces as being particular sites of the practice of embodied power, we then have to ask about the ethics of that power being exercised in ways that privilege heterosexuality and disadvantage non-heterosexuality.

This raises issues in relation to person-centred care, which underpins the social and health care policies of many countries. In person-centred care, each individual is supposed to receive care that is tailored to that person's unique set of needs and circumstances. Care where some individuals do not feel safe to demonstrate their true selves and/or where those true selves are not recognised cannot, by definition, be person-centred. Related to this are sexuality-blind models of 'off-the-peg' care, as in a 'one size fits all' approach to domiciliary and/or residential care provision which fails to take into account the sexuality/sexual identity diversity among older people who need care. This, again, cannot be person-centred. In the UK, personal budgets are available to enable an individual to buy in packages of care. These were heralded as having great potential for older lesbians and gay men to purchase lesbian- and gay-'friendly' home care. However, if no such support is available, having a personal budget with which to purchase it is meaningless.

The spatial inequalities raised here might be challenged in a wide range of ways. Sandra Fredman (2014) has recently proposed that there are four main dimensions involved in achieving substantive equality: redressing disadvantage; addressing stigma, stereotyping, prejudice and violence; embracing difference and achieving structural change; and enhancing voice and participation. In terms of redressing disadvantage, embracing difference and achieving structural change, Westwood *et al.* (2015) synthesised a range of good-practice guidance documents to identify seven key areas in which mainstream social care spaces for older people could be improved for older LGBT (lesbian, gay, bisexual and trans) people: inclusive consultation in service design and delivery; appropriate equality and diversity and LGBT-specific policies; creating a safe working and living environment for LGBT staff and service users; a robust staff training strategy; encouraging staff to use appropriate inclusive language and cultural representation; person-centred assessment and care planning; setting and auditing standards. Westwood and Knocker (2016) have also highlighted the importance of making substantive organisational and systemic changes that require more than one-off training, rather than using ongoing organisational consultancy.

In addition to making mainstream care provision more responsive to the needs of older lesbians and gay men, there is also the need for: greater choice in housing and care provision; a range of alternative housing with care for older lesbians and gay men; and for systems to enable older people, including older lesbians and gay men, to be supported in setting up, and maintaining, care co-operatives and self-directed projects. The current lack of such alternatives in the UK profoundly disadvantages older lesbians and gay men, in comparison with their overseas counterparts, given that such provision exists in parts of Europe, North America and Australia (Westwood 2015a). It also disproportionately affects older lesbians, given that they are more likely to occupy older-age care spaces than gay men (because women live longer than men) and because they are more likely to want alternatives to mainstream provision than gay men (Gabrielson 2011).

To enhance voice and participation, there is a need for greater research to inform and support social policy makers, commissioners and service providers

(Kimmel 2014). In particular, older lesbians' and gay men's fears and concerns about care provision need to better heard, better understood and better addressed. Policy makers and providers should consult closely with older lesbians and gay men, nationally and locally, about what they want and need from health and social care provision. There is also a need for greater advocacy, not just for older lesbians and gay men, but for all older people in closed care spaces. As the extracts have highlighted, some older people can be reluctant and/or feel unable to assert their rights. This, together with limited legal protections for older people in care spaces and the paucity of non-statutory advocacy, means that many of formal law's protections relating to care standards and equalities and human rights have only limited applicability to those older people living in those spaces. There is, then, a need to bring law into older-age care spaces in an ongoing way, via routinised, personalised, advocacy in order to ensure that the human rights of older people, including older lesbians and gay men, are respected and maintained.

Bringing law into care spaces is important for addressing stigma, stereotyping, prejudice and violence towards older lesbian and gay people. Although training and education, and strong policies and procedures have a key role to play, so too does formal law. Homophobic harassment is defined in the UK as a form of elder abuse (Dept of Health 2000, para 2.7). Care environments in which homophobia can flourish and/or in which staff fail to appropriately challenge not just overt acts of homophobic abuse, but also more subtle forms of everyday homophobia are, in effect, spaces in which such elder abuse is not only allowed, but is facilitated. Not only is this unethical, it is, in many countries, unlawful. It is only due to a lack of advocacy, so far, that these ethical (and potentially unlawful) care deficiencies have been able to continue. This serves to re-emphasise the importance of impartial advocacy for older lesbians and gay men occupying spaces of care for older people.

Conclusion

This chapter has highlighted how older lesbians' and gay men's concerns about future care needs are spatial and temporal concerns, in relation to the occupation of care spaces necessitated by older-age needs. These spatial concerns relate to: the social reproduction of heteronormativity and heterosexism; heightened exposure to prejudice and discrimination; and constraints upon lesbian and gay resistance to each of these. The findings also demonstrate how care spaces are sexualised spaces, privileging older heterosexual people and disadvantaging older lesbians and gay men. This has profound implications for the ethics of older-age care spaces and the affective inequalities which are reproduced.

There is a need to: redress disadvantage, embrace difference and achieve structural change, through the implementation of a wide range of practice improvements; increase choice of older-age health and social care spaces and the availability of specialist provision; and enhance voice and participation through a) consultation with older lesbians and gay men about the health and social care spaces they want, b) increased research, and c) improved advocacy services for all older people, including older lesbians and gay men.

Notes

1 Thanks to Ruth Fletcher and Rosie Harding for their excellent PhD supervision, and to the editors for their very helpful feedback on an earlier draft of this chapter.
2 The Older Women's Co-Housing project (www.owch.org.uk/).

References

Barnes, M. (2012) *Care in Everyday Life: An Ethic of Care in Practice*. Bristol: Policy Press.
Braun, V. and Clarke, V. (2006) Using thematic analysis in psychology. *Qualitative Research in Psychology*, 3(2), 77–101.
Browne, K. (2007) (Re) making the other: Heterosexualising everyday space. *Environment and Planning A*, 39(4), 996–1014.
Browne, K. and Bakshi, L. (2011) We are here to party? Lesbian, gay, bisexual and trans leisurescapes beyond commercial gay scenes. *Leisure Studies*, 30(2), 179–196.
Butler, J. (1999) *Gender Trouble*. Second Edition. London: Routledge.
Butler, J. (2008) Sexual politics, torture, and secular time. *The British Journal of Sociology*, 59(1), 1–23.
Casey, Mark (2013) Belonging: Lesbians and gay men's claims to material spaces. In Y. Taylor and M. Addison (eds) *Queer Presences and Absences*, pp. 141–158. Basingstoke: Palgrave Macmillan.
Coates, J. (2013) The discursive production of everyday heterosexualities. *Discourse & Society*, 24(5): 536–552.
Cooper, D. (2004) *Challenging Diversity: Rethinking Equality and the Value of Difference*. Cambridge University Press: Cambridge.
Cooper, D. (2007) 'Well, you go there to get off': Visiting feminist care ethics through a women's bathhouse'. *Feminist Theory*, 8, 243–262.
Department of Health (2000) *No Secrets: Guidance on Developing and Implementing Multi-Agency Policies and Procedures to Protect Vulnerable Adults from Abuse*. London: The Stationery Office.
Dyck, I., Kontos, P., Angus, J., and McKeever, P. (2005) The home as a site for long-term care: meanings and management of bodies and spaces. *Health & Place*, 11(2), 173–185.
Ewick, P. and Silbey, S. (1998) *The Common Place of Law: Stories From Everyday Life*. Chicago: Chicago University Press.
Fredman, S. (2014) *Substantive Equality Revisited*. Oxford Legal Studies Research Paper No. 70/2014. [Online] Available at: http://dx.doi.org/10.2139/ssrn.2510287 [Accessed 12th August 2015]
Gabrielson, M. L. (2011) 'I will not be discriminated against': older lesbians creating new communities. *Advances in Nursing Science*, 34(4), 357–373.
Gorman-Murray, A. (2013) Liminal subjects, marginal spaces and material legacies: Older gay men, home and belonging. In Y. Taylor and M. Addison (eds) *Queer Presences and Absences*, pp. 93–113. Basingstoke: Palgrave Macmillan. Kindle Edition.
Gough, B. (2002) 'I've always tolerated it but...': Heterosexual masculinity and the discursive reproduction of homophobia. In A. Coyle and C. Kitzinger (eds) *Lesbian and Gay Psychology: New Perspectives*, pp. 219–238. Oxford: Blackwell.

Grossman, A. (2008) Conducting research among older lesbian, gay and bisexual adults. *Journal of Gay and Lesbian Social Services*, 20, 51–67.

Herek, G. (2004) Beyond homophobia: Thinking about sexual prejudice and stigma in the twenty-first century. *Sexuality Research and Social Policy*, 1(2), 6–24.

Hubbard, Phil (2013) Kissing is not a universal right: Sexuality, law and the scales of citizenship. *Geoforum*, 49, 224–232.

Johnston, L. and Valentine, G. (1995) 'Wherever I lay my girlfriend, that's my home: The performance and surveillance of lesbian identities in domestic environments.' In D. Bell and G. Valentine (eds) *Mapping Desire: Geographies of Sexualities*, pp. 88–103. London: Routledge.

Kimmel, D. (2014) Lesbian, gay, bisexual, and transgender aging concerns. *Clinical Gerontologist*, 37(1), 49–63.

King, A. and Cronin, A. (2016) Bonds, bridges and ties: applying social capital theory to LGBT people's housing concerns later in life. *Quality in Ageing and Older Adults*, 17(1), 16–25.

Kitzinger, C. (2005)'Speaking as a heterosexual': (How) does sexuality matter for talk-in-interaction? *Research on Language and Social Interaction*, 38(3), 221–265.

Kontos, P., and Martin. W. (2013) Embodiment and dementia: Exploring critical narratives of selfhood, surveillance, and dementia care. *Dementia*, 12(3), 288–302

Lynch, K., J. Baker and M. Lyons (eds) (2009) Conclusion. In K. Lynch, J. Baker and M. Lyons (eds), *Affective Equality: Love, Care and Justice*, pp. 216–236. Basingstoke: Palgrave Macmillan.

Mallett, S. (2004) Understanding home: A critical review of the literature. *The Sociological Review*, 52(1), 62–89.

Milligan, C. (2012) *There's No Place Like Home: Place and Care in an Ageing Society*. Farnham: Ashgate. Kindle edition.

Milligan, C. and Wiles, J. (2010) Landscapes of care. *Progress in Human Geography*, 34(6), 736–754.

Monk, D. (2011) Challenging homophobic bullying in schools: The politics of progress. *International Journal of Law in Context*, 7(2), 181–207.

Orne, J. (2012) 'You will always have to "out" yourself': Reconsidering coming out through strategic outness. *Sexualities*, 14(6), 681–703.

Peel, E. (2001) Mundane heterosexism: Understanding incidents of the everyday. *Women's Studies International Forum*, 24(5), 541–555.

Phillips, J. (2007) *Care*. Cambridge: Polity

Podmore, J. (2013) Critical commentary: Sexualities landscapes beyond homonormativity. *Geoforum*, 49, 263–267.

Price, E. (2012). Gay and lesbian carers: ageing in the shadow of dementia. *Ageing and Society*, 32(3), 526–532.

Robson, R. (1992) *Lesbian (Out)Law: Survival Under the Rule of Law*. Ithaca, NY: Firebrand Books.

Seidman, S., Meeks, C. and Traschen, F. (1999) Beyond the closet? The changing social meaning of homosexuality in the United States. *Sexualities*, 2(1), 9–34.

Simpson, P. (2015) *Middle-aged Gay Men, Ageing and Ageism: Over the Rainbow?* Palgrave Macmillan.

Valentine, G. (2007) Theorizing and researching intersectionality: A challenge for feminist geography. *The Professional Geographer*, 59(1), 10–21.

Ward, R., Vass, A. A., Aggarwal, N., Garfield, C. and Cybyk, B. (2005) A kiss is still a kiss?: The construction of sexuality in dementia care. *Dementia*, 4, 49–72.

Westwood, S. (2015a) *Ageing, Gender and Sexuality: Equality in Later Life*. Thesis for PhD in Law, University of Keele, UK.

Westwood, S. (2015b) Dementia, women and sexuality: How the intersection of ageing, gender and sexuality magnify dementia concerns among lesbian and bisexual women. *Dementia*, doi: 1471301214564446.

Westwood, S. (2015c) 'We see it as being heterosexualised, being put into a care home': Gender, sexuality and housing/care preferences among older LGB individuals in the UK. *Health and Social Care in the Community*, doi: 10.1111/hsc.12265.

Westwood, S. (2016) *Ageing, Gender and Sexuality: Equality in Later Life*. London: Routledge.

Westwood, S. and Knocker, S. (2016) one day training courses on LGBT* awareness – Are they the answer? In S. Westwood and E. Price (eds), *Lesbian, Gay, Bisexual and Trans* Individuals Living with Dementia: Concepts, Practice and Rights*, pp. 145–159. London: Routledge.

Westwood, S., King, A., Almack, K. and Suen, Y-T. (2015) Good practice in health and social care provision for older LGBT people. In J. Fish and K. Karban (eds), *Social Work and Lesbian, Gay, Bisexual and Trans Health Inequalities: International Perspectives*, pp. 145–159. Bristol: Policy Press.

Wiersma, E. and Dupuis, S. L. (2010) Becoming institutional bodies: Socialization into a long-term care home. *Journal of Aging Studies*, 24, 278–291.

Chapter 15

Beyond care and vocabularies of altruism

Considering sexuality and older people

Chris Beasley

Introduction

In the wide-ranging international literature on care (which includes scholarship on law, education and health, amongst others[1]), care has been associated with attempts to value social life in ways that foreground interconnection and thus offer a critique of the encroaching spread of competitive instrumentalist individualism – an individualism typically linked with neo-liberalism and/or 'moral decline'. Care has, in short, been a means to envisage an alternative direction for social life, indeed an alternative politics. On this basis, the language of care offers both advantages and problems and has, not surprisingly, been the subject of considerable heated debate.

A fundamental premise of this volume is that the concept of care is deployed in *socially critical* literature, such as feminist approaches to social interconnection. However, the debate about care's possibilities raises theoretical and practical questions for such socially critical approaches. Notions of caring social connection are not only linked to progressive social visions. For instance, in previous co-authored work by Beasley and Bacchi (2007, 2012), the term care and associated languages are considered to invoke what might be deemed regressive from a feminist perspective. *The key objective of this chapter is to draw upon, refine and extend that earlier assessment.*

The chapter initially insists upon the significance of the term care. In exemplifying the advantages of care, I outline care's location as a response to the embrace of 'modernisation' and to 'moral decline' critical perspectives. This positioning involves a rejection of individualisation and validates a revaluation of social connection. In particular contexts, care and associated languages appear to offer *resistance* to theorising and social developments around individualisation typically related to late modernity. Care in such contexts provides a potential platform for feminist concerns regarding sociality and feminist alternative political imaginaries.

However, in the second section I assert – in keeping with previous work – that, nevertheless, care provides a *limited ethico-political starting point* for feminist aims. In this context, I summarise *problematic elements* in the literature on care. The emphasis here is upon what is delimited by care and aligned vocabularies with regard to power relations and social change. In the third section, I then *illustrate* care's limitations by focusing upon sexuality and older people in the instance of what I describe as 'the double bed problem'. This finally returns me, in concluding remarks, to the advantages of a more thoroughly *alternative approach*.

Part 1: care as resistance – its advantages

Care's possibilities as a means of 'resistance' to hegemonic understandings of sociality in modernity must be located with regard to major macro-level frameworks about social interconnection – that is, relationality, intimacy and (inter-)subjectivity. A range of scholars has registered new prevailing modes of legitimate social connection and closeness in modern 'western'/northern societies.[2] Many of them have noted how 'family' can no longer be seen as the unproblematic centre of such analyses[3] and instead have been inclined to move towards other ways of capturing what is deemed to characterise modern 'western'/northern sociality.[4] The major accounts of modern interconnection may be briefly summarised along the lines of two broad camps outlined below.

1. Modernisation promoters

- neo-liberal ascendency – the ascendency of competitive market-centred individualism, signalling *the growth of social and personal freedom*
- 'transformation of intimacy'/'reflexive modernisation' (Giddens/Beck) such that 'westerners'/northerners forgo traditional hierarchical or collective values, instead choosing *personalised individual experiences of intimacy*

2. Modernisation critics: moral decline thinking

- cultural pessimists – critique of anti-authoritarian 1960s/70s social transformation, associated with the decline of traditional forms of authority; westerners/northerners become individualistic *narcissists concerned with self-fulfilment*
- communitarians – critique of 1980s loss of moral centre and privileging of market associated with the decline of community and shared morality; westerners/northerners become *individualists who fail to care or be responsible for others*.

Hookway 2013

These theories offer accounts of late modernity which have significant implications for feminist concerns around social connection and equitable gender relations. All, despite their differing social visions and political agendas, offer versions of an individualisation thesis in which gender hierarchy is passé because in modernity individuals rule. Care comes to figure in relation to such analyses as a powerful means for resisting the rhetoric of individualisation; it becomes both a means to counter individualisation as a political imaginary and to counter the assumed actuality of the universal hegemony of individualisation. To outline responses drawing upon the language of care, it is helpful to consider briefly the particularities of the major accounts of the individualisation thesis.

Some of the modernisation promoters *positively* embrace what is seen as the rise and rise of individualistic neo-liberal social modes of practice and subjectivities which mirror the competitive atomism of market exchanges. As an example, universities are social organisations which are increasingly urged by those who accept the notion of the neo-liberal academy to strive for competitive cognitive betterment and indeed corporate revenue production.[5] Care has been actively deployed in response to this support for the neo-liberal ascendency approach. A very substantial, indeed vast, body of interdisciplinary scholarship has arisen on neo-liberalism's negative impact upon organisations such as universities and their social interactions and subjectivities.[6] In this setting, concerns about wellbeing and the consequences of competitive individualism within the neo-liberal academy amount to employment of a *care-based* model of social interconnection, and often one entwined with an awareness of ongoing inequitable gender relations. Care-based responses become the means of providing critical analyses and political strategies of resistance.[7]

If the promoters of neo-liberal ascendency actively embrace individualisation – within organisations like the academy and elsewhere – other supporters of individualising modernity tend to focus more specifically upon the positive possibilities for subjectivities and intimate relationality. Anthony Giddens and Ulrich Beck have both offered macro-scale theories concerning 'late modern societies' which assert that this is an age of weak social bonds. In this new age individuals are able to float free of the ties of traditional societies and set social roles, and hence from bodies marked by restrictive gendered assumptions, to embark on their own self-reflexive personalised projects (Giddens 1992). Late modernity here, as in the neo-liberal ascendency literature, is promoted as enabling a brave new world of individual 'pure' choice (Beasley *et al.* 2012, p. 38–47). There is little sense here of collective social requirements, obligation, dependency or coercion. Unsurprisingly, the 'transformation of intimacy'/'reflexive modernisation' approach has been subjected to robust criticism and such criticism frequently takes the form of drawing attention to ongoing embedded and embodied connections between people (Budgeon 2008; Smart 2007). Claims about *caring bonds* come to symbolise resistance to ambitious assumptions about individualisation. Here, once again, the concept of care is often aligned with a feminist politics of challenge regarding triumphant theorisations of modernisation (Mulinari and Sandell 2009).

When we come to those commentators who are *unsympathetic* to modernisation, care's potential as a language of 'resistance' to hegemonic understandings of sociality in modernity is plainly evident. By contrast with the pro-modernisation scholars, the *modernisation critics* bemoan the losses they associate with modernity and in the process offer two main versions of *'moral decline'* thinking, that is, cultural pessimism and communitarianism (Hookway 2012). In the case of the cultural pessimists, epitomised by commentators like Reiff ([1966] 1987), Lasch (1979) and Bell (1976), there is a shared nostalgia about the loss of traditional/religious/

paternal authority in the face of the 'moral impoverishment of modern culture' (Hookway 2012, p. 2). Such conservative commentators are dismayed by what they see as the loss of modes of social repression and consequent collapse into an amoral and, importantly, uncaring world.

While the communitarians are somewhat less inclined to catastrophic visions of the present,[8] they share with cultural pessimists a sense of the substantial dangers of a waning moral consensus, in their view resulting specifically from weakened community (Putnam 1995; Etzioni 1994; Taylor 1992; MacIntyre 1985, Walzer 1990). They assert from various points of view that the rise of individualism in modernity offers a diminished conception of the self and that social interconnection and social commitment is fundamental to subjectivity and meaning. Communitarian antagonism to individualism and focus on community is implicitly,[9] and sometimes specifically, tied to a care-centred ethic and community life (Khatchadourian 1999). These writers are not necessarily inclined to uphold gendered paternal authority as foundational, though they do often appear to be nostalgic about unselfish community connections and care which were, and are, largely upheld by models of femininity and women's labour (Beasley *et al.* 2012, p. 41).

In summary, in both positive and negative accounts of modernity, care appears as resistant, as against the grain, and hence it suggests another direction for sociality, a potential platform for alternative political imaginaries. Care is deployed to present a socio-political framework attentive to gender, a gender-contextualised language which highlights the importance of social connection to wellbeing and draws attention to ongoing bonds and obligations, while also offering a critique of the dangerous impact of individualism on societies, institutions, relationships and individuals without reverting to a past in which care was at the cost of women.

Theories of modern individualisation and care as a feminist alternative platform

Accounts of late modernity provided in the individualisation thesis are more focused on *describing what* change is deemed to have occurred and are not especially geared to explore *how* change occurs. These accounts also tend – despite being about social life, relationality and forms of subjectivity including gender identities – to be rather removed from the *micro-politics* of intimate everyday life and operate at the level of the rhetorical and schematic. Yet, as Jane Kenway (1997) has noted, this is an issue which is decidedly crucial for any analysis of changing patterns of social connection:

> a particular difficulty which all commentators face is how best to understand the relationship between the big material and structural shifts to everyday and to changed structures of feeling. What is needed is a theory which considers the relationship between globalizing influences and personal dispositions, *the reordered conditions of individual and collective life.*
>
> Kenway 1997, p. 3, emphasis added

Approaches to modernising individualisation do offer perspectives on 'reordered conditions'. However, they tend to be inattentive at the macro level of national identities and the global/international. More importantly, given their inclination to describe sweeping changes, such as an overall shift to individualisation, they provide rather thin theorising about small-scale and interpersonal aspects of social life and how change might proceed from these aspects in a bottom-up rather than a top-down fashion. Relatedly, these analyses often show a decidedly limited grasp of gendered power and its ongoing significance, presuming that individualisation is universal and experienced in a disembodied gender-neutral fashion (McNay 2000). For example, Beck and Beck-Gernsheim assert that 'people are being released from the constraints of gender … axes of (socially organized) difference', such that their activities 'are more a matter of individual decisions' (1996, p. 29).

In what way is care an alternative to this? The specific strategic advantages of care, in the context of analyses of modernisation approaches, arise in its avowed rejection of individualisation combined with its capacity to enable a focus upon both macro and micro politics, upon everyday intimate modes of (gendered) social interconnection. Concern with the micro offers space for recognition of bottom-up trajectories for social change. Care's rejection of current schematic and broad-brush theorisations of individualisation and its counter insistence upon the irreducible sociality of human subjects,[10] demonstrates its location as a language of resistance. In this context, care provides a platform for feminist alternative political imaginaries.

Two examples are illustrative of its political usefulness for feminist approaches to social interconnection. The first is its use by Swedish scholars to argue against the ascendency of a neo-liberal focus upon measurable, documented aspects of the preschool, preschool teaching and preschool management (Löfdahl and Folke-Fichtelius 2014).[11] Care is deployed in a range of studies of Swedish preschools to denote an alternative feminist-inflected approach in which intimate relationality is stressed as core to preschool activities, rather than being viewed as peripheral and taking time away from cognitive activities that can be documented and evaluated to demonstrate progression. As Margaret Sims has noted, early childhood is an arena of policy, funding and service delivery which 'is intensely political' (2014a, 2014b). These scholars mobilise an alternative politics about the key value of preschools around the terminology of care.

The second instance is the example of the use of the language of care in relation to dementia. An array of commentators (for instance, in the UK and Australia) have employed care as a terminology to enable an explicitly feminist analytical framework, which can evaluate the adequacy of the ethical decision-making and practical care offered to people dealing with dementia.[12] The use of the term is often aimed at strengthening opportunities for participation and inclusion of those with dementia, facilitated by professional and lay carers (see Brannelly 2006). This political focus on care as a means to facilitating 'social justice' (Barnes and Brannelly 2008) and 'social citizenship' (Bartlett and O'Connor 2010) arises in the face of increasing neo-liberal pressures towards the marketisation of healthcare and the management of a biomedicalised commodification of ageing. As Barnes and Brannelly put it, feminist-inflected understandings of care are intimately linked with political concerns regarding social equity and thus are identified with a critique of neo-liberal managerialist 'efficiency':

> [t]he re-emergence of a concern with the value base of social and health care practices and policies can be considered as a reaction to the dominance of managerialism within human service organizations and to case management as the pre-eminent model of practice
>
> 2008, p. 384; see also Kenner 2008

These practical instances reinforce the general analytical point that care as a terminology of social connection can provide resistance to neo-liberal promotion of competitive individualism (see also Chapter 5, Baker *et al.*).

Part 2: care as a problematic ethico-political starting point for feminist aims – its limits

Despite the advantages of the language of care, I have intimated that there are important limits on this terminology, and other associated terms promoting social connection. Care, in my view, offers a decidedly restricted ethico-political starting point for revaluing the feminist agenda of social connection and thus envisaging an alternative politics. This critical consideration of care, as noted in the introduction to this volume, rests upon questioning its progressive credentials and raising doubts about the degree to which this language – and the claims it makes regarding the crucial significance of caring bonds – reiterates rather than departs from, let alone resists, neo-liberalism.

Mitchell Dean has made the point that current neo-liberal understandings of sociality as matters of individual choice and 'rational' (read self-interested, disembodied/cognitive) decision-making offer a distinct political ethos (Dean 1997 in Larner 2000, p. 19). Feminist debates have identified care as of central significance in the development of a contesting political ethic. The term care thus involves a feminist articulation of the value of challenging the neo-liberal ethos of atomistic individualism and the accompanying problems of attending to social interconnection.

This challenge is also evident in a variety of other allied approaches – signalled by terms like trust, respect, responsibility and generosity, amongst others. Some of these terms (like trust and respect) primarily focus on the dangers of excessive individualisation as a threat to social order and stable government – arguments in certain ways aligned with the cultural pessimists outlined earlier. By contrast, other terms, like care and generosity, are crucially concerned to enable more humane social relations (see Diprose 2002) – arguments more often linked with the communitarian approach described previously. However, the vocabularies are by no means entirely discrete and indeed share certain problematic political and moralistic assumptions.

In previous co-authored work by Beasley and Bacchi (2007; 2012) care and associated languages are considered to reinstate aspects of social hierarchy and, relatedly, an attenuated and moralistic account of social connection. These linked inclinations towards buttressing hierarchy and a particular restricted, as well as prescriptive, understanding of connection are by no means opposed to neo-liberal conceptions of social relations. Indeed, care in this perspective supports neo-liberal understandings of social relations as necessarily asymmetrical and unequal exchanges, and as only embodied in certain acceptable respects.

The limitations of care as a feminist political ethic may be described in shorthand terms as *the problem of altruism*. Such limitations raise serious doubts about its capacity to achieve the feminist goal of providing a contesting political ethic in which reconfiguring exploitative social relations is associated with valuing embodied social interconnection between people. The analysis provided here upholds this vital feminist goal while advancing the third key theme announced in the 'Introduction' to the volume – that of articulating 'the limitations of care' (and associated vocabularies) 'as a normative and conceptual framework'. As outlined in Part 2 of this chapter, it is important to acknowledge the contribution of care to challenging the hegemony of neo-liberalism in certain respects. All the same, care and related languages may also be viewed as simultaneously mimicking elements of neo-liberalism. Precisely because I wish to give value to embodied social interconnection – that is, what stands under the 'sign' of the term care – it is important to question its problematic associations and reconfigure a more adequate feminist vocabulary. Care, I would argue, provides a significant but flawed feminist political ethic, whose limits require that its use be subject to contingent assessment. This broad argument has been outlined in several settings in previous work (see Beasley and Bacchi 2007). Hence, I will not detail the critique but rather pull together certain strands of it, in order to move to application and illustration in the final sections of the chapter.

In general, care ethicists mount a rather more substantial challenge to the rational disembodied atomistic individualism of neo-liberalism than those who, for example, employ vocabularies like trust or respect. Individualism is offered a more critical challenge by those who employ the language of care because it necessarily attends to (certain) bodily interactions, in particular related to the caring responsibilities of women/mothers. Yet care's refusal of disembodied individualism in a neo-liberal competitive hierarchical society is not as complete as it would appear.

Early care thinkers tended to see care as moral disposition. The hierarchical nature of many caring relationships, including mothering, went largely unnoticed (Shakespeare 2000; Hughes *et al.* 2005). More recent versions, such as those developed by Selma Sevenhuijsen (1998a) and Joan Tronto (1995; 2013), insist that care is an important social practice, shifting discussion from one-to-one caring relationships to institutional caring arrangements, including those I have outlined within preschool education (see also Engster 2004). However, despite expressed desires to avoid paternalism, a moral and asymmetrical relationship is constructed between those needing care and those delivering care, even in these more socially framed analyses, undermining the egalitarian potential of the terminology. Relations of dependence and vulnerability are presupposed (see Sevenhuijsen 1998b, p. 7–8).

This distinction between the needy/vulnerable, and those attending to their needs, also appears in most postmodern attempts to ground a new ethical sociality around the social relations of care. For example, the work of Emmanuel Levinas is often employed in this context. Levinas does not use the word care, but his focus on 'responsibility' and compassion for the 'other', replicates the concerns of care scholar ethics. Yet he, like care thinkers, assumes a 'radical asymmetry' between carer and those requiring care (Dunphy 2004 p. 3). Displaying related ideas, Margrit Shildrick (2001, p. 238) and a range of others engage with the language of 'vulnerability' (MacKenzie *et al.* 2013; Fineman and Grear 2013). There is a democratising concern in writings linked to Levinas' work on responsibility for the other and in the various uses of vulnerability, since these approaches highlight that all of us need care and are vulnerable. However, the emphasis is upon bodily need and the possibility of the suffering of the other making unavoidable claims upon those who are required to provide care. Despite some differences in these accounts, the caring 'exchange' is viewed consistently as a form of altruism (see Beasley and Bacchi 2007).

Establishing altruism towards the vulnerable as an ethical starting point typically involves the promotion of care as a desirable moral quality or disposition held by 'responsible' individual citizens, and connects these care-based literatures with the 'moral decline' thinking outlined earlier. Care ethicists can be credited therefore with offering a critique of the rational atomistic self/citizen associated with neo-liberalism in their emphasis on an embodied altruistic politics. However, in important ways the asymmetry at the heart of the political vision of care ethics tends to leave in place this active independent subject/citizen of neo-liberalism, who is distinguished from dependent others.[13] The twinning of care and vulnerability gives force to moral claims of accountability and obligation that are a feature of moral decline thinking, but also animates notions of liability and blame – a 'responsibilisation' project (Lemke 2001, p. 201) that seems most troublesome for a feminist agenda. Indeed care's hierarchical altruism comes with a moralistic sting for both carer and those who receive care.

Even if care, at times, offers a more thoroughly social reading of connection than neo-liberal individualism, the radical democratic potential of care thinking is also undermined by its rather limited conception of embodied sociality. In the case of care-receipt (the experience of being cared-for), the moralistic asymmetry at the heart of care as altruism not only functions to disable those who receive care as 'the needy', but also constitutes their need in relation to only certain kinds of embodiment that are apparently deemed appropriate to provoke altruism.

In this context, fleshly interconnection/sociality is understood largely in terms of moments of dependency, and indeed in terms of certain forms of legitimated dependency when those who remain independent should care. Hence, while care takes notice of bodies, it is a language which deals only with quite specific aspects of embodiment – in particular those to do with bodily maintenance and nurturance.

The needy are very commonly equated with physical dependency. Care is constituted as arising in relation to lapses in individual autonomy. Rather than as a thoroughgoing alternative to neo-liberal individualism, care functions as its support structure. The body tends to enter the room only in relation to childhood, older age and ill-health, such as in child care and elder care (Beasley and Bacchi 2007; Bacchi and Beasley 2005). This limited focus continues to emphasise the dichotomy between those who care and those cared for, highlighting an ongoing asymmetry which an alternative feminist-inflected politics might wish to counter. Indeed, the rational self of neo-liberalism appears to return in the role of carer, while those who are cared for become the repository of bodies. Bodies are only truly conceptualised as vulnerable, never as demanding, challenging, pleasurable or desiring. Care is not as challenging to neo-liberal rational selfhood as it appears.

Moreover, the combination of the moralistic sting and limited corporeality which comes with care's hierarchical altruism produces a rather emaciated, sanitised and hygienic conception of care as altruistic philanthropy. Care in the scholarly literature never strays towards mention of sexuality as *doing sex*. Sexuality, it seems, can only occasionally be mentioned in relation to care when the subject of care is identified in relation to subordinated (disadvantaged) sexualities, which can therefore presumably still, to some degree, be cast as 'in need'. Care's links with maintaining the helper/helped hierarchical dichotomy can perhaps allow glimpses of LGBTIQ communities, but its associations with a sexless moral respectable altruism resist reference to sexual practices of whatever form. Thus, even these limited glimpses of sexuality within care seem less about acknowledgement and more along the lines of a 'beneficent' silencing.

Part 3: care as sexless moral respectability; care is not good in the bedroom

It is scarcely surprising, given the restrictive conceptualisation of the body and evasion of sexual practices in the care *scholarly* literature, that similar problems with the vocabulary of care also arise within medical and institutional policy and practice settings. I will use the example of sexuality and older people to develop this point.

The general inclination to perceive older people as asexual in many western societies, including the UK, USA and Australia, continues to haunt residential care for the elderly in Australia and elsewhere (Shuttleworth *et al.* 2010, 191–92). However, there is growing evidence that sexuality remains a significant aspect of life for many people 'well into old age and potentially to the end of life' (Radoslovich 2015; Yee 2010). Longer life expectancies also mean that intimate relationships are frequently maintained in later life. The 2006 Australian census, for example, shows that 57 per cent of citizens aged 65–84 and 26 per cent of citizens aged 85 or more were legally married (65 per cent of the latter group were widowed). And even these figures underestimate the numbers of older people who continue to be in intimate relationships which do not involve marriage (AIHW 2007, 10–11).

Despite this, sexuality remains relatively new and underdeveloped territory in the medical, service and policy industry that provides care to older people or advocates on their behalf. Medical practitioners continue to have limited knowledge or practice in integrating sexuality into their care practices (Benbow and Beeston 2012; Callan and Mitchell 2007; Choi *et al.* 2011; Taylor and Gosney 2011), and limited training (Synder and Zweig 2010). Nurse training and ongoing attitudes to sexuality in nursing practice remain less than attuned to a concern with sexual expression (Elias and Ryan 2011; Mahieu *et al.* 2011). Only very recently have there been any attempts to introduce practical manuals for the care industry on this issue (ILC UK 2011).[14] Practice guidelines in Australia remain a relative rarity and, even if they exist, are unlikely to be implemented given institutional mission-statements which do not mention sexuality.[15] Moreover, COTA Australia – the peak national policy body of the eight State and Territory Councils on the Ageing – which aims to 'promote, improve and protect the rights of all older Australians ... and promote effective responses to their needs', makes no mention of sexuality at all, despite its relevance to health, wellbeing, rights, housing and mental health (COTA 2013).

The invisibility of sexuality is not, however, absolute. The particular experiences of LGBTIQ communities in care institutions have been identified as a problem in a range of studies (see Chapter 14 by Westwood). However, these often have a particular focus on broader social acceptance – including within service industries such as the aged care industry (Almack *et al.* 2010; Averett *et al.* 2012). While it is evident from such research that same-sex attracted people are likely to be required to hide their sexuality in the setting of residential care, this is not the whole picture and is not *simply* another example of the discrimination which haunts non-hegemonic sexualities. It is important to note once again – as in the case of the scholarly literature on care – that sexuality as *doing sex* is rendered invisible in discussions of *institutional care*. Sexuality as sexual practices is virtually disavowed for all older people in institutional care environments.

My own research on residential institutions for older people reveals that sexuality, whether it is associated with minority or dominant social status, disappears when care is evoked. Heterosexual older people will almost invariably be disallowed sexual expression, along with their LGBTIQ peers. Older people whatever their relationship situation, in the Australian context for example, will be placed in single beds. The disappearance of the double bed in residential care – what I would call the 'double bed problem' in keeping with Halberstam's naming of the 'bathroom problem' as signifying gender binarism (1998, 22) – is one very practical sign of an age-based sexual binarism. It indicates how care is implicated in enforcing a certain kind of altruistic paternalism that is *specifically desexed and sanitised*. As Davina Cooper noted in relation to her study of a lesbian bathhouse, care is a terminology with specific cultural links to Christian ideals of *agape* and *caritas* which incline it towards the idealisation of self-sacrificing charity towards the needy and away from *eros* (2007) – and, I would add, away from fleshly pleasure (Beasley and Bacchi 2012).

Conclusion: beyond altruism, an alternative imaginary – the ethic of 'social flesh'

This exemplar returns me to the advantages of more thoroughly alternative approaches. While the insights associated with use of the language of care are crucial, I wish to push these insights further. What is required is a vocabulary revaluing what stands under the sign of care without its connotations/associations – in particular without care's regressive complicity in hierarchy, its moralistic sting and its desexed sanitised understanding of corporeality. The aim is not to stress shared vulnerability and responsibility for the dependent other, but rather a fully embodied coexistence, an engagement with the visceral fleshliness of sociality which can also encompass our mutual reliance on the materiality of our global environment. Visions of a transformative politics and advancing an ethical global community require a more expansive conception of embodied interconnection than care commands.

The 'ethic of social flesh' – a terminology coined with my co-author, Carol Bacchi, in previous works – offers an approach which is concerned to challenge the privileging of individualist, hierarchical and body-averse moralistic accounts in order to develop a more adequate language for understanding social relations. There is no sense in this terminology of givers and receivers; rather, we are all recognised as necessarily both through cycles of care over our lifetimes. The objective is to go beyond defending a politics of 'assisting' the 'less fortunate', who are simultaneously cast as desexed dependents.

As an ethico-political starting point, 'social flesh' highlights human embodied interdependence. It rejects neo-liberal conceptions of the autonomous self and removes the always already given (and morally-inflected) distinctions between strong and weak, and between those designated as having 'control over body' and those viewed as 'controlled by body' (Bacchi and Beasley 2002, 2005). The term social flesh involves refusing the residues of a puritan *noblesse oblige* that still appear to linger in the language of care, vulnerability and altruism. Instead, social flesh puts into question the social inequality which gives rise to the need for altruism and promotes a questioning of paternalistic altruism directed at worthy – that is, sanitised – bodies. This terminology can therefore better inform new feminist-inflected directions in scholarship, policy and institutional care.

The ethic of social flesh offers an 'other' framing which foregrounds a political imaginary, agenda and putative practice founded in a revaluation of social connection. That revaluation stands sharply at odds with the 'modernity as individualisation' thesis, and its links to neo-liberalism and moral decline thinking, with which this chapter began. Moreover, the framing of social connection upon which this ethic rests moves well beyond the cognitive deliberative visions of a civic polity (and its associated vocabularies of trust, respect and responsibility), to embrace an affective, erotic and visceral social corporeality without veering into understandings of emotion, touch and embodiment as only the negativity of suffering, fragility and vulnerability. The double-bed problem in institutional care settings for older people arises within a context in which certainly there are questions raised regarding loss of civil status, rights and other attributes of the democratic polity, while also evidently evoking questions regarding loss of bodily security, privacy, capacity and integrity. However, the means to the re-configuration of the double-bed problem in theory, governance and practice is not to be found in these civic/body restatements of the mind–body divide (which either tend to focus on the cognitive citizen or upon an attenuated understanding of embodiment as fragile flesh). Rather, the double-bed problem requires a bringing together of the dynamic creativity of the socio-political and a fully realised account of positive embodiment (Beasley and Bacchi 2007). Employment of the ethic of social flesh evokes precisely this integrative vision, providing a position of alterity and 'critical agency' (Boyer 2003),[16] which apprehends both social organisational and corporeal contingencies germane to older people in institutional settings, yet also deals in the close-up practical detail, the very literal furniture, of everyday life. In this sense, social flesh, in its promulgation of human embodied and inter-subjective entwinement, connects with Braidotti's refusal of political melancholia and her insistence upon an 'affirmative politics' (Braidotti 2010, 42–6; see also Braidotti 2006, 2013). The double-bed problem is a characteristic instance of that melancholia and the ethic of social flesh its affirmative rebuttal.

Notes

1 Nedelsky 2012; Grummell *et al.* 2009; Fox and Thomson 2013; González and Ifford (2014); Van Heijst 2011.
2 See for example, Bauman 2007; Beck and Beck-Gernshiem 1995; Edwards and Gillies 2012; Fineman 2004; Gilding 2010; Roseneil and Budgeon 2004; Sevenhuijsen 1998a; Tronto 2013.
3 My thanks to Henriksson (2014) for his discussion of this point; see also Smart 2007.
4 In using the term 'western' I aim to acknowledge the, often under-recognised, cultural implications of the individualisation thesis, given its inclination to presume a universal shift in direction of the shape of social life. However, as an Australian and for a range of other reasons, I also find this term presumptuous, transatlantic-centred and one-way in its account of change, and simply geographically inaccurate for a range of cultures. Connell spells this point out in more detail and reinterprets 'western' as 'northern' (Connell 2007).
5 Gibb *et al.* 2013; Allen ed. 2007; Abbott and Doucouliagos 2003; Ayers 2005.
6 Harvey 2005; Giroux 2005; Thornton 2012, p. 16; David and Naidoo 2013; Heath and Burdon 2013.
7 Collier 2014; Davies and Bansel 2005; Gill 2009; Johnson 2014; Mountz *et al.* 2015.
8 For example, though Charles Taylor draws attention to the dangers of modernity's emphasis upon individualisation, he has also called for a freeze on cultural pessimism (Taylor 1992).
9 The communitarian concern with the 'downward spiral of contemporary societies … into atomized individuals' (Helly 2003, p. 20) may reference care, or other related terms like trust and respect.
10 Mackenzie and Stoljar 2000; Westland 2009.
11 See also Lofdahl 2014; Lofdahl and Prieto 2009.
12 See for example, Harding 2014; Peel and Harding 2015.

13 It seems possible that Sara Ahmed's reanimation of the term responsibility and how it comes into existence as a response to fragility, along with her associated understanding of the will as socially distributed and not merely a matter of individualism, may parallel usage of terms like care and vulnerability. My own more critical reading of the terms responsibility and fragility involve concerns outlined in this paper about care and its connection with 'responsibilisation' (Ahmed 2014a, 24 and 28, see also Ahmed 2014b).
14 I would like to acknowledge the ongoing work of Katherine Radoslovich in undertaking literature reviews of this material
15 This assessment derives from my ongoing work on the marketing strategies and public documents of a range of companies specialising in residential care for the elderly in Australia – such as Resthaven, Uniting Communities, Anglicare and Helping Hand – as well as from continuing postgraduate research in South Australia, undertaken by PhD candidate Kathy Radoslovich.
16 Boyer 2003, cited in Dunbar-Hester 2011, pp. 206–7 and Dunbar-Hester 2014, p. 550.

References

Abbott, M. and Doucouliagos, C. (2003) 'The efficiency of Australian universities', *Economics of Education* 22(1), February: 89–97.
Ahmed, S. (2014a) *Willful Subjects*, Durham and London: Duke University Press.
Ahmed, S. (2014b) 'Willful subjects: Responsibility, fragility, history', AWGSA Public Lecture, 24 June. Australian Women's and Gender Studies Association, Biennial Conference, University of Melbourne, 23–25 June.
AIHW (Australian Institute of Health and Welfare) (2007) *Older Australia at a Glance*, 4th edition. Canberra: AIHW, Department of Health and Ageing.
Allen, M. ed. (2007) *The Next Generation of Corporate Universities: Innovative approaches for developing people and expanding organizational capabilities*. San Francisco: John Wiley & Sons.
Almack, K. Seymour, J. and Bellamy, G. (2010) 'Exploring the impact of sexual orientation on experiences and concerns about end of life care and on bereavement for lesbian, gay and bisexual older people', *Sociology* 44: 908–924.
Averett, P., Yoon, I. and Jenkins, C. (2012) 'Older lesbian sexuality: Identity, sexual behaviour and the impact of aging,' *Journal of Sex Research* 49(5): 495–507.
Ayers, D. F. (2005) 'Neo-liberal ideology in community college mission statements: A critical discourse analysis', *The Review of Higher Education* 28(4), Summer: 527–549.
Bacchi, C. and Beasley, C. (2002) 'Citizen bodies: Is embodied citizenship a contradiction in terms?' *Critical Social Policy* 22(2): 324–352.
Bacchi, C. and Beasley, C. (2005) 'Biotechnology and the political limits of "care"', pp. 175–194. In M. Shildrick and R. Mykitiuk eds, *Rethinking Feminist Bioethics: The challenge of the postmodern*. New York: MIT Press.
Barnes, M. and Brannelly T. (2008) 'Achieving care and social justice for people with dementia', *Nursing Ethics* 15(3): 384–395.
Bartlett, R. and O'Connor, D. (2010) *Broadening the Dementia Debate: Towards social citizenship*. Bristol: University of Bristol, Policy Press.
Bauman, Z. (2007) *Liquid Love*. Cambridge: Polity.
Beasley, C. and Bacchi, C. (2007) 'Envisaging a new politics for an ethical future: Beyond trust, care and generosity towards an ethic of social flesh', *Feminist Theory* 8(3), December: 279–298.

Beasley, C. and Bacchi, C. (2012) 'Making politics fleshly', pp. 99–120. In A. Bletsas and C. Beasley eds, *Engaging with Carol Bacchi: Strategic interventions and exchanges*. Adelaide: University of Adelaide Press.

Beasley, C., Brook, H. and Holmes, M. (2012) *Heterosexuality in Theory and Practice*. New York and London: Routledge.

Beck, U., and Beck-Gernsheim, E. (1995) *The Normal Chaos of Love*. Cambridge: Polity.

Bell, D. (1976) *The Cultural Contradictions of Capitalism*. New York: Basic Books.

Benbow, S. and Beeston, D. (2012) 'Sexuality, aging and dementia', *International Psychogeriatrics* 24(7): 1026–1033.

Boyer, D. (2003) 'The social context of critical intellectual agency: The shifting fortunes of the German educated bourgeoisie and the criticism of modern society' (paper presented at the Society for the Humanities, Cornell University, May 2003), cited in C. Dunbar-Hester (2011) 'Drawing and effacing boundaries in contemporary media democracy work', pp. 195–210. In S. C. Jansen, J. Pooley and L. Taub-Pervispour eds, *Media and Social Justice*. New York: Palgrave Macmillan, and cited in C. Dunbar-Hester (2014) *Low Power to the People: Pirates, protest, and politics in FM radio activism*. Cambridge, MA. and London: MIT Press.

Braidotti, R. (2006) 'Affirmation versus vulnerability: On contemporary ethical debates', *Symposium: Canadian Journal of Continental Philosophy* 10(1), Spring: 235–254.

Braidotti, R. (2010) 'On putting the active back into activism', *New Formations: A Journal of Culture/Theory/Politics. Special Issue: 'Deleuzian Politics?'* 68, June: 42–57.

Braidotti, R. (2013) 'Transitzone/conversation with Rosi Braidotti'. Interview with Sarah Posman, *nY* 19 June [www.ny-web.be/transitzone/conversation-rosi-braidotti.html – accessed May 2016].

Brannelly, T. (2006) 'Negotiating ethics in dementia care: An analysis of an ethic of care in practice', *Dementia* 5(2), May: 197–212.

Budgeon, S. (2008) 'Couple culture and the production of singleness', *Sexualities* 11(3): 301–325.

Callan, M. and Mitchell, A. (2007) '"It's none of my business": Gay and lesbian clients seeking aged care services', *Geriaction* 25(3), September: 31–33.

Choi, K. Jang, S., Lee, M. and Kim, K. (2011), 'Sexual life and self-esteem in married elderly', *Archives of Gerontology and Geriatrics* 53(1), July–August: 17–20.

Collier, R. (2014) '"Love law, love life": Neoliberalism, wellbeing and gender in the legal profession – the case of law school', *Legal Ethics* 17(part 2): 202–230.

Connell, R. (2007) *Southern Theory: The global dynamics of knowledge in social science*. Sydney: Allen & Unwin.

Cooper, D. (2007) 'Well, you go there to get off: Visiting feminist care ethics through a women's bathhouse', *Feminist Theory* 8(3): 243–262.

COTA Australia (National Council on the Ageing) (2013) *COTA Australia Federal Election Platform: A new deal for older Australians*, August. COTA Australia: Adelaide.

David, M. and Naidoo, R. (2013) *The Sociology of Higher Education: Reproduction, transformation and change in a global era*. Oxford and New York: Routledge.

Davies, B. and Bansel, P. (2005) 'The time of their lives? Academic workers in neoliberal time(s)', *Health Sociology Review* 14(1): 47–58.

Diprose, R. (2002) *Corporeal Generosity: On giving with Nietzsche, Merleau-Ponty, and Levinas*. New York: State University of New York Press.

Dunbar-Hester, C. (2011) *Low Power to the People: Pirates, Protest, and Politics in FM Radio Activism*. Cambridge, MA and London: Inside Technology Series, MIT Press.

Dunbar-Hester, C. (2014), '"Being a Consistent Pain in the Ass": Politics and Epistemics in Media Democracy Work', *Journal of Information Policy* 4: 547–569.

Dunphy, F. B. (2004) 'Post deconstructive humanism: The "New International" as an-arche', *Theory and Event* 7(2) [muse.jhu.edu/journals/theory_and_event/v007/7.2dunphy.html – accessed 18 August 2004].

Edwards, R., and Gillies, V. (2012) 'Farewell to family? A reply', *Families, Relationships and Societies* 1(3): 433–436.

Elias, J. and Ryan, A. (2011) 'A review and commentary on the factors that influence expressions of sexuality by older people in care homes', *Journal of Clinical Nursing* 20: 1668–1676.

Engster, D. (2004) 'Care ethics and natural law theory: Toward an institutional political theory of caring', *The Journal of Politics* 66(1): 113–135.

Etzioni, A. (1994) *The Spirit of Community*. New York: Touchstone.

Fineman, M. (2004) *The Autonomy Myth: A theory of dependency*. New York: New Press.

Fineman, M. and Grear, A. eds. (2013) *Vulnerability: Reflections on a new ethical foundation for law and politics*. Farnham, Surrey: Ashgate.

Fox, M. and Thomson, M. (2013) 'Realising social justice in public health law', *Medical Law Review* 21(2): 278–309.

Gibb, A., Haskins, G. and Robertson, I. (2013) 'Leading the entrepreneurial university: Meeting the entrepreneurial development needs of higher education institutions', pp.9–48. In A. Altmann and B. Ebersberger eds, *Universities in Change: Managing higher education insititutions in the age of globalization*. New York: Springer.

Giddens, A. (1992) *The Transformation of Intimacy: Sexuality, love and eroticism in modern societies*. Cambridge: Polity.

Gilding. M. (2010) 'Reflexivity over and above convention: The new orthodoxy in the sociology of personal life, formerly sociology of the family', *British Journal of Sociology* 61(4): 757–777.

Gill, R. (2009) 'Breaking the silence: The hidden injuries of neo-liberal academia', pp. 228–244. In R. Flood and R. Gill eds, *Secrecy and Silence in the Research Process: Feminist reflections*. London: Routledge.

Giroux, H. A. (2005) 'The terror of neo-liberalism: Rethinking the significance of cultural politics', *College Literature* 32(1): 1–19.

González, A. M. and Ifford, C. (eds) (2014) *Care Professions and Globalization: Theoretical and practical perspectives*. Basingstoke, Hampshire and NY: Palgrave Macmillan.

Grummell, B., Devine, D. and Lynch, K. (2009) 'Gender, care and new managerialism in higher education', *Gender and Education* 21(2): 191–208.

Halberstam, J. (1998). *Female Masculinity*. Durham and London: Duke University Press.

Harding, R. (2014) 'Dementia and carers: Relationality and informal carers' experiences', pp. 379–391. In C. Foster, J. Herring and I. Doron eds, *The Law and Ethics of Dementia*. Oxford: Hartfordshire.

Harvey, D. (2005) *A Brief History of Neoliberalism*. Oxford University Press.

Heath, M. and Burdon, P. (2013) 'Academic resistance to the neoliberal university', *Legal Education Review* 23(2): 379–401.

Helly, D. (2003) 'Social cohesion and cultural plurality', *Canadian Journal of Sociology* 28(1): 19–44. Translated from the French by R. F. Barsky and P. Foxen.

Henriksson, A. (2014) *Organising Intimacy: Exploring heterosexual singledoms at Swedish singles activities*. PhD Dissertation, Department of Social and Psychological Studies. Karlstad: Karlstad University Studies.

Hookway, N. (2013) 'Emotions, body and self: Critiquing moral decline sociology', *Sociology* 47, August: 841–857.

Hughes, B., McKie, L., Hopkins, D. and Watson, N. (2005) 'Love's labours lost? Feminism, the disabled people's movement and an ethic of care', *Sociology* 39(2): 259–275

ILC UK (International Longevity Centre, UK) (2011) *The Last Taboo: A guide to dementia, sexuality, intimacy and sexual behaviour in care homes.* London: ILC UK.

Johnson, C. (2014) 'Hard heads and soft hearts', *Australian Feminist Studies* 29(80): 121–136.

Kenner, A. M. (2008) 'Securing the elderly body: Dementia, surveillance, and the politics of "aging in place"', *Surveillance & Society* 5(3), 255–269.

Kenway, J. (1997) *Education in the Age of Uncertainty: An eagle's eye-view.* Deakin University, Victoria: Geelong, Centre for Education and Change.

Khatchadourian, H. (1999) *Community and Communitarianism.* New York, Bern and Berlin: Peter Lang.

Larner, W. (2000) 'Neo-liberalism: Policy, ideology, governmentality', *Studies in Political Economy* 63: 5–25.

Lasch, C. (1979) *The Culture of Narcissism: American life in an age of diminishing expectations.* New York: W.W. Norton.

Lemke, T. (2001) 'The birth of bio-politics: Michael Foucault's lectures at the College de France on neoliberal governmentality', *Economy and Society* 30(2): 190–207.

Löfdahl, A. (2014) 'Teacher-parent relations and professional strategies – a case study on documentation sand talk about documentation in the Swedish preschool', *Australasian Journal of Early Childhood* 39(3), September: 103–110.

Löfdahl, A. and Folke-Fichtelius, M. (2014) 'Preschool's new suit: Care in terms of learning and knowledge', paper presented at a joint seminar for educational studies and gender studies, Karlstad University, 'Theoretical and political reflections on the concept of care', October 16.

Löfdahl, A. and Prieto, P. (2009), Between control and resistance: Planning and evaluation texts in the Swedish Pre-school', *Journal of Education Policy* 24(4): 393–408.

MacIntyre, A. (1985) *After Virtue*, 2nd edition. Notre-Dame: University of Notre-Dame Press.

MacKenzie, C., Rogers, W. and Dodds, S. eds (2013) *Vulnerability: New essays in ethics and feminist philosophy.* Oxford: Oxford University Press.

Mackenzie, C. and Stoljar, N. eds. (2000) *Relational Autonomy: Feminist perspectives.* Oxford and New York: Oxford Uinversity Press.

McNay, L. (2000) *Gender and Agency: Reconfiguring the subject in feminist and social theory.* Cambridge: Polity Press.

Mahieu, L. Elssen, K. Gastmans, C. (2011) 'Nurses' perceptions of sexuality in institutionalised elderly: A literature review', *International Journal of Nursing Studies* 48: 1140–1154.

Mountz, A., Bonds, A., Mansfield, B., Loyd, J., Hyndman, J., Walton-Roberts, M., Basu, R., Whitson, R., Hawkins, R., Hamilton, T. and Curran, W. (2015) 'For slow scholarship: A feminist politics of resistance through collective action in the neoliberal university, *ACME: An International E-Journal for Critical Geographies* 14(4): 123559.

Mulinari, D. and Sandell, K. (2009) 'A feminist re-reading of theories of late modernity: Beck, Giddens and the location of gender', *Critical Sociology* 35(4), July: 493–507.

Nedelsky, J. (2012) *Law's Relations: A relational theory of self, autonomy and law.* Oxford: Oxford University Press.

Peel, E. and Harding, R. (2015) 'A right to "dying well" with dementia? Capacity, "choice" and relationality', *Feminism & Psychology* 25(1), February: 137–142.

Putnam, R. D. (1995). 'Bowling alone: America's declining social capital', *Journal of Democracy* 6(1), January: 65–78.
Radoslovich, K. (2015) 'Research proposal', PhD thesis work, Department of Gender Studies and Social Analysis, University of Adelaide, South Australia.
Reiff, P. ([1966] 1987) *The Triumph of the Therapeutic: Uses of faith after Freud.* New York: Harper and Row.
Roseneil, S. and Budgeon, S. (2004) 'Cultures of intimacy and care beyond "the family": Personal life and social change in the early 21st century', *Current Sociology* 52(2): 135–159.
Sevenhuijsen, S. (1998a) *Citizenship and the Ethics of Care.* London: Routledge.
Sevenhuijsen, S. (1998b) 'Too good to be true? Feminist considerations about trust and social cohesion', *IWM Working Paper No. 3.* Vienna: Institute for Human Sciences.
Shakespeare, T. (2000) 'The social relations of care', pp. 52–65. In G. Lewis, S. Gewirtz and J. Clarke eds, *Rethinking Social Policy.* London: Sage.
Shildrick, M. (2001) 'Reappraising feminist ethics: Developments and debates', *Feminist Theory* 2(2): 233–244.
Shuttleworth, R., Russell, C., Weerakoon, P. and Dune, T. M. (2010) 'Sexuality in residential aged care: A survey of perceptions and policies in Australian nursing homes', *Sexuality and Disability* 28: 187–194.
Sims, M. (2014a) 'Editorial', *Australasian Journal of Early Childhood*, 39(3) September [www.earlychildhoodaustralia.org.au/our-publications/australasian-journal-early-childhood/index-abstracts/ajec-vol-39-3-september-2014/contents/].
Sims, M. (2014b) 'Is the care-education dichotomy behind us? Should it be?' *Australasian Journal of Early Childhood* 39(4), December [www.earlychildhoodaustralia.org.au/our-publications/australasian-journal-early-childhood/index-abstracts/ajec-vol-39-no-4-december-2014/care-education-dichotomy-behind-us-full-free-text-available/–accessed January 2015].
Smart, C. (2007) *Personal Life: New directions in sociological thinking.* Cambridge: Polity.
Synder, R. and Zweig, R. (2010) 'Medical and psychology students' knowledge and attitudes regarding sexuality and aging', *Gerontology and Geriatrics Education* 31: 235–255.
Taylor, A. and Gosney, M. (2011) 'Sexuality in older age: Essential considerations for healthcare professionals', *Age and Aging* 40: 538–543.
Taylor, C. (1992) *The Ethics of Authenticity.* Harvard: Harvard University Press.
Thornton, M. (2012) *Privatising the Public University: The case of law.* Oxford and New York: Routledge.
Tronto, J. (1995) 'Care as a basis for radical political judgements', *Hypatia* 10(2), May: 141–149.
Tronto, J. (2013) *Caring Democracy: Markets, equality, and justice.* New York: NY University Press.
Van Heijst, A. (2011) *Professional Loving Care: An ethical view of the healthcare sector.* Leuven: Peeters.
Westland, A. (2009) 'Rethinking relational autonomy', *Hypatia* 24(4): 26–49.
Walzer, M. (1990) 'The communitarian critique of liberalism', *Political Theory* 18: 6–23.
Yee, L. (2010) 'Aging and sexuality', *Australian Family Physician* 39(10), October: 718–721.

Index

A Local Authority v TZ (No. 2) 115, 124–6
Aboriginal Legal Rights Movement (ALRM) 68–70
Aboriginal Medical Service (AMS) 68, 70–1
Abortion Support Network (ASN) 16, 19–20
abortion trail: challenging trouble 23–6; conclusions 26–7; displacement 18–20; introduction 14–18; providing a 'home' 20–3
'abortion trail' term 15
activism 16; Allen, Margaret 72–6, 78; Baker, Jenny 66, 67–72, 78; conclusions 78–9; Dyer, Maureen 76–8, 78–9; introduction 65–6
Adelaide Working Women's Centre 75
Ahmed, Sara 14, 18, 68
Aintree v James 121
All Souls Local Action Network (ASLAN), London, UK 57
altruism (feminist political ethic) 148, 149, 155, 157, 161, 239–41, 243
Alzheimer's disease 198
Amnesty International 18
animal companions and the homeless: conclusions 111–12; contemporary society 98–100; disruptive social power 107–11; homeless people and pets 104–5; introduction 97–8; theoretical concerns 100–7
Animal Rights Action Network (ARAN) 109
antiretroviral (ARV) medication 33, 34, 39
Aries, Philippe 86
asymmetry 1, 14, 17, 23, 97, 109, 117, 240–1
'austerity' 4

Beasley, Chris 23, 76
behavioural and psychological symptoms of dementia (BPSD) 206–7, 210, 211
Bob (cat) 110–11
Bowen, James 110–11
Bringing Them Home Report (Aboriginal/Torres Strait Islanders) 69
British Pregnancy Advisory Service (BPAS) clinics 17, 24–5
Brody, Elaine 198

Cardiff CC v Ross 115, 124–6
Care Act, 2014, UK 149, 156–7
Carer's Allowance, UK 4
Carers Australia 81
carers as legal subjects: asset rich – property 158–60; care economy and social enterprise culture 150–1; caring for the unproductive – labour market 152–5; conclusions 160–1; introduction 148–9; state welfare 155–8
caring for the homeless (Westminster City Council, London, UK): bye-law proposal 54–60; conclusions 60–2; homelessness organisations 52–4; introduction 48–50; modern punitive turn in law 50–2
caring for the unproductive: care workers providing SR in exchange for remuneration 154–5; carer/worker claiming SR through remuneration 152–3
Cathedral Piazza, London, UK (soup runs) 56–7, 60–2
connect/connection 14
Cooper, Davina 15, 23, 215, 217, 227, 242

Index

COTA (Council on the Ageing) in Australia 242
Council of Europe: sex equality 135
Court of Protection 121, 125
cycles 14

'damage of dementia' 199
Dangerous Dogs Act, 1991, UK 99
Dean, Mitchell 238
dementia care: conclusions 211; duties to care and dementia talking 201–3; 'Duties to Care' Project 200, 201; familial relationships 203–7; introduction 198–201; language 237–8; parentification and infantalisation 209–11; sibling conflict/collaboration 207–9; UK statistics 198
depletion 150–61
Diagnostic and Statistical Manual (DSM) 199
Disadvantaged Schools Program (DSP), Australia 78
'Duties to Care' Project (dementia) 200, 201

economic 'rationalism' 66
embodiment (Fletcher, Fox and McCandless) 6
equality 1, 3, 122, 131–2, 135, 140–4
Equality Act, 2010, UK 153
ESCORT (Liverpool-based support group for abortion) 16–17, 19, 21, 24–5
'ethic of social flesh' 243–4
'ethics of care' 1–2, 5, 14, 35, 49, 62, 101, 117, 120, 165, 170
European Convention on Human Rights (ECHR): abstract rights 133–4; carers' rights 61; private life 59; service and forced labour 155; subsidiarity principle 133
European Court of Human Rights (ECtHR): response limitations 3; *see also* 'new fathers'
European Union (EU): Charter of Rights 179; 'new fathers' 134; Pregnant Workers' directive 131

'families of choice' 183
feminism 1, 7, 16, 66
Foster, Charles 118
Foucault, Michel 86
Franzway, Suzanne 75

Fraser, Nancy 179
'friend and family' (pets) 105

Gilligan, Carol 117
Grayling, Chris 6
Guardian 110
Gunaratnam, Yasmin 17
Guyer, Jane 43

Harding, Rosie 89, 200
Herring, Jonathan 118, 148
'Hidden Injuries of Class' 71
'home' 18, 20–3, 26–7
Homeless (Homeless Persons) Act, 1977, UK 52
Hounga v Allen and Anor 155
Housing Justice (national Christian umbrella group), UK 58, 60
Human Rights Act, 1988 50, 59

ILO Domestic Workers Convention, 2011 160
Inquiry into Health Services for the Psychiatrically Ill and Developmentally Disabled (Australia) 82
Irish Constitution, 1937 165–6, 169, 172–3, 177–9
Irish Family Planning Association (IFPA) 16–17, 18, 24–5
Irish Women's Abortion Support Group (IWASG) 16, 18

Kenway, Jane 236
Konstantin Markin v Russia – anti-stereotyping reasoning 134–5, 138–41, 141–3

Lane/Power report (soup runs) 57
LGBTIQ (lesbian, gay, bisexual, transgender, intersex questioning) 241, 242
Liberty (civil-rights organisation) 58–9, 61
Limited Access study, Australia 76
Lowth v Minister for Social Welfare 172

Marie Stopes clinics 17
Mental Capacity Act (MCA), 2005, England and Wales 9, 114–15, 120–4, 126–7
Mental Health Act, 1959, UK 120
Mental Health Act, 1983, UK 120
'Mother/Child' dyad 172

Narayan, Uma 65, 71
National Aboriginal Health Strategy (NAHS) 70
National Living Wage (NLW), UK 154, 160
National Minimum Wage (NMW), UK 154, 160
Nedelsky, Jennifer 5, 166, 169, 172, 176–8
'new fathers' and right to parental leave (ECtHR): conclusions 141–4; gender stereotype 134–5; introduction 131–4; *Konstantin Markin v Russia* – anti-stereotyping reasoning 134–5, 138–41, 141–3; *Petrovic v Austria* – male breadwinner model 134, 135–7, 139, 141–2, 143; *Weller v Hungary* – 'magnifying effect' of Article 14 134, 137–8, 141, 144
Newton, Judith 73
'No Second Night Out' policy, UK 53

older lesbians and gay men – spatial inequalities: conclusions 229–30; constraints upon resistance 222–5; discussion 225–9; introduction 215–17; methodology 217–18; prejudice/discrimination 221–2; social reproduction of heteronormativity/ heterosexism 219–20
Older Women's Co-Housing project, London, UK 225
O'Reilly v Limerick Corporation 175

'Pack of Two' (pet relations) 105–6
Peel, Elizabeth 216
Petrovic v Austria – male breadwinner model 134, 135–7, 139, 141–2, 143
Port Adelaide Methodist Mission 73

R. (Countryside Alliance) v A-G, 2008 59
R. (McCann) v Manchester Crown Court, 2002 51
relationality 5, 9, 37, 44, 97, 102, 114–27, 170, 236–7
revaluing care: cycles of care 6–7; introduction 1–2; legal, social and political responses to care needs/ provision 3–4; theoretical engagements with care/connection 4–6

ReValuing Care network 1–2
Riggs, Damien W. 200
Rough Sleeping Strategy, 2007 (Westminster City Council, London, UK) 55
Royal Commission into Aboriginal Deaths in Custody, 1991 69

Saunders, Sandra 66, 67–9, 71
Schaffer, Kay 74–5
sexuality and older people: care as problematic ethico-political starting point 238–41; care as resistance – advantages 234–8; care as sexless moral respectability 241–2; conclusions – beyond altruism and ethic of 'social flesh' 243–4; introduction 233–4
Sloan, Brian 148, 158–9, 160
social caring – journeys to activism: Allen, Margaret 72–6, 78; Baker, Jenny 66, 67–72, 78; conclusions 78–9; Dyer Maureen 76–8, 78–9; introduction 65–6
Social Exclusion Unit, UK 52–3
social reproduction (SR) 1, 14, 149–51, 152–5, 160, 166, 168, 215, 219–20
soup runs in Cathedral Piazza, London, UK 56–7, 60–2
South Africa – HIV/AIDS global health intervention: care-giving 32–6; care-giving and 'caring with' vibrant matter 36–42; carrying on seen anew? 44–5; introduction 31–2; stabilisation via 'caring with' 42–4
South Australian College of Advanced Education (SACAE) 75–6
'space of care' concept 48–9
state support for care: care as constitutional right 174–7; care work in constitutional order 168–72; conclusions 177–9; constitutional convention 172–3; introduction 165–6; unpaid care work – rights 166–8
Stewart, Ann 1
strangeness/stranger 14–27
subsidiarity principle (ECHR) 133

terms of endearment (Australian family life): conclusions 195–6; discussion – policy/practice 194–5; extended family members 190–4; family meaning 184–90; introduction 182–4; methods 184

The Future Project (The Project, South Africa HIV/AIDS) 31–2, 33–4, 34–6, 39–40, 44–5

Unemployment Benefit Act, 1977 135
United Nations (UN): Convention on the Rights of People with Disabilities (CRPD) 5, 9, 114–27
United States (US): anti-discrimination law 131

Valentine, Gill 227
'vibrant matter' concept 5, 32, 36–45
Vietnam War 72
Vine, Jeremy 110–11

Weller v Hungary – 'magnifying effect' of Article *14* 134, 137–8, 141, 144

Westminster Housing Commission, 2006 (report) 55
Who Do You Think You Are? (television programme) 187
Women's Information Network (Ireland) 15, 18
Women's Study Research Centre, Adelaide 66, 74
'work/care balance' 160
World Health Organization (WHO) 33

young carers: conclusions 92–3; introduction 81; research 85–92; role 81–2; victims 82–5